D0794352

The
SWEETEST
ROSE

150 years of Yorkshire County Cricket Club
1863-2013

David Warner

Foreword by David Hopps

GREAT NORTHERN

Great Northern Books
PO Box 213, Ilkley, LS29 9WS
www.greatnorthernbooks.co.uk

© David Warner, 2012

Every effort has been made to acknowledge correctly and contact the copyright holders of material in this book. Great Northern Books apologises for any unintentional errors or omissions, which should be notified to the publisher.
All rights reserved. No part of this book may be reproduced in any form or by any means without permission in writing from the publisher, except by a reviewer who may quote brief passages in a review.

ISBN: 978-1-9050803-1-1
Design and layout: David Burrill

Printed and bound by CPI Group (UK) Ltd, Croydon, CR0 4YY

CIP Data
A catalogue for this book is available from the British Library

for Sylvia
for never doubting

Acknowledgements

This book has taken almost three years to research and write and I am grateful to many people for their encouragement and support, particularly James Greenfield, production editor of the Yorkshire Yearbook, who gave invaluable help in liaising over the pictures and freely made his time available whenever his assistance was sought.

In order not to show favour to any one player's or official's viewpoint, I deliberately did not seek their own opinions while compiling this history, the exceptions being Michael Crawford and Ted Lester, whose recollections go back much longer than most and for many years were at the nub of Yorkshire's affairs. I very much appreciate how readily they agreed to be interviewed and how honestly they answered my questions.

Fearful of being influenced by the views of recent eminent Yorkshire cricket writers, I have not sought reference to either John Callaghan's Yorkshire Pride or Derek Hodgson's The Carnegie Official History of Yorkshire County Cricket Club, both of which, I would like to stress, are excellent publications.

Delving into the more distant past, I was helped in my research by the History of Yorkshire County Cricket, 1833-1893, by the Rev. R.S. Holmes, History of Yorkshire County Cricket 1903-23, by A.W. Pullin, Recollections and Reminiscences, by Lord Hawke (published 1924), the History of Yorkshire County Cricket, 1924-1949, by J.M. Kilburn, and Kilburn's Yorkshire County Cricket (published 1950). It goes almost without saying that editions of the Wisden Cricketers' Almanack and the Yorkshire County Cricket Club Yearbook were indispensible.

Also of great help to me were the volumes, Yorkshire Cricketers 1839-1939, by Peter Thomas, A Who's Who of Yorkshire County Cricket Club, by Tony Woodhouse, and Yorkshire's 30 Championships, 1893-2001, by Paul Dyson.

The fact that I had a wide variety of photographs to select from to illustrate the work is due entirely to the generosity and assistance of The Yorkshire Post, the Telegraph & Argus, Simon Wilkinson, of SWpix.com, Dave Williams, of cricketphotos.co.uk, Mick Pope, of Adelpharchives.co.uk, Brian Sanderson of the Yorkshire CCC Archives, Patrick Eagar, James Buttler and Jeremy Jones, with apologies to any others I have omitted to mention.

I would like to thank Great Northern Books for their friendly enthusiasm, sports journalist and author, Andrew Collomosse, for going through the book with a fine toothcomb and providing thoughtful and welcome advice, Yorkshire statistician, Roy Wilkinson, for his research, and my predecessor as Yorkshire cricket correspondent for the Telegraph & Argus, David Swallow, for both his cuttings and his clear memory of bygone events.

Finally, I have been genuinely touched by the interest shown by so many people during the writing of this book and would particularly like to mention Tony and Maureen Loffill and my first Sports Editor at the Telegraph & Argus, Peter Royston, who was a fine judge of a good story and whose continuing support I very much value.

CONTENTS

FOREWORD

The task of writing a history of Yorkshire cricket must be a petrifying thought. Not only is there a need to pay respects to a great tradition, you must pick your way through a variety of disputes that have dogged the county through the ages. It is a task that demands meticulous research, a dogged perseverance and above all a high level of integrity. David Warner is well equipped on all three counts.

The world of Yorkshire cricket can be a volatile one. It is a world with a healthy sense of entitlement, unflinching in defending what it believes to be right. It can display great camaraderie just as much as it can squabble self-destructively over trivialities. It can be heartening and maddening in equal measure.

David "Plum" Warner has observed Yorkshire cricket in all these guises since the mid-1970s. Not just observed it, but cared for it. He can say with total conviction that he has been blessed with great fortune and that he can think of nothing he would rather have done with his life. Remarkably, in all that time, I can't remember him making an enemy, not even for a day or two. In a world where fall-outs are a fact of life, and cricket journalists are often regarded as part of the problem, Plum has been widely respected for his fairness and balance.

Few cricket writers have passed through the county press boxes for long without figuring in one of the countless anecdotes that are part of Plum's day. Some, he will admit, are on their umpteenth telling and they are no worse for that. So it would be wrong not to include at least one in which he plays a role. I remember bumping into David Bairstow in Scarborough as he walked to the ground for a championship match in the mid-1980s. It was not a good day to bump into him because Bluey, one of Yorkshire's most popular cricketers of all time, was volcanic over something I had written in the Yorkshire Post. As we marched along North Marine Road, he interspersed friendly "good mornings" to passing holidaymakers with a fearsome upbraiding. His ability to switch from charming conversation with passers-by one second to a ferocious verbal assault upon me the next, without once losing his thread, caused me to laugh at the absurdity of it all. "I don't know what's wrong with you," concluded Bluey. "I give you the biggest bollocking you have ever had in your life and you can't stop laughing. You should write like David Warner."

In all his years covering Yorkshire cricket, Plum has been scrupulously fair-minded and accurate. His priority has always been to report the story of the day and he has done it well, never slanting or twisting it for extra effect. When he has felt the need to criticise, he has done so gently and even-handedly. As the cricket correspondent for the Telegraph and Argus, he has had a natural pride when a Bradford lad did well. Players through the generations have respected him for his decency. He is a good man to trust with a Yorkshire history. And he was a good man to trust for guidance when I began on the Yorkshire Post as "The Boy Hopps" in the mid-80s.

But the most striking fact about Plum, as far as I am concerned, is that he has never once been late for a match. He shudders at the thought. As somebody not so blessed, I find this level of professionalism quite astonishing. I have countless memories of rushing into cricket grounds to find Plum already well into his day. Occasionally, he would look at me with the subtlest expression of disapproval. I remember having a puncture on the way to a vital audience with Viscount Mountgarret, a former Yorkshire president, in his home at South Stainley, and arriving red-faced and covered in oil to find that Plum's notebook was already full of the shorthand that would bring him an exclusive story the following day. On another occasion – a story he relates regularly – I was lost in Glasgow on my way to Hamilton Crescent with a colleague's mobile phone in my boot and could repeatedly see the ground but could never quite reach it. We had left the hotel at the same time and he beat me to his post by at least an hour. There is something to be said for such an ordered way of living.

The camaraderie on the county circuit has always been important to Plum as it has been to many of us. It is a lifestyle which does not suit everybody. Sometimes its relevance to the outside world can be hard to fathom, but it is a gentle, companionable place, and there is cricket to watch, too. It suits a man whose wife, Sylvia, insists is one of the least practical people around. He has always been entirely at home on the long summer days in a county box whether it was relishing the closeness to the action and mild eccentricities in the old press box at Hove or the acerbic wit and repartee at Derby. Until newspapers began to pare back coverage of county cricket, the sizeable Yorkshire press contingent could be domineering, but Derby always gave as good as it got.

And that is about it. My words are up and somewhere in them there will be an error which Plum, before he read this, will have spotted and corrected. In nearly 30 years since I first met him, Plum has been a font of good sense and a good thing for the game. He has had more stories than me and I have had more hangovers; he has had more thank-yous and I have had more rows. As I write these words, I have yet to read his history, but even before I do I know that you can trust its intentions. And in the grand scheme of things, you can't say much better than that.

David Hopps
UK editor, ESPNcricinfo
Bramham, West Yorkshire
May, 2012

INTRODUCTION

The purpose of this book is to celebrate the 150th anniversary of Yorkshire County Cricket Club but when I was born in the Bradford suburb of Baildon in May, 1942, I don't suppose it could have been taken for granted that Yorkshire CCC or, indeed, cricket at large, had much of a future left.

The Second World War was then at its height and the prospects of a free United Kingdom must have looked pretty grim.

Had we finished up on the losing side the country would not have been the same as when the war began, that's for sure, and I feel certain that cricket would not have been allowed to resume again in its old familiar form once the conflict was over.

Cricket is too free a spirit to be blessed by a Nazi regime and too complex a game to be understood by conquering invaders. I have no doubt at all that cricket would have re-surfaced at some later stage because the game is part of the nation's indomitable spirit but it would have taken time.

It may seem trivial to some to list the survival of cricket as being one of the benefits to be gained from winning the war but the game is so much a part of our heritage that it goes hand-in-hand with freedom and perhaps it is not surprising, therefore, that the crowds flocked to see it when it returned on a competitive basis.

The war was not allowed to stop various forms of cricket being played throughout the country during those dark years and following Germany's surrender in May, 1945, it was, for many, a pleasurable means of celebrating the forces of good over evil.

The Australian Servicemen in that summer embarked on a programme which involved them in nearly 50 fixtures, including the five England v Australia Victory matches, which were played out to capacity crowds with 67,660 spectators paying the shilling admission charge over the three days of the First Test at Lord's.

The second of those Victory Tests was played at bomb-scarred Bramall Lane in Sheffield and around 50,000 Yorkshire folk – again over three days – watched on joyously as England won by 41 runs to level things up after Australia had won at Lord's by six wickets.

How that Bramall Lane game must have comforted the Yorkshire crowd in the knowledge that things were back to normal again both nationally and locally because there, right at the top of the England batting order, was their hero from the 30s, Len Hutton.

And the lad from Pudsey, who made that epic record score of 364 against Australia at The Oval in 1938, was once again helping his country to victory on the cricket field. Walter Hammond's century in the first innings was a masterpiece and Cyril Washbrook's 63 was courageous but it was Leonard's top score of 46 in the second dig that ensured England had sufficient runs to defend.

A fortnight later, the Australians were at Bradford Park Avenue in the first match staged by Yorkshire since 1939 and again Hutton was the complete master, his 82 out of 122 while he was at the crease being scored on a pitch made treacherous by warm sun following a deluge.

Like so many matches at Park Avenue before and since, bad weather had the final say but it did not matter. League cricket had gone on uninterrupted during the war but now Yorkshire were back in business. There was no Hedley Verity, alas, but there was, for a while, the likes of Arthur Mitchell, Wilf Barber, Maurice Leyland and Bill Bowes.

And a new generation of players were coming through and later on new trophies would be added to the glory years that had already helped to make Yorkshire the greatest cricket club in the world.

So, despite two World Wars, the game of cricket continues its journey and Yorkshire County Cricket Club, born in 1863, remains as robust as ever in 2013, 150 years on. It's an anniversary worth celebrating because the club has a history which few others can get close to matching – as I hope this book will show.

*   *   *

The telephone rang on the Sports Desk at the Telegraph & Argus office in Hall Ings, Bradford.

"Sport," I said as I picked up the handset.

Any one of five or six of us could have answered it but the telephone was nearest to me, so I did.

It was a call which changed my life more than I could ever have imagined and it came right out of the blue.

"Is David Warner there?" asked a voice which I knew belonged to the editor's secretary.

"Speaking."

"The editor would like to see you in his office."

"Oh, when would be convenient?"

"Right now."

I had an uneasy feeling in my stomach as I walked along the corridor towards his door. Every journalist did, I suspect, when they received such a summons. I was sports subbing at the time and I wondered if I had put an unsuitable headline on a story. Or had I been sending copy down the chute and into the composing room too late, causing deadlines to be missed? That sort of thing was going through my head.

His door was ajar and three small raps were answered with "Come in" and then I was facing Arnold Hadwin, who was sat at his desk smoking his pipe.

He began to re-ignite it and as this prevented any further speech at this point he motioned me to take a seat opposite him.

I watched two or three clouds of smoke head for the ceiling and then he said, with no preamble at all: "David Swallow wants to pack up doing Yorkshire cricket at the end of the season. Would you like to take over?"

I was completely taken aback. I wanted to say "yes" there and then but I knew I should discuss it at home first with my wife, Sylvia. "Thank-you very much for the offer, Mr. Hadwin, can I give you a definite answer tomorrow?" He nodded through fresh clouds of smoke.

It was in the late summer of 1974 that all this came about and I was 32 years old. It was also the last year in which I ever took a summer holiday because I naturally said "Yes" the following morning and from then on I was living and breathing Yorkshire cricket from the beginning of April to the end of September – and for most of the winter months as well, as you will find out.

I had wanted to be a newspaper reporter from about the age of eight or nine when I was old enough to be aware of the uncomfortable fact that I was not cut out to earn a living in any other way. So, from the day I started work at the age of 16 as a junior reporter on the Shipley Guardian, journalism was my main priority with a love for cricket not very far behind. To be able to marry the two together was unimaginably gratifying and the greatest pleasure has always come from getting a good story out of the cricket rather than from just watching the cricket itself.

And, believe you me, I was pitched into good stories with Yorkshire County Cricket Club from the moment I took up my post. Stories which, for a decade and more, were of interest not only in Yorkshire or even England but around the cricketing world. Now the heat may be less intense but Yorkshire CCC is still recognised around the globe as one of the game's greatest centres and the place where cricket has been fashioned into what it is today.

From my earliest days I had always loved cricket and this passion came from my mother, who never missed a ball whenever it was on the radio, and my bachelor uncle, who spent endless hours playing the game with my brother and me, either with a tennis ball on our narrow pathway at home or in what was called "the bottom field" at Baildon when we played on rough grass and used a corky ball.

At home, we propped up the stumps against the front step and bowled from the drainpipe at the other end of the house. The house wall prevented any strokes through the off-side, apart from square or late cuts which went into the front garden.

One day, my uncle bowled to a friend who leaned back and struck the ball straight through the lounge window with shards of glass going into the goldfish tank. My friend's mother got to hear about this and in the evening came round to offer to pay for the fresh pane of glass. My uncle refused point blank. "Oh no, madam, he was not to blame," he insisted. "It was a genuine square cut, not a slog."

There was a snicket ran alongside our garden path and on many a day the great Arthur Mitchell walked past while my brother and I were playing cricket. We were in awe that a man from our small town, who lived just up the road in Maude Avenue, should have played for Yorkshire and England and that he was now the County coach. I think we tried that bit harder when we saw him coming but he never even seemed to notice us as he walked slowly and stiffly by.

My international heroes were Denis Compton and Keith Miller and I soaked up information in the early to mid 50s from publications such as the Boys' Book of Cricket and the Denis Compton annual. And then there was county cricket on the radio, not great chunks of it but perhaps half an hour from mid-day and broadcasts of a similar length at three o'clock and six o'clock.

Some of the names I picked up from these commentaries were not Test stars but I was just as fascinated by them and they were equally revered. I had my own mental picture of what the mysteriously named Phebey and Fagg looked like as they walked through the gate to open an innings for Kent and then there was Constable of Surrey – not a man to take liberties with – Parkhouse of Glamorgan, Gardner of Warwickshire, Gerry Lester, curiously of Leicestershire, and similarly wonderful names attached to all 17 of the counties.

Nearer to home, a young man called Brian Close was making a name for himself and he became a hero and remains so to this day. I remember that when I was about ten he umpired – for some reason – a celebrity match at Baildon's Jenny Lane ground. He was stood at the bowler's end when back came a fearsome straight drive and Closey automatically flung out his right arm and caught the ball. What greater illegal act of heroism could a lad witness on his home ground?

Around this time, I was at Headingley in June, 1952, on the day that Freddie Trueman became really famous. My best friend and I and our younger brothers had been taken by our mothers to watch the First Test between England and India and in the Tourists' second innings they lost their first four wickets without scoring a run, Fiery Fred picking up three of them in eight balls. I remember the explosions of applause from all around but did not see much of the action because my friend and I were weaving our way through the crowd trying to find his lost brother.

As I grew older, I watched Yorkshire, mainly at Bradford Park Avenue, but was not fanatical about them. I just liked all cricket, from grass roots right to the top. When I started work at the Shipley Guardian (I was based mainly at the Bingley office which was shared with Bingley Guardian staff) I got my first taste of cricket reporting by covering Bradford League matches and this continued when I moved to the Bingley office of the Telegraph and Argus a couple of years later.

From there I went to the T&A's Shipley branch in Kirkgate and at the start of the 70s I agreed to join the sports department at head office to fill the gap left by the departure of Don Warters, who had moved to the Yorkshire Evening Post to cover Leeds United.

For the next four years, I was responsible for the Bradford League coverage in the newspaper, writing a weekly column in The Yorkshire Sports (The Pink) during the summer months. I thoroughly enjoyed this and at the Bradford League's annual dinner just before joining up with Yorkshire I received a cut glass rose bowl from the League as a farewell gesture. It was handed over by their guest speaker, Vic Feather, general secretary of the TUC.

Up to this point, I also played cricket at every available opportunity – helping Baildon Methodists rise up through the divisions of the Bradford Mutual SS League and enjoying a full programme of friendly midweek and quite often Sunday matches with the Bradford Press Cricket team and then, following an amalgamation, with the West Yorkshire Press.

None of which is at all important except that it explains that as well as being a qualified journalist I was also devoted to cricket when I got that fateful call from the editor.

Covering Yorkshire county cricket became a way of life and I would not have wanted it any other way, despite all those summers with hardly any time to do anything other than watch and write.

From 1975 up to the start of the 2008 season, I reported on virtually every Yorkshire match for the Telegraph & Argus and its sister papers, The Yorkshire

Evening Press, and The Northern Echo, and since then I have continued to cover all of the home games for the Press Association as well as editing the Yorkshire CCC Yearbook since 2009.

I think I can lay claim to have watched more Yorkshire matches over the past 38 years or so than anyone else and possibly more county cricket during that period than anyone else in the country.

I confess that I was not steeped in the history of Yorkshire cricket when I first stepped out on this road but I have grown to be absorbed by it and I jumped at the opportunity to write this book on the 150th anniversary of Yorkshire County Cricket Club.

I make no apologies for stating that I do not intend this to be an A-Z of all the players that have passed through Yorkshire's great doors since 1863 and neither will I be giving all of their statistics. These things have been so adequately done already by many writers and statisticians, right from the Rev. R.S. Holmes at the start of the 20th century up to Derek Hodgson with his revised and updated Carnegie Official History of Yorkshire County Cricket Club in 2009.

My aim is to follow the general path which Yorkshire has taken since 1863 and then stride out in greater detail from the time that I became involved in 1975. Along the way, my intention is to unearth the reasons for Yorkshire's pre-eminence in the world of cricket.

Yorkshire cricket, particularly during my early experience of it, is an emotive subject and the Geoff Boycott controversies of the 1970s and 1980s split the club down the middle. On this, and on all other issues, I do not wish to take sides, only to tell the story as it unfolded at the time.

I still have a letter which I received from my editor in early December, 1983, which says: "Congratulations on your coverage of the Boycott Affair. You have led the field throughout the summer and have managed to keep a proper balance between the two sides, while at the same time never missing a news angle."

That meant a lot to me. I will try to be just as evenly balanced in the pages which follow.

CHAPTER ONE

BEFORE THE BEGINNING

The 150th anniversary of Yorkshire County Cricket Club is an event well worth celebrating but don't be misled into believing that when the birth took place in 1863 it marked the beginning of county cricket in Yorkshire. Far from it.

Yorkshire cricket before 1863 is not the main concern of this book but it would be wrong to ignore it entirely because the embryo game in its various forms around the county helped to establish the firm belief that cricket in the broad acres meant more than it did anywhere else.

That belief was deeply embedded by the beginning of the 20th century and, surprisingly, many are the people who are envious of the White Rose birthright which they do not possess themselves. From the earliest of days right up to the present time some of those who have made vast contributions to Yorkshire cricket are not Yorkshiremen themselves.

Among their numbers, some would have dearly loved to be Yorkshire born and bred and it would not surprise me even if Lord Hawke, one of Yorkshire's greatest ever figures, both on and off the field, had not fallen into that category. His Lordship was born at Willingham Rectory in Lincolnshire but his heart and soul was in Yorkshire.

That was certainly the case with the Rev. R.S. Holmes who tells us so much about early cricket in the county in his History of Yorkshire County Cricket 1833-1903, a book he compiled at the request of the Yorkshire CCC committee in 1904.

In his preface, the good Reverend confesses: "It is the writer's misfortune, not his fault, to be unable to style himself a Yorkshireman born and bred; but 13 years' residence in the West Riding, and constant association with Yorkshire cricketers of all degrees, had already made him three parts a Yorkshireman. The compiling of this book has completed his naturalisation."

And in an Introduction to the book, Lord Hawke makes it clear what he believes Yorkshire cricket means to the nation. "Yorkshire cricket is a thing of which not only every Yorkshireman but every Englishman must feel proud," writes the then Yorkshire captain and Club president.

He goes on: "I am very proud to have had some share in the splendid achievements which can be set to the credit of the county team, and what ever I have been able to do for the players or the game has been literally a labour of love."

At the time that Hawke wrote these words he had already been Yorkshire captain for 20 years and he would continue as such until 1910. "It is a post I would not exchange for that of captain of England," he said – and meant it.

Cricket in Yorkshire can be traced back to around 1750 but in rummaging through old Yorkshire newspapers from 1737 to just after the turn of the 19th century Holmes discovered only a few references to the game – not too surprising, perhaps, in view of how much hard news there was to cram into the four-page weekly sheet, plus reports on the most popular sports of the day, boxing and cockfighting.

Even so, the amount of public interest in a 'big match' was quite amazing. In 1825, All England for the first time played the Rest of Yorkshire in Sheffield and on the second day there were between 14,000-20,000 spectators present. The contest was staged at Darnall, on the outskirts of Sheffield in the direction of Glossop, and was played out for the staggering sum of 1,000 guineas – or at least that was the prize money advertised. Convert that into today's money, play the match at Headingley Carnegie and you would have agents of all the top players desperate to get their clients a game!

The cricket ground at Darnall had been opened three years earlier and its popularity as a venue at that time was partly why Sheffield was able to establish itself as one of the most important areas in the county for the staging of games. Those who either played on the ground or came as spectators were of the opinion that it was superior to all others and it began to attract cricketers from outside the county as well as those born within its borders.

Darnall's facilities, however, did not bear comparison with those at the Hyde Park ground which opened in 1826 after costing over £4,000 to develop and as it was situated only a mile and a half from the Sheffield city centre – Darnall was three miles away – it soon became accepted as the home of Yorkshire cricket.

That continued to be the case until the Bramall Lane ground became established and in 1855 the first match of importance was staged at the venue when Yorkshire entertained Sussex. Later, crowds of 60,000 could be accommodated in the ground. How today's Test venues would love to be able to boast such a capacity for England v Australia matches.

In 1851, the Sheffield authorities had "engaged professional cricketers to amuse the populace, and so draw them from cockfighting exhibitions". Cricket was also establishing itself in other parts of Yorkshire at this time but a firm foundation had already been laid in Sheffield.

Exactly 80 years earlier, the best cricketers from around Yorkshire had travelled to play for Sheffield against Nottingham and these fixtures continued to take place now and again right up to 1860. There were 26 matches in all, Nottingham coming out the stronger with 14 wins to Sheffield's nine, three of the games ending in draws.

It was in the 1826 clash in this series of matches that Sheffield-born, Tom Marsden, entered cricket folklore and became one of the first Yorkshire heroes of the game, even though Yorkshire County Cricket Club was still 37 years away from coming into existence.

Sheffield had been strengthened for this game by also including Leicester players but it was chiefly Marsden who routed Nottingham for 101 with four wickets. His greatest achievement, however, which would be passed down from generation to generation, was yet to come.

Pitches in those days were pretty rough strips of grass and heavy scores were largely unknown and it was about par for the course that Sheffield and Leicester should have lost four wickets fairly cheaply by the time the youthful Marsden strode to the middle. He was just 21 years of age and as this was his first appearance in this fixture perhaps not too much was expected of him.

But heroic deeds are rarely anticipated, they are conjured up, as if by magic, and Marsden's bat was a wand on this occasion as he occupied the crease for eight hours while making an astonishing 227 out of 379. It was said that the fact he batted for eight hours was testimony to the fine bowling of Clarke and Barker because Marsden was known as a free-scoring left-hander who was not slow in going for his shots.

Marsden's double century was only the second ever recorded in first-class cricket – the first one being William Ward's 278 for MCC against Norfolk at Lord's in 1820 – and as news of it spread the whole of Yorkshire began to rejoice.

A local poet even immortalised the great innings in a poem of 13 stanzas, each finishing with a chorus, and it included the lines:

Then Marsden went in, in his glory and pride,
And the arts of the Nottingham players defied.
Oh! Marsden at cricket is Nature's perfection
For hitting the ball in any direction.
He ne'er fears his wicket, so safely he strikes,
And he does with the bat and the ball as he likes.

And so the first Yorkshire cricketer had become immortalised and many more were to follow with the formation later in the century of Yorkshire County Cricket Club.

That, of course, was in 1863, but almost 100 years earlier cricket was establishing itself in several parts of the county, including Leeds, and on July 7, 1761, the Leeds Intelligencer announced that a game would take place on July 9 at Chapeltown.

This was the first publicised game in the Leeds area and four years later, on September 5, 1765, the London Chronicle reported that a "great match" had taken place at Chapletown Moor on August 26 between Leeds and Sheffield and that Sheffield had won "with great difficulty". For cricket in Yorkshire to attract the attention of readers in London shows that even in those far distant days the games were of national interest.

In 1833, the first match was played by Yorkshire and organised by the Sheffield Wednesday Club. The contest was against Norfolk, who had among their ranks the greatest batsman of the day in Fuller Pilch who was born in the county but had later spent quite a bit of time in Yorkshire, learning his cricket at the Wednesday club where he was a member.

Yorkshire emerged easy winners by 120 runs and although Marsden was out for a duck in the first innings he set his side up for victory in the second innings with 53, the top score of the match.

Fuller Pilch contributed only 10 and 23 and he was outplayed by Marsden on this occasion but in the same year Pilch and Marsden were matched for the Championship of England with no fielders being allowed on either side and in each game Marsden was soundly beaten.

But Marsden epitomised Yorkshire cricket and it is significant that in 1842 when Sheffield were looking to strengthen their team by widening the net for the

Nottingham match they rejected a proposal to include Pilch on the grounds that he was not a local man. Already, it seems, there was a reluctance to bring in players from outside the county and this view gained in strength as time went on.

By the early 1860s, Yorkshire were very much a proper team but without a club and although a Public Match Fund Committee had been formed at Sheffield in 1861 it was not seen as representing the county as a whole. Funds were so tight that in 1862 an invitation from the Manchester club for Yorkshire to play Lancashire home and away had to be turned down.

This was nothing short of a humiliation and at the end of the season it was a London journalist's impassioned appeal to do something about it which drew a positive response – another early instance of an "outsider" rallying to Yorkshire's cause.

He wrote: *Yorkshire, you are wanted, that is, the leading men and cricketers of Yorkshire are wanted, to bestir themselves, beat up the wealth, rank and influential men of their shire, and establish a County Cricket Club. Good cricket grounds you have already in various parts of the county. Cricketers are ready at hand of that metal and ability that even under the present disorganised – or, rather NO – state of things, were found an eleven that could beat Surrey....*

To let a county droop in the cricket world that has found an eleven which can beat Surrey, (they had done so at Bramall Lane in 1861) appears to us a burning shame. Why, even the Yorkshire eleven, that were beaten by the Surrey team at the Oval, bowled, fielded and played their up-hill game so pluckily and well as not only to obtain the public compliments of their opponents, but a reward (10s.) from the Surrey club for each man of the eleven.

It is our opinion that if Yorkshiremen would but establish on a proper basis a County Club, they would in a year or two be able to bring such an eleven into the field as would make Yorkshire a cricketing county second to none in England, and Yorkshire-trained cricketers as famous as Yorkshire-trained racehorses. Firmly raise that: elect an active, popular, persevering secretary; back him up with a well-filled exchequer; and when you match, always play the full strength of the County.

These words of a visionary London journalist were not lost upon those who read them or heard of them 150 miles up the road in Sheffield. The time had come for action.

CHAPTER TWO

EARLY DAYS

The New Year had barely been rung in and the Christmas decorations taken down when Yorkshire County Cricket Club came into being on January 8, 1863, the small but distinguished group which met at the Adelphi Hotel in Sheffield resolving "That a County Club be formed".

In view of the sharp focussing in the years running up to this meeting of Sheffield being the nerve centre of Yorkshire cricket, it is hardly surprising that all 12 members of the committee came from the city of steel.

The Rules adopted were succinct and entirely sensible. Matches would not be staged on any one ground but should be spread around the county; recommendations from local clubs of young players considered good enough to add to the strength of the County would be earnestly invited; in negotiating with any local club or district for the site of a match the Managing Committee "shall either accept a sum of money to be agreed upon from such club or district, or the ground on which the match is played shall be surrendered absolutely and unconditionally for the match days".

It was agreed that the County Club should consist of an unlimited number of members and that the lowest subscription should be 10s. 6d (in today's money just over 52p).

A glance at the list of officials of Yorkshire County Cricket Club will show that Thomas R. Barker was elected the first president in 1863 and Michael J. Ellison the first treasurer, but it is possible that Ellison also served as president from the beginning right up to his death in 1898.

Although T.R. Barker's name appears as president in the minutes book, there is no record of him thereafter attending any meeting and a year later M.J. Ellison is marked down as serving as both president and treasurer, the latter post remaining his until his son took over in 1894.

T.R. Barker was elected the sixth Mayor of Sheffield in 1848 but he was no Yorkshireman, having been born at Bakewell, Derbyshire, in 1833, and neither was M.J. Ellison, who was born at Worksop, Nottinghamshire, in 1817. Both of them, however, had appeared in the Yorkshire side on various occasions, Barker turning out in nine games in which he scored 121 runs and took 38 wickets, and Ellison in 16 matches, scoring 195 runs and claiming a solitary wicket.

Ellison cut an imposing figure with his watch chain and long white beard but his long tenure in office suggests he was regarded as a benevolent dictator by the majority of cricketers who began to assemble under his wing.

An agent to the Duke of Norfolk estates in Sheffield, Ellison did much to put Sheffield on the map by persuading the Great Northern Railway to include the city on the main line to London. He was an unwavering supporter of Yorkshire cricket and was deeply admired by the shooting fraternity for never having missed a "Twelfth" on the grouse moors from 1832-97 – a record most probably without equal.

George Padley, who had been secretary of the Match Fund in its second year, was Yorkshire's first secretary but he, too, lasted for only 12 months before stepping down because of his appointment as Borough Accountant.

His successor was J.B. Wostinholm who for 38 years "served Yorkshire cricket with an ability and enthusiasm beyond praise," according to the Rev. R.S. Holmes. Undoubtedly Ellison and Wostinholm were the two men who virtually ran Yorkshire County Cricket Club for its first three decades and more. Although Ellison was no Yorkshireman he still advocated that only Yorkshire-born cricketers should represent Yorkshire CCC. Later on, when it was pointed out to him that Lord Hawke had been born in Lincolnshire he turned a blind eye to that small inconvenience. Perhaps who you were born mattered a little more than where you were born.

We have seen that Yorkshire were fortunate to have some strong and influential characters governing their cricket in the early days and the County Club were also splendidly served on the field by their first captain, the popular and extremely capable Roger Iddison, who hailed from Bedale, as did his team-mate at the time, George Anderson, a powerfully built batsman.

Iddison, a butcher by trade, was something of a cricket mercenary in a colourful career which began in 1853 and lasted for 23 years. An effective right-hand batsman and a round-arm and under-arm quick bowler, he played in eight pre-county games for Yorkshire and 64 between 1863-76, captaining the side until the end of the 1872 season.

But Iddison performed wherever he was able and he was also a member of Lancashire's team for 16 matches between 1865-70, sometimes representing both the White Rose and the Red in the same season. He captained both sides on occasions but always led Yorkshire in the Roses encounters.

On August 7 and 8, 1865, he played for Lancashire against Middlesex at the Cattle Market ground in Islington – Lancashire losing by ten wickets with a day to spare in the three-day match – and a few weeks later he was back with Yorkshire for the clash with Cambridgeshire at Ashton-under-Lyne in which the celebrated George Freeman made his debut.

Iddison was with both Roses teams again the following season when he opened the batting for Lancashire against Surrey and scored 49 and 106, his maiden century, before leading Yorkshire against Nottinghamshire at Trent Bridge in the game which marked the great Tom Emmett's debut.

Perhaps his allegiance to both counties was understandable because his brother, William Holdsworth Iddison, was a Lancashire player between 1867-68. Roger Iddison's other teams included an All England XI, England (on three occasions), Married Men, North of England and Players, so it can be seen that he got around a bit.

Yorkshire's first match under the banner of the newly constituted club was against Surrey at the Oval on June 5 and 6 and although the Rev. R.S. Holmes said that Yorkshire were captained by George Anderson other records indicate that Iddison led the side.

The team came home with a creditable draw under their belts and it was a well-balanced side, despite the new county's home being in Sheffield. The players and the towns and cities from which they came were: John Thewlis (Lascelles Hall), John Berry and Edwin 'Ned' Dawson (Dalton), Iddison and Anderson (Bedale), George Atkinson (Ripon), Isaac 'Ikey' Hodgson (Bradford) and Edwin 'Ned'

Stephenson and William Slinn (Sheffield).

Hodgson and Slinn were the first of Yorkshire's really effective bowling partnerships and each made his mark in that opening game at the Oval by claiming five second innings wickets as Surrey were sent back for 60 but Yorkshire never got the chance to chase the 119 they needed for victory and they had to be content with the draw.

Even though Yorkshire County Cricket Club were now up and running they were by no means responsible for organising all of Yorkshire's matches. Four games were held in that initial season of 1863 but only the home and away fixtures with Surrey came under the umbrella of the County Club, their first home game, therefore, being the one at Bramall Lane which Yorkshire won by three wickets.

The Slinn-Hodgson combination was well supported by Iddison, the trio having an equal share in nine of the first innings wickets as Surrey were dismissed for 201, and Iddison then kept Yorkshire's head above water by making 51 of his side's 172 in reply. Slinn and Hodgson again took three wickets apiece to restrict Surrey to 144 and a further half-century from Iddison, aided by 65 from Sheffield-born Joseph 'Old Tarpot' Rowbotham, saw Yorkshire over the line.

Nothing ever is or ever has been straightforward in the White Rose county and the two other Yorkshire matches in 1863 were arranged by Bradford Cricket Club, established in 1836. They were both against Nottinghamshire and the home match was played at the Great Horton Lane ground.

With York also prominent in arranging top quality matches, confusion began to arise as to just who the proper parties were for organising Yorkshire games and in 1864 Kent wrote to Yorkshire CCC asking just that question. Kent must not have been fully convinced by the answer they received because they paid a visit that season to the Swatter's Carr, Linthorpe Road East Ground at Middlesbrough where the Yorkshire side beat them by three wickets. This was the first of three first-class fixtures to be played at the venue before it was sold off for building in 1874.

The doubt over which, exactly, was the County Club, prompted an article in the Cricketers' Companion which read:

At present it is difficult to define which is the County Club, as York, Bradford and Sheffield aspire to that honour. That at York is more properly a gentleman's club, and includes most of the amateur talent of the County. At Bradford there is a most energetic Committee and a liberal subscription list, and for several seasons the matches with Nottinghamshire and Cambridgeshire have been played there. The ground, though good and advantageously situated (in Horton Lane) is too confined for first-class matches; indeed, only square hits can be run out. An enlargement is contemplated, and this done, Bradford will enjoy, as it deserves, a fair share of county cricket. Bramall Lane is a splendid area, with ample accommodation of every kind. Except Nottingham, there is no town in England where spectators are so numerous, or enter so thoroughly into the spirit of the game.

The doubts over who was actually running Yorkshire's affairs then became even more complex when five Yorkshire players lay down their bats, as it were, and went on strike. The stubborn and determined streak that has long been a characteristic of Yorkshire cricketers was already beginning to surface.

CHAPTER THREE

TROUBLE AT T'MILL

The cause of the problem was complicated and it went back to 1862 when Edgar 'Ned' Willsher was no-balled six consecutive times for bowling overarm by umpire John Lillywhite while playing for the All England XI against Surrey at The Oval.

Yorkshire's Bedale pair, Iddison and Anderson, were playing alongside Willsher in the match and they and the other professionals in the team were convinced that Surrey had pressurised Lillywhite into calling Willsher, the upshot being that the eight professionals all walked off in protest and the game was unable to resume until the following day.

Perhaps not surprisingly, ill-will between players from the north and south had been building up steadily and this latest incident worsened the situation to such an extent that when Iddison, in 1864, was asked to get together a North team to play the South at Islington he failed to turn up and a Southern amateur had to be drafted in as a substitute. The South responded during the match with a statement which said that they would refuse to play the North in a match scheduled for Newmarket.

All Southern players went on to withdraw their services from the All England and United All England teams and instead played for the newly-formed United South of England Eleven which W.G. Grace later began to 'grace' with his presence.

The row continued to simmer and its repercussions were felt by the Yorkshire County Club the following season when five of their leading players refused to play against Surrey at Bramall Lane, the quintet in question being Anderson, Atkinson, Iddison, Rowbotham and Stephenson.

Later in the summer, Yorkshire entertained the All England Eleven at Bramall Lane but the game attracted little interest because the five agitators were not allowed to play by the Sheffield committee, one member of which suggested that the five should never play on the ground again. There was, however, considerable public support for the absentees and a benefit match on their behalf was arranged for the September.

As a result of all this trouble and strife, Yorkshire did not win any of the matches arranged by the County Club in 1865 and the situation became so serious that the Club did not organise any games at all the following year. In the February the general committee had decided "That it be left to the discretion of the Committee to determine whether any and what Matches shall be played during the ensuing season but that it be a distinct instruction to the Committee that Anderson, Atkinson, Rowbotham and Stephenson be excluded from any Match which the Committee may make."

What a relief for the club, therefore, that in April, 1867, the committee decided that the offending players should be allowed to play against Surrey. Even so, the affair appears to have rumbled on between Yorkshire and Surrey for quite a time and even in this day and age there is not much love lost between the two counties.

Perhaps it all goes back to those days in the mid-1860s without anyone now realising it!

It was also resolved early in 1867 that "the choice of players in the coming season be left in the hands of the Committee, and they are empowered (if they think well) to play those cricketers who refused to play in the past season, on their expressing regret for what has occurred." All, apparently, did so.

The ending of the wrangle was described in words by the Rev. R.S. Holmes which may bring a smile to the faces of Yorkshire cricket followers blessed with the gift of hindsight. He wrote: "Ever since that year there has reigned the most perfect harmony between the Committee and cricketers of the Yorkshire County Cricket Club." It was a happy situation which would certainly not last for ever.

But history has shown that the loyal support originally shown for Willsher from Iddison and Anderson and Co was well placed. In 1864 the MCC wisely changed the Laws and overarm bowling was sanctioned.

And history has also shown that not everything went sour on the Yorkshire team in 1866 because, as already mentioned, Tom Emmett made his debut in the match against Nottinghamshire at Trent Bridge arranged by the Bradford Club and he announced himself by claiming 5-33 in the first innings as Notts were sent back for 91. The home side still went on to win by nine wickets inside two days, Emmett picking up the solitary wicket to fall in their second innings.

Tom Emmett

Born in Halifax on September 3, 1841, Emmett was one of the first great Yorkshire cricketers and to this day he is considered one of the fastest left-arm bowlers the county has ever produced.

Although he slowed down to some extent and displayed more cunning when he grew older, his round-arm action produced searing pace when he started out in the game and for several years he was acknowledged as being one of the most dangerous bowlers in England.

His speciality was a ball which pitched on leg and whipped across the batsman to hit the off bail. For some reason known only to Emmett he called it his "sostenuter" and it was lethal enough to dismiss W.G. Grace more than once.

The great W.G. rightly had every respect for Emmett and he was gracious enough to remark that in his opinion Emmett and his Yorkshire fast bowling partner, George Freeman, were the best two bowlers in the country.

Emmett played in 299 matches for Yorkshire between 1866-88 and he holds the distinction of being the county's first bowler to capture 1,000 wickets, his final tally standing at 1,216. None of the 12 other bowlers in Yorkshire's history to have claimed 1,000-plus wickets has done so at such miserly cost as Emmett's 12.71 runs per wicket and the only bowler with at least 500 wickets to his name to have been fractionally less costly was Ted Peate at 12.57.

Quick and dangerous as he was, Emmett was nevertheless a charming man with a bubbling personality and few, if any, other professionals at the time were more popular either with their team-mates or the crowd. When Emmett was awarded a benefit match in 1878 it raised the princely sum for those days of £616 13s. 1d.

He went on to serve as Yorkshire captain from 1878-82 but without any great success, his friendly and easy-going personality perhaps not making him the tough sort of leader to get the best out of his men.

Emmett reached his pinnacle for Yorkshire in 1886 when he took 112 wickets and it was the following summer at Sheffield that he destroyed Surrey by grabbing six wickets for seven runs. On five other occasions, including the Australians at Bradford in 1882, he captured six wickets in an innings at fewer than four runs each.

His best return was 9-23 against Cambridgeshire at Hunslet in 1869 when he took 16 wickets in the day. The previous year he had sent back nine Nottinghamshire batsmen for 34 at Dewsbury, and he was able to boast eight wickets in an innings on six other occasions.

Emmett was no mean batsman, either, and he registered a fighting 104 off Gloucestershire's attack at Clifton College in 1873.

His all-round skills earned him seven Test matches with England and he went on three tours of Australia, playing in the first-ever Test between the two countries which was staged at Melbourne in 1877. In all, however, he managed only nine Test wickets but six of them came for 68 runs against Australia at Melbourne in 1879 and in practically every other match in which he played against the Australians he enjoyed remarkable success.

It was fortunate indeed for Yorkshire that Emmett should appear on the scene to boost morale and divert attention from the players' strike which was threatening to tear the county club apart.

Also taking part in two of the three Yorkshire matches arranged in 1866 was another player who would become a household name – George Freeman, from Boroughbridge. He had made his debut against Cambridgeshire in the previous year, his appearance serving as a beacon of hope during that generally gloomy time, and his haul of 4-29 was an indication of what was to come later.

For a relatively brief period, Freeman was lightning quick with the ball and although he played in only 32 matches for the Yorkshire County Club he took an amazing 209 wickets at just under ten runs apiece. Is it any wonder that W.G. Grace said of him that he considered Freeman to be the best bowler he had ever faced?

Freeman was wicketless in the two matches in which he played in 1866 but come the following summer he and Emmett took the cricketing world by storm, Freeman helping himself to 51 wickets for Yorkshire at 7.4 runs per wicket while Emmett bagged 30 wickets at 5.2 runs apiece. Batsmen simply could not cope with this battering which they received from the awesome pair and so lethal were Freeman and Emmett together that Yorkshire were triumphant in all seven of their matches that season when they did the double against both Cambridgeshire and Lancashire, Freeman's figures in the innings victory in the Roses game at Whalley being 22.1-14-10-7 and 31-14-41-5. Emmett, however, did not play in this fixture and Freeman and Luke Greenwood bowled unchanged throughout, Greenwood enjoying match figures of 7-76 in what was his most successful season. To end the campaign with a 100 per cent winning record is something which Yorkshire have never done since and they will almost certainly never do so again.

Freeman and Emmett were just as fearsome in 1868 but Yorkshire were not able to maintain their almost impossibly high standards of the previous season and they won four and lost three of their seven matches. Even so, Freeman continued his total domination of Lancashire matches, helped this time by Emmett. At Holbeck, Lancashire decided to bat first on winning the toss and were sent back for 30 with Freeman's figures showing 13-8-11-8 and Emmett 12.2-8-11-2. Yorkshire made 250 and routed Lancashire again, this time for 34 with Freeman 16-11-12-4 and Emmett 15.2-9-13-6.

The dynamic duo bowled unchanged throughout this match and Freeman captured the first hat-trick in Yorkshire's history. Almost beyond belief, the pair again bowled unchanged in the next match against Middlesex at Bramall Lane and Freeman again floored his opponents with a hat-trick. Middlesex were first bowled out for 79 (Freeman 29.3-17-29-7, Emmott 29-11-42-3) and then 59 (Freeman 22.3-10-32-5, Emmott 22-16-16-3).

Some years later, Freeman recounted a tale about the Holbeck match which shows how intense the Roses rivalry had become yet how honourable were those who played in or watched the games.

He was taking a drink in a hotel in Thirsk, the town where he lived, when he struck up a conversation with a stranger. The subject inevitably turned to cricket and it soon became apparent that the visitor was a Lancastrian and an avid supporter of the Red Rose. Yorkshire were very much the inferior side, in his opinion, and after listening to him for some length of time, Freeman cut in to say that he thought there had been a match in which Lancashire had twice been dismissed for under 50, but he was unsure as to the exact detail.

Impossible, said the stranger, and slapped a sovereign on the table as a wager which Freeman accepted before the former famous cricketer made off to re-acquaint himself with the scores.

Once Freeman had left the hotel, someone who had overheard the conversation told the man exactly who Freeman was and said that he had played in the match in question.

Freeman was later told that the man responded by saying: "Then I may as well stump up at once." He did so most honourably by leaving the money at the bar and Freeman never saw him again but he respected him for ever more.

As we know, from 1863 to 1874, not all of Yorkshire's matches were arranged by the Yorkshire County Club but Freeman and Emmett were running riot in the mid-part of that period regardless of who was responsible for organising them. They were putting Yorkshire cricket on the map.

CHAPTER FOUR

LASCELLES LIONS

The standard of pitches in those early years was well below what is expected today which is one of the reasons why the likes of Emmett and Freeman were so dominant and why scores were generally on the low side.

But Yorkshire were also bringing on batsmen who became household names and three of the earliest had strong associations with Lascelles Hall.

John Thewlis was born in 1828 at Kirkheaton – the Huddersfield suburb which was to become even more renowned later on as the birthplace of the incomparable George Hirst and Wilfred Rhodes – but moved to Lascelles as an eight-year-old. The young Thewlis refused to go to school because he was self-conscious of his white hair and he taught himself to read and write as well as to play cricket.

He went into the Yorkshire County Club side as soon as it was formed and he was the only player not to miss a single game during the first three years of its existence.

On July 24, 1868, Thewlis opened the batting for Yorkshire against Surrey at the Oval in a game of huge historical significance because going in first with him on his debut was his nephew, Ephraim Lockwood, who was affectionately and mysteriously known by his team-mates as Mary Anne.

Uncle and nephew put on 176 together before Lockwood was dismissed for 91 but Thewlis went on to make 108 to become the first Yorkshire CCC batsman to record a century. He was related to two other notable Yorkshire cricketers from Lascelles Hall in David Eastwood, who represented his county from 1870-87, and the immensely talented all-rounder, Willie Bates, who earned his place in the side in 1887 by virtue of taking all ten wickets for Yorkshire Colts v Nottinghamshire Colts with his off-spinners.

A hard-hitting batsman, Bates played each of his 15 Test matches in Australia and there was a sad irony about his death in early January, 1900, at the age of 45. Just before Christmas he had attended the funeral at Lascelles Hall of his uncle but he caught a cold which proved fatal.

As for Lockwood, he rightly earned the tag of being Yorkshire's best batsman so far but to do so he had to shrug off the comments of spectators and opposition players at the commencement of his career, remarks brought about by his rustic appearance.

Yet there was nothing farmer-like about his batting and one of the Australian party of 1878 told the Rev. R.S. Holmes that the Aussies considered that Lockwood had a greater variety of strokes than any other English batsman, apart, that is, from W.G. Grace. He could even do what W.G. did not attempt, and that was to cut balls off the middle stump, and when he made his biggest score of 208 against Kent in 1883, the recipient of much of the mayhem, Jimmy Wootton, said it was the finest display of cutting he had ever seen.

Lockwood's younger brother, Henry, also from Lascelles Hall, managed a few

innings and six in the second – and every one of them was cleaned bowled. It is difficult to imagine a more stunning introduction to county cricket. He bowled unchanged with Emmett in the first innings as Surrey were dismissed for 111 and he helped send them back for 72 in the second, Yorkshire winning by ten wickets. Hill's match figures were 12-57 and he also shone with the bat, top-scoring with 28 in Yorkshire's first innings knock of 100.

A Yorkshire supporter presented Hill with a silver cup to mark his triumph but it is not only his performance in this match for which he is remembered because he is also credited with the first wicket and the first catch in Test cricket – against Australia at Melbourne in 1877 when he bowled opener Nathaniel Thompson and almost immediately afterwards held a catch from Thomas Horan. He also played in the second Test on Lillywhite's tour and this proved to be his last but in an 11-year career with Yorkshire he captured 542 wickets at a frugal 12.91 runs apiece.

The replacement of Freeman by Hill meant bowlers remained very much on top for Yorkshire in 1871 but perhaps the team were not playing as a unit because they won only three of their seven matches and their record was even more dismal the following summer when they won two out of ten while suffering seven defeats. Whatever the reasons for the decline, luck was seldom on their side because they invariably lost the toss.

It was not Yorkshire but the legendary W.G. Grace that was the top attraction for spectators attending Bramall Lane in 1872 who witnessed his first appearance at the venue in a County match, his previous visit there being in 1869 when he scored 122 out of 173 for South v North.

On this later occasion he was with Gloucestershire on their initial visit to Bramall Lane and once again the good doctor was in tremendous form, dominating proceedings with both bat and ball – as he was prone to do. Opening the batting with Tom Matthews, the pair put on 238 before both fell in quick succession, Matthews for 85 and Grace for 150. W.G. then bowled unchanged with his brother, Edward, to claim 8-33 as Yorkshire crashed to 66 all out and he followed this up with 7-46 out of a total of 116, Gloucestershire going home with victory by an innings and 112 runs under their belt.

The most significant development in the history of county cricket occurred in 1873 – ten years after the formation of the Yorkshire Club – with the opening of the County Championship. Yorkshire folk may be reluctant to admit it but they have to thank Surrey for their initiative in getting the competition started by requesting the MCC to "remove the prevailing laxity in the matter of county qualification". MCC seemed prepared only to endorse what the counties themselves wanted and so the leading counties met in late 1872 and agreed the qualifications for a county cricketer.

It was an extremely complicated competition in the early years with no firm rules or regulations on how the Championship should be determined and with complex rules on the distribution of points. This unsatisfactory state of affairs lasted until 1894 when the MCC took the matter in hand and sorted things out properly.

But at least we had got Championship cricket up and running and Yorkshire followers, particularly, can toast its birth, because their team have taken the title more times than anyone else.

CHAPTER FIVE

HARD TIMES

Yes, toast the birth of the County Championship, by all means, but then put the champagne on ice for a while because there will be little else to celebrate until quite a few years have passed. Yorkshire may have won the Championship title more than anyone else over the past 150 years but they took a long time to settle in and a decade or so was to pass before there were signs that a firmer foundation was being laid.

On the face it, Yorkshire should have been successful right from the start of the Championship because they still had some marvellous players but they lacked team discipline and direction and were a bit like a powerful ship without a rudder.

Iddison had been a popular captain of the County Club from 1863-72 but, as we have discovered, in those years he also played for other prominent teams, including Lancashire, and it is doubtful if he had ever considered it his duty to build up a strong Yorkshire team of the future.

The Championship put a different perspective on things and what Yorkshire really needed was a resolute captain who could see further ahead than the next match and who cared passionately about the men under his command. It was a time yet before that man stepped forward.

Iddison gave up the captaincy ahead of that first Championship season and was replaced by Joe Rowbotham who was certainly respected by his team-mates, having played in the first Yorkshire match organised by the County Club ten years earlier and who in 1869 became the first Yorkshire batsman to make two centuries in the same season.

Finding a long-term captain was proving difficult because Rowbotham was in charge in 1873 and again in 1875 while sandwiched in between was Luke Greenwood, now coming up 40, the first Yorkshire player from Lascelles Hall. This also proved to be his last season with Rowbotham also calling it a day two years later.

Another Lascelles Hall native, Ephraim Lockwood, was appointed captain for 1876-77 and the job was handed to that most loyal of Yorkshire servants, Tom Emmett, from 1878-1882. But Emmett was too modest a member of the team and too jovial a personality to rule with the iron hand that was required.

All of the captains Yorkshire turned to at this period were thoroughly good professionals but, the class system being what it is in this country, the team would probably have felt they could have been pushed harder if an amateur, with firm but fair discipline, had been their leader.

Similar thoughts evidently entered the head of the County Committee because there exists a minute from 1878 which says: "That T. Emmett be made captain in the absence of a gentleman". Not the most tactful way of putting it, perhaps, but we know what was meant.

Yorkshire's task was not made any easier in that first season of 1873 by the retirement of Freeman, but Emmett's star still shone as brightly as ever on the field of play and Lockwood was considered the best professional batsman in England. Pinder was as fine a wicketkeeper as any side could want and Allen Hill, who had replaced Freeman, grabbed 81 wickets at 12 runs per wicket, 60 of them being cleaned bowled

Rowbotham, despite his advancing years, was considered still to be in his prime as a batsman and Greenwood continued to be reliable with the ball while a trio of Colts in Alf Smith, George Ulyett and Louis Hall all looked extremely promising youngsters.

Undoubtedly, Yorkshire had plenty of quality players to call upon in 1873 and in the seasons which immediately followed it, yet they performed only adequately and could not take the new Championship competition by storm in the first few years of its existence.

Nine counties started out in the Championship but in its inaugural year Yorkshire could only finish a respectable third behind the mighty Gloucestershire (or Gracetershire!) and Nottinghamshire and they held the same position the following summer when Derbyshire won the title with Gloucestershire their nearest rivals.

Yorkshire dropped to fourth in 1875 and after going up a position in 1876 they slumped to seventh in 1877, the table of merit at the time being determined not by most points gained but by fewest losses sustained. This system was flawed and the Champion County was not necessarily the best side. In 1883, for instance, Yorkshire won nine matches, lost two and drew five of their 16 games but they still finished second to Nottinghamshire whose record was four wins, one defeat and seven draws.

Regulations are regulations, however, and Yorkshire yearned to head the table but were unable to do so. How strange that history should repeat itself 100 years later when Yorkshire were again in a vain struggle for supremacy but the tension was probably greater in the 1970s because by then the team had a big reputation to try and live up to – and they failed to do so.

Although Yorkshire were unable to dominate in the 1870s they were still quite capable of playing wonderful cricket – they even beat Gloucestershire and the Graces for the first time in 1875 – and some of the players were showing encouraging signs of development, not least Ulyett who decided to concentrate mainly on his batting seeing that there were plenty of other top-class bowlers around.

Ulyett did not entirely desert his bowling, either for Yorkshire or England, achieving a hat-trick against Lancashire in 1884 when he also took 7-36 against Australia at Lord's, but it was as a batsman that he mainly held centre stage and the crowds loved him. He was known to them as "Happy Jack" and when he was granted a benefit they responded so generously that he became the first Yorkshire player to receive a four-figure sum.

Twice Ulyett carried his bat, making 146 out of 248 against MCC at Scarborough in 1884 and 199 out of 399 against Derbyshire at Bramall Lane in 1887. His dashing style contrasted perfectly with that of his opening partner, Louis Hall, who can safely be tagged as the Geoff Boycott of the 19th century.

Hall was cautious and properly careful, a reliable and solid batsman among many cavaliers, and he just loved to occupy the crease – which he did more successfully than any other batsman in Yorkshire's history, carrying his bat on 14 occasions between 1878 and 1891. Much later, Len Hutton achieved the feat six times and Boycott eight.

Other bowlers continued to make their name in the 70s, notably Tom Armitage, who bowled lobs as well as round-arm, and that member of the Lascelles Hall mafia, Willie Bates, who played all of his 15 Tests in Australia. In 11 seasons for Yorkshire from 1877-1887 this magnificent all-rounder scored 6,499 runs, most of them with truly aggressive intent, and knocked back the stumps of 637 batsmen. Tragically, he lost an eye while practising in the nets on his last tour of Australia and his first-class career came to an abrupt end while he was still in his pomp.

Right at the very end of the 70s, Yorkshire gave a debut to Ted Peate and although they did not realise it then they had found the first in a series of left-arm slow bowling wizards which no other club anywhere in the world would be able to match. Nothing in Yorkshire's history gives the club's followers greater pride than the chain of left-armers which came off the production line, Peate being the very first link.

And even before Peate's career was prematurely brought to a halt when Lord Hawke considered his services were no longer required, the second link had already been attached with the appearance of Bobby Peel, whose early demise was even more dramatic.

Peate started off as a quick bowler but in a shed where he worked as a warp twister at Yeadon – for whose cricket club he took hundreds of wickets – he began practising slow bowling and discovered he had much greater command of length and line.

In 1878 he played in a match against Scarborough, who had the Rev. E.S. Carter in their side, and he was so impressed with Peate that he several times urged Yorkshire to give him a try. The following year, Peate was given a game with the Colts and he returned almost unbelievable figures, capturing all ten wickets for 11 runs in the first innings and 7-23 in the second, in addition to scoring an unbeaten 25.

That was good enough for Yorkshire who had no similar bowler in their ranks and after his first two outings had been badly hit by the weather he returned match figures of 12-77 against Kent at Sheffield. The same opponents were blitzed again three years later when Peate achieved a most noble hat-trick by sending back Lord Harris, Lord Throwley on his debut and Edward O'Shaughnessy. That was in the second innings when Bates claimed 6-12 but it was Peate who was chief destroyer in the first innings with 7-31 to Bates' 3-47. They would have shared all 20 wickets but for a run out.

Peate took 8-5 against Surrey at Holbeck in 1883 but it was often against the Australians that he was at his most devastating, whether for England, Yorkshire or other sides. In 1884 he accounted for 55 Aussie wickets at 14.02 runs apiece, yet it was his remark as a batsman that became part of cricket folklore.

Playing in The Oval Test in 1882, he was last out in an England defeat which saw the birth of the Ashes following the mock obituary in the Sporting Times which read: "In affection remembrance of England cricket which died at the Oval, 29th August, 1882. Deeply lamented by a large circle of sorrowing friends and acquaintances. R.I.P...N.B. The body will be cremated and the Ashes taken to Australia."

Going in at the fall of the ninth wicket, Peate had joined the redoubtable Charlie (C.T.) Studd with nine wanted and Peate had scored two of them when he was dismissed attempting to attack too boldly. He was approached in a rage by Isaac Walker, an MCC stalwart and noted Middlesex player, and asked why he had not played safe and let Charlie get the runs? His reply was: "I couldn't trust Mr. Studd." Peate's reasoning was that in the rising tension before either had gone in, the Yorkshireman had seen Mr. Studd walking around with a blanket over his head.

When Peate's services were deemed to be no longer required at the end of the 1887 season he had taken 794 wickets in 154 matches for Yorkshire at 12.57 runs apiece but the man who had joined him in the side – and is alphabetically next to him in the directory of Yorkshire players – would play in around twice as many games for the county and end up with 1,311 wickets at 15.74, plus 9,322 runs with six centuries.

Opinion was almost equally divided as to whether Peate or Peel was the greater bowler but everyone was agreed that both were out of the top drawer and that either could land the ball on a sixpence – although Peate shrugged off such claims by saying that no-one could consistently do that.

Like Peate, Peel decimated the Australians, taking 102 wickets in 20 Tests with a best haul of 7-31 at Old Trafford in 1888, and his figures for Yorkshire were just as stunning. In that same year he weighed in with 8-12 and then 6-21 as Nottinghamshire were sent packing for 24 and 58 at Bramall Lane and in 1895 he returned 9-22 v Somerset at Headingley. In the following summer he scored an unbeaten 210 against Warwickshire at Edgbaston when he went on to finish the season with 1,193 runs.

He managed 100 wickets in seven seasons, his best being in 1895 when he bagged 155, and his career with Yorkshire would have gone on quite a bit longer than 1897 had he not enjoyed drinking just as much as he enjoyed bowling.

Like many professionals at that time, Peel was not averse to taking a glass or two but when he rolled up late and very drunk one morning and staggered on to the outfield it proved to be the final straw as far as Lord Hawke was concerned.

There has been much confusion over exactly which match it was that the sensational incident took place and although it is hard to credit now it may be that the newspapers did not consider it all that newsworthy in those days.

Another interpretation could be that there was a conspiracy of silence. Hawke had considerable influence and may have applied pressure on the Press to steer clear of giving precise details.

More than half a century after the event, George Hirst recounted his version to A.A. Thompson for his book Hirst and Rhodes, but Hirst's memory faltered over some of the detail. He thought the match took place at Chesterfield and that Peel came down to breakfast in the professionals' hotel quite the worse for wear on the day that play was due to begin, but first class cricket was not even played at Chesterfield until 1898.

The match is assumed by many to have been Yorkshire v Middlesex at Bramall Lane on August 16, 17 and 18 but the scenario described by Hirst does not quite fit into the pattern of that particular game – Peel's last for the county.

Peel undoubtedly played an active part in the first innings of the Sheffield game, first of all scoring a capable 40 and then picking up 5-71 as Middlesex were bowled out for 247 to leave Yorkshire with a lead of 119 which they extended to 301 before declaring on 182-6. Middlesex rallied to 219-2 to draw the match and Peel bowled only seven overs in their second innings.

But Peel could not have wandered on to the outfield on the first morning – as Hirst states – because Yorkshire batted first. And Peel was still involved in the game on the final day because Middlesex did not begin their second innings until then and Peel bowled seven overs.

In fact, Peel WAS told to leave the field later that very day because of his condition but it was the FOLLOWING morning that he made his way, with unsteady gait, on to the field at Bradford Park Avenue as the match against Derbyshire was about to begin. And it was then that he was ordered off and his career with Yorkshire was finished.

Although time may have dimmed Hirst's memory to some extent, his account of the Peel episode brings an instant smile to the faces of all who read it, despite everyone feeling it was a tragic way for such a gifted and likeable cricketer to end up.

Hirst says he was having breakfast in the hotel before setting off for the ground when Peel staggered towards him "in a proper condition." So concerned was the kindly Hirst to protect his friend and team-mate that he helped him back to bed, tucked him up and when he got to the ground (Park Avenue, not Bramall Lane) he told Hawke that Peel "had been taken very queer in the night and won't be able to turn out this morning."

Hawke sympathised, called up the 12th man and led his team on to the field but at that point Hirst noticed, to his dismay, that Yorkshire did not have 11 men on duty but 12.

"There, his face red, his cap awry, the ball in his hand, stood Bobby Peel, in an even 'properer' condition than before," said Hirst. He heard Lord Hawke say: "Leave the field at once, Peel," to which Peel replied: "Not at all, my Lord. I'm in fine form this morning." Peel then turned away from the wicket and delivered "an elaborately cunning ball" in the direction of the sightscreen.

Hirst was not quite sure exactly what happened next but he believed that Peel might have been led quietly away with few people realising that a serious breach of discipline had occurred.

Another story has it that Peel also urinated on the field before making his exit but there is no reference made to this by Hirst and it is probably just part of the folklore which has built up over the years.

Something serious had certainly occurred at Bramall Lane because in its review of the 1897 season, Cricket, a Weekly Record of the Game, reports: "Peel showed good form both with bat and ball, but, owing to an illness and the "contretemps" at Sheffield, played little after the first half of the season."

Peel had indeed missed the six matches leading up to the Sheffield game, his previous appearance being in the Roses encounter at Bradford when, significantly or otherwise, he was "absent hurt" in the second innings when the last pair of Schofield Haigh and David Hunter clung on for the draw.

So, sadly, the curtain came down on Peel towards the end of 1897 and amazingly, incredibly, it went up the following season on yet another left-arm spinner, the greatest bowler in Yorkshire's history, Wilfred Rhodes.

Despite the emergence of the splendid players already mentioned – and several others besides – in the 1870s and 1880s, Yorkshire were still not the best team in the land at this time but two significant events in 1883 would lead to them establishing their reputation beyond any doubt ten years later.

The first was the reconstitution of the Yorkshire Committee which, up to and including 1883, had been comprised entirely of men from Sheffield and this was hardly surprising in view of the fact that the club originated in Sheffield at the instigation of the citizens of Sheffield.

It was now felt that the Committee could be too parochial and not truly representative of the county as a whole. As a consequence, a resolution was passed that the Committee was willing to allow a representative from each of five places in Yorkshire. In the end, seven towns or cities were allowed a representative: Bradford, Dewsbury, Halifax, Huddersfield, Hull, Leeds and York, with Barnsley, Wakefield and Scarborough being added over the next few years, so that by 1892 the committee comprised 22 representatives, 13 of them from Sheffield and nine from other areas, although Scarborough was omitted for some reason.

In 1893 further changes took place in the constitution of the committee, Sheffield's power being eroded yet again by a reduction to seven representatives while Bradford and Leeds were allotted three seats each. Other minor changes were made over the years but the committee system continued to serve the club for 110 years before a newly formed Management Board effectively carried out a *coup d'état* in order to save the club from possible bankruptcy.

And what was the other significant thing which occurred in 1883 and was responsible more than anything else for the rise to pre-eminence of Yorkshire cricket? The appointment as captain of the Hon. Martin Bladen Hawke.

CHAPTER SIX

TAKING CHARGE

But for the grandly named the Rev. Edmund Sardinson Carter, the history of Yorkshire County Cricket Club may have meandered down a very different course because it was he who was responsible for Lord Hawke making his Yorkshire debut against the MCC at the Scarborough Cricket Festival in 1881. And Hawke came to look upon Carter as a father figure so far as cricket was concerned.

Born in Malton in 1845, Carter gained a double blue at Oxford and went on, like his father before him, to become vicar of Malton and Slingsby. Although he played in 14 matches for Yorkshire between 1876-1881, he was best known for his involvement with the renowned Yorkshire Gentlemen band of cricketers and for his great work in organising the Scarborough Festival, along with Lord Londesborough.

Hawke, himself a cricket blue and captain at Cambridge University, often played for Yorkshire Gentlemen at York, first turning out for them during the holidays when he was at Eton. He quickly caught the attention of Carter who happily marked him down for his county debut in the 1881 Festival at North Marine Road.

It was an inauspicious start by Hawke, who, batting at No 7, twice had his stumps wrecked by Nottinghamshire and England's William Barnes – for four in the first innings and a duck in the second as Yorkshire crashed by an innings and 26 runs.

But here was the man of pedigree that Yorkshire had been seeking ever since the introduction of Championship cricket. Hawke played for them several times in 1882, mainly under the captaincy of Emmett who did offer him the post but he chose not to accept it at that stage, preferring instead to get the feel of things while Emmett directed operations. His introduction to county cricket came against Surrey at Bramall Lane when he opened the batting with Ulyett and made 20 before being dismissed, his partner going on to make 120. This was Peel's debut match, which he celebrated with nine wickets, and it also provided Hawke with a huge learning curve so far as Championship tactics were concerned.

Only 44 were needed for a Yorkshire victory when Hawke opened the second innings with Ulyett but there was a mere half an hour in which to get the runs and Surrey's wily captain, John Shuter, instructed his bowlers to bowl wide of the stumps. The ploy was so successful, if not quite in the spirit of the game, that the frustrated batsmen could only muster 35 before time ran out on them.

Hawke played in three matches for Yorkshire against the Australians in 1882 and when the annual fixture against the MCC at Scarborough came round once more, he was handed the captaincy by Carter. Again, personal success eluded him for when he opened the innings he was bowled by another Nottinghamshire and England man, Fred Morley, for only four.

His was not the only failure, however, because the match was monopolised by

Emmett, who captured 8-52 to bowl out MCC for 115. He then top scored with 51 in Yorkshire's reply of 265 before taking 5-31 as MCC were skittled for 80, Peate bagging the other five.

In 1883, Emmett continued to serve as captain until after the Varsity match at which point Hawke, then an undergraduate at Cambridge, took charge, and he maintained his iron grip on Yorkshire cricket for the next 55 years, leading them on the field until 1910 and serving as Club president from 1898-1938.

Now Lord Hawke was intensely proud of his Yorkshire heritage but if he had one big regret in life it was that he himself was born outside Yorkshire – at his father's rectory at Willingham, Gainsborough, on August 16, 1860.

How ironic 'that the man who so fervently espoused the cause that only Yorkshiremen should play for Yorkshire was not actually Yorkshire-born himself, but Hawke was always at pains to point out that his Yorkshire ancestry went way back into the mists of time.

He spoke glowingly of his ancestor, Admiral Lord Hawke, who secured a great naval victory over the French at the Battle of Quiberon in 1759, and he considered him to be second only to Lord Nelson in his strategies and skills.

The Admiral's wife had been associated with Yorkshire "from time immemorial", as Hawke put it, and the link remained very strong but there was great misfortune for Hawke's father, Edward Henry Julius Hawke, who seems to have been shabbily treated in a family wrangle and who later acceded to the peerage but without receiving any of the estate.

He became curate of Stonegrave, near Helmsley, Yorkshire, before moving to become rector of Willingham where he lived until he inherited his title and retired in 1874. That was where the future Yorkshire captain was born, along with seven of his nine brothers and sisters.

Upon his retirement, the rector moved with his large family into Wighill Park at Tadcaster, and it was in this rented Georgian house that Lord Martin Bladen, the 7th Baron, was to live for the next 50 years, succeeding to his father's title in 1887. Hawke loved Wighill Park and once he was established as Yorkshire captain he took the professionals there annually for dinner – and the pros were happy to sit at the table of their master.

During his long career, Hawke played in five Tests for England and although he was a more than capable batsman he was not out of the top drawer, his first-class record showing 16,759 runs at 20.15, with 13 centuries, while for Yorkshire he made 13,133 runs at 20.26, with ten centuries.

He had, however, the authority and the willpower to mould his Yorkshire professionals into a powerful fighting unit. Yorkshire needed a disciplinarian then just as they did in the 1930s when Brian Sellers took command to lead his men into another era of greatness. Like Hawke, Sellers was a determined rather than naturally talented cricketer and the same was true of Ronnie Burnet when he led Yorkshire out of the wilderness in 1959.

And nobody was ever more courageous or more determined than the 1960s captain, Brian Close, yet in his case he also had an abundance of ability and was the best-loved captain Yorkshire have ever had.

Hawke may have had the right qualities and the ideal background that Yorkshire were looking for in a captain but he was unable to press a magic button in 1883 and make everything come right at once.

For a start, Hawke was a young captain whose men were very much his senior and the professionals were a motley bunch who were not going to change their attitudes or their lifestyles overnight.

The stars still shone brightly, but singly rather than in a cluster, and nobody radiated more energy and light than George Puckrin "Shoey" Harrison before suddenly fizzling out.

Harrison, a shoemaker in his home town of Scarborough, shot to prominence in that significant year of 1883 while playing for Colts of the North against Colts of the South at Lord's. Never before had he travelled so far away from home and he was so wary of arriving in the capital on his own that he requested Henry Perkins, the secretary of MCC, to meet him at King's Cross station. His introduction to cricket's headquarters, however, was almost without parallel. He did not bowl in the first innings but when he was given a chance in the second he responded with 9-15, striking the stumps all nine times with thunderbolts, four wickets coming in four balls and six wickets in seven.

This stunning performance saw the raw youngster selected to play at Lord's again a few days later but this time for the Players v the Gentlemen and he was cut to ribbons. W.G. Grace said he wanted to take first strike in order to see what Harrison was about and within 15 minutes he had knocked the stuffing out of him, so paving the way for a century from Edward Tylecote. In all, Harrison bowled 53 overs and ended up with what would seem these days to be reasonable figures of 3-108 but the youngster was so distraught that he took himself off to bed that evening and wept uncontrollably.

Despite this setback, Harrison recovered his poise quickly enough to take 100 first-class wickets that season at just 13.26 runs apiece and 88 of his dismissals were for Yorkshire at fewer than 12 runs each.

Unfortunately, Harrison never quite managed the searing pace of that season again owing to a shoulder injury sustained while returning the ball from the deep and in ten seasons for Yorkshire between 1883-1892 he claimed 226 wickets at 14.9. Still great figures, but not as great as they might have been.

Harrison's form deserted him entirely in 1884 but Hawke continued to build for the future and for a while it looked as if Baildon born and bred Fred Lee would play a significant part in the county's fortunes.

An enterprising batsman who mixed big hitting with a wide range of orthodox strokes, he headed Yorkshire's batting averages from 1879-1881 before dropping out of the side through poor form and then returning in 1884 and going on to hit 165 in the Roses match at Bradford Park Avenue in 1887 when he piled up 280 for the second wicket with Louis Hall.

Lee was unable to sustain this high standard, however, and it seems likely that he fell victim to Hawke's weeding out process because he was only 33 when he was considered surplus to requirements in 1890.

Irwin Grimshaw, from Farsley, was another of Yorkshire's rising stars of the 1880s who did not do quite enough to satisfy Hawke that he could help him win titles and his county career ceased in 1887 at the age of 30. He hit four centuries for Yorkshire before the axe fell and enjoyed several outstanding innings but he did not have the consistency which his captain was looking for. Like certain others among his professional colleagues, Grimshaw was not averse to taking alcohol and this side of his character would certainly not have won Hawke's approval.

If Grimshaw did not go on to realise his full potential, then the same can definitely be said of Joseph Preston who had it in him to be a really great all-rounder and many were of the opinion that he was one of Yorkshire's finest cricketers in the 1880s.

Preston's life was short and often tragic. A couple of years before first playing for Yorkshire in 1885 he is reported in Tony Woodhouse's A Who's Who of Yorkshire County Cricket Club to have killed a certain A. Luty while bowling to him. For Yorkshire he had a best score of 93 against Derbyshire at Bramall Lane in 1887, when he added 150 with Ulyett for the sixth wicket, and against the MCC at Scarborough in 1888 he bowled splendidly to return figures of 9-28. In addition, Preston was superb in the field which is more than can be said of many of his team-mates.

The demon drink was a problem for Preston also and although Hawke believed he stood alongside Billy Bates – Yorkshire's leading all-rounder at the time – in ability, he still had his reservations. Hawke later said of him that he was "an irresponsible individual who, had he possessed the least self-restraint, might have become one of the finest cricketers Yorkshire ever produced... but he had too many friends."

Ah, those friends of professionals in the 1880s! Willing to buy their heroes a drink whenever an opportunity arose – and it frequently did – but in so doing hastening the end of their careers.

Despite Preston's fine bowling achievements in 1888 when he captured 102 wickets at 13.05, his form deteriorated rapidly the following summer and Hawke dropped him and ended his first-class career. His life was also coming to a close: he died in 1890, aged 24, at his father's home at the Blue Bell Inn, Windhill, in Bradford, having caught a chill. How great Preston might have been, had things worked out differently, we will never know.

Preston's final season was a disastrous one for Yorkshire who propped up the table for the first two months of the '89 campaign and finished last but one. They would have been bottom of the pile had they not played Sussex for the wooden spoon at the end of August and won.

Their situation would have been bleaker still but for the continuing brilliance of Peel who headed the batting and bowling averages. He scored the only century of the season and took almost three times as many wickets as any of his colleagues.

The likes of Emmett, Bates and Peate had by now gone and even the emergence of the great wicketkeeper, David Hunter, the courageous batsman, Robert Moorhouse, and the famed opener, J.T. Brown, could not at this stage save Yorkshire from ignominy.

There was something of a recovery in 1890, the year of the county debuts of two stars of University cricket in F.S. Jackson, of Cambridge, and Ernest Smith, of Oxford, but the team plummeted again in 1891 when they lost twice as many matches as they won and there were mutterings of discontent in the Press and among the fans. The situation was so bleak that members' subscriptions brought in just £90.

Nothing much changed in 1892 when Yorkshire could only move up into sixth place while all-conquering Surrey lifted their third consecutive title. With little alteration to the playing staff in 1893 many followers of Yorkshire cricket firmly believed that another dreary season lay ahead – but how spectacularly wrong the Jeremiahs were!

CHAPTER SEVEN

ON THE MARCH

Yorkshire not only won the County Championship in 1893 but they won it by a country mile, being streets ahead of all their rivals. Of their 16 matches in the competition, they were victorious in 12 and suffered only three defeats and a draw.

In the previous season, Yorkshire had got off to a splendid start and they did not taste defeat until the middle of June but from that point on they faded away and ended up a disappointing sixth.

Fatigue was probably one of the reasons for their decline in 1892, the first-class programme being so demanding that the players barely had a day's rest from the beginning of May to the end of August. Some things, seemingly, do not change.

They were, however, unfortunate, to lose to Surrey on the new Headingley ground which they had played upon for the first time in 1891 when they went down to Derbyshire by 45 runs. There were just three minutes remaining when Surrey crossed the line by 17 runs on their way to yet another title, the incomparable George Lohmann, in his last truly great season before illness set in, destroying the batting with 6-37 and 8-70 after the first day had been wiped out by bad weather.

Yorkshire made another fine start to the season in 1893 but this time they kept the momentum going and most of the country rejoiced when they took the title to end Surrey's domination. The White Rose county were generally much admired for the spirit in which they played the game and for their uncompromising attitude.

It was the beginning of a glorious decade of Yorkshire cricket in which they won the Championship six times and earned the respect of the whole nation. Yorkshire cricket had truly established itself under Hawke and the pride and passion which the team generated lives with us to this day.

The strength of the Yorkshire team from 1893-1902 can be gauged by the fact that of the 243 Championship matches which they played, 146 were won, 68 drawn and only 29 lost – and several of those defeats were, strangely, to much inferior sides.

Another significant feature of 1893 was the publication for the first time of the Yorkshire County Cricket Club Yearbook and its birth could not have been better timed because the following year it was able to print the scorecards of that great Championship-winning season in very much the style which exists to this day.

It showed that Yorkshire began at a cracking pace with five consecutive victories and if Lord Hawke's presence was felt it was certainly not on the field of play because he was absent from all of these successes.

Victory in the first match of any season is always important because it raises confidence and sets the tone for the months ahead and Yorkshire could not have enjoyed a better opening than in 1893 when they beat Gloucestershire, W.G. Grace and all, by an emphatic nine wickets at Gloucester.

The star of the show was not John Tunnicliffe or the emerging all-rounder, Ted Wainwright, or the cunning Peel or the acting captain Ulyett, but the much less gifted Thomas Wardall, who had a match to remember and was responsible for getting the ball rolling with a momentum which could not be stopped.

Wardall, from Middlesbrough, played only 45 matches for Yorkshire between 1884-1894 and was considered a sound but over cautious batsman who also bowled slow donkey drops which could occasionally be useful.

They could never have been more useful than in this game because after two early wickets had fallen, W.G. Grace and John Painter settled into a profitable stand for Gloucestershire and it was in some desperation that Ulyett called upon Wardall to ply his particular trade.

The move proved inspirational as W.G., having completed his half-century, gave a return catch to Wardall which was gratefully accepted. Whatever the type of ball it was has been lost in the mists of time but one can only speculate on how apoplectic the good doctor must have been had he patted back a donkey drop.

Wardall, having done his job, retired from the attack with figures of 6-5-4-1, but his exploits were far from over. Opening the batting with Tunnicliffe in reply to Gloucestershire's 235, he scored 106 out of 385 and Wainwright then captured 6-56 as the home side folded.

In 12 other Championship innings that season, Wardall scraped together only a further 88 runs and after bagging a pair against Surrey at The Oval in late June and making four in his next innings against Nottinghamshire at Bradford he faded away entirely and did not re-appear that summer. Yet Wardall had made his mark at exactly the right time and who knows for sure how things would have turned out had he not dismissed W.G. and gone on to score a gutsy century?

Another event occurred in that match which virtually went unnoticed at the time but was an indication that some of Hawke's men were on the threshold of greatness. When George Hirst bowled Octavius Radcliffe in the Gloucestershire second innings it gave him his 50th first-class wicket – one of the first milestones for him to pass on his epic journey through cricket.

Yet the main reason why Yorkshire were crowned Champions in 1893 was not through any dazzling individual brilliance but rather because the team played as a unit – very much in the style of England when they held on to the Ashes in Australia in the winter of 2010-11. There was no batting Colossus, indeed no-one averaged even 30, and only two centuries were registered after Wardall's opening effort and both of these came from Arthur Sellers, the father of Brian.

But there was consistency in the bowling, with Wainwright leading the way with 90 dismissals, followed by Peel with 70 and Hirst with 59. And Hirst was beginning to blossom with the bat as well as the ball. In Gloucestershire's return match at Huddersfield he made an unbeaten 35 out of 162, prompting W.G. to remark to the Rev. Holmes: "I had no idea the beggar could bat so well." To which the reply was: "You shouldn't be surprised if he should turn out to be a greater batsman than bowler." A shrewd observation but it was Hirst's prowess with both bat and ball that made him one of the great all-rounders of all time.

Winning was beginning to matter more to Yorkshire than most other counties and Middlesex were surprised and unhappy to see Wainwright on the team sheet when they came to Bradford in mid-August. Middlesex were without that sporting Titan, A.E. Stoddart, who was playing for England in The Oval Test, and they fully expected Wainwright to be representing his country also but the Yorkshire committee had refused to release him to play.

From Yorkshire's point of view it was a canny move because Wainwright scored a valuable half-century and then claimed three wickets, including both of Middlesex's openers, as his side gained a useful first innings lead and went on to win by 145 runs.

In 1894, Yorkshire once again enjoyed 12 wins and they experienced one fewer defeat than the previous year but they still could not prevent their arch rivals Surrey from snatching the title off them. Atrocious weather did not help, the Kent game being abandoned without a ball being bowled, but they had no just cause for complaint because their only two beatings were both at the hands of Surrey.

Sellers bowed out of cricket for business reasons before the start of the season but the family name was to remain a household word among the Yorkshire cricket fraternity for many years to come. New boys in the side included Frank Mitchell, the Cambridge undergraduate and brilliant bat who was to play for both England and South Africa, and David Denton, who became the second heaviest scorer in Yorkshire's history with 33,282 runs and 61 centuries.

The pair were only scratching the surface in 1894, however, and the most impressive aspect of Yorkshire's cricket in that season was their magnificent fielding. For holding on to their catches and saving runs it was felt that they had no equals.

In 1895, Derbyshire, Essex, Hampshire, Leicestershire and Warwickshire were all promoted to the Championship and Yorkshire's programme, like that of title-holders, Surrey, included matches against all 13 opponents. Once again, however, Surrey held the upper hand with Lancashire coming in second and Yorkshire third. Hawke's men paid the price for a bad beginning and end to the campaign and they were also deeply embarrassed by losing twice to newcomers, Derbyshire.

The season was a disappointing one in the Championship for Driffield's J.T. (John Thomas) Brown senior, who had batted so brilliantly for England in Australia during the winter of 1894-95, but he still managed Yorkshire's highest innings of 168 against Sussex at Huddersfield. Jackson showed all-round excellence, Hawke, Denton and Robert Moorhouse all piled up the runs and Peel's skills were not diminishing after 14 years of toil, the left-armer gathering in 136 wickets, with his 15-50 analysis in the match against Somerset at Headingley being the best performance of the season the length and breadth of the country.

If Yorkshire failed to reach the peaks of 1893 in the two seasons which followed, they scaled new heights in 1896 when they once again ousted Surrey at the top. Brown and Tunnicliffe, now a regular opening pair, made an early impression against Middlesex at Lord's with century stands in each innings to bring a ten-wicket victory, and the runs continued to flow for the side as the summer wore on.

There were several massive totals, the biggest of all being the 887 against Warwickshire at Edgbaston which remains the highest score in county cricket and beaten in this country only by England's 903-7 declared against Australia at The Oval in 1938 when Len Hutton compiled his amazing 364.

White Rose fans were given a fright when Lancashire threatened their long-standing record at The Oval in 1990 before ending on 863 and Somerset racked up

850-7 before declaring against Middlesex at Taunton in 2007.

The Edgbaston rampage established another cricketing record at the time as four batsmen each completed centuries, Peel smacking an unbeaten 210 batting at No 7 with Hawke (166), Wainwright (126) and F.S. Jackson (117) following in his wake.

Hawke and Peel put on 292 together for the eighth wicket, which remains the highest ever recorded for that wicket in this country and the third highest of all time – although Robin Martin-Jenkins and Mark Davis came within a run of equalling Yorkshire's achievement for Sussex against Somerset at Taunton in 2002.

Quite remarkably, none of Yorkshire's four centurions had made it to three figures the previous season and for once Hawke was more anxious for Yorkshire to post records than he was for them to go on and win the match. This was the second game of the season and the only one of the first seven that they did not win but Hawke's decision can be justified in that the huge score added to Yorkshire's growing reputation as the most formidable of sides – and the achievements of that team are still there for all to see.

During the course of the season, a suggestion that Hawke should be granted a testimonial for his services to Yorkshire cricket rapidly gained public approval and resulted the following summer in his Lordship receiving from club president, M.J. Ellison, his (Hawke's) portrait in oils and a service of plate.

Six thousand spectators were present at the match with Somerset at Headingley for the presentation and there were several eloquent speeches, including one from F.S. Jackson who said that having played alongside Hawke for seven years he had witnessed at first hand his untiring devotion to Yorkshire cricket and he felt that no testimonial could adequately repay him.

In the winter between claiming the Championship title and receiving his testimonial, Hawke persuaded the county committee to give winter pay of £2 per week to the professionals in order that they could maintain themselves adequately and it was Hawke, also, who went on to bring in benefits.

The loyal Ellison died in 1898 after serving Yorkshire with such devotion since the club's formation 35 years earlier and there was only one man deemed sufficiently worthy to follow him – Lord Hawke.

Now Hawke had complete control both on and off the field and to this day he remains the most influential figure in the club's history. Yet there was to come a time when the professionals were keen to show that so far as leadership was concerned they were the equal of the old-style amateurs.

Len Hutton, of course, never captained Yorkshire but he was immensely proud to become the first regularly appointed professional captain of England, winning back the Ashes in the Coronation year of 1953 and successfully defending them in Australia in 1954-55.

That doyen of cricket writers, John Woodcock, was quoted in the Wisden Cricketer in March, 2010, as saying that in his opinion the happiest tour of all was the one under Hutton to Australia.

He went on: "The heavy defeat in the first Test at Brisbane and the three victories that followed it made an amazing story. One had become so fond of the players, partly through getting to know them well on the ship going out."

Woodcock was quite ill on the tour and confined to his hotel room before the start of the decisive fourth Test in Adelaide but Hutton, preparing to leave for the ground, knocked on the writer's door and insisted that he be looked after in the comfort of the players' dressing room.

It was from there that Woodcock saw the Ashes retained and he witnessed a rare unguarded moment from Hutton. "As Godfrey Evans hit the winning run, Len caught my eye and said in that quizzical way of his: 'I wish that booger 'awke were 'ere'."

The reason for Hutton's cynicism was that Hawke had once famously remarked: "Pray God, no professional shall ever captain England." Now was the moment that cricket began to look forward rather than back and a Yorkshireman was leading the way, just as a great Yorkshire figure had also done in the past.

Hawke was the face and voice of Yorkshire cricket for nigh on 40 years and although the team were happy to prove later on that they could fight their battles without him he has, to this day, retained the deepest respect of all who are connected with the club.

Yorkshire were to win the Championship title four more times under Hawke after 1896 and three consecutive table-topping seasons from 1900-1902 meant that with the ushering in of the 20th century their own reputation had been well and truly secured.

CHAPTER EIGHT

THE TRINITY

We have already seen how cricket became a passion inside Yorkshire, the early seeds bursting forth with the formation of the county club in 1863 and the roots being permanently strengthened by the appointment of Lord Hawke as captain in 1883.

But would it ever have taken hold to such an extent without the rare chemistry which built up between the aristocrats and the working class who came together in the side in the 1890s?

Hawke was the respected leader who cared for his flock like a shepherd but the toff in the team was S.F. Jackson, one of the greatest amateurs of all time and deeply admired by all who played with or against him.

Jackson possessed both flair and orthodoxy in abundance and was scrupulously honest in playing the game but cricket for him was only one part of a full and varied life.

He and Hawke were the elite of Yorkshire cricket in the '90s but had their like flooded the team then the balance would have been wrong and the working class spectators would have felt that the game was not for them.

But this did not happen because first George Hirst entered the team in 1891 followed by Wilfred Rhodes towards the end of the decade. The duo, from Kirkheaton, Huddersfield, were ordinary young men in the sense that they came from humble backgrounds but they were not ordinary at cricket. They were extraordinary. The two greatest players in Yorkshire's history. And they rubbed shoulders with Hawke and Jackson and on the field of play everyone was equally respected and everyone had a particular task to fulfil in the quest for team supremacy.

THE Rt. Hon. Sir Frank Stanley Jackson

F.S. Jackson, known as 'Jacker' in the world of cricket, was, among many other things, the younger son of the Rt. Hon. W.L. Jackson, the first Lord of Allerton, who was a cabinet minister in Lord Salisbury's Government.

Besides being one of the greatest all-rounders in the golden era of amateurs, he was also an influential man of business and politics, representing North Leeds as M.P. and serving as Financial Secretary to the War Office. He was for a time Chairman of the Conservative Party, a Privy Councillor and Governor of Bengal from 1927-1932.

Born at Allerton Hall, Chapel Allerton, Leeds, on November 21, 1870, cricket was of secondary importance to Jackson and yet he was one of the best ever to play it. He was a natural. Returning from active service in the Boer War, he was very much out of practice and suffering from enteric fever but in his only innings in two years he scored a dashing century for the Gentlemen v The Players at Scarborough, gracing that fixture from 1891-1906.

Earlier on, he had been in the team at Harrow and it was at Cambridge University where the nickname 'Jacker' stuck. He made his debut for Cambridge University against C.I. 'Buns' Thornton's XI at Fenner's in 1890 and went on to captain the Light Blues.

Jackson was in Hawke's party which toured India in 1892-1893 and he lit up the England side from 1893-1905 with batting which touched on genius and with deadly accurate bowling which was quickish off a short run-up and contained a dangerous off-break.

Batting for England against Australia at The Oval in 1893 he raced to his century in 135 minutes and was the first batsman to reach three figures in this country with a hit over the boundary – four runs being given rather than six in those days.

Four years later on the same ground he put on 185 with Tom Hayward for the first wicket. It was a record partnership for any wicket in a home match for England and a record stand for either side in England v Australia Tests.

One of England's finest sides decimated Australia at Edgbaston in 1902, the Yorkshire trio of Jackson, Hirst and Rhodes annihilated them for 36, which remains Australia's lowest total. This time Rhodes was the destroyer-in-chief with 7-17 with Hirst mopping up the remainder.

But when the Australians came up against Yorkshire at Headingley in that season they fared even worse, being dismissed for 23 in their second innings with Jackson taking 5-12, including four wickets in five balls. The other five wickets went to Hirst at a cost of nine runs. Jackson had already picked up four wickets in the first innings as the Australians fell for 131, one of his victims being Victor Trumper after he had top scored with 38. Three days had been reserved for the match but it was all over in two, Yorkshire winning by five wickets.

Jackson succeeded to the England captaincy in 1905 and, as if it were his right, went on to win the toss five times out of five against Australia. At Headingley he thrashed 144 not out in 268 minutes to record the first Test century on the ground and at Old Trafford he became the first batsman to complete five Test centuries in England.

Jackson was 'Botham-like' in his instinctive all-round prowess and at Trent Bridge in the same series he decided to bring himself on "for a bit of a bowl" and promptly dismissed Monty Noble, Clem Hill, and captain, Joe Darling, in the space of six deliveries.

Darling had led Australia to Ashes success in the two previous tours of 1899 and 1902 but this time Jackson and his team came out on top with three wins and two draws, the inspirational leader heading England's batting and bowling averages.

Towards the end of the tour, the two great captains came face to face again at the Scarborough Cricket Festival and the powerfully-built Darling greeted Jackson with a towel round his waist, declaring: "I'm not going to risk the toss this time except by wrestling." But when Jackson replied that if that were the case he would call upon George Hirst to act for him, his opponent backed down. The coin was *duly tossed and 'Jacker' won it again.*

Hawke's long tenure of office meant that Jackson never got the opportunity to captain Yorkshire on an official basis but he was elected president of MCC in 1921 and took over as Yorkshire president from Hawke in 1939 and remained in that office until his death in 1947.

Business commitments and Parliamentary duties meant he only played regularly for Yorkshire in four seasons and in his early cricketing days he performed much better for country than county. Yet in a Yorkshire career spanning 1890-1907 he still rattled up 10,371 runs with 21 centuries and claimed 506 wickets at fewer than 20 runs apiece. In 20 Tests he scored 1,415 runs, with five centuries, and took 24 wickets.

Clearly, Jackson greatly assisted Hawke in spicing up Yorkshire's image for playing adventurous cricket and it must have helped Hawke a great deal to know that here was a man who did not need looking after or caring for in the same way as did many of the professionals.

But neither were Yorkshire a one-man show. There were too many other great players in the side, including that illustrious pair from Kirkheaton.

Lightning doesn't strike twice, they say, but it did in that Huddersfield village of Kirkheaton, first on September 7, 1871, when George Herbert Hirst was born, and then again on October 29, 1877, when Wilfred Rhodes came into this world.

By the turn of the 20th century when both of them were in their pomp, the good folk of Huddersfield were able to proclaim that opinion may be divided upon them as to who was the greatest cricketer in the land but they knew for sure that he batted right-handed and bowled left – and that he came from Kirkheaton. From the day that Hirst made his Yorkshire debut in 1891 to the day that Rhodes played his last match in 1930 one or the other was to be seen gracing the cricket fields of England – and very often and dynamically, both of them together.

George Hirst

Jackson may for a while have been the most naturally gifted player in the country, Rhodes may have done more for Yorkshire and England than anyone else, but the true embodiment and soul of Yorkshire cricket was George Herbert Hirst, the most popular and best-loved Yorkshireman ever to wear the White Rose.

Jackson was at his best on the big stage, the Colossus of Rhodes could perform on either but Hirst reserved most of his blood, sweat and tears for Yorkshire.

When it comes to studying the record books, Hirst and Rhodes are bracketed together as among the greatest of all time and when one considers that Jackson, Wainwright and Schofield Haigh are also in the list of Yorkshire's top eight all-rounders – the only ones to score at least 10,000 first-class runs and also take in excess of 500 wickets – it shows how mighty Yorkshire were with all eight of the octet playing together in the same side.

Hirst is credited with Yorkshire's highest individual score of 341 against Leicestershire at Aylestone Road, dragging his side from the depths of 74-5, and it *is testimony to how his aura has stood the test of time that when that brilliant Australian, Darren Lehmann, amassed 339 for Yorkshire against Durham at Headingley Carnegie in 2006, he told the Press in all seriousness that he was happy to let the record stay with Hirst "because he was a better player".*

Who was the more gifted batsman we shall never know but taking all-round qualities into consideration then Lehmann was spot on and if Hirst were looking down from some Elysian Field that day he would have been much touched by the honest comments of this modern day sporting genius.

Herbert Sutcliffe (38,558), David Denton (33,282) and Geoff Boycott (32,570) head the list of Yorkshire's most prolific batsmen and they are followed by the indomitable Hirst, the only one of the top four to be classed as a genuine all-rounder. He hit 32,024 runs in 1,050 innings with 56 centuries for an average of 34.73 and he is immediately followed by Rhodes, hot on his heels with 31,075 runs. Rhodes, however, had 145 more innings and scored ten fewer centuries for an inferior average of 30.08 which would suggest that Hirst just shaved it as a batsman.

The opposite is true when one compares their bowling because Rhodes sits unchallenged at the top with 3,598 wickets for Yorkshire at 16.01 while Hirst is immediately beneath him with 2,481 victims at 18.02. Schofield Haigh (1,876) and Raymond Illingworth (1,431) join them in the stratosphere looking down on all of the rest. Hirst's career-best bowling figures of 9-23, however, were a shade better than Rhodes' (9-28) and the elder of the two did also play in 167 fewer matches.

In 24 Test matches – he really should have played in more – Hirst made 790 runs with a top score of 85 v Australia at Adelaide in 1898 and he reeled in 59 wickets, including 5-48 against Australia at Melbourne in 1904. In the first Ashes Test at Edgbaston in May, 1909, Hirst and Colin Blythe shared all 20 of Australia's wickets, Hirst taking 4-28 in the first innings and following up with 5-58, England cruising home in three days by ten wickets.

But Hirst did not become the most popular cricketer in the land through his Test exploits: it was his amazing excellence for Yorkshire and the stamina and conscientiousness which he showed day in and day out which led to him being so admired.

In all, he completed the double 14 times – just two fewer than Rhodes – and in 1906 he set himself upon a pedestal where he is likely to stand for all time as the only cricketer to score 2,000 runs and take 200 wickets in a first-class season – 2,385 for an average of 48.86 and 208 at 16.50 runs per wicket to be precise.

If Hirst were left with one slight regret after his career was over it may have been that he never quite managed all ten wickets in an innings. Four times he had nine and when he registered his career-best 9-23 in the Roses match at Headingley in 1910 he rattled the stumps eight times. Haigh picked up the remaining wicket. Fearing he would never manage all ten he asked to keep the ball as a memento. "Nay, nay, cut the ball in half, we bowled 'em out atween us, George," grinned Haigh. No fawning in the Yorkshire dressing room. Never has been and never will be. Even George Herbert Hirst was not allowed to get too big for his boots, not that he would ever for a moment have wanted to do so.

One of the reasons why Hirst did not always take wickets in Australia is because the ball did not swing so much for him as in England, but in home conditions he was dynamite and opposing batsmen said that he got so much inswing that when the ball hit the stumps it was as if it had been thrown in from the covers.

Apart from one appearance for Yorkshire against the MCC at the end of the 1929 season, Hirst wrapped up his career in 1921 when he became coach at Eton for the next 17 years. He also coached at Yorkshire and Scarborough for many years and was loved by all for his devotion and kindness. No wonder Hawke described him as "the greatest county cricketer of our time."

Wilfred Rhodes

Throughout its 150 years' history, Yorkshire has produced many great players but the greatest of them all, without a shadow of doubt, is Wilfred Rhodes – and the record books prove it.

For a start, over a 32-year period, Rhodes played in far more matches for Yorkshire than anybody before him or since and it is safe to say that nobody will get even close to his 883 appearances. The demands of Test and one-day international cricket, the burn-out of modern day players and the much-reduced first-class programme are all good reasons why Rhodes' record will stand for ever.

His friend and team-mate, George Hirst, is closest to Rhodes with 717 appearances but David Denton (676) and Herbert Sutcliffe (602) are the only others to make it beyond the 600 mark.

Only in the art of making runs and taking wickets was Rhodes remotely like Hirst for whereas Hirst was extrovert and constantly cheerful Rhodes was introvert and constantly serious as he worked remorselessly on exploring and exploiting the weaknesses of opposing batsmen and bowlers. Chalk and cheese, maybe, but both fascinating and extraordinary characters.

Rhodes made his first-class debut as a 20-year old for Yorkshire v MCC at Scarborough in 1898 and by the end of that initial season his canny left-arm spin had brought him 141 wickets for Yorkshire and 154 all told. The following year at North Marine Road he registered his career-best bowling figures of 9-24 for C.I. Thornton's XI v the Australians as well as producing his best bowling figures for Yorkshire of 9-28 against Essex at Leyton.

In 1905, Rhodes hit a double century off Somerset's bowling at Taunton and he remained at the top of his game for so long that it was 16 years later that he made his career best score of 267 not out against Leicestershire at Headingley.

His overall statistics are quite staggering. His first-class haul of 4,187 wickets (3,598 of them for Yorkshire) has never been matched anywhere in the world and his 16 doubles of 1,000 runs and 100 wickets has also been out of the reach of anyone else. In all, he passed 1,000 runs 21 times, 17 for Yorkshire, and completed 100 wickets in 23 seasons.

Rhodes bagged 100 wickets in a season for Yorkshire on 22 occasions and he was at his peak in 1901 and 1902 when he helped himself to 240 and 253 respectively. He claimed seven wickets or more in 70 innings and six times he bowled unchanged in a match, three times with Hirst and three with Schofield

Haigh. Like Hirst, it is surprising that Rhodes never managed to take all ten wickets in an innings but he did achieve a couple of hat-tricks – against Kent at Canterbury in 1901 and against Derbyshire at Derby 19 years later, just to prove that he had lost none of his competitive edge.

England first called upon Rhodes in 1899 and his exploits for his country were no less amazing. After starting out batting at No 11 for Yorkshire he went on to open for England against Australia and South Africa with the great Jack Hobbs. In the first Test v South Africa at Johannesburg in 1909-1910 he put on 159 with Hobbs and in the fifth Test at Cape Town the pair added 221 together. Two years later against Australia in Melbourne they created the then England first wicket record of 323, Rhodes ending with 179.

His most successful bowling returns for England were 8-68 against Australia at Melbourne in 1903-1904, when he also became the first bowler to take 15 wickets in a match between the two countries, and 7-17 in that remarkable performance against the Aussies at Edgbaston in 1902 when they were bowled out for 36 and Hirst claimed the other three. Rhodes' figures remain the best in Test matches on the ground.

At Johannesburg in 1913-1914 he took his 100th Test wicket, completing the first double ever recorded for England in 44 matches, and at Sydney in 1920-1921 he became the first player to score 2,000 runs and take 100 wickets in Test cricket.

And it was at The Oval in 1902 that Rhodes, along with Hirst, entered cricket folklore. Rhodes, last man in, joined Hirst at the crease with England still needing 15 to beat Australia. Hirst, legend has it, approached his partner and said: "We'll get these in singles." They did win the game, if not exactly in that manner, but anything other than victory would never have entered the heads of either of them.

It is a sobering thought that Rhodes, Yorkshire's greatest cricketer, may never have played for them at all. Starting out as a youngster with Kirkheaton – as Hirst had before him – he was recommended by the club to Galashiels in Scotland where he became their much respected professional. He was then rejected by Warwickshire upon going for a trial and it was only in that match against MCC at Scarborough that Yorkshire finally came to their senses.

The Rhodes Collection

The sterling deeds of Rhodes between 1898-1930 are well documented in the record books and in many other publications which have focused on this great player, but the past truly caught up with the present in 2010 when a vast collection of unique cricket memorabilia, which was built up over the years by Rhodes, was most generously gifted to Yorkshire CCC by his granddaughter, Mrs. Margaret Garton, the sole surviving member of the Rhodes dynasty.

The collection, consisting of 293 separate items, including an album containing 305 photographs taken by Rhodes on his travels to India and Australia in the 1920s, had never previously been seen outside his family, and, most fittingly, it came into Yorkshire's possession a few weeks after the opening of the club's new £300,000 cricket museum at Headingley Carnegie.

Each item and each scrap of paper was lovingly listed and referenced for archives purposes by Yorkshire cricket archivist, Ron Deaton, a long-standing member of Yorkshire CCC.

Ron spent six weeks sifting through every item and afterwards he said: "I have never seen anything like this before, it is just a dream. I consider it an honour and a privilege to have done this work on what must be one of the most wonderful cricket collections in existence. Every piece is an absolute treasure and for me it was like gazing at the crown jewels for the first time.

"It is the crème-de-la-crème of cricketing memorabilia from the greatest Yorkshire cricketer of the 20th century and the cricket-loving community throughout the world will be fascinated by this collection, as will all Yorkshire members."

The piece de resistance, according to Ron, is Rhodes' autograph book which the archivist describes as "priceless". It contains the players' signatures from the 45 Test and county teams that Rhodes played against and includes all the county sides of the 1908 season as well as several of Australia's Test sides.

Also of major significance are five cricket balls with engraved shield-shaped silver plaques which were presented to Rhodes upon the completion of some of his most notable achievements. They are the balls in use for his 100th Test wicket at Adelaide, his Test stand of 221 with Hobbs in Cape Town, his hat-trick for Yorkshire v Derbyshire, his wicket with his very first delivery on England's tour of Australia in 1903, and his career-best figures of 18.4-10-24-9 for Yorkshire v the Australians in 1899.

In mint condition is a leather casket, shaped like a giant cricket ball which was presented to Rhodes by Lord Hawke, then Scarborough president, on Rhodes' retirement from first-class cricket at the Scarborough Jubilee Festival in 1930.

Filled with chocolates at the time, it was handed over by Hawke on behalf of Rowntrees of York in appreciation of his great career, and preserved with it was the newspaper cutting and photograph of the event which appeared in the Yorkshire Evening Press on Saturday, September 13, 1930.

But the most fascinating aspect of the whole collection is the wide range of photographs taken by Hirst and which show him in a much rosier light than the rather sombre one in which he is usually cast. Here he is often seen smiling and in a relaxed mood and the methodical nature of the collection shows just how seriously he took his hobby, for which he converted an attic at his home in Marsh Grove Road, Huddersfield, into a photographic studio.

Rhodes' Yorkshire and England caps, ties and badges are sealed in plastic containers and also perfectly preserved are letters which the great man received from royalty and prime ministers – including Harold Macmillan – begging for an audience.

The museum was already bursting with historical items and information concerning many of the main personalities that have graced Yorkshire cricket down the years but nothing can surpass these vivid flashbacks to the life and times of Wilfred Rhodes.

CHAPTER NINE

A LESSON LEARNED

As we have seen, Yorkshire had stars aplenty by the time of their Championship triumph in 1896 but success in cricket can never be taken for granted. Just as they were unable to hold on to the title in 1894 after winning it for the first time so they were unable to do so again in 1897.

Surrey had bounced back on the first occasion and now it was Red Rose rivals Lancashire who finished top of the pile with Yorkshire having to make do with fourth place.

The season was not without incident, however, and Yorkshire were given a salutary lesson in May that no victory is guaranteed until either the winning runs are hit or the last wicket taken and the umpires are removing the bails.

Yorkshire were playing Somerset at Taunton, with Jackson leading the side in the absence of Hawke, and the skipper opened the first innings and made 124 out of 385, passing 7,000 first-class runs on the way. The home side were bowled out for 223, Wainwright claiming 5-53, and following on they fared only marginally better, reaching 276, the wickets being shared by that formidable quartet of Hirst, Haigh, Peel and Wainwright.

Just 114 were needed by Yorkshire and Jackson, probably with an early getaway in mind, instructed J.T. Brown to open the second innings with John Tunnicliffe.

The pair added 62 together and with victory seemingly a foregone conclusion Jackson packed his bag and left for Taunton railway station, taking another professional, the young Frank Milligan, with him. Poking his head through the carriage window as the train departed, Jackson saw to his horror that Yorkshire had suddenly become 85-5 and he knew that David Hunter would be of little use with bruised hands or Wainwright with a strained arm. That Jackson did not end up with egg on his face was due to two reliable professionals, Haigh and Hirst, who knocked off the remaining runs.

Milligan would be tremendously relieved that his captain was with him on that early train home, otherwise he would have felt the full wrath of his team-mates. Less than three years later, the much-loved Milligan was dead, killed in action in the Boer War while serving under Colonel Herbert Plumer and trying to relieve Mafeking.

A devil-may-care batsman who delighted in hitting the ball as high into the heavens as he possibly could and an erratic but sometimes dynamic fast bowler, Milligan was hugely popular with the public at large and he earned the admiration of Hawke who said that his 64 against Essex at Huddersfield in that 1897 season was one of the finest instances of brilliant hitting he had ever seen.

Four other Yorkshire cricketers – Fairfax Gill, Jimmy Rothery, Major Booth and Hedley Verity – were also to die as a result of war wounds and they are all remembered in a plaque to commemorate those who made the ultimate sacrifice which was unveiled at a ceremony just inside the Hutton Gates at Headingley in August, 2007, on the first day of the Roses match.

Booth, a volunteer in the Leeds Pals, died near La Cigny, France, on July 1, 1916, on the first day of the Somme offensive; Gill, a gunner with the 21st Trench Mortar Battery, Royal Field Artillery, died in hospital in Boulogne of war wounds on November 1, 1917; Rothery, a private in the 1st Battalion East Kent Regiment, died of war wounds in Beckett's Park Hospital, Leeds, on June 2, 1919; and Verity, a captain in the Green Howards and the greatest cricketer of all of Yorkshire's fallen, died in a prisoner of war camp in Caserta, Italy, on July 31, 1943, after being mortally wounded in an attack in Sicily, his last reported words to his Company being "keep going".

Yorkshire continued to have action-packed matches in 1897 and Hunter, who was a good enough No 11 to enjoy several last-wicket century stands during his career, was the hero with the bat at Derby. He came in on the final day with 16 still needed and promptly knocked them off.

Having missed all the excitement at Taunton and Derby, Hawke was not there, either, when Brown amassed 311 off Sussex's attack at Bramall Lane, putting on 378 for the first wicket with Tunnicliffe (147), the third highest opening partnership in Yorkshire's history. The following year, Brown, whose batting could be tentative one minute and aggressive the next, assembled another triple century, this time against Derbyshire at Chesterfield, when he and Tunnicliffe hit 554 together – the second highest opening stand in world cricket and top of the list until Herbert Sutcliffe and Percy Holmes pipped it by one run against Essex at Leyton in 1932.

True cricket enthusiasts revel in seeing outstanding batting or bowling performances, even when directed against their own team, and this proved to be the case at Harrogate when spectators were held in awe by Gilbert Jessop who thrashed 101 for Gloucestershire in 40 minutes of mayhem. But the home fans were overjoyed at Bradford to be looking on as Schofield Haigh completed the hat-trick against Derbyshire.

Hawke was in the hot seat in more ways than one against Essex at Huddersfield late in the 1897 season when he, too, found himself at the wicket with only the last man to come in and six still needed. Unfortunately, Hunter was not playing in this game and his understudy, Sandy Bairstow, was a reliable wicketkeeper but a hopeless batsman. He survived for a while but with one needed to tie and two to win he was given out lbw by Lancashire umpire Dicky Barlow – and Lancashire went on to win the title. There were no complaints from Hawke who was keen to point out that it was a perfectly proper decision.

Many years later, Yorkshire were to snatch the Championship in similar circumstances when a Yorkshire-born umpire raised his finger to an opposing batsman. That was against Surrey at Hull in 1968 and only a couple of minutes remained with the Brownhats' last pair at the wicket when Arnold Long feathered Tony Nicholson to wicketkeeper, Jimmy Binks. There was great excitement as Yorkshire appealed in unison and then cast their gaze anxiously in the direction of the umpire at the bowler's end who was none other than that giant of a man from Northallerton, Albert Gaskell, a Yorkshireman through-and-through – and proud of it.

Gaskell's finger shot skywards and his feet left the ground as he jumped with joy. "That's out….and we've won the Championship," he boomed. Surrey were not too pleased about this. Mind you, they wouldn't be, would they?

But there was no Championship for Yorkshire in the year under review and it ended unhappily with the sacking of Peel. The good news, of course, was that it led to the emergence of Wilfred Rhodes.

And Rhodes was straight out of the blocks in the first match of the following season, 1898, impressing everyone with his 4-24 against a very strong MCC side. 'Everyone' included his captain, Hawke, and W.G. Grace who was playing for MCC and immediately admired Rhodes' rhythmic action and the skilful variety of his deliveries.

If the young Rhodes had a worry over how his future would map out it may have been that he did not wish his bowling to be seen as being far more important than his batting. Rhodes loved batting even more than he did bowling but Hawke believed his bowling was more important to the side in those days and he did not always wish to see him spend too long at the crease.

But when Hawke once lightly remarked during a match that he did not wish to see Rhodes score more than 20, back came the reply: "I hope that some day I shall be played for England for my batting." Ability, determination and strength of character saw Rhodes achieve his ambition but even he could not have anticipated that he would form with Hobbs one of England's greatest opening partnerships.

In the summer of 1898, however, Yorkshire's concern was that Rhodes should go on taking wickets and he did not let them down, picking up 126 of them at 13 runs apiece to help regain the Championship title, assisted in no small measure by Jackson and Tunnicliffe who both enjoyed a runs bonanza with Jackson also taking 91 wickets. Tunnicliffe was not only a great opening batsman but one of the finest slip fielders of his time or any other. If only we could wave a magic wand and see Tunnicliffe and Philip Sharpe, who caught them as easily as shelling peas from the late 1950s to the mid 70s, standing side by side, what a fascinating sight it would be.

Brown and Tunnicliffe's world record-breaking opening stand of 554 at Chesterfield was another highlight of a superb season but the innings as a whole reflected Yorkshire's soaring team spirit under Hawke rather than just being an affair dominated by two batsmen. At the fall of Tunnicliffe for 243, Hawke asked his men to go hell for leather and he led by example by sacrificing his own wicket early on. A tiring Brown knocked down his stumps upon reaching 300 and the innings was over an hour after Tunnicliffe's departure.

Meanwhile, Tom Hayward was shaping a massive innings of his own for Surrey against Lancashire at The Oval and telegrams kept arriving at Chesterfield from Kennington enquiring of Brown's score. Hayward was allowed to go on and overtake Brown, making 315, but the length of his innings was not in the best interests of the game and Surrey could not force the win they were seeking.

Champions again, Yorkshire began well in 1899 but faded towards the close, despite the flowering into full bloom of Denton, who scored 1,595 runs to give him the third of his 20 seasons in which he exceeded the 1,000 runs mark. Rhodes worked his socks off again and Hirst hit three consecutive centuries in August but for the second time in a few years Surrey were to take the title away from them.

It would have been comforting to have ended the 19th century in a blaze of glory but it did not quite happen. The start of the 20th century was quite a different story.

CHAPTER TEN

HAPPY NEW YEARS

If Yorkshire welcomed in the 20th century with a New Year wish that they would regain the County Championship then that wish certainly came true – and this time they did not relinquish their grip the following season or the one after that.

It was a golden age of milk and honey when Yorkshire reigned supreme and cricket gossip did not ask who would win the title but who would finish second to Hawke's mighty team?

Lancashire came closest to Yorkshire in 1900 but they lost two of their 28 matches whereas Yorkshire were unbeaten with 16 victories and 12 draws.

Hirst led the way with the bat, followed by Tunnicliffe and Denton, each of the trio going well beyond the 1,000 runs mark, and although Hirst had an indifferent year with the ball it did not matter because Rhodes stepped up with 206 wickets at 12.29 runs apiece (261 wickets in all cricket) and Haigh managed 145 at 14.16. The other J.T. Brown, from Darfield, collected 23 wickets with a season's best of 6-34 but the truth of it was that the Kirkheaton duo so monopolised the scene that other bowlers hardly got a look-in. In 21 of the games, Rhodes claimed five wickets in an innings and on six occasions he bagged ten in the match, while Haigh took five wickets in an innings ten times and had one match return of ten wickets.

Another player to enjoy success that year was Headingley-born Tom Taylor who made useful runs. Taylor was primarily a top-class wicketkeeper and a fine batsman but his chances behind the stumps were limited because of the towering presence of David Hunter.

Taylor, educated at Uppingham and Cambridge University, was a multi-talented sportsman who gained a Blue at cricket and hockey and also excelled at rugby and tennis. He would have been Hawke's preferred choice to follow him as captain had the family engineering business not got in the way and although he left county cricket early he returned to Yorkshire CCC as president in 1948 and served until his death in 1960 at the age of 81. He was at various times president of Scarborough Cricket Festival and of the Yorkshire Lawn Tennis Association.

There had been fears before the season began that the absence of both Frank Mitchell and Jackson, who were away fighting in the Boer War, would drag the side down, but those fears proved unfounded, just as they did 110 years later when Test stars Michael Vaughan and Matthew Hoggard had both departed. In the event, they were barely missed and Yorkshire would have been Champions in 2010 had they won on the final day instead of going to pieces against Kent.

There was also sadness before the start of the 1900 campaign with the news that Frank Milligan had perished in the attempt to relieve Mafeking and so deeply felt was his loss that his team-mates clubbed together to give a cot to Bradford Children's Hospital. Kids doted over Milligan and he was never happier than when playing among them. It was felt that he would have much appreciated this gift in his name to the hospital.

Once Yorkshire got on the field they never looked back or paused for breath all season but no victory was more dramatic than in their opening game against Worcestershire at Bradford. It was all done and dusted within the day, Yorkshire sandwiching 99 in between their opponents' scores of 43 and 51, Rhodes and Haigh bowling throughout both innings to return figures of 11-36 and 7-49 respectively.

Hirst and Haigh rarely bowled well together, it was said, and in 1901 it was Hirst who gave Rhodes much the stronger support by taking 135 wickets to his partner's 196.

The batting that year was led by Mitchell who plundered 1,674 runs – the highest aggregate yet recorded in a Yorkshire season – and the England cricket and rugby international hit seven centuries, including four in as many matches, and six half-centuries. A couple of years later, the Boer War veteran returned to South Africa to live and he came back to England in 1912 as the Springboks' captain in a three-match series in which England, under C.B. Fry, won every match. Mitchell only played in the first Test, however, before Louis Tancred took over.

Yorkshire's record was phenomenal in 1901 because they won 20 and lost only one of their 27 matches. They began the season at a cracking pace by winning their first eight contests and none of the other counties ever had the slightest chance of taking the title away from them.

They were brilliant but not quite invincible and it was lowly Somerset, who unexpectedly and much to their own surprise, found a chink in their armour at Headingley. So far under the cosh were Somerset at one stage that they made arrangements for their saloon to take them home on the second evening but in the event they won the game by the enormous margin of 279 runs on the third day.

Bowled out in their first knock for 87, thanks mainly to Rhodes' 5-39, they found themselves trailing by 238 after Yorkshire replied with 325, Haigh top-scoring with a then career-best 96 which saw him top 3,000 first-class runs. But Lionel Palairet (173) and Len Braund (107), who had both been out for ducks in the first innings, then put on 222 in 140 minutes for the first wicket, their centuries being followed by one from Frank Phillips (122). The bowling for once went to pieces, the middle order continued to rattle up the runs and Somerset finished with 630. On a crumbling pitch on the final day, Yorkshire were dismissed for 113.

This capitulation was in sharp contrast to virtually everything else which happened in 1901 and only a month earlier Yorkshire had run complete riot at Trent Bridge where they routed Nottinghamshire for 13, the second lowest total in the history of the Championship and the lowest until Northamptonshire were dismissed for 12 at Gloucester six years later.

After Yorkshire had posted a modest 204, Rhodes grabbed six wickets for four runs and Haigh four for eight to dispose of Notts within the hour and it was Hirst's 6-26 that then spurred the visitors on to victory by an innings and 18 runs.

Hawke's team had by now really got their act together and their leader was also responsible for making sure his boys were properly looked after in other areas off the field. They toured the country in 1901 in a saloon carriage hired at the club's expense and at the close of this and the next two seasons a cheque was added to the players' bonus fund which had been set up in 1897, the year after winter pay of £2 per week had been brought in for the professionals. Yorkshire were looking after their players like no other county and the players were showing their appreciation by earning every penny of their money.

Yorkshire's supremacy was again never questioned in 1902 when they made it a hat-trick of Championship wins but once more the only fly in the ointment was put there by Somerset. As in the previous year, they were the only side to defeat Yorkshire and they had the proud boast of being the only team to conquer them in the first three years of the 20th century. Eighty matches since the turn of the century and only two defeats. Never had Yorkshire shone brighter.

Taylor, in what was his last season before going into the family business, was the leading batsman in 1902 with 1,276 runs and although it was back to Rhodes and Haigh being the principal wicket-takers, the finest piece of bowling in Hawke's opinion came from Jackson in the Roses match at Sheffield which Yorkshire won by an innings and 22 runs. Lancashire were sent back for 72 and 54 and the unplayable Jackson had three for five and five for eight to give him match figures of 8-13.

Irving Washington, Wombwell born and bred, and the first left-hander to be picked by Yorkshire solely as a batsman, made a good impression by contributing 906 runs in the Championship and 1,022 altogether in what was by far the better of his two seasons of first team cricket with the White Rose.

One of the red-letter moments of the season came at Lord's on August 23 when Tunnicliffe caught Middlesex captain Gregor MacGregor off Rhodes to bring the slip fielder his 500th victim. At the close of his career, Tunnicliffe had pouched 665 catches and this record for a Yorkshire fielder as opposed to a wicketkeeper may stay with him for all time. Rhodes, who played in over 400 more matches than Tunnicliffe, stands next to him with 586 catches and the only others with 500-plus are Brian Close (564), Philip Sharpe (525), Vic Wilson (520) and Hirst (518).

Another momentous milestone was reached on Yorkshire's visit to Cheltenham which the visitors won by an innings and 102, the outstanding feature being the dismissal of Walter Troup in the second innings to give Rhodes his 1,000th first class wicket.

Yorkshire's achievements in 1902 were all the more remarkable in that Test calls once again took a heavy toll with Jackson, Hirst and Rhodes featuring so strongly in the five-match series against Australia that the trio topped the England batting averages. And it was in the final Test, remember, that the last wicket pair of Hirst and Rhodes calmly knocked off the last 16 runs in singles in front of a highly charged crowd which could hardly bear to watch, so intense was the excitement.

No wonder that such a marvellous season should see the whole team rewarded for their brilliant performances by being entertained by the Society of Yorkshiremen in London when Hawke was given an ovation lasting for several minutes before he could begin his speech and when every guest was presented with a white rose.

A poem was read out which went:

We're proud as Yorkshiremen of the honours you have won,
And of the brilliant feats which from time to time you've done,
And we see no earthly reason why with such a gallant band
The Cricket County Championship should e'er be wrested from your hand.

Being merely mortal, the title was wrested from their hand by Middlesex the very next season but they were to remain a power in the land for many years to come and the 'pride' mentioned in these lines is still very much with them to this day.

CHAPTER ELEVEN

A TOUCH OF CLASS

It is the English fascination with the class system which has attracted millions of television viewers to tune in to programmes like *Upstairs, Downstairs* and *Downton Abbey*.

Likewise, the early popularity and success of Yorkshire County Cricket Club was partly due to the upper, middle and lower classes working together to make their side the elite of the land so far as cricket was concerned.

In Society, of course, those who existed downstairs only moved higher up the house when ordered to do so – and then merely for the benefit of the upper classes who resided there.

With Yorkshire, as we have seen, it was different in that all classes worked together in a common cause (if we may call it that) and a century or five wickets was seen to be of equal value whether it came from a lord or a chimney sweep.

So Hawke, flushed with success from a hat-trick of Championship titles, continued to be the automatic choice as leader as Yorkshire worked their way through the 'Noughties'. Already president of the club, his contributions to cricket were recognised by an even higher authority in 1914 when he was elected president of the MCC in the famous club's centenary year and he remained in office during the dark years of the Great War.

Back at Yorkshire, J.B. Wostinholm retired from his 38-year stint as secretary in 1902 and was to be followed in that position by Frederick Charles Toone, later to become Sir Frederick.

Another reason why Yorkshire's backbone has always been so strong is because the club has been guided by a remarkable handful of long-serving secretaries who have carried out their duties with the utmost loyalty and devotion.

Toone was secretary for 27 years until his death in 1930 and he was followed by John Nash who served for 40 years from 1931-71. Joe Lister, the only ex-first-class cricketer to fill the role, was appointed from 1971 until he, too, died in office in 1991 and he was succeeded by David Ryder from 1971 up to the ending of that job title in 2002 when he continued in a pivotal role first as the club's accountant and then as stadium facilities manager.

It is testimony to the exemplary way that they have carried out their duties that from 1864-2002, a period of 138 years, Yorkshire should have cause to engage a total of only five secretaries.

Toone's appointment in 1903 certainly meant that the club continued to be administered by the upper and middle classes and this point is emphasised in a photograph taken in 1908 at Hawke's residence at Wighill Park, Tadcaster, where he is pictured in the doorway with three other worthies in Charles Stokes, treasurer from 1899-1912 and a committee representative for 36 years, ex-secretary J.B. Wostinholm and the then current secretary, F.C. Toone.

Although Toone was no cricketer himself, his skills as an organiser were unsurpassed and he came to Yorkshire from Leicestershire CCC where he had been secretary since 1897.

After the war had ended, Toone was entrusted by the MCC to manage three England tours of Australia and his strong character and impeccable organisational qualities proved that he was exactly the right man for the job.

On his return to England from his last tour 'Down Under' in 1928-29 he was knighted in recognition of his great work in fostering relations between "the Dominions and the Mother Country."

Toone was only the second person to be knighted specifically for services to cricket and he followed Sir Francis Lacey who had been a reasonable cricketer but first and foremost was secretary of MCC for 28 years.

When Ian Botham was knighted in 2007 he became the 21st person directly associated with cricket to be so honoured and the list includes a dozen or so Englishmen with Sir Frederick Toone's name probably escaping the tip of the tongue more frequently than any of the others in that select band.

Having lost only two matches out of 80 in the first three years of the century, it must have come as a shock to Yorkshire to be defeated five times in 1903 when they handed over their title to Middlesex with Sussex finishing in second place.

It was a season in which Yorkshire blew hot and cold – or rather cold and hot – because by the end of June they had succumbed to four southern counties in Somerset (inevitably), Middlesex, Sussex and Surrey. The pendulum then swung dramatically the other way and from the beginning of July until the third week in August, Yorkshire were back to their best form, either winning easily or just being thwarted by lack of time in which to make the final thrust.

Suddenly, the Championship was within their grasp again until Kent got the better of an exciting draw at Canterbury and Sussex claimed the double over Yorkshire for the first time in their history when they won the last match of the season at Brighton.

Many factors combined to unsettle Yorkshire that summer when Taylor was absent through business and Washington was unavailable because of injury. Jackson was present only rarely, Hawke missed several matches through injury and Brown, the bowler, fell in a heap and damaged his shoulder at Taunton in only the third game and his career was over. On top of all this, Hirst's leg gave way just when he was at his brilliant best with bat and ball and he had to be sidelined for three weeks.

Yet there was one aspect of their cooling-off which Yorkshire could not in the least excuse and that was in the sharp decline of their fielding which had been such a strong feature of their play over the previous few years. Not only were the younger players to blame because quite a number of the spilled chances slipped through the fingers of those whose hands should have been as safe as houses.

Despite Hirst's leg injury he still topped Yorkshire's batting and bowling averages, scoring 1,535 runs and capturing 121 wickets, while Rhodes got fully into his stride with the ball after a slow start, taking 8-12 against Worcestershire on a bad wicket at Huddersfield and 13-152 against Lancashire on a batsman's paradise at Headingley. He ended with 169 wickets and, like Hirst, was now an automatic selection had he been just a specialist batsman or bowler.

Yorkshire could only finish second to unbeaten Lancashire in 1904 but one of the highlights of the season was the Roses clash at Headingley which Hirst took as his benefit and the fans flocked in their thousands to pay homage to their hero who at this time was considered the best all-rounder in the world. The total number of spectators over the three days of the August Bank Holiday period was 78,792, more than 31,000 converging on the ground on each of the first two days. Hirst raked in £3,703, a figure which stood as a record Yorkshire benefit until the ever-popular Roy Kilner received £4,106, 21 years later. It is said that Hirst's smile stretched from one side of his face right round to the other. If he did permit himself a frown, it would only have flickered briefly across his brow when Lancashire managed to cling on for the draw.

The month before Hirst's bonanza, the papers were full of quite a different story, Yorkshire's match against Kent at Harrogate being abandoned on the second day following allegations that the pitch had been "doctored" during the night. The truth of the matter never did emerge but Kent's captain, Cloudesley Marsham, later claimed that some person or persons had "rolled, watered and doctored" the wicket, a charge which was strenuously denied by the groundsman and Harrogate Cricket Club.

The umpires and captains agreed that the game be abandoned as a first-class fixture but to appease the crowd play continued on a 'friendly' basis for much of the day and the home fans had the consolation of watching Haigh perform a hat-trick with slow leg-breaks. The MCC turned down Harrogate's suggestion of an enquiry into the whole affair, saying that little purpose would be served by one, but they added that the captains were justified in calling the game off after the umpires made it known they believed the pitch had been tampered with.

Also in 1904, Yorkshire met Nottinghamshire at Headingley in the first time limit fixture ever to be played, with each innings limited to four-and-a-quarter hours and with the match to be decided by the number of runs scored, irrespective of wickets lost. It is believed the captains agreed to stage this non-first-class encounter as an experiment to test the water as there had been some calls for reforms when perhaps none were needed but, as it turned out, the time limit never entered a game which Yorkshire won by 71 runs.

This practical demonstration was deemed a huge and pointless flop and it was never repeated but perhaps it is also true that the Yorkshire club and players were traditionalists by nature and not always the first to take change on board – as was to be the case with their slow response to limited overs cricket in the 1960s.

Around the same time in the early 20th century, Yorkshire were vocal in their opposition to suggestions that county matches should start on Wednesdays and Saturdays and they were powerful enough for a majority to go along with them for a while but when the change was eventually made it was an obvious success and Yorkshire's earlier resistance was quickly forgotten.

Having lost Brown the bowler in 1903, Yorkshire now lost Brown the bat who was reluctantly and sadly forced to retire through ill-health and who, to the anguish of everyone, was buried later that year. In addition to heart problems, he contracted terminal cancer in May, 1904, and died in the November of congestion of the brain and heart failure at Dr. Kingscote's Medical Home in London. The sting was further taken out of the bowling through Rhodes becoming less effective that season as his batting improved still further. He was one of five players to top 1,000 runs but the batting honours once again went to the invincible Hirst who became Yorkshire's first all-rounder to score 2,000 runs and take 100 wickets in one English summer.

It may not have been Yorkshire's best season with the ball but it was much better than it would have been without the appearance on the scene of Hubert Myers who weighed in with 78 wickets at 20.41 runs apiece. Such an introduction by a young player these days would probably see him straight into the England reckoning but the general standards were much higher in the 1900s.

Myers, a fast bowler and useful bat who hailed from Yeadon, had played on only a few occasions for Yorkshire before 1904, and his regular appearance in the side was due to a recommendation from their former player, Frank Mitchell, who was now touring with South Africa but still found time to turn out for Yorkshire on a few occasions in early season.

Mitchell gave it as his opinion that Myers was probably a better bowler than Yorkshire understood him to be and that he could send down a swinging ball that was almost as difficult to play as Hirst's. As the season advanced, Myers often shared the attack with Hirst and against Gloucestershire at Dewsbury his 8-81 was the club's best return of the season.

Not everything always went right for Yorkshire in 1904 but they did shake off one monkey which had been clinging to their backs. They beat Somerset not only once but twice!

Even though nobody begrudged Lancashire their Championship success it was with some relief on the east side of the Pennines that Yorkshire replaced their Red Rose opponents at the top of the table in 1905 to record the seventh of Hawke's eight title wins. His Lordship was mildly surprised by his side's success on this occasion because, having stressed the importance of England selecting the strongest possible team for F.S. Jackson to take on Australia with, he felt that Yorkshire may, consequently, be considerably weakened.

That was indeed the case but Yorkshire responded by playing bright and positive cricket and they won their first four matches, including the one against Leicestershire when Hirst initiated the fightback by hitting what remains the highest score in the club's history of 341, of which 212 of his runs came from boundary hits. It is recorded that he played only one flawed shot in this epic assault and the inbred honesty of the man is revealed in his later remark that he thought he may have been lbw before he had scored, but that the umpire was of a different opinion.

As we have already seen, it is not always the brightest button that proves to have the strongest thread in an hour of need and when Yorkshire staved off defeat against Essex at Leyton to secure the Championship they had cause to be grateful to Morley-born amateur all-rounder Ernest Smith who was a valued member of the side for about ten years from 1888.

Batting first, Essex piled up 521 through centuries from captain Frederick Fane and Charles McGahey and they may well have made more but for Smith taking three wickets with the best analysis of the innings. Despite 40 from Denton and 36 from Hawke, Yorkshire were bowled out for 98, "Johnny Won't Hit Today" Douglas at one stage striking the stumps five times in eight balls, Rhodes, Haigh and Myers comprising the hat-trick victims.

Following on 423 behind, Yorkshire had already lost a wicket by the start of the third and final day and they knew they had to bat out time to save the match and bring home the title. They were helped by Hirst, who passed 2,000 runs for the season on his way to 90, but over an hour still remained when Smith strode to the crease at 213-6 and was later joined by Hawke.

It was Smith's usual style to give the ball a good crack but this time he resisted all such temptations and he was still not off the mark when the stumps were pulled out of the ground, having nothing tangible to show for one of Yorkshire's most valuable-ever scoreless knocks.

Smith, an Oxford Blue, who went on to become headmaster of a preparatory school at Eastbourne, was physically very fit and he continued playing cricket long after his Yorkshire days were over. He made first-class appearances for Leveson-Gower's XI at Eastbourne right up to 1928 when he was 58.

So Yorkshire clung doggedly on to top the table in 1905 but the reason they could not emulate this achievement the following year was, astonishingly, due to just one run – the margin of the defeat they suffered against Gloucestershire at Bristol when they only needed draws in this match and the final one against Somerset to retain the title.

Captained by Ernest Smith in Hawke's absence, Yorkshire met with unexpected resistance from Gloucestershire and they trailed by five runs on the first innings after George Dennett had gathered up eight of the wickets that were included in his haul of 160 dismissals that season. The home side replied with 228 which left Yorkshire needing 234 to win but panic set in and last man, William Ringrose, appeared with 11 still required.

Nine of these were scored by his partner, Myers, but then Jessop brought himself on to bowl to Ringrose with just one run separating the teams. His first delivery was wide down the legside and it was only a despairing and brilliant stop by wicketkeeper John Board that saved the extras which would have won Yorkshire the match. Two balls later, Jessop rapped the unfortunate Ringrose – who had taken five first innings wickets – on the pads and the appeal was upheld, so giving the Championship to Kent for the first time.

Yorkshire were certainly not at their strongest in 1906, having to rely too heavily on Hirst, Rhodes, Denton and Tunnicliffe, and in trying to plug some of the gaps they called upon 27 players at some stage or other during the season.

Some were more successful than others and one who dazzled like a shooting star before fizzling out after all of three matches was Herbert Sedgwick. On his debut against Worcestershire at Hull he took five wickets for eight runs as the visitors were demolished for 25 and when they followed on he then performed the hat-trick. A few days later he got among the wickets against the West Indians at Harrogate and then in the Roses game at Old Trafford, in John Tyldesley's benefit match, he caused a stir by opening the bowling and knocking back Archie MacLaren's stumps before he had scored. That was his last scalp in a contest which Yorkshire won by 107 runs and little else was heard of him, his first-class career comprising of 16 wickets at 20.43 runs apiece.

An even briefer Yorkshire career was that of Ces Parkin whose debut in 1906 against Gloucestershire at Headingley proved to be his only match – and not because he failed to score and only picked up a couple of wickets. It came to Yorkshire's attention after the game that Parkin had been born at Eaglescliffe on the Durham side of the Tees and 100 yards away from the Yorkshire border, which meant he was not qualified by birth to play for the White Rose county. He was dropped forthwith and it was noted that "the Yorkshire committee and Lord Hawke did not require to be told their duty in the matter."

Yorkshire's loss, though, turned out to be Lancashire's gain because after returning home to play for Durham for a while he moved over the Pennines and in 1914 he featured in the first of his 157 matches for the Red Rose. He played in ten Tests for England, concluded his career with over 1,000 first-class wickets and when he died his ashes were scattered over Old Trafford where his wife also planted two rose bushes.

A reminder, once again, not to suppose that Parkin was by himself in slipping through a net already breached by Hawke who always thought that he alone should be the exception to this policy of which he was so proud.

So many others wriggled out for one reason or another that by the time that the boundaries were officially opened up in 1992 with the signing of Sachin Tendulkar no fewer than 29 non-Yorkshiremen had represented the county.

CHAPTER TWELVE

HAWKE'S FINAL FLING

So, Yorkshire were second best in 1906 and the same applied in 1907 when they were pipped by Nottinghamshire in a summer of depressingly dreadful weather which prevented them from getting a positive result for a whole month. Neither were they able to test their strength against the unbeaten new champions because their fixture at Trent Bridge came to a soggy end with Yorkshire on 47-1 and not a ball was bowled in the return game at Huddersfield in early July.

But the weather was not wholly to blame for a general decline in Yorkshire's high standards. Some of the older players were beginning to creak and the younger ones who came in were unable to take much of the weight off the backs of their more seasoned colleagues.

At the end of the season, the faithful Tunnicliffe reluctantly acknowledged in a letter of resignation that "time waits for no man" and the shadows were also beginning to lengthen around Hawke who kept indicating at various official functions that his playing days were drawing to a close.

Hawke was adamant that he would have been gone altogether by now had Tom Taylor, his favoured successor, been around to take over the captaincy but Taylor was lost to business and Hawke soldiered on because no suitable alternative could be found. Also, whenever the subject of retirement cropped up, his players made it quite clear that they wanted their skipper to keep going.

And not only did Hawke keep going but he even added to his esteem by winning the Championship again in his milestone year of 1908, the perfect way in which to celebrate 25 years of captaincy.

Doubts about Yorkshire's ability to last the pace with an ageing side soon evaporated as they galloped unbeaten through the season but their resurgence still came as something of a surprise far and wide. Incredibly, they enjoyed exactly the same record as they did at the start of the century, winning 16 of their 28 matches and drawing the other 12.

Just as Midgley had shot briefly to the fore in 1906, so did John Newstead now but his fame lasted all season rather than for just three matches. Newstead could hardly be classed as "new blood" because he was 25 when he played his first game for Yorkshire in 1903 and 30 before he took his first wicket.

The late developer hardly put a foot wrong during a summer in which his medium-quick bowling, very much in the style adopted almost half a century later by Bob Appleyard, brought him 131 wickets, each costing him only 15.94 runs. In addition he scored an unbeaten century against Nottinghamshire at Trent Bridge and only narrowly failed to complete the double. He was named one of Wisden's Five Cricketers of the Year and had there been a Test series the general consensus was that he would almost certainly have been picked.

For some reason which was just as perplexing to him as to others he could never repeat that form in future years and he slid quietly into oblivion. Yet his sudden burst of activity with the ball in 1908 was particularly valuable as it relieved the pressure on Hirst and Rhodes and helped Yorkshire overcome the handicap of losing Haigh with a broken finger for several weeks.

Most of the batsmen made runs steadily and they were assisted by another one-season wonder in William Wilkinson who had taken over Washington's role as a genuine left-hander. He chipped in with a useful 1,282 runs but was never as effective again and after making a maiden century against Sussex at Bramall Lane the following season he was never able to pass the 30 mark.

By mid-July it was obvious Yorkshire were going for glory once again which meant that a presentation of mementos to Hawke during the Nottinghamshire match at Headingley to mark his 25 years of captaincy was able to be such an enjoyable event. Funds opened up by Yorkshire CCC and the Yorkshire Evening Post raised £1,000 and £824 respectively from which Hawke was to purchase articles that became family heirlooms. The funds were subscribed to by all classes of cricket followers.

And at the presentation ceremony, performed by the Earl of Wharncliffe in front of a big crowd, Hawke was given a reminder by a member of the working class that you don't get owt for nowt in Yorkshire. Responding to many speeches singing his praises, Hawke said he did not know how to reply to what had been said. Back came a voice: "Get a good score and tha'll be right."

What a unique web we weave in bringing together the many strands that make Yorkshire cricket what it is.

There were now just two seasons to run of Hawke's great tenure of captaincy but his glory days were behind him and there was to be no fairytale ending for his team who finished third to Kent in 1909 and eighth to the same opponents in 1910. Hawke himself featured only occasionally in the first of these seasons and even more rarely in the second, at the end of which he formally resigned.

In 1909 he became ill after the first match and left England to recuperate until into August but he was then involved in the debacle against Surrey at The Oval when they were fired out on a rain-affected pitch in their second innings for a humiliating 26 in 16.1 overs, Thomas Rushby claiming 5-9 and William "Razor" Smith 5-12.

This was the lowest score in Yorkshire's history and it was to remain so until Hampshire destroyed them for 23 at Acklam Park, Middlesbrough, in 1965.

Not only were Hawke's playing days almost over but so were David Hunter's at the close of 1909 and the ending of his active service must have been keenly felt by Hawke. Like Tunnicliffe, Hunter was one of Hawke's most deeply-respected team members and with both of these old comrades put out to grass, Hawke must have felt the world was changing around him as his 50th birthday loomed.

When David Hunter first came into the side in 1888 he maintained the high standards already set behind the stumps by his brother, Joseph, and George Pinder. During David's 21 years of service there were always reliable deputies to fill in whenever he was unavailable and this quality of understudy has always been equally as high throughout the club's history.

From David Hunter onwards, Yorkshire have been fortunate to get long and outstanding service from their wicketkeepers who, between them, would have played far more often for England had Kent not been even stronger in this department.

Hunter was followed by the splendid Arthur Dolphin, who beat off strong competition from Howard Watson, and after him came the likes of Arthur Wood, Jimmy Binks, David Bairstow and Richard Blakey, all of them being fine exponents of their art. It would be hard to argue, however, that any one of them was better than Hunter whose 1,186 dismissals, comprised of 863 catches and 323 stumpings, has never quite been reached, although Binks and Bairstow got pretty near.

Unlike many wicketkeepers, Hunter was seen but not heard on the field of play – more a Blakey than a Bairstow – but he was as keen as mustard and the proudest of No 11 batsmen. He and Hawke more than once figured in last-wicket century partnerships and their 148 stand against Kent at Sheffield in 1898 remained a county record for the tenth wicket until Geoff Boycott and Graham Stevenson exceeded it by one run against Warwickshire at Edgbaston in 1982.

It was obviously a difficult time for Yorkshire officials in 1910 with the team floundering and Hawke virtually retired in all but name and had there been an obvious successor to the great man that summer they would no doubt have been eager to appoint him.

But no amateur of similar standing to Hawke as a cricketer was around and it was left to Sir Everard Radcliffe, whose family came from Rudding Park, near Knaresborough, to stand in for Hawke – and here was another non-Yorkshireman, Radcliffe being born at Hensleigh, near Tiverton, in Devon.

A graduate of Oxford University, but not a member of the cricket team, Radcliffe had only three moderate seasons with Yorkshire during their period of decline. Perhaps he was of reasonable club standard as a batsman but he was certainly not county class as his figures of 826 runs in a total of 64 matches for an average of 10.86 clearly indicate.

Radcliffe did a difficult job to the best of his ability and he could not have been without a sense of humour, either, as is shown in his remarks after captaining Yorkshire in the 1910 Roses match at Old Trafford in which Yorkshire were trounced by an innings and 111 runs and Lancashire's cricket and rugby international, Reggie Spooner, made an unbeaten 200 out of 395-5 declared.

With only two wickets to his name in his entire career, Radcliffe brought himself on as the eighth bowler for a solitary over with Spooner near to his double century. "I shall never be convinced that I did not have him lbw when he had made 199!" he said with mock hurt.

Spooner's 200, incidentally, remains Lancashire's highest individual Roses score on their home soil, although at Headingley Stuart Law racked up 206 in the 2007 Championship match while in a first class game outside that competition Graham Lloyd plundered 225 ten years earlier.

In the November of 1910, with Hawke beyond his 50th year, he officially handed in his resignation as captain after being the guiding hand for 28 seasons and completely transforming the club. His achievements for Yorkshire, England and the game internationally cannot be over-estimated.

A man who put team before self-interests and the spirit of the game before all else, he also improved the lot of Yorkshire cricketers by raising the wages of his professionals and making sure that financial benefits were in place after retirement.

His own contributions to the game should also be recognised because although not a batsman off the top shelf, he was still very good over an extremely long period and able to make significant contributions even when he had introduced into Yorkshire's ranks run-scorers of the highest calibre.

In many respects, Hawke's grip and influence on Yorkshire cricket remained as strong as ever because in addition to being club president he was also a trustee and chairman of the cricket, finance and ground committees. Nothing could be signed, sealed and delivered without having Hawke's thumb mark on it – and that was how it was to remain up to and during the period between the two World Wars.

CHAPTER THIRTEEN

TRIUMPH AND TRAGEDY

The immediate concern of Hawke's following his retirement was who to appoint as captain in 1911 and with no obvious leader to call upon the job was this time handed on an official basis to Radcliffe. But he could bring about no immediate improvement and seventh place in the table was the best that Yorkshire could manage.

Hawke had, however, started a weeding-out process in the spring, getting rid of Myers and the gifted but erratic batsman James Rothery and giving a decent run to the up-and-coming Major Booth and Alonzo Drake who were gifted bats and exceptional bowlers.

In a short space of time, Booth and Drake formed a great bowling partnership together, vindicating Hawke's decision to give them their fling, but how quickly and tragically they were cut down and their huge potential never fully realised. Had things been different they could have gone on to be mentioned in the same breath as Hirst and Rhodes.

As already recorded earlier on, Booth was killed in action near Serre, France, while Drake, who suffered bouts of depression and was rejected from war service, died at his home in Honley, Huddersfield, in February, 1919, at the age of 34.

Booth, one of that select band of genius cricketers to come from Pudsey, showed his ability with the bat in his first regular season of 1911 by hitting a career-best 210 off Worcestershire's attack at New Road, but in his few brief years it was his bowling which was the more eye-catching.

Nine times he trawled in ten or more wickets in a match, including his best figures of 14-160 against Essex at Leyton in 1914, and on four occasions he bagged eight wickets in an innings. In addition, he twice did the hat-trick – against Worcestershire at Bradford in 1911 and against Essex at Leyton the following year, both of these opponents having good reason to feel heartily sick of the sight of him.

Booth, who played in two Tests for England against South Africa in 1913-1914, topped 100 wickets for Yorkshire in three seasons from 1912-1914, with 167 in 1913 being his best, and his loss to both county and country in tragic and heroic circumstances can only be imagined.

But Drake's loss, too, was incalculable and his bowling record was just as dramatic as his team-mate's. In 1914, he became the first of three Yorkshire bowlers to take all ten wickets in an innings in a first-class match (Hedley Verity was to do it twice) with his 10-35 return against Somerset at Weston-super-Mare when his match analysis was 15-51. And in the same season he became the only Yorkshire bowler ever to take four wickets in four balls in the match with Derbyshire at Chesterfield. In 1912 he had secured a hat-trick against Essex at Huddersfield.

Drake, like Booth, claimed 100 wickets in 1913 and 1914, with 158 in the latter year being his best, and he completed the double in all first-class matches in 1913.

On pitches which suited him, Drake was totally unplayable and the Yorkshire club and all of its followers were just as devastated by his untimely death as they were by Booth's.

If it merits a special note that Drake and Booth both firmly established themselves in 1911 then it is also equally necessary to add that another great player made his debut for Yorkshire in that summer and that he, too, was to have his career cut short by a premature and much-lamented death.

Roy Kilner was and remains a figure of folklore proportions in and around his home patch of Wombwell and was one of the most popular men ever to don a Yorkshire sweater.

The son of a miner, who was later licensee of the Halfway House in Wombwell for 30 years, Roy was the elder brother of Norman, who batted with distinction for Yorkshire before making a bigger name for himself with Warwickshire, and the nephew of Irving Washington.

Like Washington, Roy was a quick-scoring left-hander and he also developed into a left-arm slow bowler of the highest quality who could mix orthodoxy with chinamen and googlies.

It was after the First World War that Kilner's fame spread and he turned out in nine Tests for England between 1924-1926 and on Arthur Gilligan's tour of Australia in 1924-25 he hit 74 at Melbourne and took 4-51 at Adelaide.

Kilner completed 1,000 runs in a season ten times and he did the double four times, his zenith being reached in 1923 with 1,404 runs for an average of 32.24 and 158 wickets at only 12.91 runs apiece.

He had a top score of 206 not out against Derbyshire at Sheffield in 1920 and his best bowling figures were acquired at Cardiff Arms Park in 1923 when he captured 8-26. In 365 first-class appearances for Yorkshire he scored 13,018 runs with 15 centuries and he took 857 wickets at 17.33. His full first-class career record shows that he topped 14,000 runs and collected just over 1,000 wickets, making him a celebrated all-rounder by any yardstick.

So popular was the short and stocky Kilner that many a proud parent named their son after him and many more would have done so had he not died in hospital in Barnsley in 1928 after spending the winter coaching in India where he caught a bug which developed into enteric fever. His passing so stunned the whole of Yorkshire and particularly his neighbourhood that over 100,000 people lined the streets to pay their respects as his funeral cortege slid silently by.

Norman Kilner was as gifted a batsman as his elder brother and he scored two centuries in his time with Yorkshire between 1919-1923. His only problem at Yorkshire was that his rival for a place was Maurice Leyland and when Kilner felt that the battle was an uneven one he moved on to Warwickshire where he played in 330 matches, taking his first-class tally to 17,522 runs with 25 centuries.

Although not at their best in 1911, Yorkshire did enjoy eight consecutive county victories in the first part of the season, this sequence culminating with the win over Leicestershire at Bradford where Cecil Wood gamely carried his bat in both innings for the vanquished with scores of 107 and 117. The worthy gentleman spent over eight-and-a-half hours at the crease while his colleagues fell around him and was on the field for each of the 1,211 runs scored in the match. Unfortunately for him and Leicestershire, Denton played superbly for an unbeaten 137 as Yorkshire successfully chased down 272.

It was a great summer with the bat for Denton, whose 2,223 runs included six centuries, but there was some disappointment for Rhodes in that the total receipts accruing from his testimonial match with Lancashire at Sheffield were only £1,179 and once all expenses had been met the net amount available for Rhodes was just over £750. But club secretary Toone and the sub-committees around the county organised subscriptions so well that the Fund was able to close on £2,202 1s. 10p.

On the field, Rhodes joined Hirst and Haigh in capturing 100 wickets and his batting continued to go from strength to strength. In Yorkshire's final match of the season against MCC at Scarborough he scored a century in each innings for the first time with knocks of 128 and 115 and a few weeks later this remarkable man repeated the feat for England against New South Wales at Sydney, hitting 128 and 115.

One other feature of 1911 was the opening of the winter shed at Headingley on the site where the club offices were to stand until the move into the new Carnegie Pavilion. It cost over £600 to erect and Yorkshire players shivered at their indoor net sessions until it closed down upon the building of new indoor net facilities at the Kirkstall Lane end of the ground in 1966. This accommodation was also less than inviting in the depths of winter and it remained in use until 1990 when the new indoor cricket school was opened in St Michael's Lane, the first piece of property that Yorkshire CCC had ever owned.

With the likes of Booth and Drake adding to the mighty power of Hirst, Rhodes, Haigh and Denton, it came as no surprise that Yorkshire should grasp hold of the Championship title again in 1912 for the ninth time in 20 years of generally stunning progress.

Radcliffe had resigned the captaincy at the end of 2011 and into the saddle leaped Sir Archibald Woollaston White who may not actually have been seen as a knight in shining armour by the general public when he accepted the role but still proved a good enough leader to bring glory to his foot soldiers.

Educated at Cambridge University, White, from Tickhill, near Doncaster, had led Yorkshire on a few occasions in Radcliffe's absence in 1911 so the job was not entirely new to him. He was a batsman of modest ability but a strong disciplinarian who put the team beyond everything else and he remained as captain right up to the Great War.

An honest man, White conceded that his Championship-winning team were not as good as some of the sides which Hawke had led but he was right in his belief that Yorkshire were very much the pick of the bunch in the wet and thoroughly miserable summer of 1912. It rained so frequently that of Yorkshire's 19 home matches only one was free of weather interference and it should be of no surprise that there was a loss on the year's working of over £948.

England calls meant Rhodes was missing from six county matches and Haigh from one but this time the junior members of Yorkshire's side gave excellent support to the more seasoned players and if 1911 had been a great summer for Denton this one was even better in terms of his mastery of the crease. Despite all the time lost to the elements, Denton emerged as the leading run-scorer in the country with 2,127 – 85 more than even the great Jack Hobbs could manage. Denton stroked a career-best score of 221 against Kent at Tunbridge Wells and his runs aggregate and average were far ahead of anyone else in the side, although Benny Wilson also played a major part by topping 1,000 runs with some solid displays.

Justified or not, Denton had been tagged "Lucky Denton" earlier in his career, when good fortune was often said to have smiled down on him, but he had now reached the stage where nobody thought luck came into it at all, just almost unrivalled batsmanship.

Wilson, from Scarborough, first joined the Yorkshire side in 1906 and gave solid if mainly unspectacular service right up to the outbreak of hostilities, exceeding 1,000 runs (often by a good distance) in five seasons and striking his career-best score of 208 off Sussex at Bradford in 1914, adding 271 for the fourth wicket with Rhodes.

Hawke was sufficiently pleased with Yorkshire's performances to tell members at the club's annual meeting that they "would have a very excellent team for many years to come" but what he did not know was that war would very shortly push cricket to the back of everyone's mind.

The new Champions were indeed a better side in 1913, winning one game more than when taking the title, but they were forced to give way to Kent, who were beaten three times to Yorkshire's four and deserved top place, even though things may have been different if Haigh and Hirst had not been forced to miss several matches for various reasons, Haigh damaging his foot when struck by a motor car.

Three matches were played against Lancashire that season, the "extra" one being a non-Championship encounter at Aigburth which was arranged to celebrate the visit of the King to Liverpool. It turned into a memorable occasion in more ways than one because Harry Dean, a left-arm pace bowler from Burnley, grabbed nine Yorkshire wickets in the first innings and eight in the second to give him match figures of 17-91, the best on record in Roses cricket. Yorkshire fans will say that it doesn't really count because it wasn't in the Championship and, therefore, cannot be taken too seriously! Lancashire supporters will offer a different interpretation and at the same time point out that in the opening Championship fixture of the season Yorkshire were bowled out on a rain-soaked Old Trafford pitch for 74 and 53, their destroyer this time being slow left-armer, Jim Heap, who claimed match figures of 11-39.

At least Yorkshire pride was fully restored at Headingley in the August Bank Holiday week when the White Rose won a nerve-tingling thriller with six minutes to spare after Lancashire had succumbed in their second innings to terrific bowling from Booth, who took 7-77 on a good batting track, followed by inspired batting from Haigh and Wilson, who put on 108 together in 50 minutes to take Yorkshire to within sight of their target.

A strange feature of 1913 was the re-appearance for Yorkshire during August of the gifted amateur all-rounder and former Cambridge University captain, E. Rockley Wilson, who went on to play one Test match for England in Sydney in 1921 at the age of 41.

On his first-class debut for A.J. Webbe's XI against Cambridge University at

Fenner's in 1899, Rockley Wilson caused a sensation by coming into the side at the very last minute and scoring 117 not out and 70. For the University he hit a century in the Varsity match of 1901 and twice in these contests he took five wickets with his slow but extremely accurate right-arm spin. On his Yorkshire debut in 1899 he scored 55 while adding 110 for the third wicket with Denton against Somerset at Anlaby Road, Hull, but he played in only nine games up to 1902 before "disappearing" until 1913. He had become a schoolmaster at Winchester, where he was also in charge of cricket, and he lived there until his death in 1957, aged 78.

Wilson and Yorkshire simply lost touch with each other and when his availability became known it seems the club were reluctant to drop someone to accommodate him until they heard rumours he was contemplating signing for Hampshire. He returned to play for his native county – he was born at Bolsterstone, near Sheffield – and after the Great War he helped to fill part of the huge void left by the deaths of Booth and Drake, one year finishing top of the national bowling averages. Few careers have been as remarkable as that of Rockley Wilson, who also owned one of the biggest known cricket libraries in existence.

Winchester was not associated merely with Wilson around this time. At the end of the 1913 season, some of the brightness went out of Yorkshire cricket with Haigh's announcement that he was retiring from the first-class game to take up a coaching appointment at Winchester College. However strong a side may be, the loss of a player who has scored nearly 11,000 runs and captured 1,876 wickets is bound to be keenly felt, particularly when he is of such a sunny nature as this son of Huddersfield.

Drake's drum beat ever louder in 1914 with his unique four wickets in four balls at Chesterfield in the midst of a spell of five wickets for six runs in three overs, but the drumbeat of war also reverberated across the nation.

A bright start by Yorkshire was followed by a bad sequence of results, brought about partly by injuries to Hirst and the reduced effectiveness of Kilner who could not shake off his serious illness of the winter. The bad patch ended as quickly as it started but Yorkshire could do no better than to finish fourth to Surrey who were trailed by Middlesex and Kent.

The assassination of Archduke Franz Ferdinand of Austria on June 28, 1914, was the trigger for the First World War and the conflict began a month later. Yorkshire's Championship match with Middlesex at Sheffield, starting on August 12, was first declared off by the visitors because of the war but they then reversed their decision and a thriller was won by Yorkshire after sparkling centuries from Denton and Patsy Hendren.

Twice Yorkshire were beaten by pending Champions Surrey, the latter occasion in mid-August being at Lord's because the military had requisitioned The Oval. Hobbs hit a masterly double century out of 549-6 declared and Yorkshire went down by an innings but it was generally agreed that nobody had their hearts in the cricket and minds were elsewhere.

As Yorkshire headed for their final match against Sussex at Brighton, Booth and Kilner made it known that they intended to enlist on their return home as they felt it was their duty and the only course of action they could take. They joined the

Leeds Pals along with Dolphin, Booth falling on the battlefield at Serre and Kilner being wounded in his right wrist.

On the penultimate day at Brighton, in a match which meandered to a draw, Booth and Drake bowled their last overs for Yorkshire after Denton had scored Yorkshire's last century for five years and Kilner, Hirst and Rhodes had all recorded half-centuries in a first innings score of 461. There was also a knock of 46 from a batsman coming in at No 8 that was a forerunner of things to come in that all-too-short space between the two World Wars. It was compiled by Percy Holmes, another Huddersfield great, who had begun his career quietly in 1913 but was to go on to form one of the greatest opening partnerships that cricket has ever known.

CHAPTER FOURTEEN

OPENERS OPEN UP

History shows that Yorkshire like to mark significant dates in the calendar by finishing top of the Championship table. Who clinched the title in the first year of the 20th Century? Yorkshire CCC. Who led the way in the first year after each of the two World Wars? Yorkshire CCC. And who took the crown in their own centenary season? Yorkshire CCC.

Of course, not everything goes quite according to plan. In the Queen's Coronation summer of 1953, for instance, they finished a humiliating 12th but they atoned for not winning the Championship in 2000 by doing so in 2001.

In 1919, everything did go according to plan and Hawke, continuing as president, was able to show over the next 20 years or so that he was just as insistent on success – and as capable of bringing it about – as he had ever been.

Yorkshire CCC had not hibernated during the war although it did not organise any matches. The early feeling that the war would be over and everything back to normal within six months soon disappeared and, taking the long view, the club appealed to members to continue paying their subscriptions in order that the wheels of finance could keep on turning.

The response was so generous that £5,560 rolled in, allowing sums to be paid to clubs which staged county matches in order that the grounds could be properly maintained and not fall into a state of neglect. There was also sufficient money in the kitty to pay allowances to Yorkshire players who were taking part in charity matches whenever their war duties would permit.

Yorkshire's offices had moved from Sheffield to Leeds following the death of J.B. Wostinholm in 1902 and they became the headquarters of the West Riding Volunteers for the duration of the conflict, Lord Hawke being appointed Major and County Adjutant and the club's secretary, Frederick Toone, becoming secretary. In May 1918, Lord Hawke was raised to the rank of Colonel and Toone succeeded him as County Adjutant with the rank of Captain, both men receiving gifts at the end of the war in recognition of their outstanding service.

The charity matches which were played raised almost £20,000 and in addition around 500 parcels of cricket equipment were despatched from the county's office to military camps at home and abroad, the many thank you letters which came back being testimony to how much all of this was appreciated.

When county cricket was able to start up again in 1919, some things remained familiar to Yorkshire spectators and other things changed. The first Championship match against Gloucestershire at Gloucester brought Yorkshire victory by an innings and 63 runs with Roy Kilner forging out 112 and Rhodes taking 7-47, so nothing much different there.

Sadly, there was no Booth or Drake or Haigh, of course, but in that first match there was Percy Holmes and there was Herbert Sutcliffe and there was Norman Kilner with Abe Waddington and Emmott Robinson also staking their claim during the summer, so ensuring that those great players of the recent past were being replaced by cricketers of equal standing.

And there was also a new captain in D.C.F. (David Cecil Fowler) Burton, who, like his immediate predecessor, Sir Archibald White, was a Cambridge University man. Born in Bridlington, Burton was from a well-known sporting family, his father possessing a private cricket ground and his younger brother, Robert Claude, having turned out a couple of times for Yorkshire in 1914.

A cricket fanatic and a decent batsman, Burton had made his debut for Yorkshire in 1907 and up to the start of the war he had played in 42 matches so he was by no means new to the county scene. He went on to lead Yorkshire more than capably for three seasons and although success was immediate it came at some personal cost to Burton in the thriller with the Australian Imperial Forces team at Sheffield when the visitors scraped home by one wicket. He was struck under the eye by a ferocious delivery from Jack Gregory which knocked him clean out and it was several matches before he was able to resume playing, Yorkshire being led in his absence by the ever-faithful Hirst.

A feature of 1919 which, thankfully, was never repeated, was the introduction of two-day Championship matches, starting at 11.30am and finishing at 7.30pm, and this format was particularly exhausting for Yorkshire who played 26 games – considerably more than most of their opponents. Placings were decided on percentages of wins to matches played and Yorkshire topped the table with 46.15% followed by Kent and Nottinghamshire, who each played only 14 matches and had 42.85% and 35.71% respectively.

Burton felt that two-day cricket helped to bring about some exciting finishes and was popular with the spectators but he admitted that three matches in a week was a draining experience for his players.

In that first Championship match of 1919 Yorkshire had one legendary pair in Hirst and Rhodes and, although it was not apparent then, the side also included another pair who would become household names in Holmes and Sutcliffe, the greatest opening combination in Yorkshire's history.

The partnership was not formed immediately, Holmes initially walking to the middle with Rhodes, but Burton agreed to the pairing after talking it over with Hirst and being influenced by his advice which was invariably sound.

Great deeds do not necessarily come about with the first experiment in cricket – often quite the reverse is true – and there was nothing to get excited over when Holmes and Sutcliffe walked out for the first time against Kent at Headingley on June 30. Holmes quickly walked back again for a duck before a run had been scored, Sutcliffe managed 20 and Yorkshire were skittled for 64, Bill Fairservice and Frank Woolley bowling unchanged to finish with 6-35 and 4-28. It was a rain-affected match and, following on, the pair had managed eight together when the game ended in a draw.

Soon they were in harmony, their first three figure stand being a splendid 279 at Northampton and there were four further century partnerships from them before the season was out.

Holmes and Sutcliffe were significant factors in the building-up of Yorkshire's reputation and each, therefore, merits special attention. You simply cannot have one without the other. Like fish and chips or steak and kidney pie.

PERCY HOLMES

Not content with merely spawning George Hirst and Wilfred Rhodes, perhaps the greatest pair of cricketers in Yorkshire's history, Huddersfield then produced, among its other illustrious sons, Percy Holmes.

Like Hirst and Rhodes, Holmes and Sutcliffe roll off the tongue as if they are one identity rather than two and although Sutcliffe may have been the greater batsman and enjoyed a far more star-studded England career it is always Holmes' name that comes first when the magic words Holmes and Sutcliffe are uttered.

Throughout the 1920s and until Holmes' retirement in 1933, the Yorkshire crowds marvelled at their achievements and if they held Sutcliffe in the deeper respect their affections were probably stronger towards his partner.

Just as Hirst was more Yorkshire than England in his finest achievements, so was Holmes who was never fully recognised by his country, mainly because Sutcliffe and Jack Hobbs had stamped their mark so indelibly on the opening spots. Just as Hobbs' opening partner at Surrey, Andy Sandham, missed out on many an England appearance because of Sutcliffe and Hobbs, so did Holmes.

Whereas Sutcliffe was refined in appearance with a touch of haughtiness at the crease, Holmes seemed a more relaxed figure, a man of the people who simply went out to do what he was paid to do – and that was to make runs in vast quantities. He did this with lightness of foot and in a jaunty manner.

One thing which Holmes was not was a boy wonder. He was 25 when he first played for Yorkshire Seconds and 27 when he made his first team debut in 1913 and it was not until after the First World War that he looked anything special.

Born in Oakes, he captained both the cricket and football teams at school but left at 13 to work in a worsted mill. He went on to join Huddersfield League clubs Paddock and Golcar before moving to Spen Victoria, then members of the Yorkshire Council, where his progress during the war showed a marked acceleration.

Holmes was in his 30s when he and Sutcliffe eventually teamed up as Yorkshire's openers in 1919 but still young enough to go on and share in 69 century opening partnerships – a number that could well have reached three figures but for the war years.

Once they came together, Holmes was the quicker scorer for quite a few years and when he was well set it was almost impossible to get him out. He hit 60 centuries for Yorkshire and these included seven double centuries and two triples, his career-best 315 not out against Middlesex in 1925 being the highest score ever made at Lord's up to that stage – and two runs more than Sutcliffe's best.

Holmes scored 1,000 or more first-class runs in a Yorkshire season on 14 occasions, reaching his pinnacle with 2,351 in 1925. He topped 2,000 runs three times and came close to doing so in several other seasons. In 1920 he totted up 2,029 runs in the Championship alone.

He scored 26,220 runs during his Yorkshire career, which gives him sixth place in the county's list of heaviest scorers, and although he was some way short of

Sutcliffe's 35,558 he had 165 fewer innings. The margin would have been considerably reduced had he made his mark earlier.

June 16 and 17, 1932, were the days on which Holmes and Sutcliffe amassed their record 555 against Essex at Leyton. It was not the easiest of starts for Holmes, who was suffering from lumbago, and he was dropped behind very early on. He managed to overcome the pain of his condition, although his movements were restricted and he was outscored by Sutcliffe on this historic occasion. Sutcliffe, on 313, virtually gave away his wicket the ball after 555 was reached, leaving Holmes unbeaten on 224.

It is quite incredible that, whatever the circumstances, a batsman of Holmes' pedigree should play in only seven Test matches, making four half-centuries with a top score of 88. But the reverse side of the coin is that Yorkshire fans were able to watch him more often than would otherwise have been the case, and they weren't complaining about that.

HERBERT SUTCLIFFE

It was not without good cause that Herbert Sutcliffe became known as the Prince of Yorkshire Cricket. He was princely, lordly, majestic all rolled into one. A mighty fine achievement for a commoner.

Whether he was batting for England or for Yorkshire, Sutcliffe gave the impression of being superior to all around him. With Hobbs for England and with Holmes for Yorkshire, Sutcliffe ruled the world of cricket. And he ruled it because he was, paradoxically, sufficiently down-to-earth to relish a good scrap and to be strong enough, mentally and physically, to come out of it on top.

If Huddersfield can claim to fashion world-class all-rounders – as well as Percy Holmes – then Pudsey is just as famous for its shaping of world-class batsmen and even though Sutcliffe was born at Summerbridge, near Pateley Bridge, he was but a baby when his family moved to Pudsey.

By the time he was six, Sutcliffe had lost both of his parents and was brought up by three aunts but his prowess at cricket was soon noted by a well-known local sportsman, Richard Ingham, and he went on to play first for the Pudsey St Lawrence club as a 14-year-old and then Britannia on his way towards the Yorkshire nets and even greater things.

For England and for Yorkshire, Sutcliffe was par excellence. In 54 Tests between 1924-1935 he made 4,555 runs at an average of 60.73 and hit 16 centuries with a top score of 194 against Australia at Sydney in 1932. With Hobbs, he figured in 26 century stands, the first being 136 against South Africa at Edgbaston in 1924. The next Test was at Lord's and the pair this time contributed 268 together before continuing their phenomenal alliance in Australia during the winter.

In Yorkshire's colours, Sutcliffe's 38,558 runs at 50.20 leave him well clear of the field with no danger of ever being caught, Denton trailing in his wake by over 5,000 runs.

In all first-class cricket, Sutcliffe glided his way regally to 149 centuries, a record 112 of them for Yorkshire. Only Geoff Boycott (103) has also completed a *century of centuries for the county. In addition to his triple century, Sutcliffe hit 15 double centuries and completely dominated bowling attacks in the entire period between the two world wars, exceeding 1,000 runs in each of the 21 seasons. His first season of 1919 saw him score 1,839 runs, a record for a Yorkshire batsman, and with the bit firmly between his teeth he never once allowed his pace to slacken.*

It is impossible to believe that Yorkshire will ever again see the likes of a combination such as Holmes and Sutcliffe and for many years these 'twins' believed they shared the same birthday of November 25 – Holmes in 1886 and Sutcliffe in 1889. Only when Sutcliffe was checking through family papers did he discover that he was actually born on November 24. They had long since established a tradition of getting together for a quiet celebratory drink on their birthdays and this continued into old age when they used to meet up at the Greyhound public house at Tong, the halfway stage between their homes in Huddersfield and Ilkley, to chink glasses and gaze misty-eyed into their great and glorious past.

The discovery by Yorkshire in 1919 of the two most awesome opening batsmen in county cricket history may not have been enough on its own to win back the Championship title but they were also blessed in other areas. True, some giants had departed, but Hirst, in his 48th year, and Rhodes, in his 42nd, remained much better cricketers than most men half their age.

With the war itself leaving such a hole in Yorkshire's side, it was a bold decision not to re-engage Benny Wilson who it was felt had, before the conflict, generally scored his runs too slowly, despite totalling 1,578 in the Championship in 1914 with a top score of 208 and three other centuries.

But as briefly mentioned earlier in the chapter, powerful replacements were on hand and in Emmott Robinson and Abe Waddington, Yorkshire could not have wished for better.

Of all the great and the good that have worn the Yorkshire colours, none played harder or with more determination or with more pride than Keighley-born Robinson who was another late developer, being 35 when he was given his debut against Warwickshire at Edgbaston.

A medium to quick bowler, who thought carefully about how each delivery would be cunningly employed, and a tenacious batsman who came good when it really mattered, Robinson was also a brilliant fielder. He became a legendary figure, partly because he was so admired by one of the greatest cricket writers of them all, Neville Cardus, of the Manchester Evening News, who famously once wrote of Robinson: "I imagine that the Lord one day gathered together a heap of Yorkshire clay and breathed into it and said: 'Emmott Robinson, go on and bowl at the pavilion end for Yorkshire'." He continued: "Often have I looked at his fine, keen face and loved the lines in it, graven by experience. He enriched the nature of cricket, put into it the humours of the soil, invested it with character."

And how Robinson loved Roses battles when no quarter was asked or given and when to concede a boundary with a loose delivery was seen as a heinous crime. No wonder that he reserved his career-best bowling figures for one such contest, taking 9-36 at Bradford in 1920.

Work your way over the tops from Robinson's birthplace of Keighley and you come to Clayton, a hilly suburb of Bradford from which Waddington hailed. His presence in the Yorkshire side was just as significant as Robinson's – and even more so in their debut season of 1919 because his 94 Championship wickets – 100 first-class – added great momentum to Yorkshire's successful Championship challenge. His impact was all the more remarkable in that he did not come into the first team until the beginning of July.

Lean of limb and blessed with a perfect action, Waddington was genuinely quick in his early days and he played for England in two Tests in Australia in 1920-21 but a subsequent loss of form and a shoulder injury took their toll and he retired at the end of 1927.

A relatively short career, perhaps, but far longer and more effective than that of Ambrose Causer Williams, who performed a near super human achievement with the ball in 1919 before stepping back into the shadows almost as quickly as he had emerged from them.

Williams had been around for a few years without suggesting he was a front-rank Yorkshire bowler but he was given another chance after doing well in a Second XI match. In the game against Hampshire at Dewsbury, Yorkshire had declared on 401-8 as a consequence of centuries from Rhodes and Burton, the captain's unbeaten 142 being one of the batting highlights of the season. On a faultless pitch, Williams then despatched the visitors for 82 by bowling with demonic fervour to claim 9-29, all but one of his victims being clean bowled. Williams also enjoyed a five-wicket return against Lancashire that season but went wicketless against Middlesex and that was his first-class career over.

So many ingredients served to make 1919 the success it turned out to be for Yorkshire but the emergence of Holmes and Sutcliffe was particularly significant and if any doubts existed at all about how gifted a combination they were then they melted away for ever in the Roses match at Sheffield when they put on 253 together, Holmes making 123 and Sutcliffe 132. It was a record first wicket stand in Roses games and the first time that each Yorkshire opener had scored a century. Many other records would be set before they were through.

CHAPTER FIFTEEN

INTO THE ROARING TWENTIES

Burton remained in charge of Yorkshire as they entered the 1920s – which also heralded the welcome return of three-day matches – but he was unable to maintain their grip on the Championship title, Middlesex stealing it from them in 1920 and holding on to it the following year, Yorkshire finishing third and fourth respectively.

There were no complaints about Middlesex topping the table in 1920 because they were beaten only twice in 20 matches but it was a close shave at Bradford where they won by four runs, Yorkshire being handicapped in the second innings by the absence of the injured Roy Kilner.

Struggling to reach a 193 target, last man Waddington joined Rockley Wilson at 148 and they bravely took Yorkshire to within five of victory when Waddington drove fiercely at a ball from Greville Stevens which had four stamped all over it until it crashed into the stumps at the bowler's end. In the same over Waddington was bowled for his highest score at that point of 25 and Yorkshire lost by four runs, despite nine wickets in the match for Wilson.

History, of a sort, was to repeat itself at Bristol in 1999 when Yorkshire lost to Gloucestershire by six runs in the semi-final of the NatWest Trophy, skipper David Byas finishing unbeaten on 71. Twice in his innings he also slammed the ball into the opposite stumps and had he missed them the result could have gone on to be very different.

Yorkshire in 1920 had started out confident of remaining Champions, their ego lifted by Emmott Robinson's career-best 9-36 in the Roses clash at Bradford, and they certainly looked the part in the opening weeks, staying unbeaten until the second half of June when they went down to Surrey at Sheffield.

Rhodes, still plugging away remorselessly, completed the hat-trick during a match return of 11-44 against Derbyshire at Derby, and Waddington also bagged three-in-three in the following match at Northampton. Burton had the hat-trick balls mounted and he presented them to the pair instead of handing over hats, as was the custom.

Rhodes and Waddington, overall, had too much work to do that season as can be seen by comparing their statistics with those of the other bowlers – 296 wickets shared by the duo while all of the rest combined could manage only 181.

Hirst by now was past his peak and his pace had slackened but more wickets could have been expected of him had he not been missing until late season because of the coaching duties he had taken up at Eton.

Yet there were encouraging signs on a new front with the introduction to Yorkshire first team cricket of George Macaulay, from Thirsk, who changed from medium fast to off-breaks to become another of Yorkshire's greatest bowlers of all time.

Macaulay, an uncle of Joe Lister, who was to take on the role of Yorkshire secretary in 1972, is placed fourth in the list of the club's leading wicket-takers with 1,774 dismissals at 17.22 runs per wicket, and he also captured 24 wickets for England in eight Test appearances.

He was unable to rock the boat in his first season, however, and he was dropped after taking 1-102 against Surrey when Wisden reported that he had neither the pace nor the stamina required for the first-class game.

Yorkshire's attack was boosted in August by a clutch of wickets for Rockley Wilson, whose Indian summer earned him a place on the MCC tour of Australia in the winter along with Rhodes, Dolphin and Waddington, but the season's highlight was supplied by Holmes in an act of revenge against Hampshire at Portsmouth towards the end of August.

At Headingley in May, Hampshire had won the toss in perfect conditions and opener George Brown made an unbeaten 232, putting on 183 for the first wicket with Alex Bowell (95) and taking the score to 456-2 declared by adding an unbroken 269 for the third wicket with Phil Mead (122*). Atrocious weather over the weekend changed the nature of the pitch and Yorkshire were bowled out for 159 and 225 to lose by an innings and 72 runs.

In the return match it was Yorkshire's turn to bat first on a splendid pitch and Holmes made Hampshire pay for their earlier romp by compiling an unbeaten 302, the highest score of the season. He and Sutcliffe put on 347 for the first wicket and Yorkshire at one stage were 456-2 – exactly the same score as the visitors had been at Headingley. They declared at 585 3 and now it was Hampshire's turn to collapse, but on a much truer wicket, and they were sent back for 131 and 219 to crash by an innings and 235 runs, Rhodes coming out of the match with 11 wickets.

Indeed, Holmes was undoubtedly Yorkshire's player of the season, scoring 2,144 runs at an average of 54.97 and hitting six other centuries as well as his triple century. He also set another Roses record at Old Trafford by becoming the first batsman in these contests to score a century in each innings. The only other batsman so far to have done that for Yorkshire in Roses games is Ted Lester on the same ground in 1948.

Yorkshire were gracious enough to admit that Middlesex were worthy champions but they felt less charitable when their rivals retained the title in 1921 because they firmly believed that rain had robbed them of three victories. A thunderstorm brought about an abrupt halt at The Oval when only two wickets needed to be taken for an innings win and similar circumstances prevailed against Lancashire and Leicestershire.

There was further ill-fortune for Yorkshire during the season and not all of it the fault of the English climate. Immediately upon retiring to their dressing room at Lord's after a beating by the champions to the tune of an innings and 72 runs, a chair collapsed under Dolphin as he reached for his locker and he suffered a broken wrist which kept him out for the remainder of the summer. The wicketkeeper's absence would have been felt all the more had Reg Allen not deputised so capably and in the best Yorkshire traditions. Allen had a huge pair of hands which he used to good effect behind the stumps and his first-class career would have stretched beyond 30 matches had he not been unfortunate enough to be on the scene at the same time as Dolphin and then Arthur Wood.

Another casualty in 1921 was Hobbs who elegantly carried his bat for 172 out of 294 in Surrey's win at Headingley in late June but this turned out to be his only Championship match of the season. He had been recovering from an accident up to this fixture and, immediately following it, he stayed on in Leeds to play in the Test match against Australia but went down with a serious illness and never got to the middle.

The loss of Hobbs to cricket must have been deeply felt, just as it was, in a different way, for Yorkshire fans when the inimitable Hirst brought his first-class career officially to a close after Yorkshire's match with MCC at Scarborough. The great man made a solitary appearance in 1929 but his true swansong was in 1921.

Once again Rockley Wilson contributed significantly to Yorkshire's great form in the latter part of the season. He claimed 51 wickets at 11.91 runs apiece to head the bowling averages while Rhodes, Waddington and Macaulay each topped the 100 mark. Rhodes was in sparkling all-round form, scoring 1,329 runs and taking 128 wickets. Five other batsmen also aggregated over 1,000 runs and Yorkshire's form in general was sure to have been well received at Lord's where F.S. Jackson, now a Leeds MP, had become President of MCC.

Burton can rightly be credited with having done a superb job as Yorkshire captain over his three years in charge, but his record cannot quite stand comparison with his successor, Geoffrey Wilson, who led the side to Championship honours in three successive seasons before standing down.

Like his immediate predecessors, Sir Archibald White and Burton, Wilson lifted the title in his first season in charge in 1922, and this sequence of instant success by amateur captains was not over yet.

Which prompts the question, will a side of extremely talented players invariably come out on top or do they need a great captain to cajole them into giving of their best? Perhaps the captain and his team need each other in order to excel. The truth is that the likes of Hawke, Sellers and Close were all acknowledged as inspirational leaders, yet each had exceptional players under his command.

Wilson certainly had the right credentials for the job at that time. Educated at Harrow, where he was captain, and at Cambridge University, where he gained a Blue, he first played for Yorkshire in 1919 when he made his top score of 70 against Leicestershire at Fartown. A brilliant fielder but modest batsman he was still good enough to score 142 not out for MCC v Victoria at Melbourne in 1923 and in his days at Harrow he made 173 against Eton at Lord's.

Just as others have maintained before and since, Wilson claimed that the spirit of the game meant more to him than the actual result, although winning was undoubtedly his second priority. It would seem, however, that in 1924 Yorkshire lost some of their reputation for great sportsmanship but more about that later.

The side he led out in 1922 had the look of Champions from the start and a team photograph taken in the early Spring shows what a confident and relaxed bunch of fellows they were. And they had every reason to be so for each one of them had a name which meant something in the world of cricket – Edgar Oldroyd, Norman Kilner, Roy Kilner, Herbert Sutcliffe, George Macaulay, Abe Waddington, Maurice (spelled Morris on his birth certificate) Leyland, Emmott Robinson, Wilfred Rhodes, Arthur Dolphin and Percy Holmes. These were the men that Wilson led into battle and although they lost the odd skirmish or two they came out triumphant in the end.

It was a season in which bowlers generally held sway and Macaulay, Roy Kilner and Waddington each contributed over 100 wickets, with none of them conceding more than 15.40 runs per victim, while Rhodes headed the averages by virtue of taking 84 wickets at 12.71. So well did the combined attack deploy themselves that the only Championship century taken off them came from Ernest Tyldesley, who hit a glorious 178 at Sheffield, but Lancashire were still beaten in the end.

Waddington was the leading wicket-taker with 127 and he also enjoyed the most extraordinary performance by picking up seven wickets for six runs in seven overs when a bewildered Sussex were torn apart for just 20, his first four victims coming before a run had been scored off him. Sussex later tried valiantly to make amends at Hove by dismissing Yorkshire for 42, their lowest score of the season, but the visitors hit back strongly to come away with the spoils.

It may well have been a summer that suited bowlers but that did not stop Oldroyd, Sutcliffe, Rhodes, Holmes and Kilner making it beyond the 1,000 runs mark, Oldroyd's 1,534 runs at 45.11 taking him to the top of the batting averages in the best season of his career.

Nor was the combined power of these mighty men sufficient to hold back one of Yorkshire's longest-serving stalwarts from making his debut. The taciturn, unsmiling, unfrivolous Arthur Mitchell, known to everyone as Ticker, was introduced to the public at large in Yorkshire's first-ever game against Glamorgan at Headingley and he would remain at the forefront of the club's affairs for practically half a century.

ARTHUR MITCHELL

Arthur Mitchell, as I have already briefly stated, was born in my home town of Baildon and it is appropriate that his birth in 1902 coincided with Yorkshire winning the Championship for a third successive time. He was very probably conscious of this fact from the moment he drew breath and his main mission in life continued to be to make sure, either by playing or coaching, that they remained the best team in the world — including Test teams! He was a man of few words on or off the field and often gave the impression of being a curmudgeonly old soul but these traits only served to endear him to the cricket-following public in Yorkshire. Cricket, after all, is a serious business, and nobody has ever been more serious about it than Ticker. A generation of Yorkshire cricketers who learned their trade under his supervision and guidance will vouch for that.

Yorkshire won by an innings and 103 runs on Mitchell's debut against Glamorgan and that was the sort of margin he would consider to be Yorkshire's right. His own contribution out of 429-7 was a mere 29 but Oldroyd, the man he would succeed at No 3, made 143. In Glamorgan's second innings, Mitchell caught Johnnie Clay off Waddington and this was the first of 406 catches he would take for Yorkshire. His resolve was such that from a below average fielder in his league days he turned himself into one of the greatest close-to-the-wicket fielders the game has ever known.

There continued to be nothing flowery about Mitchell – he didn't like reading Cardus because that's what he considered him to be – and the story of his Test debut against South Africa at Headingley in 1935 proves the point. His Yorkshire team-mate, Leyland, had to pull out of the England side at the very last minute through illness and a messenger was despatched to Mitchell's home to tell him that he was replacing Leyland and should report to the ground immediately. The urgent message was given to Mitchell in his garden where he was working on the soil. "Tell them I'll be along presently, once I've gotten missen tidied up a bit," he said.

With his domestic chores done, Mitchell duly arrived at Headingley and went on to score 58 at No 5 in his first innings before opening in the second and contributing 72 to a first wicket stand of 128 in 110 minutes with Derbyshire's Denis Smith. In addition, he fielded magnificently throughout the drawn match.

In 479 innings for Yorkshire, Mitchell hit over 18,000 runs, including 39 centuries, and in his 18 seasons with the club he was a guiding influence in them winning the Championship 11 times during one of their greatest periods. He retired in 1939 and after the Second World War he returned as Yorkshire's first full-time Coach, a position he held until his retirement in 1970.

Mitchell and Leyland together put scores of young cricketers through their paces when they were invited to the Headingley nets and more than one of them breathed a sigh of relief when they discovered it was Leyland who would be instructing them rather than his dour and rather uncompromising friend. Nevertheless, Mitchell's overall contribution to Yorkshire cricket was immense and his personality perfectly reflected what a serious and honourable business it is to represent the White Rose.

By 1923, Wilson's team had become one of the strongest ever put out in county cricket and they demonstrated this not by words but by deeds, winning 25 of their 32 Championship matches and losing only one – and that by just three runs against runners-up Nottinghamshire at Headingley. So dominant were Yorkshire that 13 of their victories were by an innings and ten of their 16 competitors were beaten at home and away.

Yorkshire were almost invincible and their power was such that they could afford to let two men go at the end of the season who had helped turn the tables on Essex at Chelmsford when defeat beckoned. With Holmes and Sutcliffe absent, Norman Kilner and John Bell were called upon as openers and in the second innings they added 117 together, each batsman making a half-century, to see Yorkshire to a seven-wicket win. This had seemed unlikely when they trailed by 99 on the first innings but Rhodes then floored Essex with five wickets for eight runs in 6.5 overs and they were toppled for 64, leaving a target of 164 which Kilner and Bell made look easy. The pair were unhappy that they could not gain regular places, however, and Yorkshire agreed to Kilner being released for Warwickshire and Bell for Glamorgan where they both forged new and successful careers.

Playing against Yorkshire that summer must have been demoralising because there was barely a chink in their armour. Not only did Rhodes and Kilner complete the double but they were joined in the 1,000+ runs class by Sutcliffe, Holmes, Oldroyd and Leyland while Macaulay was the leading wicket-taker with 149 at

13.34. In addition, Emmott Robinson had 95 victims and Waddington, despite being sidelined for the second half of the season with a shoulder injury, managed 57.

Holmes and Sutcliffe both continued on their merry way and were so dynamic together for Yorkshire that many a follower of the game wondered why Holmes was not getting the same recognition at England level as was his county partner.

Yorkshire were at the height of their popularity and fame and how those in charge of the club's affairs now would love to see the same volume of spectators these days that flocked to watch them 90 years ago. The Roses match of 1923 at Bradford Park Avenue, for instance, attracted a crowd of 26,000 on August 6, with thousands unable to get into the ground.

Wilson completed his hat-trick of Championship title wins in 1924 and if his team did not quite live up to their reputation of the previous season they were still a very considerable force with the public interest just as high as ever. After their opening tour, they were welcomed back by 25,000 fans on the first day of their match with Surrey at Headingley but bad weather ruined the game as a contest.

There is also evidence to suggest that Yorkshire lost some of their team harmony and certainly the spirit in which they played their cricket was brought into question. Wilson may not have managed to impose the same order that Hawke would have brought to the side and the rumpus which erupted during games with Middlesex and Surrey could have had something to do with the captain standing down at the end of the season.

Before these matches, Yorkshire were dealt a mighty blow to their ego in the Whitsuntide Roses fixture at Headingley. The game had failed to ignite in either of the first innings when slow scoring and poor weather put a damper on things but four wickets each for Macaulay and Kilner then sent back Lancashire for 74, leaving Yorkshire to make a token 57 for victory.

As often happens, the most thrilling and unexpected triumphs or disasters are witnessed by only a handful of people because few bother turning up when a certain conclusion appears inevitable and such was the case on the final day of this encounter.

Yet the small band of spectators were suddenly bolt upright in their seats as Parkin and Dick Tyldesley exploited a difficult batting surface to maximum effect to destroy Yorkshire for 33, Tyldesley collecting 6-18 and Parkin 3-15 in an unbroken spell of sustained hostility. It remains Yorkshire's lowest total in the history of Roses cricket.

Whether this humiliating setback had a bruising effect on team spirit is open to conjecture but another heavy defeat, this time by an innings and 152 against Middlesex at Lord's, when even Rhodes was smote for four sixes, led to acrimony in the return match at Sheffield.

Although Middlesex were put in to bat there was never any chance of anything but a draw on a docile pitch and as the visitors dragged out their innings to 358 the crowd began barracking, spurred on, it seems, by Waddington's attitude towards some of the umpiring decisions.

The umpires, Harry Butt and Bill Reeves, protested in a letter to Lord's about Waddington's behaviour and the Yorkshire Committee asked the MCC's Cricket

Committee to investigate the matter – but not before Middlesex had stated they would not play Yorkshire the following season.

The MCC's report backed the umpires and suggested that Waddington be told to keep his feelings under control. Sufficient pressure was applied on Waddington for him to write to the MCC apologising for his behaviour and this action resulted in Middlesex reversing their decision not to play Yorkshire. But relations between the two clubs remained strained for some while.

A month or so later there was another shemozzle over Yorkshire's match against Surrey at The Oval when a London newspaper, in a strong article, said that incidents during the game reflected long-standing differences between the sides. The furore soon died down and no official complaints were made but Yorkshire's reputation was again tarnished.

So did Wilson always manage to maintain discipline within his team or did the professionals sometimes do what they wished rather than what their captain wanted? There was an earlier incident in 1922 which suggested that the workers could sometimes disobey their master.

In the game with Essex at Harrogate, it had been agreed to change the hours on the final day so that Yorkshire could catch the evening train to London on their way to Maidstone for their game against Kent. At the time so arranged, Essex had nine down and required 60 to avoid an innings defeat and Yorkshire's professionals felt keenly that an extra half hour ought to have been claimed. By way of protest, they made no effort to catch their train and they were forced to travel through the night to Maidstone, arriving just before breakfast time.

Wilson's hat-trick of Championship title successes was a fine achievement and one can only speculate over whether he would have continued in the hot seat in 1925 had certain attitudes not always been to his liking.

CHAPTER SIXTEEN

HONOUR RESTORED

Wilson's resignation opened the way for Major Arthur William Lupton to take over as captain in 1925 at the age of 46 – 17 years after he had first turned out for Yorkshire against Leicestershire at Aylestone Road.

The Major was well past his prime – and, indeed, he was no more than a useful fast bowler in his younger days – but he was a disciplinarian who cared for those under his command and they responded by giving of their best.

Their best was so superior to all other counties that Yorkshire galloped to their fourth consecutive Championship win and Lupton became the fourth consecutive leader to see the side to the title in their first season in charge.

Yorkshire conquered their opponents in 21 of their 32 matches and no side was able to lower their colours all season. This outstanding record delighted Hawke but he was even more pleased with the way Yorkshire acquitted themselves under Lupton.

After the unsavoury events of the previous year, Hawke had been forced to use his considerable influence to prevent Yorkshire from becoming outcasts in the eyes of the MCC and to keep them on reasonable terms with Middlesex, both of which bodies carried an awful lot of weight.

Yorkshire were so dominant and so well-behaved that their supporters had the confidence to question MCC's judgment in not having included Holmes and Macaulay on Gilligan's tour of Australia during the winter just gone.

Both players responded to this snub by enjoying an extraordinary summer for Yorkshire, Holmes amassing 2,123 Championship runs at an average of 62.44, including his career-best unbeaten 315 at Lord's, and Macaulay heading the bowling list with 176 wickets at 15.21 runs apiece, his tally being exactly 200 in all first-class matches.

Sutcliffe, Leyland, Rhodes and Oldroyd also scored well in excess of 1,000 runs and Roy Kilner, Rhodes, Waddington and Robinson supported Macaulay so efficiently that between them the quintet accounted for 564 of the 570 wickets to fall. No wonder Yorkshire were able to 'carry' Lupton, whose only real contributions were as a leader of men, and how well he fulfilled those duties.

In his epic triple century at Lord's, Holmes featured in several notable partnerships and his opening stand with Sutcliffe had reached 140 when Sutcliffe had to retire hurt on 56 with a damaged thumb. Sutcliffe did not return until the score was 404-4 but he was only able to add a couple of runs before he was out. Before Sutcliffe's re-appearance, Holmes had dominated a second-wicket partnership of 166 with Oldroyd (61) and he later put on an unbroken 100 for the seventh wicket with Robinson, whose contribution was 21. The declaration came at 538-6 and Yorkshire went on to win by an innings and 149 runs.

As Yorkshire continued piling up runs and picking up wickets that season they were a big attraction wherever they played and this ability to pull in the crowds on their travels has never left them. Even in the present day and age, opposition venues relish the opportunity to stage 'the Yorkshire match' because they know it will pull in bigger crowds and greater income than can be expected from any other county.

Their popularity meant big gates were guaranteed at the end of the 1925 season for the Champion County v The Rest of England match at The Oval but on this occasion the master batsman was playing for the opposition, Hobbs stroking his 16th century of the summer. There were also centuries for Sutcliffe and Frank Woolley before the game ended in a draw.

Yorkshire in 1926 held on to their unbeaten tag but they were forced to finish second to Lancashire, who emerged with a slightly higher percentage after winning their last three matches of the season. They were, however, beaten twice and one of their defeats resulted from a comprehensive thrashing by Yorkshire in the Whitsuntide Roses match at Headingley when the Red Rose was crushed by an innings and 94 runs. Just as Yorkshire had ruled the roost for the past three years, now it was Lancashire's turn to be cock-a-hoop with four more titles in the next eight years – although it was 2011 before they would win the Championship outright again.

The season had begun well enough for Yorkshire but they flagged later on without ever looking in any serious danger of losing a match. Lancashire, on the other hand, won six of their August matches while Yorkshire lost momentum by only drawing several of theirs. Holmes and Sutcliffe led the way among the six batsmen to pass 1,000 runs in first-class matches but Macaulay and Rhodes, each with 100 or more wickets, did not quite receive the support from their fellow bowlers that might have turned one or two stalemates into victories.

Yorkshire slipped down a further place in the third and final year of Lupton's command and on May 24, 1927, they suffered their first defeat in a Championship match in almost three years. They were undone at Hull by Warwickshire, who captured the last four second innings wickets just in time to claim the extra half hour and knock off the required 42 runs with minutes to spare. Poor batting was generally to blame for Yorkshire's downfall but there was still an audible sigh of relief within the camp that they no longer had to go into every match with the added pressure of trying to extend their unbeaten run.

Macaulay continued to be the linchpin of Yorkshire's bowling and his all-round strength in the side was never better emphasised than against Worcestershire at Headingley. Bowling unchanged throughout the contest, he and Robinson destroyed their opponents for 46 and 81, Macaulay's match figures being 12-50, and in the Yorkshire innings he scored 67 in an eighth-wicket stand of 163 in 85 minutes with Waddington, who recorded his one and only century. With Macaulay in this sort of form it is no surprise that Worcestershire capitulated inside two days.

Champions Lancashire and Middlesex were the other teams to beat Yorkshire in 1927 and it was in the return fixture with Middlesex at Sheffield that Leyland plundered his side's highest score of the season of 204 not out. A superb second innings batting display on a difficult pitch at Northampton by Sutcliffe, coupled with a doughty knock from Holmes, dramatically turned the tables on Northants towards the end of July but it proved to be the last victory for a month because dreadful weather then had the final say until the last match against Sussex at Hove, when Kilner scored an unbeaten 91 and claimed eight wickets in a nine-wicket win.

Yorkshire's batting that season appeared as strong as ever but cracks were beginning to appear in the bowling, despite the best efforts of both Macaulay and Robinson. Rhodes was still chugging along nicely, but coming up 50 he was hardly operating at full steam, while Kilner's spin had lost some of its sharpness and Waddington was not quite the threat of recent years.

And so it proved that important changes came about during the following winter. Waddington, never a man to be trifled with, was offered new terms but declined to accept them and a career which had started with a bang ended with more of a whimper. Dolphin also decided to hang up his gloves after 23 seasons of immaculate service but the news coming out of the club that really grabbed the attention of the sports journalists was that Herbert Sutcliffe might be asked to succeed Lupton as captain.

Hawke's trenchant views on his preference for amateur captains were well known but times were changing and pressure was beginning to build to put a professional in charge.

Neither Hawke as President nor Toone as Secretary aired their own views in public on the matter but the pro-professional lobby was so strong that after a committee meeting in early November a letter was sent to Sutcliffe in South Africa, where he was on tour with the MCC team.

It was penned by Toone and said: "At the committee meeting yesterday you were appointed Captain for 1928 without your status being altered.

"It is hoped that this will be agreeable to you and that you will accept the same and be happy and successful in your new and honoured position."

But all was not 'agreeable' to Sutcliffe and his reply, in a cable to Hawke, was negative. It read: "Official invitation received yesterday. Many thanks you and committee great honour. Question carefully considered. Regret to decline. Willing to play under any captain elected."

Sutcliffe's despatch prompted the calling of a special committee meeting at which the captaincy was offered to Captain William Worsley, later to become Sir William Worsley Bart., the father of Yorkshire's Patroness, Katharine, H.R.H. The Duchess of Kent.

The decision to turn down the captaincy was not taken lightly by Sutcliffe, who would have faced controversy on a couple of fronts if he had accepted it and might, as a consequence have suffered a loss of his batting form. First, as Yorkshire's first professional captain since Peate, his every move would have come under the microscope, and second, he would have had to appease those county members who felt the job should go to the senior professional – and that was Rhodes.

There can be little question that from a playing point of view Sutcliffe did the right thing because 1928 turned out to be the first of five years in which he was at his very peak as a batsman. He began his period of supreme mastery by hitting 13 centuries in a total of 3,002 first-class runs – 2,418 of them for Yorkshire at 83.38 – and in two other seasons during this time he exceeded the 3,000-run mark, his golden form taking him to the top of the England batting averages in three consecutive seasons from 1930-32.

With Worsley rather than Sutcliffe in charge, Hawke probably got the captain he privately preferred because Yorkshire continued to be guided by an amateur with plenty of status attached. And, to be fair, Yorkshire players also enjoyed the advantages which were to be had through having the popular and loyal Worsley as their leader, not the least of which were visits to Hovingham Hall, the home of the Worsleys since the early 18th century.

Educated at Landgrave School and Eton, Worsley was a hard-hitting batsman of no exceptional ability, but his commitment to Yorkshire cricket and the game in general could not be questioned. After his two seasons as captain, he joined the committee in 1931 and 30 years later he was elected President, a position he held with great pride until his death in 1973.

It can be seen that there had been no shortage of stories coming out of Yorkshire CCC during the winter of 1927-28 and before the new season could begin there was the biggest shock story of them all with the death, on April 5, of Roy Kilner, the beloved son of Wombwell, in Barnsley Fever Hospital. His premature death left countless runs still unscored and wickets untaken.

Without Kilner, Yorkshire's bowling was further weakened in 1928 and Worsley saw them slip to fourth in the table, their lowest position since being similarly placed in 1920. The veteran Rhodes headed the club's bowling averages and he was mainly aided by Robinson and Macaulay who struggled with a foot injury in May when he gathered in only 14 of his 120 wickets. Thomas 'Sandy' Jacques, a well-liked fast bowler, was given some opportunities but he could not fill the void entirely and neither could Leyland or Frank Dennis, who would become the brother-in-law of Len Hutton and uncle of Yorkshire left-armer, Simon Dennis.

There was no doubting Leyland with the bat, however, and he came second to Sutcliffe in the Championship averages, although his 1,451 runs were still some way short of the 1,882 made by Holmes, who played in nine more matches than the graceful left-hander. So swift was Leyland's advance that he was selected for the Gentlemen v Players match and for the Rest in the Test Trial before winning his England cap at The Oval and going on to tour Australia.

Another good sign that the batting was in safe hands was the progress made by Mitchell, who broke free of what had often been 12th man duties to register 1,190 Championship runs and 1,308 first-class. And safe hands, or safe gloves, were stationed behind the stumps in the form of Arthur Wood, who so capably took over the wicketkeeping duties from Dolphin and held on to them until after the Second World War, his 855 victims being testimony to his high standards.

If Sutcliffe set the standards in the art of batting, Holmes was not far behind him and in the latter's benefit match against Middlesex at Headingley, the pair saved Yorkshire after the follow-on by adding an unbroken 290 of which the dashing Holmes made 179 by way of celebration. The following month, Holmes achieved Yorkshire's highest score of the season with a brilliant and faultless 275 against Warwickshire at Bradford, an innings which contained 49 fours.

Yorkshire shared second place with Lancashire in 1929 when Nottinghamshire finished top and once again it was the weakness of the bowling which was their Achilles Heel. Rhodes, though, refused to let age be a barrier to success, topping the county's Championship averages with 85 wickets at 17.22 runs apiece. Dennis weighed in with 76 while Macaulay and Robinson had 95 and 72 respectively.

Rarely a season went by around this time without an exciting new prospect appearing on the scene and the one to surface in 1929 was the gentle giant, William Eric Bowes, universally known as Bill Bowes, who was to become among the greatest ever to play for Yorkshire or England and whose love of the game was second to none. He bowled in only 13 innings in his maiden season but his 40 wickets were more than enough to announce that he had arrived.

The batsmen were again up to the task but at the end of the season – and the end of the Twenties – there was yet another captaincy change as Worsley decided to stand down. The Thirties beckoned and with them a fresh period of Yorkshire greatness before the country was at war again.

CHAPTER SEVENTEEN

THE THRIVING THIRTIES

In terms of performance, Wilfred Rhodes had stood unchallenged both as Yorkshire's greatest cricketer and their king of left-arm spin. As the monarch began to make plans in 1930 to vacate his throne, a crown prince arrived on the scene in the guise of Hedley Verity, whose own similar style bowling quickly confirmed the line of succession would continue uninterrupted.

Rhodes may have been gradually bowing out in this, his 53rd summer, but Yorkshire were eager to look forward rather than gaze back and a new captain in Sheffield-born A.T. (Alan) Barber, assisted by exciting new players such as Bowes and Verity, took Yorkshire to the very brink of their latest period of supreme domination.

It was proving to be a time of significant change in the history of the club and 1930 also brought the death, while still in office, of secretary, Sir Frederick Toone, who passed away in Harrogate on June 10, just days short of his 62nd birthday. One of the greatest organisers cricket has ever known, Sir Frederick was succeeded as Yorkshire secretary the following year by his young assistant, John Nash. Just as Verity followed Rhodes, so did Nash follow Toone and he was the reserved behind-the-scenes guiding hand of the county for the next 40 years.

More of Nash shortly, but the long rule in their own particular fields of the likes of Hawke, Rhodes, Hirst, Toone and Nash, with others to follow them, certainly brought stability to the club and helped in no small measure to shape its destiny.

The willingness, albeit sometimes reluctantly, of great Yorkshire diehard professionals to accept the rule of young and relatively wealthy amateur captains was also a significant factor in the club's unstoppable march forward and never was this more clearly demonstrated than in 1930 when the 25-year-old triple Oxford Blue, Alan Barber, was put in charge of Rhodes and Co.

Differences of opinion were bound to occur – and they did – but the professionals held a grudging admiration for Barber who had already earned himself the reputation of being a brilliant all-round sportsman by achieving Blues in cricket, soccer and golf, which he played off a two handicap. In addition he played football for Corinthians and Barnet as well as being skilled at hockey and an Eton Fives player.

Having captained Oxford University at cricket and soccer he was young and adventurous when he first turned out for Yorkshire in 1929 and by the time he was appointed captain, the players under him were in no doubt either as to his prowess as a sportsman or his keenness for Yorkshire to succeed as a team.

In June, 2010, Alan Barber's nephew, Richard Barber, gave a splendid address at the Sir Leonard Hutton 364 Club annual luncheon at Headingley and here was a link in a fascinating chain which went right back to within a year of Yorkshire CCC's foundation.

His uncle led a Yorkshire team which included the veteran Rhodes who at that time was the only current cricketer to have played against W.G. Grace, whose first appearance at Lord's was in 1864, the year after Yorkshire's birth. The county club's origins may sometimes seem to be in the dim and distant past but when one goes back step by step the timescale does not look all that great at all.

From what Richard Barber was able to reveal about his uncle we can see that he was a young man with the strength of character to control from the off a world-class team which contained no fewer than nine who had or would play for England in Sutcliffe, Holmes, Leyland, Mitchell, Macaulay, Robinson, Bowes, Wood, and, of course, the silent manipulator, Rhodes, who, certainly under Major Lupton, would move the field around himself.

In Barber's first match in charge, he decided to bat on after lunch, only to be told by one of the other Yorkshire players: "But skipper, Mr. Rhodes has declared." It was important to Barber that he should be seen not to kowtow to Rhodes or anyone else and he swiftly reversed the decision.

Rhodes was still not fully prepared to accept that his young captain's word was law, however, and matters came to a head immediately following the match against Essex at Dewsbury when, in the dressing room, the revered senior statesman criticised Barber for not having made a bowling change. He was supported by Wood, who said: "Tha wants to listen to Wilfred, skipper, he's got a wise old 'ead on 'is shoulders."

Barber's authority was clearly being challenged and he replied: "Wilfred, I know that you were playing cricket for England before I was even born – but I am the captain."

And his next move was even more dramatic and daring. He instructed Rhodes to pack his bags and leave for home and he despatched a telegram to the office calling up a young substitute for the game which began the following day against Leicestershire at Hull.

The substitute's name? None other than Rhodes' great successor, Hedley Verity, whose only previous first team appearance had been just over a week earlier in a three-day friendly with Sussex at Huddersfield.

Verity fully justified Barber's courageous act by emerging with match figures of 8-60 to hurry Yorkshire to victory by an innings and 163 runs.

Rhodes was recalled for the next game against Hampshire at Bradford but the memory of Barber's bold action had been imprinted on his memory for life. Upon being introduced by his father, Bertie, to the now old and virtually blind Rhodes at Headingley in the 1960s, Richard asked him if he remembered his uncle, Alan Barber? "Aye, 'im that sent me 'ome," was his reply.

Having fully established his authority, Barber injected a spirit of adventure into Yorkshire's play and, in contrast to so many other White Rose captains, he was prepared to take risks in order to achieve wins. This is borne out by the fact that he declared 13 times in 1930, winning seven of these matches and losing none of them.

Barber made such an impact that summer that towards the end of the season he was approached by the selectors to captain the MCC in the West Indies in the coming winter. But the dashing young sportsman had chosen teaching as his career and his appointment at Ludgrove School had already been confirmed. Reluctantly he decided his career must come first and he turned down MCC's invitation, leaving for ever the world of first-class cricket which he so loved.

So, Barber's stay with Yorkshire was a brief one and although they finished in third place in the Championship table they were only five points adrift of title-holders Lancashire and two points behind Gloucestershire. More importantly he had moulded his men into a potentially lethal force and he had hastened the inevitable baptism of Hedley Verity.

HEDLEY VERITY

Greatly admired and held in genuine affection in an all-too-brief life and proudly remembered as a war hero in death, nobody was more courageous in battles against friends and foes alike than Hedley Verity – a true Yorkshireman in every respect.

And how much greater would his cricketing exploits for Yorkshire and England have been if the Second World War had not cut into his career at exactly the time he was at the peak of his bowling skills at the age of 34?

Even the years eaten away by the war would not have spelled the end of Verity's glittering career had he survived the action because he would surely still have had some time ahead of him at the top of his profession.

Captain Verity, of the Green Howards, is buried in the military cemetery at Caserta, near Naples, having died of wounds after bravely leading a night attack on the German position at Catanca, Sicily, in July 1943, and suffering severe injuries which were to prove fatal.

He rests in foreign fields but in life he could not have been closer to the bosom of Yorkshire cricket, born at 4 Welton Grove, Burley, an address which is within a stone's throw of Headingley cricket ground where he immortalised himself by twice taking ten wickets for his beloved county, a double feat achieved by none of his colleagues either before or since.

It was generally assumed at the time that his 10-36 against Warwickshire in 1936 would go down in the annals as his finest figures but the following year he captured 10-10 against Nottinghamshire, the best bowling statistics ever recorded in world cricket.

Having cut his teeth with Rawdon Cricket Club, where Brian Close and Bryan Stott were also to start out, Verity moved on to Horsforth Hall Park where he was observed by George Hirst and invited to summer trials at Headingley. In those days he was a fine young all-rounder who bowled mainly medium-paced swing but it was when he crossed over the Pennines to fulfil professional engagements, first for Accrington in the Lancashire League and then Middleton in the Central Lancashire League, that he changed to the style for which he became famous.

It was at Middleton that he was allowed to follow Hirst's advice to bowl more in the manner of Rhodes and from that point on he was on the path to glory, although, like his illustrious predecessor, he was first rejected by Warwickshire following a trial at Edgbaston.

This snub only acted as a spur to secure his future with Yorkshire, who had been typically over-cautious in showing any positive intent, but there was no hiding his ability in 1929 when he played for the Second XI against Yorkshire Amateurs at Harrogate in the latest in a number of occasional games. Verity took one for 17 in the Amateurs' first innings but swept them away in the second with five wickets for seven runs in 11.2 overs, seven of which were maidens.

After his First XI debut in 1930, Verity finished the season at the top of the club's averages with 52 wickets at 11.44 runs apiece. He played in ten of the Championship matches and his first appearance alongside Rhodes was against Gloucestershire at Bristol in July when the pair shared 14 of the 20 wickets as Yorkshire made it by an innings and 187 runs.

Now Rhodes knew deep inside that he could retire gracefully, happy in the knowledge that Verity was there to continue to spin sides out, and he did exactly that from 1931-39, the golden period in which Yorkshire were county champions in seven of the nine seasons.

In his ten seasons with Yorkshire, Verity played in 228 Championship matches, taking 1,304 wickets at an average of 13.20, and he scaled the heights throughout this period, his most prolific season being his last in 1939 when he gathered in 165 wickets at 12.69.

In all first-class matches for Yorkshire he claimed 1,558 wickets at 13.70 to place himself sixth in the club's list of leading wicket-takers, while his record for England was also of the highest standard with 144 wickets in 40 matches at a cost of 24.37 runs per wicket.

No wonder the depth of sorrow felt throughout Yorkshire and the whole nation when Verity did not return from the war in which he had proved himself so gallant and so brave a leader of men.

It is entirely appropriate that on the club's Yorkshire Regiment Day on July 31, 2009, a blue plaque at his birthplace in Welton Grove should be unveiled by his proud son, Douglas, with Yorkshire President, Brian Close, and the Regiment's bugler among the party in attendance. After the ceremony was over the group moved on to watch the start of the Roses match at Headingley. Nothing could have been more fitting.

Although Yorkshire's team of 1930 lacked some fine tuning, they may still have won the Championship if they had not been the victims of appalling weather, nine consecutive fixtures being ruined in one period and two games in succession ending without a ball being bowled at Chesterfield and Harrogate, followed by only a half a day's play at Sheffield.

The weather was certainly cruel on Yorkshire's fans who also had another distraction that summer in the form of a thrilling Ashes series during which Bradman hit his 334 at Headingley, where he was always revered in a two-way relationship which culminated in him being elected a vice-president of Yorkshire CCC, an honour he always kept close to his heart.

What with Bradman's name on everyone's lips and Yorkshire losing several of their own top players to the Ashes series, it is little wonder that in a summer of such dismal weather, Yorkshire were not always the focal point. But at least the regulars had the satisfaction of bidding Rhodes farewell and warmly welcoming Verity.

With the sudden standing-down of Barber, Yorkshire turned in 1931 to Frank Greenwood, a Huddersfield industrialist of average cricketing ability who had, nevertheless, caught the eye with an unbeaten 104 against Glamorgan at Hull in 1929.

His young team responded by winning the Championship and repeating their success the following year when Greenwood led the side on only a handful of occasions because of business commitments.

Greenwood was the new face in charge on the field in 1931 and the new face off it was John Nash who steadfastly and with a minimum of fuss carried out his duties as club secretary for the next 40 years – three years longer than his predecessor, Sir Frederick Toone.

It is quite astonishing that from Wostinholm becoming secretary in 1864 to Joe Lister's death in 1991 only four men should fill the post over a period of 127 years and this long spell of sound management is an important reason why Yorkshire became such a solid institution.

The line of faithful and long-serving secretaries would undoubtedly have continued but for the restructuring of the club and it would be nice to think that David Ryder would have held the job for the past two decades or so had the old system prevailed. As already mentioned, Ryder was a most capable assistant secretary to Lister and he took over as secretary upon Lister's death. But then Yorkshire went on to appoint Chris Hassell as the club's first chief executive and Ryder's role was to change several times over the years, yet he remained the one that office staff invariably turned to for help and advice.

Down the years, of course, Yorkshire have endured more rows and controversies than any other county cricket club but they have always sailed through them without too much internal damage, thanks to those charged with the responsibility of navigating these stormy seas.

Of all the people at the heart of Yorkshire cricket, none rode the crest of the wave more effectively than Nash who was at the centre of things during two of the county's greatest spells, first in the 30s and then in the 60s.

It is worth at this stage looking more closely at his role and nobody is better suited to talk about Nash than my close friend, David Swallow, who was my predecessor as Yorkshire cricket correspondent at the Telegraph & Argus. He recalls:

Nash joined the club at their headquarters in Old Bank Chambers in Park Row in the centre of Leeds in his mid-teens and he served a sound apprenticeship under Fred Toone who set him a worthy example.

But it was not first his intention to stay with Yorkshire for long. When he left Pudsey Grammar School the idea was to follow his father into engineering and perhaps become a draughtsman.

In a newspaper article for the Telegraph & Argus, Nash told me: "When Mr Toone came back from his second trip to Australia as manager I was thinking of leaving but he told me there was a probability I would become assistant secretary and so I stayed."

Hawke was not in favour of Nash taking over from Toone at first, believing he

BENEVOLENT DICTATOR: Michael J. Ellison - First Treasurer and the first 'proper' President.

DANGEROUS DUO: George Freeman (right) and Tom Emmett... considered by W.G. Grace to be the best two bowlers in the country.

THE GREATEST: Lord Hawke – the most influential and significant figure in the history of Yorkshire CCC – and a non-Yorkshireman at that! Captain from 1883-1910, President from 1898-1938.

GRATEFULLY RECEIVED: Lord Hawke thanks subscribers at his testimonial presentation at Headingley on July 14, 1908. The fund raised £1,842 and gifts chosen by Hawke included a diamond tiara, a George III silver soup tureen dated 1817 and a pair of Purdy guns. His players presented him with George III and George IV silver tea services.

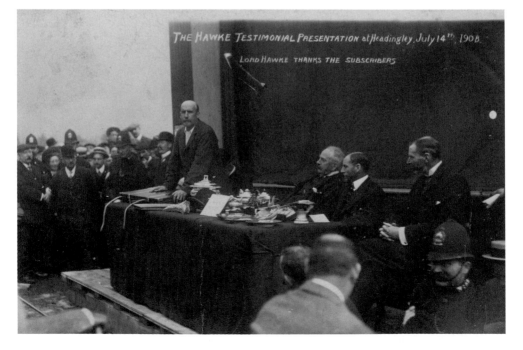

AMATEUR PAR EXCELLENCE: Rt. Hon. Sir F.S. Jackson – Brilliant amateur all-rounder, England captain and Yorkshire President, plus great Parliamentarian, chairman of the Conservative Party and governor of Bengal. Pictured here bowling and as Yorkshire President.

YORKSHIRE 1875:
A varied assortment
of players in a team
still a few years away
from being knocked
into shape by Hawke.
They won six of their
12 first-class games
and finished fourth in
the Championship
table to
Nottinghamshire.
Back row (from left):
G. Martin (umpire)
and John Thewlis;
middle: George
Pinder, George
Ulyett, Tom
Armitage, Joe
Rowbotham, Allen
Hill and Andrew
Greenwood; front:
Tom Emmett, John
Hicks, Ephraim
Lockwood and
Charlie Ullathorne.

YORKSHIRE SECONDS 1908. A rare picture from that era of the Second XI before playing Staffordshire at Rotherham in a two-day match in the Minor Counties' Championship. Back (from left): Umpire, Benjamin Wilson, Major Booth, William Brown (brother of J.T. Brown junior), Alban Turner and Alfonso Drake; middle: Horace Rudston, Robert Frank (captain) and Harold Harrison; front: Arthur Dolphin, Charles Grimshaw and William Micklethwait.

FRONT OF THE QUEUE: Ted Peate – first in the line of a series of slow left-arm bowling wizards for Yorkshire.

GEORGE HIRST AND (opposite page)WILFRED RHODES: Each of them a Colossus and each of them from the Huddersfield village of Kirkheaton.

THE GENTLE TOUCH: Rhodes
shows his grandson, Wilfred Rhodes
Burnley, how to hold the bat correctly.

FAMILY ALBUM: Photography was Rhodes' main hobby and these are a selection of the many pictures he took while touring India with England. The shot of the elephant rolling the pitch is of particular historical interest.

RIGHT ARM OVER: Hirst coaches a Yorkshire hopeful in the art of bowling.

JOURNEY'S END: Rhodes (centre) during his last game for Yorkshire against MCC at Scarborough in 1930 with his old team-mate, Hirst, who was umpiring the game, and Yorkshire President, Lord Hawke. Rhodes scored 41 and captured five wickets in the drawn match. He played in two further games at the Jubilee Festival before the curtain finally came down.

SWEET MEMORIES: A leather casket in the shape of a cricket ball which was presented to Rhodes by Lord Hawke upon his retirement at the Scarborough Jubilee Festival. The casket was made by Rowntrees of York and filled with chocolates.

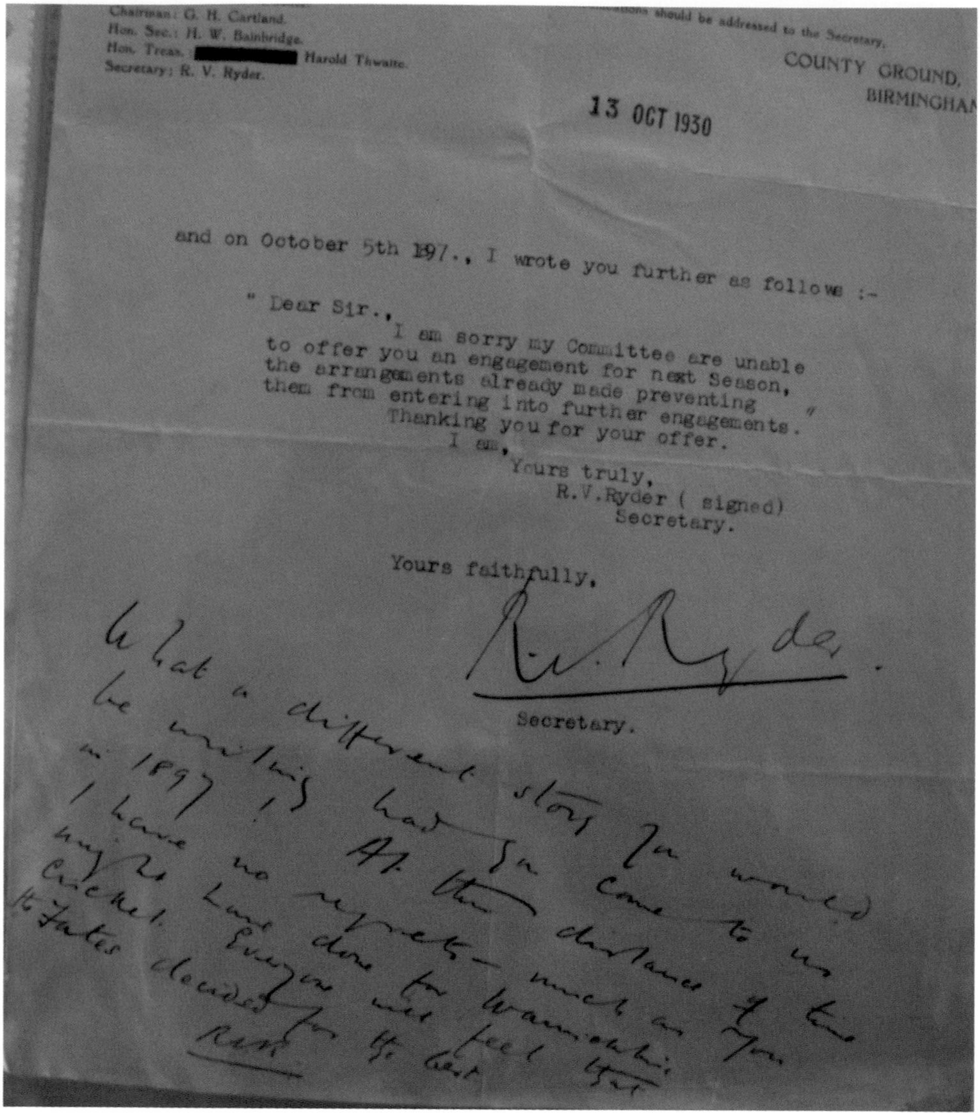

Chairman: G. H. Cartland.
Hon. Sec.: H. W. Bainbridge.
Hon. Treas.: ████████ Harold Thwaite.
Secretary: R. V. Ryder.

...ions should be addressed to the Secretary.

COUNTY GROUND,
BIRMINGHAM

13 OCT 1930

and on October 5th 197.., I wrote you further as follows :–

" Dear Sir.,
        I am sorry my Committee are unable
to offer you an engagement for next Season,
the arrangements already made preventing
them from entering into further engagements. "
        Thanking you for your offer.
        I am,
                Yours truly,
                R.V.Ryder (signed)
                Secretary.

        Yours faithfully,

                [signature: R. V. Ryder]

                Secretary.

[handwritten postscript in margin]

NO REGRETS: In 1897, Warwickshire CCC, in a letter from secretary, R.V. Ryder, turned down Rhodes' invitation to join the club and 33 years later the same secretary reproduced the letter for Rhodes, who was writing a book, and added the postscript: "What a different story you would be writing had you come to us in 1897. At this distance of time I have no regrets – much as you might have done for Warwickshire Cricket. Everyone will feel that the fates decided for the best".

PERFECT PLANNING: Yorkshire Secretary for 27 years from 1903, Frederick Charles Toone had unsurpassed skills as a planner and he went on to manage three England tours of Australia. He was to be knighted in recognition of his great work in fostering relations between "the Dominions and the Mother Country".

J. Bacon & Sons, Leeds.

FOLLOWING ON: John Nash succeeded F.C. Toone as secretary and served for even longer – 40 years.

WOMBWELL HERO: All-rounder, Roy Kilner, was a figure of folklore proportions around his home patch and when he died of a fever at the age of 37, over 100,000 people lined the streets for his funeral.

OPENING UP: Percy Holmes and Herbert Sutcliffe (left) (their names always said in that order) were the greatest pair of opening batsmen in Yorkshire's history, featuring in 69 first wicket century stands together. On the opposite page, they are seen in front of the scoreboard at Leyton in 1932, having put on a record 555 against Essex.

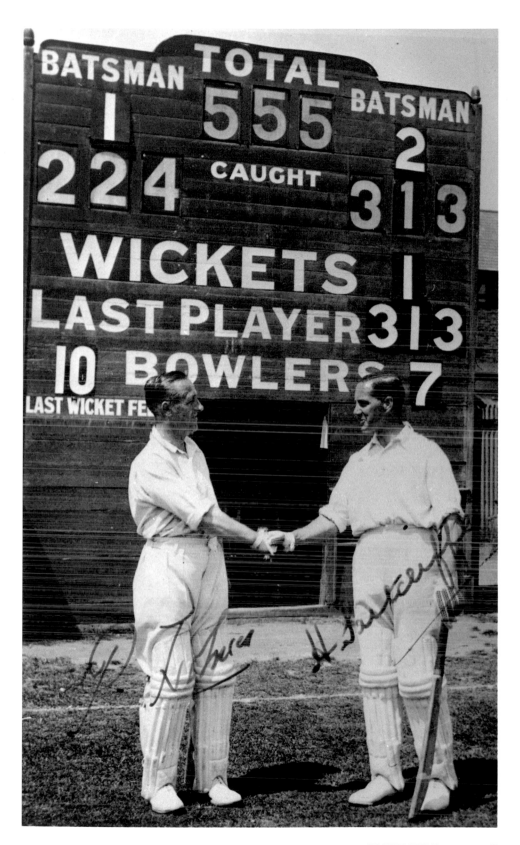

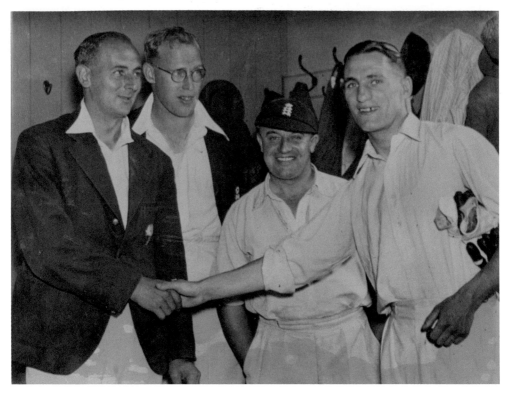

TEN OUT OF TEN: Hedley Verity, war hero and bowling giant. The only Yorkshire bowler twice to capture ten wickets in an innings, his 10-10 v Nottinghamshire at Headingley in 1932 still standing as a world record. Verity is pictured, above, with Yorkshire and England colleagues Bill Bowes, Arthur Wood and Len Hutton, and, below, with Norman Yardley playing for the Green Howards in Ireland in 1941, the last picture to be taken of Verity in cricket flannels. Two years later he died of war wounds sustained in Sicily.

PUTTING ON THE STYLE: Verity shows off his action to the camera

I'M IN CHARGE: On and off the field, Brian Sellers ruled Yorkshire cricket with an iron hand. One of the greatest ever captains, Yorkshire won the Championship five times under his leadership in the 1930s and again in 1946. The two portraits show him as player and later as cricket chairman and he is also pictured leading out his team against Sussex at Hove.

was too young, but he voted with the committee to make the decision unanimous.

Nash, a studious and thorough young man, turned out to be ideal for the top job when it so suddenly came along. With an eye for careful detail and an unflappable manner, he settled into the secretary's chair with ease.

Hailing from the Pudsey and Farsley area, he was to play as important a role in the fortunes of the club as the long list of players. He was close to Herbert Sutcliffe and Len Hutton and perhaps his connection was even more so with Raymond Illingworth.

In 1951, Illingworth was doing National Service in the RAF when Nash put a call in to the Station Commander at Dishforth (Group Captain Nash but no relation). He asked if Raymond could be released to play for Yorkshire in the last home match of the season at Headingley. That was against Hampshire and the start of an illustrious, if sometimes controversial, career.

Later Nash played the organ at Raymond's wedding to Shirley Milnes. And some years later Mr and Mrs Illingworth bought the Nash home in Stanningley!

Subsequently, the two men were involved in one of the most discussed events in Yorkshire's history. When the player asked for a contract the secretary had to tell him the committee was unwilling to agree.

So Raymond handed in his notice at Park Avenue in July, 1968, to Mr Nash. The aftermath is documented elsewhere.

After completing almost half a century with YCCC, 40 of them as secretary, he became the longest serving administrator with the club.

Like his predecessor he took an England side to Australia and New Zealand, joint manager with Brigadier Green at the start of the 1950s of Freddie Brown's team.

He once admitted to rarely seeing a full day's play because of office work. But he represented a link with Yorkshire stretching from Hawke and including the likes of Rhodes, Hirst, Sutcliffe, Hutton, Brian Sellers, Close and Boycott.

He could have written a book about all the famous names and the many events surrounding them. However, he kept his counsel and was much respected for that. On retirement he admitted that he had once tried to persuade the committee to move Yorkshire away from Headingley! It may sound like sacrilege but being a Pudsey-Farsley man he appreciated in the early 1930s the potential of the area known as Dawsons Corner.

Even in the 1930s it was known that the area was ripe for development with rail and road connections. At that time it was a green belt buffer between the conurbations of Leeds and Bradford. Not surprisingly, perhaps, the suggestion was rebuffed and today there is a huge retail complex and business park on the site.

Away from cricket he was secretary of the Parochial Church Council at St John's Church, Farsley, for many years. He played the organ with skill and passion, once persuading Donald Bradman to join him at service.

There was a dry, whimsical sense of humour lurking behind his public front. Once at Bramall Lane he appealed over the public address system for spectators not to hurl cushions around. There are different versions of the story. One claimed that a wag shouted out "There'll be repercussions if they don't." The other said it was John Nash himself who eased the tension with the remark.

He died of a heart attack in April, 1977, safe in the knowledge that he had served Yorkshire cricket well.

With Nash in charge of the admin and Greenwood in charge of a bourgeoning team, Yorkshire had high expectations of success in 1931 and these were realised to an extent that few could have dreamed of.

With Sutcliffe and Holmes supplying the bulk of the runs and the now nationally-acclaimed Bowes and Verity to the forefront among the wicket-takers, Yorkshire had the Championship title firmly in the bag by the time they embarked on their Southern tour in mid-August – and this despite several weeks of depressing weather early in the campaign.

It was fine enough in mid-May, however, for Verity to bag his first all-ten by scything through the Warwickshire second innings at Headingley but the general disruption caused by the weather meant that Yorkshire were still only eighth in the table when they went to Lord's on June 20.

They were then in such complete control that they won their next five matches by an innings, the final one being Macaulay's benefit match against Surrey at Bradford when the visitors were swept away for 61 in their second innings, Verity taking 6-11 and Bowes picking up the remainder.

Rain prevented a result in the next game with Nottinghamshire at Sheffield but then Yorkshire went on the rampage again with five consecutive victories to give them ten wins from 11 matches.

Only once were Yorkshire beaten all summer and this was in an eyebrow raising game with Gloucestershire at Sheffield when the enterprising Greenwood boldly went along with a plan thought up by the visitors' captain, Beverley Lyon, aimed at extracting a positive result from a fixture which had seen the first two days washed away by rain.

The regulations allowed for 15 points for an outright win but only five points for a first innings lead and with only a day remaining that appeared to be the inevitable conclusion until Gloucestershire went in to bat to get the game started. The crowd thought the rain had quickly returned when the players ran off after Emmott Robinson's first ball to Alfred Dipper went for four byes and their astonishment was even greater ten minutes later when Holmes and Sutcliffe came out to bat and the process was repeated after Wally Hammond's first ball to Holmes also brought four byes.

The cunning plan meant the game could then start proper, with the winners picking up 15 points. And these went to Gloucestershire who made 171, despite Verity's 7-64, and then sent Yorkshire back for 124.

Greenwood adopted the same principle against Northamptonshire at Bradford in August and this time Verity's seven wickets set up a Yorkshire win but the authorities were generally unhappy with the procedure and although it was adopted on a few other occasions by other sides it soon fizzled out.

By the end of 1931, Yorkshire were recognised as the best team in the land and only one piece remained to be placed in the jigsaw before the full picture of their mightiness could be seen.

CHAPTER EIGHTEEN

THE STORYBOOK YEARS

A glance at the list of Yorkshire captains down the years will show that Frank Greenwood was again in charge to retain the title in 1932 – perhaps the biggest headline making year in the club's history – but this was only partly true.

An increased workload of business commitments meant that Greenwood was only available to Yorkshire for seven matches, the first of his absences being in the curtain-raiser against Oxford University in the Parks.

Into his shoes stepped Keighley-born Arthur Brian Sellers and, after a century from Holmes, the visitors went on to win the game by 162 runs. Thus one of the greatest captains the game has ever known and one of the most significant figures in Yorkshire's history had presided over the first of his many victories. He went on to captain Yorkshire in 25 matches in that initial season – and did not lose one of them!

In all but name, Brian Sellers (known either as Crackerjack or Abscess – from his initials ABS) was the real leader of Yorkshire in 1932 but from the following year until 1947 he was the colonel-in-chief, guiding his team to six Championship titles. Or was he really the Sergeant Major?

The captains before Sellers had often been well-connected men who were accepted as leaders because they had been successful in other areas of life and at least had some knowledge of the game of cricket.

Sellers too was successful in business and he certainly had the right connections within the club, his father, also Arthur, in the 1890s being a brave and fearless Yorkshire batsman in the same style as his son and later a committee member and vice-president, while his elder brother, Godfrey Sellers, also served on the committee.

Arthur Sellers Snr was chairman of the cricket committee when Brian first deputised for Greenwood and his appointment as vice-captain in 1932 must also have had the stamp of approval of the president, Lord Hawke, and vice-president, Lt-Col the Rt. Hon. F.S. Jackson, so he had obviously got extremely influential backing.

But Sellers was no throwback to Hawke or Jackson because here was a man who could be just as colourful in language or as sharp of tongue as any of those under his command. On one occasion when Major Lupton was captain, Rhodes steered him gently into the outfield in order that he should not be offended by some of the riper words floating around; now Sellers himself would make himself clearly understood in the most basic of terms.

And in no way did Sellers wish to be seen as superior to his men in background or pedigree. As a batsman he was capable and tenacious but not gifted like those around him, yet he was fearless and brave both at the crease and in the field and his word was law.

It was Hawke who was responsible for moulding a disparate group of cricketers into a famous fighting unit but Sellers' role was entirely different because his troops were already an elite force when he joined them. His skill was in keeping them all as sharp as razors and in preserving and indeed strengthening their love and pride in the county of their birth.

Educated at St Peter's School, York, Sellers was a major in the Royal Artillery during the war, winning the MBE, and after giving up the Yorkshire captaincy at the end of the 1947 season he remained the most powerful figure in the club, calling the shots as cricket chairman for 13 years and remaining in close touch with events until his death in 1981.

But not all of his decisions off the field were as well received as those on it and he became something of a dinosaur in later years. His stubborn refusal to introduce contracts for players led to the departure of Raymond Illingworth to Leicestershire in 1968 and there was even greater uproar over his sacking of Brian Close, who moved to Somerset in 1970.

Illingworth's exit opened the door to the England captaincy and Close, deeply upset at his enforced departure, became an icon at his new county. But neither of these two illustrious players should have been treated in the way they were and perhaps it is no coincidence that the last truly great period in Yorkshire's history was drawing to a close by the time both of them were gone.

None of this, however, diminishes Sellers' achievements with Yorkshire or moves him off the pedestal upon which history has placed him. And nobody can ever argue that whatever Sellers did for Yorkshire, right up to the very end, was not what he believed to be in the best interests of the team and the club.

Sellers' achievements were duly recognised in 1940 when he was chosen as one of Five Cricketers of the Year in the Wisden Cricketers' Almanack after leading Yorkshire to three consecutive Championship titles right up to the war and many considered he was the finest technician in the game. It was only that his own batting was not of the very highest standard that got in the way of his chances of taking on the England captaincy but he later became a very influential figure at Lord's, sitting on several committees and serving as a Test selector.

As we have seen, Greenwood was officially Yorkshire's captain again in 1932 but the push towards the Championship title was really led by the emerging Sellers, even though it cannot be doubted that the same result would most likely have been attained by Greenwood had he featured regularly.

In truth, Yorkshire were now approaching the peak of their powers and in no season was the story of their success more remarkable than in 1932 when both batting and bowling achievements were more the stuff of fiction than of fact and much has already been written in great detail in other books about these exploits.

Two substantial figures had bowed out at the end of the previous season in Emmott Robinson and the low-profile but nonetheless high-quality batsman, Edgar Oldroyd, but such was the overall strength of the team that they were barely missed.

Once again Sutcliffe was in such phenomenal form that he topped 3,000 runs in all first-class cricket for the second consecutive year and 12 of his 14 centuries – five more than any other batsman in the country – were for Yorkshire. Leyland, Holmes, Mitchell and Barber also made it into four figures in all Yorkshire matches while Bowes and Verity were such a menace that they took 352 wickets between them.

So mighty were Yorkshire that Sutcliffe, Verity, Bowes and Leyland were all selected for England's Bodyline tour of Australia in the winter of 1932-33 but the decision to take Bowes, despite his 168 county wickets, was left so late that he only had five days in which to collect his kit and make personal arrangements, which included postponing his wedding. The hesitancy over taking him on board might have been because he had attracted criticism in some quarters for testing the courage of batsmen by bowling bouncers but this trait of the gentle giant's would unquestionably have received the full approval of England's captain, Douglas Jardine.

Yorkshire were on top of the world in 1932 and the world looked on as batting and bowling records were smashed.

First up was the first-wicket stand of 555 by Holmes and Sutcliffe against Essex at Leyton in mid-June, beating by one run the record set 34 years earlier by those two other great Yorkshire openers, Tunnicliffe and Brown.

There was drama throughout with Holmes being dropped behind the wicket when only four and then settling in with great determination despite suffering constantly from lumbago.

With the magical figure of 555 being reached at almost one o'clock on the second day, Sutcliffe, on 313 compared to his partner's 224, gave away his wicket unaware that Sellers would have declared at the end of the over in any event. Sutcliffe was soon regretting his actions because the scorers found themselves busily searching for a run which had been 'lost' in their books and at one stage the board slipped down to 554.

The 'missing' run was eventually 'found' – it had to be, hadn't it? – and the record was confirmed. Sutcliffe, on this occasion the more dominant of the two, packed his innings with 33 fours and a six, and the physically more restricted Holmes managed 19 fours.

A month later, immediately after the tension-packed match at Bradford where Bowes bowled Goddard with the first ball of the final over to give Yorkshire victory over Gloucestershire by 133 runs, the focus switched to Verity and his phenomenal 10-10 at Headingley.

Nottinghamshire were very much on top of this game on the second afternoon before a thunderstorm abruptly ended play for the day with Yorkshire 163-9 in reply to 234, their chief destroyer being Harold Larwood (warming up for Australia) with five wickets.

When play was able to resume on the final day, Sellers gave an early indication of his shrewdness by declaring and accepting defeat on the first innings. Nothing out of the ordinary occurred up to lunch when Walter Keeton and Frank Shipston – who was to die in July, 2005, just short of his 100th birthday – had opened up with 38 together.

But it was a different story in the afternoon as Verity grabbed all ten wickets while only 29 were being added to the lunch score. Virtually unplayable, he did the hat-trick, twice took two wickets in two balls and finished up with the stunning figures of 19.4-16-10-10.

His son, Douglas, revealed only recently that his dad had told him that while congratulations were being showered on him from all sides, Wilfred Rhodes sidled up and said: "It should have been ten wickets for six runs, Hedley. You bowled a full toss which was hit for four."

Hard to please, Wilfred. We wouldn't want him to have been any different.

Just one footnote from this amazing season. Despite the dominance of Verity and Bowes, the Championship bowling averages were topped by neither of them, the honours going to the left-arm medium pace of Horace Fisher who gained his place towards the end of the season and cashed in with 19 wickets.

A month after Verity's ten-for-ten, Fisher himself performed a then unique hat-trick against Somerset at Sheffield, each of his victims being trapped lbw. Horace's family three years ago donated the hat-trick ball to Yorkshire and now it is proudly displayed in their museum at Headingley. I was present at Cheltenham 47 years on from Fisher's achievement when Yorkshire were this time on the receiving end of a similar hat-trick from Gloucestershire's South African captain, Mike Procter.

The hat-trick theme continued in 1933 when Sellers by now was officially in charge. In uncompromising style he led his men to their third Championship title success and, along the way, Macaulay's off-breaks earned him two hat-tricks for him to become the first Yorkshire player to perform the feat twice in the same season – he was joined by Don Wilson in 1966.

Macaulay's first was against Glamorgan at Cardiff in May when Yorkshire won by 166 runs and, strangely, they were his only wickets in the match, ten of them being claimed by Bowes and six by Verity. The second occasion was in the Roses tussle at Old Trafford, which Yorkshire won by 156 runs in two days, and there was no doubting Macaulay's dominance this time as he weighed in with seven for 28, including the hat-trick, and five for 21.

Before Macaulay twice got to work on a broken and dusty pitch, however, Yorkshire were put in command by Mitchell who hit a near-miraculous 123 out of 341. It was an unforgettable display of batting on a pitch which held so many potential demons that Holmes, upon his departure, opined that the game would be all over within the day.

Only Macaulay and Fred Trueman have picked up four hat-tricks for Yorkshire but Macaulay's two three-in-threes were by no means his only highlights of the season.

Less than a fortnight after crushing Lancashire he shot out Leicestershire for 27 at Kettering with 7-9 in 14 overs and then followed up with 4-25, the home side this time being routed for 68 to lose by an innings and 206 runs by 1.22pm on the second day.

Macaulay's contribution to Yorkshire's cause should never be under-estimated. He retired in 1935 and joined the RAF at the start of the war but, tragically, he contracted pneumonia while serving in the Shetlands in 1940 and died there shortly after his 43rd birthday.

Mitchell, who was rapidly establishing himself as one of the greatest fielders and catchers in the world, made it well past the 1,000 runs mark, along with Leyland, Sutcliffe and Barber, and the Baildon man also enjoyed a remarkable Scarborough Festival in which he plundered 158 against the MCC and 100 not out in each innings for Leveson-Gower's XI v the MCC Australian XI.

The only downside to 1933 was the diminishing form of Holmes who had made it known he would retire at the end of the season long before he clocked his first 50 on August 17 in the final home game against Nottinghamshire at Park Avenue. It proved to be an occasion full of nostalgia because Holmes and Sutcliffe's 141 together was the last of their 69 century opening partnerships.

And so, come September, Yorkshire's greatest opening pair were parted for ever, but as so often has happened in Yorkshire's history the ending of one great career saw the birth of another. Holmes quit the stage and on to it, in 1934, stepped Len Hutton.

LEN HUTTON

In writing this profile, I had to think long and hard over whether to give him his full Christian name of Leonard or to call him Len. In the end I decided on Len because it was as Len Hutton that he was known to hundreds of thousands of cricket followers around the world.

But to most of his team-mates and to those who knew him closely he was almost invariably referred to, whether in his company or not, as Leonard. Brian Close and Raymond Illingworth, who were to follow him as distinguished captains of England, always called him Leonard, and still do, as did the likes of close colleagues Bob Appleyard and Ted Lester. And Freddie Trueman, never a man to stand on ceremony or to mince his words, would always refer to him in reverential tones as Leonard.

It was a natural mark of respect for a batsman they knew from experience and instinct to be a cut above all others in their midst. Leonard was the master and even great players themselves were in awe of him.

No fairytale story enveloped the lad from Pudsey when he first appeared on the Yorkshire scene. Indeed, he began with a duck, ignominiously run out against Cambridge University in an innings in which he saw Sutcliffe and Wilf Barber both score immaculate centuries.

But his peers in the game instinctively knew from his earliest days that here was a star in the making and Hutton was shrewd enough to take their advice to concentrate on occupying the crease and to develop his game without worrying too much about going for his shots.

And as his game developed so did his strokes, particularly the breathtaking cover-drive which became his trademark and also the ability to place the ball with the greatest of precision between two fieldsmen.

As far as the cricket paying public of Yorkshire was concerned, Hutton was a source of immense pride in the brooding days before the 1939-1945 war and in the brighter times which followed it. And he was a figure of optimism and hope for the whole nation.

From a batting perspective, his finest moment was his epic record-breaking score of 364 against Australia at The Oval in 1938 when he overhauled Bradman's unbeaten 357 for South Australia in 1935-6 and Bobby Abel's similar score for Surrey in 1899, in addition to Bradman's record Test innings of 334 at Headingley in 1930. But cricket is a team game and Hutton's most notable achievement after becoming England's first professional captain of the 20th century was to win back the Ashes in that historic sporting summer of 1953 and to retain them in Australia in 1954-55.

Just as he launched his county career with a duck, Hutton also failed to score on his England debut against New Zealand at Lord's in 1937 and in the second innings of that match he was out for only one. But in the next Test at Old Trafford he scored a century and was on his way to stardom.

Many a sportsman wins the hero worship of fans because of an extrovert personality which is in keeping with the way they play the game but in Hutton's case entirely the opposite was true.

Reserved, modest and veering towards shyness by nature, he had a quiet charm which instantly appealed and a steely determination which made Yorkshire folk very proud of him indeed. England's call was answered by 'Our Len' and he achieved everything that his country asked of him and plenty more besides.

And everyone knew that all this was accomplished despite the handicap throughout much of his career of having to bat with his left arm a couple of inches shorter than his right, the result of a serious injury sustained in 1941 when, while serving with the Army Physical Training Corps, he was doing commando training in a gymnasium. Attempting a fly spring the mat slipped from under him and he fractured his forearm and dislocated the ulna at the base of his wrist, injuries which required an operation and three skin grafts.

The accident occurred in the March but after months of hospital treatment Hutton was back with his unit and playing cricket for both the Army and his own club, Pudsey St Lawrence, in the Bradford League.

Already made an honorary life member of MCC while still playing, Hutton retired at the end of the 1955 season and was soon knighted for his services to the game.

In 79 Tests he scored 6,971 runs with 19 centuries and he was captain in 23 of them, winning 11, drawing eight and losing only four. For Yorkshire he compiled 19,361 Championship runs with 63 centuries at an average of 52.04 and in all first-class matches for his county he made 24,807 runs with 85 centuries at 53.34. Taking all of his career matches together he scored 39,950 runs in 810 innings and struck 129 centuries and 177 half-centuries.

Deeply upset by Yorkshire's troubles in the 1980s, Sir Leonard went a long way towards healing the wounds by accepting the presidency of the club in 1990. He was the perfect ambassador but, sadly, his days in office were relatively few because he died on September 6 of that year shortly after suffering a heart attack.

The retirement of Holmes did not mean that Sutcliffe was without a reliable opening partner in 1934 because Mitchell was immediately successful in the role, scoring centuries in the first two Championship matches against Glamorgan at Swansea and Lancashire at Sheffield, where he made 121 and the White Rose won by an innings and three runs.

But Yorkshire could finish the season no higher than sixth place, their worst performance in 23 years, and this was attributed in part to losing so many key players to the Ashes series, Leyland and Verity being called upon for all five Tests, Sutcliffe for four and Bowes three. The evidence bears this out because four Championship matches were lost while Tests were also taking place. They were not helped, either, by a serious decline in the form of Macaulay who could only manage 49 wickets in the competition. Hutton was by no means the finished article yet but the polish was being applied and his maiden century was a gem of an innings – 196 in the ten-wicket victory over Worcestershire at New Road.

Yorkshire were masters of all they surveyed again in 1935 and from then until the outbreak of war they confirmed their status as one of the greatest county sides ever seen. In 148 Championship games during this golden period they won 87 and lost only 11 and they clinched the title in each year except 1936 when they finished third to Derbyshire, who came out top for the only time in their history so far, with Middlesex being the runners-up.

It took them some time to thaw out in 1935 because May was one of the worst cricketing months for many years with bitter winds sweeping the country and at Chesterfield on May 14 their match against Derbyshire was abandoned in a snowstorm.

But then came a sequence of five consecutive wins, including the dramatic contest with Kent at Bradford which Yorkshire won by two wickets late into the second day. Kent, after gaining a first innings lead of 51, were further boosted by a glorious exhibition of batsmanship from Frank Woolley, who made 73, but once he had gone Verity and Macaulay rapidly collected five wickets apiece, leaving Yorkshire 192 to win. Sutcliffe responded to Woolley's genius with a masterpiece of his own and upon reaching his century there was quite a delay as spectators went wild in their acclamation. Seven runs from victory, Sutcliffe was out for 110, Verity was bowled first ball and the result remained in doubt until Sellers swept 'Tich' Freeman for four.

Yorkshire's reputation for suddenly losing a match right out of the blue was maintained at Huddersfield when they suffered their only defeat of the season, Essex firing them out for 31 in a game dominated by Stan Nichols and 'Hopper' Read who shared all the wickets in steamrollering Yorkshire by an innings and 204 runs. As well as recording figures of 4-17 and 7-37, Nichols also lashed 146 out of a total of 334.

The humiliation was soon forgotten, thanks in the main to Bowes who gathered up six wickets in each innings of the Roses clash at Bradford. A month earlier, Bowes had responded to being left out of the Lord's Test by annihilating Northamptonshire at Kettering with match figures of 16-35, the second best in Yorkshire's history.

It was a difficult summer for Macaulay, poor health restricting him to eight Championship matches and a mere 23 wickets and prompting his announcement that he would retire at the end of the season, but things went well for Wood, who became the first Yorkshire wicketkeeper to make it to 1,000 runs.

With Hawke's views on professional captains well known, an eight-week tour of Jamaica by Yorkshire from early February, 1936, was led by the young and rather shy Paul Gibb in the absence of Sellers, who was unable to make the trip because of business commitments.

Gibb had announced himself with 157 not out on his Championship debut the previous summer and he did an outstanding job in what for him must have been difficult circumstances, Yorkshire becoming the first side to beat Jamaica on their home soil in ten years.

A graduate of Oxford University, Gibb was an interesting character. He was a sound if somewhat unspectacular opening batsman and a very efficient wicketkeeper who went on to play in eight Tests for England before losing his place behind the stumps to Godfrey Evans. He then severed his connection with Yorkshire and went as a professional to Essex in the 1950s, becoming a first-class umpire for ten seasons from 1957.

Whether pre-season tours have any real merit in preparing teams for the summer ahead is a subject which attracts differing views but the Jamaica visit did nothing special for Yorkshire who slipped into third place in 1936, partly as a result of an unusual number of injuries and partly through a rather lacklustre final Southern tour when they were unable to step up their momentum.

Leyland headed the batting averages in an inclement summer and only Sutcliffe and Hutton went beyond the 1,000 runs mark with him in the Championship, although they were joined by Mitchell in all first-class matches. Frank Smailes, with a grand total of 125 wickets and 561 runs, established himself as the team's leading all-rounder, while the two other main bowlers were Verity and Bowes, who managed 113 first-class wickets despite being unable to shake off niggling injuries for much of the time.

From 1937 up to the war, Yorkshire looked down on all their rivals as they enjoyed an uninterrupted period of supremacy. They were not, however, invincible and in 1937 they experienced two wounding defeats, losing by an innings and 22 runs to Middlesex at Lord's and to Lancashire by five wickets at Sheffield.

In mid-August, in the thick of the battle for the Championship, Sellers received a telegram from Middlesex captain R.W.V. Robins which threw down the gauntlet and asked for a challenge match between the two great sides to round off the season.

The challenge was accepted and there was widespread interest in the game which was scheduled over four days at The Oval from September 11. The challengers were firmly put in their place and the fourth day was never needed, Yorkshire romping home by an innings and 115 runs after an immaculate 121 from Hutton and a second innings haul of 8-43 from Verity.

Yorkshire pride in 1938 was not limited to Hutton's 364 for England at The Oval because the white rose blossomed in all its glory despite heavy Test calls and they took the Championship for the first time in an Ashes summer since 1912. Verity and Bowes again topped the bowling averages but there were 100-plus wickets, also, for Smailes, who completed the double, and the clever off-spinner and splendid fielder, Ellis Robinson, who was rewarded with his county cap.

May was a merry month for Hutton who collected 733 first-class runs in nine completed innings but, like several of his colleagues, his season was interrupted for a while by injury. He broke a finger on a spiteful pitch at Lord's which also claimed two further casualties in Leyland, with a broken thumb, and Gibb, with a split head.

War clouds may have been gathering in the spring of 1939 but a more relaxed and confident set of young men is hard to imagine than those who posed for the camera for the Yorkshire pre-season team photograph. How sleek and composed looked Sutcliffe and Norman Yardley in the centre of the front row as they flanked their captain, Sellers, whose hair was as sharply parted as ever; how relaxed but eager seemed Hutton and Smailes on the back row, how absolutely certain appeared the whole group that they would succeed in their mission to complete a hat-trick of Championship titles.

And, indeed, 1939 brought about the last triumph of one of the greatest teams of all time. In match after match there were achievements which suggested, or rather proclaimed, that they were in their pomp.

The outbreak of war meant that the whole Championship could not be completed but Yorkshire made absolutely sure of first place before the abandonment and they were noble winners.

Gloucestershire beat them twice but it was generally accepted that Sellers' men were the team of the year, winning 20 out of 28 matches. In Bowes they had the best new-ball bowler in the world, in Verity the finest left-arm spinner and no other team in the universe had close-in fielders who could rub shoulders with Mitchell, Turner, Sellers, Robinson and Yardley.

Bowes, Verity and Robinson grabbed 363 wickets in the Championship alone and Verity led the full first-class averages with 191 wickets at 13.13 while Hutton, Sutcliffe, Leyland, Barber and Mitchell all had 1,000 Championship runs with Yardley joining them from all games. Hutton had ten centuries for Yorkshire and two for England and was the unchallenged master of playing the turning ball; Sutcliffe, hindered by injuries in the later part of the season, completed 1,000 runs by mid-June and successive innings brought him scores of 165, 116, 234* and 175. Not without justification had he become known to his colleagues as 'The Maestro'.

By the time Yorkshire began their end-of-season southern tour in the last week in August, the outbreak of war was beyond any doubt and when they stepped out against Kent at Dover on August 23 it was felt it could start at the next tick of the clock. Cricket became small talk among players and spectators but Hutton helped cause a distraction with a century and Verity did likewise with nine wickets in the win by an innings and 14 runs on the second day.

Another innings victory inside two days followed against Hampshire at Bournemouth, Verity destroying the hosts first time round with 6-22. Sutcliffe received instructions from the War Office and did not travel to Hove for the final game. The gloom descended further with news that the Scarborough Cricket Festival had been cancelled.

Yorkshire agreed to play at Sussex partly because Sellers had received no order to the contrary and partly because it was Jim Parks' benefit match and they did not want to let him down.

But for the circumstances, the twists and turns of the match would have been the sole topic of conversation in cricket circles. Sussex batted first and George Cox took complete control with a mighty 198 out of 387. But centuries from Hutton and Yardley gave Yorkshire a five runs lead, yet when they went out a second time they only needed 29 to win. This was because Verity, opening the bowling in his last appearance for Yorkshire, returned figures of 6-1-9-7 and Sussex were skittled for 33. In his final moments, both at cricket and in life, Verity was a true hero.

With rail travel in chaos, Yorkshire arranged to travel home on their final journey by coach and with a blackout in force they made an overnight stop in Leicester.

Early the following morning they were in Yorkshire again. Their journey home was described most evocatively by J.M. Kilburn, the esteemed Yorkshire Post cricket correspondent, and I think it only fitting to conclude this chapter with the following paragraph of his:

Halts began, one passenger dropping off here, another there. Finally came journey's end in City Square, Leeds, and then departed their several ways one of the finest county teams in all the history of cricket. It never assembled again.

CHAPTER NINETEEN

THE MEMORY MEN

Cricket on the wider stage spluttered back to life, growing stronger and stronger with each passing day, following Germany's surrender in May, 1945, and Yorkshire hearts were filled with pride as Hutton headed England's run chart with 380 in the five Victory Tests against Australian Services.

Yorkshire's faithful members did not forsake their county during the dark years of war and they responded generously to the club's appeal for them to continue paying their subscriptions even though there was no cricket to watch.

The reason for this request was that it soon became obvious that a good deal of money would be required to re-launch cricket on the various home grounds once the hostilities ceased. Most of the bigger venues were requisitioned by the military and there was considerable damage to the structure and playing area at Bramall Lane when Sheffield was blitzed in December, 1940.

War in Europe ended too late for Yorkshire to organise a full programme in 1945 but they managed to arrange a couple of two-day matches against Derbyshire at Bramall Lane and Chesterfield and a three-day Roses game at Park Avenue, which was played for the benefit of the dependants of Verity, proceeds amounting to around £3,000 despite rain decimating the final day. The cricket was as dour as history demanded from these contests and the weather for the most part was drab. Normal service had indeed resumed.

And so had Hutton's zest for runs. His 111 for Yorkshire came hard on the heels of Keith Miller's identical score for Australian Services in the two-day draw at Sheffield in July and the following month he hit 55 and 73 for a Yorkshire XI v RAF at Scarborough.

Much to its credit, the Bradford League kept going throughout the war – exactly as it had done in 1914-18 – and not only did this provide a much-needed diversion for the sports-minded population of the West Riding but it also meant that the many first-class cricketers who were drawn to it were able to keep in good shape and form.

In a splendid book published in 2009, Tony Barker lists all the great names that were drawn to the Bradford League and the clubs they played for. Wilf Barber, Arthur Booth, Bill Bowes, Horace Fisher, Paul Gibb, Harry Halliday, Len Hutton, 'Sandy' Jacques, Maurice Leyland, George Macaulay, Arthur Mitchell, Ellis Robinson, Brian Sellers, Frank Smailes, Abe Waddington, Arthur Wood and Norman Yardley were among the Yorkshiremen in the League while, from farther afield, came the likes of Les Ames, Bill Copson, George Cox, Jack Crapp, George Duckworth, Arthur Fagg, Cliff Gladwin, Alf Gover, Arthur Jepson, Eddie Paynter, Winston Place, George and Harold Pope, Bill Voce and Cyril Washbrook.

A couple of years ago, for the express purpose of this book, I went to interview two doyens of Yorkshire cricket whose association with the club in one form or another stretched back longer than almost anyone else.

Michael Crawford, the Second XI captain who later held high offices within the club, including treasurer and then chairman during controversial times, was born on July 30, 1920, and Ted Lester, the hard-hitting batsman who later became first team scorer, was born on February 18, 1923.

Their early impressions of Yorkshire cricket were formed well over 75 years ago and they have maintained their close interest in the club throughout the second half of its existence.

No pair could be better qualified to cast their minds back and give an honest appraisal of Yorkshire CCC but where should they be inserted in this narrative? I decided here was the appropriate place because although they were still making their way after the 1939-45 war they were, at the same time, old enough to be fully appreciative of Yorkshire's great past.

And old enough, too, to recall some of the magical moments now etched deep in his memory is the Morley-born cricket writer and author, Derek Hodgson, who for many years reported for several national newspapers, including The Daily Express and The Independent. It is always nice to get a view from the other side of the fence, as it were.

MICHAEL CRAWFORD

Michael was called up to captain Yorkshire in Norman Yardley's absence in one Championship game in 1951, scoring nine and 13 in a thrilling match with Worcestershire at Scarborough which the visitors won by eight runs. A well-organised batsman, he played for the Yorkshire Second XI from 1947-53 and was captain in 1951 and joint-captain with Ronnie Burnet in 1952.

He captained Leeds CC for 14 seasons from 1949-1962, leading them to their first Yorkshire League title in 1958 and their third Yorkshire Council Championship in the same year.

Michael took over as Yorkshire treasurer in 1963 from A. Wyndham-Heselton, who had held the post for 30 years, and he gave continuous service until 1980 when he became club chairman for the next three years and chairman of the cricket management committee.

A member of Yorkshire's general committee from 1954-1983, he was a trustee of the club from 1963-1985, elected a vice-president in 1979 and an honorary life member in 1983.

Educated at Shrewsbury School and Magdalene College, Cambridge, Michael was also an outstanding amateur soccer player, obtaining a Blue and scoring a goal against Oxford University in 1946-47 and playing in the same University side as Trevor Bailey and Doug Insole.

In 1939, he said au revoir to Cambridge and spent the next five years in the Army, serving in the Middle East and Italy as a captain in the Royal Artillery and being mentioned in despatches. He returned to Cambridge in 1946 and scored all four goals in the University's 4-3 win over Tottenham Hotspur. It was reported in the local newspaper: "The man of the afternoon was M. Crawford who can surely have few superiors as an outside left in amateur football today. He scored all four of the Cambridge goals; all of them really first-class and three after being sent away all on his own." Michael's soccer career also included spells with Cambridge Town, Corinthian Casuals and Old Salopians.

Michael was a chartered accountant with John Gordon, Harrison, Taylor and Co which merged to become Spicer and Pegler and later part of Touche Ross and then Deloitte. He retired at 60 in 1980 and ran a property and investment company from 1980-95.

His wife was formerly Miss Hazel Cameron and is a cousin of former South Africa wicketkeeper, Jock Cameron, who once clouted Hedley Verity for so many runs in an over at Sheffield that wicketkeeper, Arthur Wood, shouted to Verity: "You've got him in two minds, Hedley: he doesn't know whether to hit you for four or six!"

What are your first impressions of Yorkshire cricket?

I was born at Moortown Corner in 1920 and I was very interested in cricket from an early age. My father took me to Bramall Lane in 1931 when I saw Yorkshire on the first day of the Roses match in which Holmes and Sutcliffe put on 323 for the first wicket and I can always remember greatly admiring Sutcliffe who was out for 195. I can remember Eddie Paynter running in from fine leg and catching him at ankle height.

As a boy, I lived for Yorkshire cricket and Sutcliffe was my favourite cricketer in those days and I always looked to see how many he had made.

There are two other pre-war matches which I can particularly remember for different reasons. The first was Yorkshire v Essex in 1935 when my brother and I took our sandwiches to Huddersfield. We went on the train and got there about 12.10pm with the game having been going on for about 40 minutes and Yorkshire were seven wickets down. I just couldn't believe it. They were bowled out for 31 in the first innings and 99 in the second. Nichols won the match for Essex. He also made 146 and Yorkshire were beaten by an innings and plenty. It was most unusual for Yorkshire to be defeated like that but things just went wrong for them. They couldn't blame the pitch because it was the same for Essex.

The second one was at Headingley in early August, 1939, when Lancashire got a first innings lead and were then bowled out in their second innings with Ellis Robinson taking eight wickets. Yorkshire had to make 147 to win and they got there, Hutton playing a wonderful innings of 105 not out. The only other Yorkshire batsman to get into double figures was Leyland with 13 and Yorkshire won by five wickets with the rain just beginning to fall. I will always remember what a wonderful innings it was by Len on a difficult pitch.

Championship cricket certainly drew the crowds in those days and there would be 10,000-15,000 for the first day of a Roses match without any difficulty. I suppose there were not so many other activities in those days and people tended to watch the major sports. Rather than being able to get into a motor-car and set off on a Bank Holiday people would go and watch Yorkshire and Lancashire at Headingley, Bramall Lane, or Old Trafford.

I knew Sutcliffe and Hutton well. I bought my bats from Herbert Sutcliffe's sports shop in Queen Victoria Street in Leeds. My father took me there and Sutcliffe was so friendly. He helped me to get some matches when I was stationed at Catterick during the war.

After Sutcliffe, Hutton was my favourite cricketer. Hutton was the more accomplished batsman but Sutcliffe had a wonderful temperament and his average of 60 in Test match cricket was proof of what a great cricketer he was.

My father was very interested in cricket as a boy, just as I turned out to be. Hirst and Rhodes were two of his favourite cricketers and they had such outstanding records for Yorkshire and England.

Who else did you particularly admire?

Bowes and Verity also stand out a mile as being some of the finest Yorkshire cricketers in my early days along with Leyland, Holmes and Sutcliffe. We produced five or six players to play for England and no doubt they were welded together by Brian Sellers, who was a wonderfully inspiring captain. I certainly owe a debt to Sellers for helping me in many ways. He helped me when I joined the Yorkshire committee in 1954 and particularly when I joined the Test and County Cricket Board Finance Committee for 16 years, which I thoroughly enjoyed.

And I always thought that John Nash was a delightful man and we got along very well together when I was treasurer and he was the club secretary.

Some people believed that Sellers was too rigid once his playing days were over and I think that is true comment. It was wrong of him to sack Close as Yorkshire captain. He was so strong that I think his own personal opinions could be detrimental to the club and he found it difficult to accept change when things around him were changing, but I still have a great admiration for him. His heart and soul were in Yorkshire cricket, there is no doubt about that.

Appleyard and Trueman were obviously very fine cricketers and both of them played in the match against Worcestershire at Scarborough in 1951 which I was asked to captain, as did Close and others.

Yorkshire, of course, in those days played only Yorkshire-born cricketers and I think this had a great unifying effect on the side's performances. I am sorry that it doesn't apply today and I don't think there is the same spirit or unifying effect. On occasions there may have been three or four non-Yorkshire-born players in the side and all probably doing very well but it is still not quite the same as a Yorkshire side full of Yorkshire-born players.

It is one of the great mysteries of cricket why Yorkshire haven't produced as many players of the same international standard as they did in the old days.

When did you first play cricket?

It was at Shrewsbury School where I first learned my cricket. I was away for the war from 1939-46 and when I came back I played league cricket for Leeds and was captain from 1949-62 when we played in the Yorkshire League.

I played on the Headingley ground every other week and other Yorkshire first team venues like Harrogate, York and Hull. Close, Trueman and Illingworth all came into the side at one time or another. I think that when they were doing

National Service and had some free time they were allocated a club by Yorkshire.

I had also been going to the Headingley nets since I was 13 or 14 when George Hirst was in charge. In 1944 I wrote him a letter saying how much I had enjoyed being under his guidance and I got a very nice card back from him.

I played one or two games for Yorkshire Seconds in 1947 when Stanley Raper was captain. I nearly got into the Cambridge University side but didn't. Geoffrey Keighley took over as captain of Yorkshire Seconds for a short time before emigrating to Australia and I was asked in the middle of 1949 if I would succeed him. I did it for two seasons in 1950-1951. I could only do it for two years as I had just qualified as a chartered accountant and I had to give it up in the second year as my boss made me available only for a certain number of matches. It didn't occur to me then that I may one day be asked to be Yorkshire captain.

Which of the younger players do you particularly remember?

Doug Padgett, Ken Taylor and Bryan Stott were all starting out at the time. They were 15 or 16 years of age and they were all wonderful cricketers. I just hope I was able to do something to help them become part of a great team. I certainly think that the grounding they received in the Second XI was a great help to them. They were players of exceptional talent and they certainly developed with two or three seasons of Second XI Cricket.

There were only two players that I wanted to bring to Leeds CC so that they could play regularly at Headingley. One was Trevor Copley and the other was Geoff Boycott when he was 16 or 17.

I can remember quite clearly that I met him in a Barnsley car park and suggested he couldn't do better than play at Headingley where he would be noticed. He did come as an opener and he did very well until he got into the Yorkshire side.

It has never been made public before but I was invited to captain Yorkshire in 1958 before Ronnie Burnet agreed to take on the job. I thought about it for a week but I had just been made a partner in my firm and I had a young family so I said 'no'. Ronnie was asked and he did it very well. He did a wonderful job at a difficult time.

I was elected to the Yorkshire committee in 1954 and served for 30 years until 1984. There were difficult times in the later years over Boycott who was a magnificent batsman as his record proved. I don't want to rake up old sores but to my mind he was the greatest of batsmen but not necessarily the greatest of cricketers. He so often seemed to play for himself rather than for Yorkshire. That was the feeling shared by many people but it is past history now. He was a very successful batsman and is now a very capable commentator. I think he is pretty good.

The early 80s were a particularly difficult time with so many on the committee feeling that strong action was required against Boycott. I was for reconciliation. He was near the end of his playing days and I thought he should have been allowed to go on. I blame myself for not having stuck out as chairman but the feeling in the committee was so strong, particularly on the cricket committee, that I am afraid the majority won the day.

One or two of us were badly hurt by what happened, including Norman Yardley who was club president at the time. I was very close to Norman and we had almost identical views about things and I consulted with him a lot when he was president and I was chairman. He was a man I had the greatest regard for: a fine cricketer with a fine cricket brain and his knowledge of cricket was very good.

What is your opinion on overseas players?

I always liked to think of Yorkshire being for Yorkshire-born cricketers but I suppose it was inevitable that overseas players would come and Sir Lawrence Byford was responsible for the change in policy in opening up the field. We had to be able to compete on equal terms and we were going through a difficult period and not winning the Championship like we used to do.

Even now I would prefer only to have Yorkshire-born players in the side. I was disappointed in 2010 when we signed Herschelle Gibbs from South Africa and Clint McKay from Australia for that season's Twenty20 Cup competition. I found it quite depressing, particularly as the young Yorkshire side were doing so well that season under Andrew Gale.

I think that all the young players that have come through in recent years justifies the setting up of the Academy in the early 1990s. We are now producing a volume of very fine cricketers who have emerged from the Academy and this is proof that it is working.

Why has Yorkshire CCC become perhaps the most famous cricket club in the world?

Yorkshire and cricket seem to gel together for some reason. Yorkshire cricket followers are always arguing about something and we will never stop arguing but the majority of members want a successful Yorkshire side and this applies more to Yorkshire than the other counties. It is difficult to pinpoint the reason but it probably goes right back to Lord Hawke and his run of wonderful successes right from winning the first Championship title in 1893. Success breeds success and like Australians, Yorkshire folk do not like losing.

Yorkshire play the game seriously and I will always remember going to the Headingley nets in 1948 when I was just out of the Army and my firm of chartered accountants let me go for a practice. I remember saying to Maurice Leyland: "I am sorry but I have got to get back to work," and he said: "Hey lad, what do you think that we are doing here?" These are sentiments which that other great coach, Arthur Mitchell, would also have endorsed.

What of the future?

There has been plenty of talk in recent years about a reduction in the amount of Championship cricket but I think it would be a great mistake to reduce the number of county matches. I think young cricketers still have the proud ambition to play for England in a five-day Test match and I don't think they would expect to make a living solely out of Twenty20 cricket alone. It is producing crowds and money but don't let it start ruling cricket and taking up the major part of the summer.

TED LESTER

Scarborough born and bred, Ted Lester has always lived in the seaside resort and he would never, even for a moment, have considered living anywhere else.

A record-breaking batsman with Scarborough Cricket Club, Ted played in 228 first-class matches for Yorkshire between 1945-1956, gaining a regular place in the side in 1948 after averaging 73 the previous season.

Things were rarely quiet when he was at the crease and he passed 1,000 runs in six seasons with his strongly attacking style, his career-best score of 186 being made against Warwickshire at, appropriately, North Marine Road, in 1949 when he added 178 for the fourth wicket with Vic Wilson, who also broke records with the Scarborough club.

Ted finished with 10,912 first-class runs at an average of 34.20 and he scored 25 centuries. He holds the distinction of being the last Yorkshire batsman to make a century in each innings of a Roses match – 125 not out and 132 at Old Trafford in 1948. The previous summer he had struck 126 and 142 at Northampton immediately after hitting 127 against Derbyshire, so becoming the first uncapped Yorkshire batsman to hit three consecutive centuries.

Increasing problems with his feet made it too difficult for him to continue at first class level and in 1958 he took over the captaincy of the Second XI from Ronnie Burnet, who had moved up to lead the First XI. In that initial season his side became the only Yorkshire Seconds' team to top the Minor Counties table and win the play-off.

He was captain for four seasons and he oversaw the development of eight budding England cricketers and eight others who went on to play first team cricket for Yorkshire.

Immediately upon his retirement at the end of 1961 he was appointed first team scorer – a position he held until giving way to John Potter at the end of 1988 – and in 1972 he became the first scorer to pass the Association of Cricket Umpires' test. The organisation has since had Scorers added to its title and Ted has served as its President for many years. He was made a life member of Yorkshire CCC in 1982 and is also a life member of Scarborough CC.

Did you learn your cricket at an early age?

I learned my cricket on the beach. I played a bit against the holiday makers. I used to go on the sands and field the ball for them and then they would ask if I wanted to have a bat? Once I had settled in they would often pack their bags and say: 'I am sorry, sonny boy, we will have to go' – and they'd walk off and set up shop further down the beach. I was talking to Jim Kilburn once when he was cricket writer on the Yorkshire Post. He said he used to do exactly the same thing and join in. I thought that was a bit strange. It seemed a bit of an anti-Kilburn thing to do.

I have no idea how or why my interest first started in cricket. My father's *eyesight was not good enough so he never played cricket. No relative ever played cricket. So I just honestly don't know where it came from.*

I joined the Scarborough club as a boy because I was born just opposite the ground. The Trafalgar Road entrance was about 100 yards away from where I lived. I spent a lot of time there as a boy and worked my way into the first team.

How did your early career go?

I played in a couple of two-day friendly games for Yorkshire against Derbyshire in 1945 but my first-class debut that year was against the RAF at Scarborough. I remember it well because I opened the batting with Len Hutton and was bowled without playing a shot. I let the ball go outside off-stump and it came back and knocked the old dolly down. It was the first time and also the last that Len gave me any advice. He just said: 'Make sure you get your pads in the way in future.'

My first Championship match was Yorkshire v Notts at Trent Bridge. It was the last match of 1946 and by then we had already retained the title. I was working in the treasurer's department at Scarborough Town Hall and in the middle of the afternoon a boy came in with a telegram for me and it was from Yorkshire. It said: 'You are selected to play at Brighton, Bournemouth and Trent Bridge.' It was difficult getting time off work to play in all of them so in the end Yorkshire told me I would be playing at Trent Bridge.

I then had my first personal experience of Brian Sellers, whom I had never met before but I had heard plenty about him from the second team lads who had played under him and had said what a bully he was. So I was obviously frightened to death. I travelled from home to Trent Bridge on the Friday night and the boys were coming up from Bournemouth so I had to wait for an hour or two before they arrived. I still didn't meet up with him that night, however, or even first thing next morning.

At Trent Bridge the amateurs stripped downstairs and professionals upstairs. About half an hour before start of play the dressing room attendant came up and said: 'Mr. Sellers wants to see you down in his room.' So that meant walking down the steps from top to bottom to meet him for the first time. How I got down those steps I shall never know, but I did.

I knocked on the door and a booming voice said: 'Come in.' I went in and for five minutes he treated me like a son. He couldn't have been a nicer fellow. I couldn't believe that this was the big bully that everybody had been talking about. And so he then says, the best of luck, blah, blah, blah and that was it.

So on the Monday morning I went out to field and I am fielding at third man and Sellers was fielding in the gully. A wicket fell and Cyril Turner had told me: 'Whatever you do when you are in the field, don't take your eyes off him. If you do and he wants to move you, you are for it.' So when the wicket fell I was still looking at Sellers and then he beckoned me to him and he gave me the biggest rollicking I had ever had. The reason being that I hadn't got my cap on straight!

Ticker Mitchell always pulled his cap over one eye and he had always been a bit of a hero of mine and I wanted to follow what he did and so I thought I would put the cap over one eye. Sellers said: 'You are not playing schoolboy cricket now, you are playing for Yorkshire.' And it went on, the rollicking went on until the next man came to the wicket. What contrasting experiences for me in so short a time. I couldn't believe in view of the way he treated me to begin with that he was the same fellow. But I wouldn't criticise him too much.

Do you think Sellers was too much of a disciplinarian and involved in cricket administration at Yorkshire for too long?

It is a difficult one is that, there are two ways of looking at it. I am a firm believer in the Sellers regime although I didn't like it at the time, I must admit. But I think discipline seems to have gone out of the window now completely.

I can understand someone who is a bit of a disciplinarian like Sellers – and I have never known a bigger one – finding it difficult once he has stopped playing. It must have reflected badly on him when he found he couldn't rule the roost like he used to do, but as far as getting results was concerned he was the best captain I ever played under. And later on when he was cricket chairman, the likes of Close, Illingworth and Trueman must have been difficult to harmonise and pull together. You might say that there were two sides to the Close affair and two sides, also, to Illingworth and the contracts.

When and how did you become a professional with Yorkshire?

In 1947, I averaged exactly 73 for the first team and 73 for the second team and that determined me to turn pro. I was in good nick then, it was an easy game in those days. I was still working at the Town Hall and I knew I had to make my mind up at the end of the season because they had told me I couldn't have any more time off to play cricket. I just didn't know what to do and I left it until the winter of 1948. The Press kept asking, what is he going to do? Is he going to play or is he not? And so it got to the middle of February and the Town Hall were having an outing to Leeds to the pantomime and Yorkshire asked if I could get over to meet them.

I had earlier written to them and asked if I packed my job up at the Town Hall could they guarantee that I would have a regular first team place? The chairman said he appreciated my position and understood the difficulties but they couldn't give me a cap straight away. They decided that if I took full-time employment, as soon as I got another century they would give me my cap. I shook hands and that was that, nothing in writing. I went to Lord's for the first match and got double figures. The next game was against the Aussies at Bradford. We were bowled out for 71 and 89 and I got 16 in the second innings and was the second highest scorer.

So that was two matches that had gone. I then went to Oxford, failed in the first innings and managed to get 149 in the second innings. I came off the field and I wondered if that was going to count. Norman Yardley gave me my cap that same afternoon. So it did count. That was something that Geoff Boycott could never manage, a century against Oxford! Yorkshire were as good as their word and I thought about this whenever players said they didn't trust the committee. But I did.

Yardley was our captain and a nicer fellow you could not wish to meet. I never had any trouble at all except once when we played at Bradford against Surrey in 1949. I was 40-odd not out, we needed four to win and I was on strike. I thought I am going to get 50 here if it is the last thing I do. So Stan Squires was bowling his *off-spin and I thought, right he is going over the top. So I tried to go over the top and holed out. And I am walking out and who is next in to bat but Norman. And he says: 'C***.' And that is all he said. I thought he could have done worse, he could have hit me with the bat!*

Was playing under Norman Yardley an enjoyable experience?

Yes, it was. It was a different experience to playing under Sellers but as for winning matches... The trouble with Norman was he was too nice a bloke and he got one or two players who took advantage of him. It was impossible to have played under two more different types than Sellers and Yardley. I don't know the ins and outs of it in those days but Alex Coxon got kicked out and he got 100 wickets. So why? I don't think Norman Yardley was behind that but Sellers could have been. He probably didn't like his attitude and the way he carried on, but there has never been a better trier for Yorkshire. When Alex got picked for England, Yardley said to me: 'Well, at least England will have one trier'.

In 1949 Yorkshire finished joint first with Middlesex but perhaps weren't at their best. You say one or two were difficult to handle. Did that reflect in results do you think?

It was a difficult season in 1949. We won seven of the last eight games. The feeling in the side was that we wanted to win it for Norman so that we could show we didn't need Sellers. Sellers was still a major force although not playing. Sellers was captain a lot in 1948 because Yardley was playing for England. The difference when Sellers played rather than Norman was incredible. We won matches and lost matches in 1948 but I think it would have been a far different outcome if Sellers had played all season. I think we would have won the title instead of coming fourth. Once Sellers had gone we had Norman full-time in 1949 and I think the boys probably enjoyed it more because discipline under Sellers was hard to imagine.

Also in 1949 at the Cambridge University match at Fenner's, Close, Trueman and Lowson all made their Yorkshire debuts. That was a significant time. I wonder why all three played in that game? I said Closey was the best 18-year-old cricketer I had ever seen and I had no reason to change my mind over the years. He was incredible. I think he would have been even better if he had not gone to Australia in 1950-1951. He had got so much potential, really, but he was badly handled in Australia and became dispirited. He said he cried himself to sleep many times in Australia – and it's not quite Close, that, really. I am certain if he had never been to Australia he would never have been out of the England side. I think he should have been in the England side a lot more in any case. They had an unfortunate habit of upsetting the wrong people.

Fred never had an extended run with us. He came in the side and had to go into the Forces and was in and out for quite a while before becoming established. He wasn't always a confident lad and it took him a year or two to really settle in. During this time we were finishing second or third to Surrey every year. I think Surrey were rather a good side and I don't think there was any great feeling that we were unlucky. I think it was accepted that although we tried like hell to upset them they were top on merit.

Who were the up and coming prospects?

In 1956, Billy Sutcliffe became captain and two years later I became second team captain and I enjoyed it very much. I had a pretty good side with a lot of promising young lads in it in 1958. We won the Minor Counties and had the likes of Philip Sharpe, Brian Bolus, Jackie Birkenshaw, Mel Ryan, Don Wilson, Bob Platt, and Doug Padgett. We also had Brian Bainbridge and I thought he was the best off-spinner we had, even better than Illingworth and Birkenshaw. I once talked to Trevor Bailey about him at Harrogate after he had bowled Essex out and I said what did you think of Bainbridge? He replied: 'It is a pity he played instead of Illy. I can always get after Illy but I can never get after Bainbridge.' In the first innings he had Trevor lbw for one and in the second innings he bowled him for ten. He took 6-58 in the first innings and 6-53 in the second. It was a pity he didn't carry on as I think he would have made the grade. He received an offer from Northants but decided to stick to his everyday job.

In the two years before I took over the captaincy and was not featuring in the first team, I got the job as senior pro to look after Ronnie Burnet. He was obviously one of those earmarked for the captaincy of the first team and they wanted him to get to know a bit more about it. When he got the first team captaincy it was automatic promotion for me. Sellers told me I could have the second team job for as long as I wanted it. So I said thanks very much. And if the scoring job hadn't come through I don't know how long I would have kept it.

That was the one thing about Sellers, I must admit, I couldn't have had a better chairman. He was super. I used to like to take the lads out now and again to see what they felt about things and Keith Gillhouley said he got better paid playing for the second team than he did for the first team. I asked Sellers about it and he said: 'Cheeky bugger, they are never satisfied.' But Keith got the pay rise next match. That was the sort of man that Sellers was because he realised that Gillhouley had a fair case.

Boycott first appeared in the side under me in around 1959. I remember when Boycs was picked for the second team and another player said: 'I gather Geoff Boycott's playing in the next match.' I said yes. He said: 'We don't want that so-and-so in our side. We have a happy side here.' I said to him: 'I can assure you that if there is any trouble he is out and I never had a scrap of bother with him. He was as good as gold.'

Boycott's reputation began early then if there were people at that time in his career who didn't want him in the side?

There was that feeling but I had no real problems with him at all. The first small difficulty I had was either in his first match or second. We were playing somewhere in Yorkshire, I think it was against Warwickshire Seconds, and we weren't doing very well. We had no chance of winning and were trying to save the game. When I went in fielders used to drop back a bit. A slow left-armer was bowling and I hit him to long off and said: 'Come one.' I got down to that end and Boycs was still there, he hadn't moved. I said: 'You had better go because you are in trouble if you don't,' so he went.

The throw went over the top of the bowler and Boycs got in. I often wonder what would have happened if he had run me out. So that was the only bit of bother I ever had with him.

How did the scoring come about?

I was Second XI captain in '60 and '61 and I had never given scoring a thought at all. But at the Scarborough festival I was having a drink with John Nash after the game and he said that when he got back to Leeds he was going to have to sort the scoring job out because Cyril Turner couldn't do it any more, he was sort of finished. So I said that I might be interested and he said he would put my name forward. I never heard another word until the middle of November when I learned I had got the job if I wanted it. It meant I could extend my Yorkshire career for a long time and so I decided to pack up playing altogether.

You have either seen or played with the great Yorkshire openers in Sutcliffe, Hutton and Boycott. What order of merit would you place them in?

I can't tell you because I don't know. I have thought about this many times and all I can say is that Herbert would have to go in at No 3. It is very nearly impossible. Talk to some like Illy and Close and they would say Boycott doesn't register but I won't have that. They seemed to think that Boycs wasn't quite as good as the other two and I find it is very difficult to draw the line and say who is the best and who isn't. They were all very good players at a different time. Herbert, what I saw of him, was a good off-side player, a good pad player. He used to leave a lot outside the off-stump which he wouldn't have been allowed to do with the new lbw rule. I think Boycs was a better player of quick bowling than Len was. You can make a case out whichever way you want. I would certainly want all three in my side.

What about your earliest memories?

I remember the Aussies coming to Scarborough to play Leveson-Gower's XI in 1930. My parents were taking in visitors at the time and one of the visitors collected me from school and took me down to North Marine Road to see Don Bradman. Now whether I can actually remember it or whether people just talked about it a lot I don't know, but he made 90-odd after being dropped by Rhodes in the first over. They argued in the ground that he had dropped him on purpose which is absolute rubbish. Bradman was always a schoolboy idol of mine. I used to read about him and what he did in Australia and this was my first recollection of seeing him play.

George Hirst was the best coach I have ever seen and the best coach I ever had. I think it was about 1936 or 1937 that I read in the local paper that Hirst would be coming to Scarborough to coach schoolboys in the afternoon and senior players at night. I had no invitation so I went down to the nets and fielded the ball and

George eventually said: *'Would you like an innings?'* And that started it off.

He said come along tomorrow, sort of style. He was the first to notice my ability. My school wouldn't let me play for Scarborough first team then because they wanted me to play for them. I played regularly in 1938 and we won the Yorkshire Council in 1939. Vic Wilson played in that year. The play-off was on the Saturday that war was declared. We spent a couple of hours on Doncaster station with kids going all over the place in trains as evacuees. We won by nine wickets and I didn't contribute anything.

Looking back over the time what players most typified Yorkshire cricket?

I think George Hirst must go out as No 1. I think one of the reasons why we were so successful before the war was because of his coaching. He coached on what was there which is what not many coaches do. I would put him as No 1 as player, coach and Yorkshire involvement. He was a super fellow.

Wilfred Rhodes on the other hand would never give credit to anybody really. He would never encourage a youngster. Before the war I played in a Colts trial match at York in which the umpires were Hirst and Rhodes. You got a fair idea of the two of them then, with one being most helpful and the other most critical. I don't think Rhodes was too concerned about other people. It is difficult to say because I only saw them early on.

Where do you think Yorkshire cricket is going now?

I think they are improving now. It seems as if they have turned the corner. I get that impression. I haven't been to Headingley for quite a few years now but from a distance it seems all right. I have seen Adam Lyth once or twice down here at Scarborough and have thought what a good player he looks.

I think they seem a more settled side now and there is no reason why they shouldn't progress because they have good players in all departments.

Has county cricket still got a place in the cricket calendar?

I think too many people are looking at Twenty20 cricket and not giving enough consideration to the proper game. I am still in favour of four-day cricket and I think now we have too many one-day games. I would hate to be a cricket coach these days because I don't know how you should coach. The emphasis is now on comic shots and I don't know how you can coach them.

DEREK HODGSON

You have had a great affection for Yorkshire cricket since boyhood. When did you first realise that it was something very special?

Young cricketers in Redcar or Wombwell or Abbeydale will have little appreciation of just how big Yorkshire were 75 years ago. Whatever Yorkshire or

Yorkshire's players did was national news: a modern comparison would be Manchester United. Let me give you a couple of examples.

My schooldays were spent in Bedfordshire, a Morley family steeped in Yorkshire cricket. Over breakfast in my grandparents' cottage in Ampthill I would listen to my father and grandfather discussing Yorkshire's performances as recorded in the morning newspaper.

Granddad would often go on about Rhodes and Hirst, dad would talk about Bowes and Verity and both were intrigued by a new young batsman called Hutton.

I vaguely remember when Yorkshire were bowled out for a low score at one of the lesser county grounds and so impressed was the newspaper that the story ran on the front page.

One morning in 1938 I was called in from the cottage garden and told to stand by the radio and NOT MAKE A NOISE. At that time Bradman's Test record score of 334 was the Mount Everest of cricket. Would anyone, ever, climb it? Hutton, a 21-year-old from Pudsey, was about to accomplish that very feat and pass Bradman.

Such significance was probably lost on an eight-year-old. I uttered not a sound until a great round of applause was heard on the wireless, as we then called a radio. Dad and granddad were clapping and I could hear the sound of bottles being opened in the kitchen. One writer was to describe the moment later as 'the time the British Empire stood still.' All over the cricket world – including liners at sea – crowds gathered around to listen for the runs that broke the record.

Move on ten years and the station adjutant at the RAF Hospital, Ely, organised a coach trip to watch Cambridge University play Yorkshire at Fenner's. The bus was full. He told us: 'You are going to see the new Lindwall. His name is Truman, like the president.' F.S. Trueman, with an e, was not the only unfamiliar name on the scorecard. Also, there were F.A. Lowson and D.B. Close. The new Lindwall was quick, aggressive but very wayward. Frank Lowson made a few runs and never looked back after that. The big impression was made by the 18-year-old Close.

My other memory of a gloriously sunny day under Cambridge trees, looking towards an old pavilion alas long since demolished, is of the size of the crowd and of overhearing a group of students a few seats away. They had hoped to see Hutton but, as one said: 'We don't get much chance to see Yorkshire down here.'

The defining week in a professional cricketer's life was all too often his benefit match and the overwhelming choice of opposition, from 1920 to 1970, to draw the biggest crowd and raise the maximum income, was Yorkshire. But since that time the world, through communication by road and television, has grown so much smaller as cricket has been strait-jacketed into a TV screen. Cricketers are immensely better off and more money than ever flows into the game – but are small boys called in from country gardens to listen for a score?

CHAPTER TWENTY

TIMES OF CHANGE

On the face of it, things appeared to be pretty much the same for Yorkshire in 1946 with the return of first-class cricket on a full-scale basis. They retained the Championship title after having won it in three consecutive years leading up to the war and Sellers was again their captain. The weather was not much different to usual either, with rain causing many a disruption, but the inclement conditions did not deter the fans and home gate receipts of almost £23,000 were a record for the club.

Of course, some changes were inevitable and obvious, the one causing most sadness being the absence of Verity who had been killed in action. Other familiar faces were missing, too, the likes of Sutcliffe, Mitchell and Wood all having retired. Bowes was still very much a part of the scene but he was not the feared fast bowler he used to be, three years in Italian and German prisoner-of-war camps having caused him to shed four and a half stone by the time he tasted freedom again. Now he bowled under medical supervision and had moved down from markedly quick to medium-paced.

Other changes had still to be made but were, nevertheless, in the air, Leyland, Barber and Turner all deciding to call it a day at the end of the summer, but one of the new faces who excelled to a remarkable degree in 1946 was, in fact, an old hand.

Left-arm spinner Arthur Booth played in two matches for Yorkshire in 1931 but this fine bowler was then kept out of the side by Verity, who had no equal, and it was only Verity's failure to return from the war that presented Booth with an extended opportunity to prove his worth 15 years later at the age of 43.

He responded to the challenge with such vigour and in such style that even Verity himself would have been satisfied with the outcome, which was 111 first-class wickets at 11.61 runs apiece, 84 of his victims coming in the Championship at 11.90. Hardly surprising that he should top the bowling averages, leaving the likes of Bowes, Ellis Robinson, Smailes and new arrival Alex Coxon in his wake.

Startling figures, indeed, but he could not emulate them the following season when he was plagued by rheumatic illness and his Yorkshire career was at a sudden end. He remained immensely proud – and rightly so – of his Indian summer and a couple of years or so before his death in 1974 I bumped into him, without realising who he was, at a Bradford League Priestley Cup final which I was covering for the Telegraph & Argus and he reminisced after the match about his golden year. Booth served on the Lancashire committee in 1970 and at one stage was also a scout for Warwickshire, which may have been a reason for his presence at the Bradford League's premier event of the season.

Booth and Coxon did more than could be expected of them in their first full summers but three other apprentices with greater futures ahead of them barely scratched the surface in 1946, captain-in-the-making Vic Wilson only twice reaching double figures in eight Championship innings, spin-wizard elect Johnny Wardle bowling just three overs without reward on his debut against Worcestershire at Headingley in his only appearance of the summer, and Willie Watson mustering a mere 221 runs with a top score of 43 in 13 Championship knocks. There was something about Watson's batting, however, that caught the eye and he was chosen for a Test trial at Canterbury without so far having a half-century to his name.

The damp weather caused runs to be at a premium in 1946 and only Hutton and Barber topped the 1,000 mark but nearly every other batsman chipped in with useful contributions at exactly the right time, and none more so than the skipper who enjoyed his best season with the blade and ended just short of the 1,000 first-class runs he undoubtedly deserved.

The last game marked the Championship debut against Nottinghamshire at Trent Bridge of Ted Lester who, as already noted, was to have one of the longest continuous associations on and off the field with Yorkshire. He made a workmanlike contribution of 47 in a match which the champions would most probably have won by an innings if rain had not intervened at the point where Booth had already added three wickets to his earlier analysis of 5-50.

Mitchell was no longer a working part of the team in 1946 but a wise decision meant that he was very much a part of the club's future. The committee appointed him as Yorkshire's first full-time coach and it meant that he was on call for various duties all the year round whereas Hirst, coach at both Eton and Yorkshire, had not been quite so freely available.

Despite all the changes going on, Yorkshire still played like the Championship-winning outfit they were in 1946 but they lacked the same staying power the following season which marked the start of a decline within the team that was to last for over a decade.

Strong leader and master tactician that he was, Sellers was unable to halt the slide into eighth place in the Championship table, Yorkshire's lowest placing in 37 years. Coxon, with 74 wickets in the competition, and Wardle, with 70, again showed their increasing authority as did Watson, with 1,301 runs, and Lester, with 657 in seven matches which included the splendid performance at Northampton when Yorkshire won by 351 runs in two days. Lester, on a pitch on which everyone else struggled, lashed 126 and 142 while the young and raw fast bowler Ron Aspinall, who later became a popular and well-respected umpire, grabbed 8-42 and 6-23 to give him overall figures of 14 -65.

Bowes, batteries now not fully charged, still headed the averages with 61 wickets at 16.98 and although there was sadness at his pending retirement there was joy at the resounding success from a financial point of view of his benefit match against Middlesex at Headingley, which drew in 41,000 spectators over the two days which it lasted. Unfortunately, Yorkshire lost the game by 87 runs and this was almost entirely due to the brilliance of Bill Edrich, who stroked 70 and 102 on a tricky surface.

Another link with Yorkshire's great side at the turn of the century was broken in 1947 with the passing of F.S. Jackson, who had taken over as the club's president in 1939 following the death the previous year of his old team-mate and captain, Lord Hawke.

The old guard from those glory years still had a powerful representative in the modern Yorkshire, however, in Tom Taylor, who was elected as Jackson's successor in 1948 and he continued to serve as president with great distinction until his own death 12 years later and just a few days before his 82nd birthday.

It says much for the loyalty and devotion shown to Yorkshire by Hawke, Jackson and Taylor that once their distinguished playing days were over they should remain leading figures in the club right to the very end of their days.

Cricket was by now becoming a game of more professionals and fewer amateurs but Yorkshire appointed another amateur captain in 1948 and no-one, then or since, ever had a wrong word to say about Norman Yardley. The number of top cricketers born and bred in Yorkshire of whom it can be said never incurred the wrath of any of their team-mates may be counted on the fingers of one hand, but Yardley was one of them.

Whether captaining Yorkshire or England, Yardley was the perfect gentleman to all under his command and some will say that had there been a tougher side to his nature he may even have got a bit more out of his men at county level.

Yardley's quiet demeanour perhaps masked what a talented sportsman he was. Another product of St Peter's School at York, where he three times headed the batting averages, he moved on to Cambridge University, captaining them in 1938 and also gaining a Blue at hockey. He was a fine rugby player at St Peter's and later six times North of England squash champion.

A stylish and fluent batsman and an extremely effective medium-pace bowler, Yardley was in good all-round form when he took on the Yorkshire captaincy, having topped 1,000 runs the previous season despite being absent during the five Tests in which he led England against South Africa.

And what a busy summer 1948 proved to be for him as he captained not only Yorkshire but also England against Bradman's mighty Australians, who won four of the Tests with the other being drawn.

Yorkshire showed some improvement on 1947 by finishing fourth, Glamorgan wearing the crown for the first time, and they may have been a more settled unit but for the chopping and changing at the helm which was forced upon them through circumstances. When Yardley was on England duty, Sellers was often in his old familiar role but when business commitments did not permit this, Smailes took over.

The team did not play as well as individual statistics may suggest and runs were not always scored and wickets taken at the most essential times. Hutton again dominated the middle with Watson, Halliday and Lester also achieving 1,000 runs, and Wardle took almost twice as many wickets as anyone else — 129 in the Championship and 148 first-class.

On occasions, Yorkshire were able to demonstrate their power even when some of their best players were elsewhere, the second Ashes Test at Lord's being a case in point. Yardley and Hutton were joined in his only Test by Coxon, a whole-hearted cricketer of fiery temperament who gave his all for Yorkshire for five years before being somewhat mysteriously sacked, as Ted Lester has indicated. Despite missing this trio they still beat Kent by six wickets at Bradford but in the next game against Derbyshire at Chesterfield they lost by 233 runs on the first innings and just held out for a draw, George Pope taking 6-12 in the first innings when they were bowled out for 44 and 4-13 in the second as Yorkshire dipped to 37 for six before stumps were drawn. Pope had also contributed 73 to Derbyshire's 277 which would have been a considerably larger score but for Wardle's 8-87.

The only tangible success for Yorkshire under Yardley came in 1949 and then it was not undiluted joy because they were forced to share the Championship with Middlesex. Even so, a side still in transition showed plenty of guts in getting over an indifferent start to win their last six matches and it was a particularly commendable effort because everyone knew that even one slip during this tense period would spell the end of their title ambitions.

Yorkshire, in all, won 14 of their 26 Championship matches – and lost only two compared to Middlesex's three – but it was the fixture with Cambridge University at Fenner's which contained something really noteworthy, although nobody at the time was aware of it.

Harry Halliday hit a century and Wardle claimed five wickets in a comfortable nine-wicket win but a closer examination of the scorecard reveals that it was also the game in which two giants of Yorkshire cricket made their county debuts in Brian Close and Fred Trueman and they were joined by another player of considerable significance in Frank Lowson.

How could whatever spectators were present have imagined for a moment that they were catching a first glimpse of one of Yorkshire and England's greatest bowlers at the same time as seeing one of their greatest captains who would also be one of the bravest cricketers ever to step on a field?

Trueman and Close were in the action straight away because they shared the new ball, Close being a quick bowler in those early days (quicker, he has claimed, than Trueman) but it was Fred who struck first blood by dismissing opener Robert Morris. Each ended up with two wickets and Close also bagged two to Trueman's one second time around. Close, batting at No 5, scored 28 before being caught and bowled by Mike Stevenson who in later life reported on cricket for The Daily Telegraph and was not slow to impart his moment of cricketing fame to Press box audiences around the country.

The best individual performance from this illustrious trio, however, probably came from Lowson who made up for his first innings failure by scoring an unbeaten 78 as Yorkshire quickly chased down their 164 target. Lowson went on to enjoy a successful Yorkshire career between 1949-1958, scoring almost 14,000 runs, and hitting 30 centuries, and he represented England on seven occasions. This Bradford-born son of Scottish parents, who moved to Yorkshire so that Frank Snr could play soccer for Bradford Park Avenue, proved to be such a high-quality batsman that spectators sometimes mistakenly thought it was Hutton they were watching at the crease.

FRED TRUEMAN

Although Trueman first appeared for Yorkshire in 1949 he did not truly arrive for another year or two yet but when he did he hogged the stage like few have done either before or since.

Not only that, but he identified with the man in the street to a greater extent than any other Yorkshire cricketer and he was revered in all parts of the county. They liked his brushes with authority, they liked the way this miner's son from Stainton, near Maltby, left the coal pits behind him and went on to rub shoulders with the world's cricketing elite and they liked how he inflicted carnage and often terror among opposing batsmen, whether it be for Yorkshire or England.

Born in a coalmining community in South Yorkshire but laid to rest in the graveyard at Bolton Priory after the historic church had been packed to the rafters on a warm summer's day for his funeral service in 2006, the lifestyle of Fredericks Sewards Trueman may have changed dramatically over his 75 years but he remained, in his own proud words, "t'finest fast bowler that ever drew breath". Few would disagree – and fewer still would have argued against this assertion in front of the great man himself.

We are reaching a time in Yorkshire's history when much of the team's character and uniqueness had already been shaped but Trueman's contribution to these special qualities was just as great as anybody who had gone before him.

Here was a young man who ticked all the boxes that the majority of the Yorkshire cricketing public wanted. This was no fancy pants with a clipped accent that went down well with the MCC, this was a full-blooded fast bowler with a jet black mane who wore his flannels and shirt like everyday working clothes yet in them still managed a run-up and bowling action which was a thing of rare beauty.

It was three years after his Yorkshire debut as a raw 18-year-old that Fred exploded on to the Test scene with blistering pace at Headingley to reduce India to four wickets lost – three of them to the young Tyke – before a run had appeared on the board. He went on to gather in 29 wickets in that five-match series at an average of 13.31 and his eight for 31 haul at Old Trafford remained the best of his career for England.

Commitments with the RAF and a preference on occasions to choose Scarborough-born Bill Foord ahead of him, meant that Fred did not become a regular fighting force with Yorkshire until 1954, although by then he had demonstrated beyond any doubt that he was no tearaway but a man with the flair and personality for the big occasion – and one who loved performing in front of the big crowds that went with them. He showed this in 1953 when, ignored for the first four drawn Ashes Tests, he was drafted in at The Oval and took four first innings wickets for 86 to restrict Australia to 275 and pave the way for the great England victory which followed.

Fred was among the very first cricketers to have what is perceived by the media these days to be star quality and how Yorkshire and England revelled in his moments of triumph, particularly against Australia. On his home ground in 1961 he reduced his pace to take five wickets for no runs in 24 balls with unplayable off-cutters and in the final Ashes Test at The Oval in 1964 he became the first bowler in Test history to claim 300 wickets upon Neil Hawke edging to Colin Cowdrey in the slips.

In all, Fred played in 67 Tests, taking 307 wickets, and in all first-class matches he scooped up 2,304 wickets at 18.29 runs apiece, 1,745 of his victims being for

Yorkshire at 17.12.

It goes without saying that he was a driving force in Yorkshire's seven Championship wins during his illustrious career in which he placed four hat-tricks, ten or more wickets in a match on 25 occasions and five wickets or more in an innings 126 times.

Upon his retirement from Yorkshire in 1968, Fred unexpectedly went on to play in half-a-dozen John Player League matches for Derbyshire in 1972 before taking his final on-the-field bow but cricket remained a huge part of his life and his fame stayed with him.

He became a much-loved part of the Test Match Special team and his puzzlement over much of what was happening in the modern game delighted his fellow commentators and listeners alike.

Fred joined the Yorkshire committee as a Craven district representative in 1979 and, inevitably, went on to serve on the cricket sub-committee but these were increasingly difficult times, with the pro-Geoff Boycott faction diametrically opposed to those who ran the club, and it was a bitter blow to Fred when he was voted off the committee in favour of Skipton printer and Boycott campaigner, Peter Fretwell, in the 1984 uprising.

Fred and Geoff in later years narrowed the gulf which had sprung up between them, but Fred's pride remained wounded by his rejection at the hands of Yorkshire members and his heart and soul were never in Yorkshire present and future to the same degree that they had been in Yorkshire past.

To the man in the street, however, and to those cricketers who had been privileged to play either with him or against him, Fred remained a towering figure that no amount of internal bickering could bring down.

In March, 2010, a bronze statue of Fred by the Yorkshire sculptor, Graham Ibbeson, was unveiled by Fred's widow, Veronica, on the Leeds-Liverpool Canal Basin in Skipton, and at Headingley in late summer the lower tier of the Carnegie Pavilion was named after him. In the following year, some of his past deeds were brought to life in the new cricket museum at Headingley Carnegie, thus ensuring that his memory will live on for future generations.

CHAPTER TWENTY-ONE

SECOND BEST

Until they won the Championship title again in 1959, Yorkshire were very much second best in the 50s, apart from on a couple of occasions when they were considerably worse than that.

This, of course, was the decade dominated by arch-rivals Surrey, who walked off with the spoils for a record seven successive seasons from 1952-1958 and had it not been for their presence Yorkshire would not have suffered nine years of famine.

Not that Yorkshire looked lightweight when it came to a comparison of the giants which both sides were able to field during this period. But Surrey gelled much better under their captain, Stuart Surridge, whose leadership skills were the equal of those exhibited for Yorkshire by Sellers before the war.

Surridge was captain from 1952-1956 and Surrey walked off with the Championship in each of those five seasons with Yorkshire finishing second on three occasions, as they had also done in 1951 when Warwickshire wore the crown.

The start of the 50s was marked by the sharing of the Championship title between the emerging Surrey and Lancashire with Yorkshire snapping at the heels of the pair of them.

Yorkshire stacked up the runs in 1950, with Hutton, Lowson, Halliday and Vic Wilson all making it beyond the 1,000 mark in the Championship and with Yardley and Lester joining them in all first-class matches for the county. Remarkably, a seventh name would have been added in Willie Watson had he been available earlier than August but the gifted cricket and soccer professional in the summer months up to then was in South America with England's World Cup football team.

Upon changing out of soccer shorts and stepping into cricket flannels, Watson marked his return to Yorkshire by hitting 122 in the six-wicket win over Somerset at Taunton and two further centuries followed on his way to heading the county's Championship averages with 636 runs in just 11 innings at 70.66.

Of the trio who made their debuts together the previous season, the one to bloom most spectacularly was Lowson, who stroked over 2,000 runs in all matches and established himself as Hutton's regular opening partner when the senior man was not on the Test scene.

The bowling was dominated by Wardle, by now having satisfied everyone that there would be no interruption in Yorkshire's long line of great left-arm spinners, and he weighed in with 144 Championship victims and 172 all told, followed by the hard-working Coxon.

If a left-arm spinner were to take 100-plus wickets in a season for Yorkshire these days, it would not worry the club a jot had they no other experienced slow bowler to call upon. It did in those days, however, and with Close generally not there to bowl his off-breaks because of National Service and injury, the club promoted Eddie Leadbeater from the Second XI to see how he would fare with his orthodox leg-breaks. He responded superbly with a total of 87 first-class wickets and went on to earn an England place on the 1951-1952 tour of India, playing in two of the Test matches.

Leadbeater did not play frequently for Yorkshire after 1952 but he still finished up with 201 wickets from his 81 matches. He was their only regular leg-spinner until the emergence of Adil Rashid in 2006 and many would say he richly deserved a first team cap but it never came his way. He continued to bamboozle batsmen in the Huddersfield League into his 60s and Bob Platt was among the former team-mates to attend his funeral when he died in the spring of 2011.

Just as the match against Cambridge University at Fenner's in 1949 became significant because of the three Yorkshire debutants, so the 1950 fixture with Scotland in Edinburgh saw the introduction to first team cricket of a Yorkshire bowler who stands comparison with the greatest the game has ever seen.

Sharing the new ball with Ron Aspinall was Bob Appleyard, from the Bradford suburb of Wibsey, who made a satisfactory start to his enhanced status with five wickets in the match for 41 runs. This was good enough for him to retain his place in the next match against Surrey at The Oval and Peter May was among his early successes in a first innings return of 4-47, Yorkshire going on to win by seven wickets.

Appleyard stayed in the side for the visit of Gloucestershire to Hull and he picked up a couple of wickets in the innings victory but it was not until the following summer that Yorkshire were fully to appreciate what an extraordinary player they had in their midst.

They were not long in making this discovery because in 1951 Appleyard scythed his way through batsmen like a knife through butter and to this day he remains the only bowler in the world ever to claim 200 first-class wickets in his first season.

BOB APPLEYARD

By normal standards, Appleyard was not a quick bowler, although he opened the bowling, and neither was he slow. He bowled sharp off-spin on an immaculate length to begin with and he could also swing the ball in and get disconcerting bounce. Never satisfied that further improvement was beyond him, he developed the leg-cutter after noting what had happened to one delivery when his grip on that particular ball had changed accidentally.

Bob's achievements in 1951 were straight out of the pages of fiction and they were made all the more incredible by the fact, not known then, that even at the height of his success he was already beginning to suffer with some of the symptoms that turned out to be the tuberculosis which ate so deeply into his career.

Feeling increasingly ill, he managed only the first match of the 1952 season before the disease took a grip and he spent the next 11 months in hospital where his surgeon, Geoffrey Wooler, removed the upper half of his left lung. The complex operation was a complete success and half a century later the surgeon and the cricketer were re-united at the launch of Bob's amazing biography, No Coward

Soul, by Stephen Chalke and Derek Hodgson.

After two years out of the game, Bob returned with a will of iron and became a key bowler with England, his resolve and determination never greater than on Hutton's Ashes-winning tour of Australia in 1954-55 when he topped the Test and tour averages, despite Tyson and Statham being in their pomp.

Further health problems brought his career to an untimely halt in 1958 and great though his Yorkshire and England figures were they would have been better still had he been able to enjoy a normal span of playing activity.

A successful business career then limited his involvement with Yorkshire for a while but he came to the fore again during the upheavals of the 1980s and he joined the general committee as a Bradford district representative in 1984, moving on to the cricket committee two years later and serving on it under Brian Close until 1993.

In 1991 he was made an honorary life member of Yorkshire CCC and he continued to serve as a Bradford representative until coming off the committee in 1994, when it was reduced from 23 district members to 12 with each of the four new districts having three representatives.

A change of policy by Yorkshire in 2006 resulted in the Club's president automatically being chosen from former players with an illustrious past and Bob became the first to be honoured under this system, serving for the new two-year period.

His many notable achievements included his tireless work in establishing the Yorkshire Cricket Academy at Bradford Park Avenue, where he also helped bring back Championship cricket for a while in the mid-1990s, and in being a key figure in the formation of the Sir Leonard Hutton Cricket Foundation which has assisted in the development of scores of budding young cricketers around the county.

Back now to 1951 and this was another season in which Yorkshire were only second best, this time to Warwickshire, despite Appleyard's avalanche of wickets and 99 for Wardle, who represented England in the series against South Africa along with Hutton, Lowson, Watson and wicketkeeper, Don Brennan, who some maintained was Yorkshire's best-ever glove man when stood up to the stumps.

Yorkshire never lost a match on the occasions that Brennan stood in as captain and as well as becoming a Test selector this Bradford wool man went on to play a big part on the county committee which he joined in 1972, serving on the cricket committee from the following year for the next decade or so and being a staunch and outspoken ally of cricket chairman, Ronnie Burnet, during the Boycott revolution.

Yorkshire in 1951 were a smart unit without being the powerhouse they would become towards the end of the 50s but small shoots were continuing to surface around this time which would be seen as mighty oaks in later years.

Raymond Illingworth, for instance, made his debut against Hampshire at Headingley in August and acquitted himself well by scoring 56 in the ten-wicket victory, although the honours chiefly went to Yardley for his unbeaten 183, to Leadbeater for his six wickets in the first innings and to Appleyard for his six in the second.

Illingworth was just turned 19 on his first appearance and he was already making a name for himself in the Bradford League with his home club of Farsley, to whom he has remained unflinchingly loyal down the years. Long after his eminent days of playing and captaining Yorkshire, Leicestershire and England were over, he was happy to be groundsman at Red Lane, tending the square and outfield with the same care he took on his own garden.

I have chosen in this book not to do separate profiles on Yorkshire's captains because they are very much part of the on-going plot in the club's history and suffice it to say that the likes of Illingworth, Close and Boycott have crammed so much into their careers that several books have already been written on each of them.

Illingworth did not bowl on that debut against Hampshire but, of course, the master off-spinner/batsman became one of only eight players for Yorkshire to perform the exceptional double of scoring over 10,000 runs and taking 500 wickets. In his case it was considerably more on each count – 14,986 runs and 1,431 wickets.

Close is the only other player since the 1939-1945 war to be in that elite band, with 22,650 runs and 967 wickets, and each of these two old comrades, of course, would have greatly enhanced their already formidable records if Illingworth had not felt forced to move on to Leicestershire and Close to Somerset.

It was entirely appropriate that when Close had served his two years as Yorkshire president from 2008-2009 he should be followed in that office by Illingworth, the pair of them having contributed so much to their native county since their teenage years.

A couple of months before Illingworth made his debut another, even younger, player enjoyed his first outing and he was to become a guiding force with Yorkshire over the next half century.

When Bradford-born, Doug Padgett, the Idle and Bowling Old Lane batsman, stepped on to the field against Somerset at Taunton, on June 6, 1951, at 16 years and 321 days, he became the youngest cricketer ever to play for Yorkshire and this most correct of technicians held on to the tag for 30 years until giving way to Paul Jarvis at 16 years and 75 days.

The latest teenage wonder is Leeds-born wicketkeeper-batsman Barney Gibson, from Pudsey Congs, who made his debut for Yorkshire against Durham MCCU in 2011 at 15 years and 27 days to become the youngest-ever first-class cricketer in the country.

It has been my good fortune since reporting on Yorkshire cricket to have become on very friendly terms with many of the past and present players and none more so than 'Padge' and his wife Pat.

Padgett, good enough to play for Idle first team in the Bradford League at the age of 13, was an integral part of Yorkshire's great side which scooped seven Championship titles between 1959-1968 and when his first-class career ended in 1971 after 22 uninterrupted seasons he had scored 20,306 runs for his county to place himself 12th in the list of leading scorers.

He then succeeded Arthur Mitchell as Yorkshire coach, a position he held until his retirement, and he further assisted the younger players in their development by taking over the captaincy of the second team.

The second team captaincy in 1951 was taken on by Michael Crawford who did the job jointly the following year with Ronnie Burnet. They continued to bring on many of those who would become household names in the not-too-distant future.

Surrey began their record-breaking run of seven consecutive Championship titles in 1952 and Yorkshire again had to be content with second place but it was a good effort considering they were without Appleyard after the first match and also Coxon, who had been sacked despite his 113 wickets the previous year. In addition, Yorkshire could only occasionally call upon Trueman because his National Service had kicked in.

India must have wished that Trueman had also been unavailable for England but that was not the case and the fiery young fast bowler's fame spread quickly as a consequence of his sensational Headingley debut and his 29 wickets in the series – nine more than his nearest rival, Alec Bedser.

Wardle once more dominated the bowling with 158 Championship wickets and now Close was able to give a helping hand more often, his mix of quick bowling and off-breaks earning him 98 wickets in this competition and 114 in all matches for Yorkshire to become the first player in the country that year to complete the double.

Several other bowlers also rallied to the cause, including Eric Burgin, from Sheffield, and Bill Holdsworth, from Armley, in Leeds, both of whom were to become proud members of the Yorkshire Players' Association when it was formed by Bryan Stott and Geoff Cope in 2005.

The pair were among the first of Trueman's fast bowling partners, so, like others who followed them, they had, as Bob Platt put it, to learn to bowl up the slope and into the wind!

Burgin and Holdsworth had similar careers, each of them starting in 1952 and finishing at the end of the following season. Burgin played in a dozen matches and in his first summer he captured career-best figures of 6-43 against Surrey at Headingley and also claimed 5-20 in the Roses match at Old Trafford when Lancashire were fired out for 65. Holdsworth made his debut against Gloucestershire at Harrogate and finished the season with 15 wickets but he more than doubled that tally the following year when he began on a high note by taking 5-21 in the opening match against Essex at Hull.

Both went on to be outstandingly successful in the leagues and Burgin was also a good footballer, who once captained York City. Neither would claim to be among the greatest bowlers Yorkshire have ever produced but both did a fine job in times of change and are very much a part of the Yorkshire tapestry.

Len Hutton and his England side added to the general euphoria in Coronation year by winning back the Ashes but Yorkshire in 1953 were quite dreadful, sliding down the Championship table and into 13th place. It was their worst effort since 1892.

The batting was hardly to blame because six of the side each managed in excess of 1,000 runs and it was the bowling which felt the strain through the continuing absence of Appleyard, the limited availability of Trueman because of National

Service, plus soccer injuries taking such a toll on Close, who played professionally for Leeds United, Arsenal and Bradford City, that he barely appeared at all.

Wardle managed 100 wickets again but the margin between him and the rest of the bowlers was a wide one, although Illingworth had matured enough to claim 69 dismissals and there were 54 for Scarborough-born Bill Foord who was another of Trueman's hard-working pace partners.

Team spirit around this time may not have been at its best and reports have suggested that some of the senior players did not always make the younger ones feel at home in the dressing room. Wardle, for one, was not the easiest of people for everyone to get along with – although some cherished his advice and none doubted his ability – and Yardley may not have had a tough enough manner to deal with any agitators. True, Yorkshire were not sufficiently strong to challenge the might of Surrey but dropping like a stone to 13th place indicates all was not well either on or off the field.

It was, however, back to second place in 1954 and the surge up the table was largely due to the return of Appleyard and the greater availability of Trueman, each of them taking over 100 wickets. Close was also fit enough to contribute important runs and wickets but the feeling still remained that this was a team of talented individuals rather than a side which achieved results through unity of purpose.

There was sadness and an acute sense of great loss at the start of the season when one of the strongest links with the past was severed during the opening Championship match with Gloucestershire at Bristol when it was learned that George Hirst had died. Yorkshire responded in the best possible way by winning the game by 80 runs, Close with 6-86 and Wardle with 4-24 wrecking the Gloucestershire second innings.

In this same game, Joe Lister made his debut for Yorkshire and he also played in the next fixture at Taunton but that was the extent of his first-class career with his native county. It was far from his final involvement with the club, however, for he returned as secretary in 1971 and guided it through its most difficult times before dying while still in office 20 years later.

After his two games in 1954, Lister moved on to Worcestershire and played for the Pear county in the same season. He brought stability to the club, captained the second team and was assistant secretary and then secretary before succeeding John Nash as secretary at Headingley.

During the 70s and 80s, running Yorkshire was something of a nightmare, with the pro-Boycott and anti-Boycott factions at each others throats and the club finding themselves involved in various legal actions. Some found Lister difficult to deal with and he was certainly a complex and rather private man but in my opinion he steered the middle course with great skill and never slipped off the tightrope on which he was forced to walk. He could on occasions be terse with the media and anyone else but he also had a generous and milder side to his nature and besides liking him, I thought he did an almost impossible job marvellously well.

From a financial viewpoint, Yorkshire were able to rub their hands in glee in 1955, the long hot summer meaning there were virtually no interruptions to the cricket and the team's rise to second place again resulting in crowds flocking to the home games. Gross gate receipts of £29,466 were a record for the county, members' subscriptions amounted to almost £20,000 and over £7,000 was received from the MCC as a share of the profits from the previous winter's England tour to Australia and New Zealand.

As there always is, there were some shadows among the sunshine and although Appleyard topped the bowling averages, he missed more matches through injury than he played and the same applied to Hutton, whose painful back restricted him to just nine games for Yorkshire and prevented him from appearing at all in the Test series against South Africa. He had been named as captain for all five Tests but his lumbago forced him to stand down just before the series began and Peter May took over the reins.

And so, at the end of 1955, Hutton's noble career came to an end and Yorkshire also had to look for a new captain with the retirement of Yardley, both players to some degree not liking the way that cricket was going with more pressure building up on winning and with fewer concerns about the spirit of the game. Hutton had the additional burden of being the batsman that all England depended upon more than any other and Yardley was expected to bring to Yorkshire the same success which Sellers had achieved. Two great Yorkshiremen could look back with pride, yet at the same time feel relieved to be no longer part of the modern game.

Another whose first team days came to an end was Lester who had not been able to play regularly because of problems with his feet. He was, though, granted a testimonial of £3,000 and his services were retained as senior professional with the second team.

The captaincy of Yorkshire in 1956 went to Billy Sutcliffe and there were good reasons for this, the main one being that since 1948 he had gradually worked his way towards a regular place in the side and had matured sufficiently to hit 1,124 Championship runs the previous summer, a figure topped only by Watson and Vic Wilson.

But the fact that he was the son of the great Herbert was to some extent a handicap because he was expected to be as good as his father and the comparisons and judgments must not have been easy for him to bear. Furthermore, he had to try and bring greater harmony to the dressing room as well as deal with the pressures which were mounting over Yorkshire being unable to offer an effective challenge to Surrey's continued supremacy. At the end of the season he could not have welcomed the committee's stated opinion that "it is considered that more matches would have been won had the players played in a more determined manner on all occasions, and a higher position than seventh attained".

The weather had reverted to type in 1956 and it marred Yorkshire's first match to be played at Acklam Park, Middlesbrough. Play was only possible with Glamorgan on the Saturday but gate money of £1,467 showed that it was well worth taking Championship cricket to this most northerly venue. This continued to be the case until Acklam Park, like other outposts, ceased to be a Yorkshire first team ground but games there were always good to watch, offering plenty for the seamers to start with before runs were easier to come by.

Surrey were at the peak of their powers in 1957, winning three-quarters of their 28 matches and finishing 94 points ahead of runners-up Northamptonshire. Yorkshire, without Trueman during the successful Test series against the West

Indies when he was England's leading bowler, showed some improvement in coming third with the rest some distance behind.

The most significant feature of the season was that many of those who would play some role in the glory days which were just around the corner made their presence felt. Illingworth, Bryan Stott, Ken Taylor, Close and Vic Wilson all achieved 1,000 Championship runs, along with Watson, who was soon to leave for Leicestershire, and although Wardle led the bowling with 92 dismissals and Appleyard had 60, they were greatly assisted by Trueman and Illingworth, with Trueman's back-up 'team' of David Pickles, Bob Platt, Mel Ryan and Mike Cowan all contributing.

Around this time, Halifax-born, Pickles, was seen as the most dynamic of Trueman's partners and he had such blistering pace in 1957 that he was regarded by some as the fastest bowler in the country. There was plenty of speculation as to what havoc Trueman and Pickles would wreak together in years to come but unfortunately Pickles was a dazzling firework that quickly fizzled out.

He was at his best in that summer of '57 and after taking three wickets on his debut against Gloucestershire at Scarborough in mid-July he continued to be given the new ball for the remainder of the season. He reached his peak in the penultimate match against Somerset at Taunton when he enjoyed overall figures of 12-133 and back at Scarborough for the festival match against MCC, he bagged three wickets in each innings, clean bowling the likes of Bill Edrich, Doug Insole and Ted Dexter.

But that was as good as it got for the Halifax flyer who was not quite the same force the following season and then, sadly, faded away. Yet he was never forgotten by those whose stumps he had plucked out of the ground before they had barely raised their bat.

One can only speculate on what would have happened if Trueman and Pickles had been a powerhouse together for the next decade but the falling-off of Pickles was less keenly felt because Ryan, Cowan and Platt were all around to become great supporting acts for top-of-the-bill Fred.

While the first team were still bent on trying to topple Surrey in 1957, something else happened that should not go unnoticed. Yorkshire's Second XI, captained once again by Ronnie Burnet, clinched the Minor Counties Championship. Strength in depth was slowly but surely beginning to return.

CHAPTER TWENTY-TWO

LAST POST, NEW DAWN

The resignation of Billy Sutcliffe as captain before the start of the 1958 season was not entirely unexpected. His two summers in charge had not been easy ones what with the younger players never really feeling comfortable alongside the older hands. Then there was the comparison everyone made with his father, Herbert, and such talk must have been widespread in 1957 when he scored only 631 Championship runs, easily the lowest aggregate of all the other batsmen who had similar opportunities.

Increasingly, the family sports outfitting business was also demanding his attention, so Billy decided to call it a day. But his departure still left Yorkshire in something of a dilemma as to who they should choose to take over.

Watson, perhaps too reserved to knock heads together in his home camp, had in any case moved on to Grace Road during the winter to lead Leicestershire, whereas Wardle, as subsequent events would show, was not exactly flavour of the month with cricket chairman Sellers and the committee.

Times were changing rapidly but the idea that Yorkshire should be led by an amateur captain still held strong and with a traditionalist like Sellers continuing to call the shots it came as no surprise that he should seek Sutcliffe's successor from outside the first team.

Soon the world knew that the job had gone to Ronnie Burnet who had built up the Second XI so well that they had just walked off with the Minor Counties title. The one doubt in Sellers' mind, however, might have been whether Burnet's own limited ability as a batsman at first-class level would handicap the team more than his skills as a captain could offset.

In any case, Sellers also seriously considered another option which was never made public knowledge until the writing of this book. While Burnet at 38 was leading the Second XI to honours in 1957, their previous captain, Michael Crawford, two years his junior, was shaping Leeds Cricket Club into such a strong fighting force that in 1958 they would win both their first Yorkshire League title and their third Yorkshire Council Championship.

To have Crawford in charge of the First XI and Burnet continuing to develop the Seconds was such an attractive proposition that this was the course decided upon and Crawford was offered the job vacated by Billy Sutcliffe. But as we now know he turned it down for business reasons.

So, Yorkshire's last post as an amateur captain was duly accepted by Burnet but there was no immediate suggestion that he and his side were standing on the threshold of a new dawn. Surrey again went on to win the title to be in seventh heaven and, in often damp and dreary weather, Yorkshire slid down to 11th.

The season began so badly for Burnet that he must have pondered over the wisdom of allowing himself to be cast into the lion's den. He started his reign by seeing his side lose to MCC at Lord's by five wickets and then after two of his young shining lights, Stott and Padgett, had helped bring an easy victory over Cambridge University, he went down injured and was forced to sit out the first seven Championship fixtures, including the eight-wicket hammering by Lancashire at Headingley when Brian Statham helped himself to 6-16 in the first innings and a further three in the second.

Then, when he did make his Championship debut, it rained so heavily in the first match that it never got beyond Northamptonshire being 196-4 and not a ball was bowled in the second against Nottinghamshire at Hull.

The clouds parted at Bramall Lane where Yorkshire overwhelmed champions Surrey to the tune of 248 runs after a second innings century from Taylor and match figures of 9-58 for Trueman, but then leaden skies returned and the next spell of decent weather saw Burnet's boys decimated at Northampton by Australian leg-spinner, George Tribe, who was unplayable. He captured 7-22 in a first innings total of 67, out of which Close scored 46, and an astonishing 8-9 in the second innings knock of 65 to land himself with Northamptonshire's best bowling figures of 15 -31. They remain the third best figures ever recorded against Yorkshire.

Another pointer to a brighter future occurred in late July when a multi-talented 21-year-old sportsman called Philip Sharpe, who had churned out runs at Worksop College and for the Yorkshire Cricket Federation, made his Yorkshire debut against Sussex at Worthing and a week later showed off his ability by opening with Taylor at Bramall Lane and scoring 141 in an innings victory over Somerset.

Sharpe's innings would have been talked about the length and breadth of Yorkshire had something genuinely sensational not occurred during the course of the game that rather blotted it out.

Johnny Wardle was sacked, abruptly and without warning, and even though Yorkshire Post cricket correspondent, Jim Kilburn, in the style of the day, barely gave the news a mention, it was the only talking point in the clubs and pubs of Yorkshire for many a day.

To be strictly accurate, Wardle was not immediately sacked, even though he never played first-class cricket again after the Somerset match when Yorkshire secretary John Nash, out of the blue, issued a terse statement which said: "The Yorkshire County Cricket Club have informed J.H. Wardle that they will not be calling on his services after the end of the season."

This match ended on August 1 and Yorkshire travelled straight to Old Trafford for the Roses game with Wardle included in the side. But before the contest could begin Yorkshire issued another statement, this time from Burnet.

It read: "J.H. Wardle has requested that he stand down from the match because of comments he intends to make about his colleagues in a newspaper article to be published while the match is in progress. He has been given permission to stand down and has left the ground."

Articles by Wardle duly appeared in the Daily Mail and they were extremely critical of his colleagues, the captain, the committee and the coaching set-up. Now MCC, with whom Wardle had been invited to tour Australia in the winter, got involved, saying they would discuss the situation on August 19.

Eight days before that, the Yorkshire committee met and the statement which followed said Wardle had broken his contract by publishing comment without permission and that his contract was now to be terminated forthwith.

The open sores which had been festering between Wardle and Yorkshire were exposed for all to see in a part of the statement which read: "In past years Wardle has been warned on several occasions that his general behaviour in the field and in the dressing room has left much to be desired. As no improvement was shown this year the decision to dispense with his services was made, as it was unanimously considered that it was essential to have discipline and a happy and loyal team before any lasting improvement could be expected in the play of the Yorkshire XI."

The death sentence on Wardle's career was then finally handed down by MCC who informed him they were withdrawing his invitation to tour Australia because his newspaper articles had done a grave disservice to the game.

And so, a man who simply loved Yorkshire and England cricket was prematurely put out to grass with 1,842 first-class wickets to his name – and with the certainty of many more to follow had he been able to continue.

It was a sad story and one which could have had a happy ending but instead finished in tragedy. As the years rolled by, the rancour and bitterness were forgotten and in 1983 Wardle was made a life member of Yorkshire County Cricket Club.

In February, 1985, Wardle was officially appointed a bowling coach for the coming season with the powers to attend games home and away whenever he wished and to do whatever he felt was necessary to improve the county's lot.

No sooner was the ink dry on his contract that day than he stepped into the Press Box at Headingley and enthralled us all with his knowledge of the game and with his unshakeable belief that he could revive Yorkshire.

I wrote at the time: "The presence of former Yorkshire and England spinner Johnny Wardle at Headingley was like a breath of fresh air sweeping the ground.

"He turned up with public relations chairman Sid Fielden to discuss the final details of his new job as a bowling coach…and within minutes of his official business being completed he was talking passionately about how he would transform Yorkshire this season.

"'Look, we have got batsmen and bowlers in Yorkshire who have the ability to be Test players and if I cannot bring out that potential then it is my fault, blame me.

"'But I will bring it out, I know I will, and I am already looking forward to it. I tell you now that Yorkshire will make more than a few teams sweat this season'."

Wardle, that day, was at peace with Yorkshire again, but even as he left the ground, he felt dizzy and unwell. It was the first sign of a brain tumour that prevented his active involvement and on July 23 he died.

Nobody mourned his death more than Geoff Cope, the former Yorkshire off-spinner, who went to Wardle at his cricket school in Thorne, near Doncaster, to re-model his action after he had been called for throwing in 1972. After spending countless hours with his young charge, Wardle predicted that Cope would go on to play for England. He was right.

Wardle was not the only senior player to take his bow in 1958 because both Appleyard and Lowson, the latter plagued by varicose veins, played only occasionally, and they were gone when the following season arrived.

Under their new captain, Ted Lester, the Second XI had once again excelled by retaining the Minor Counties title, helped in no small measure by the man destined to step straight into Wardle's shoes, Don Wilson – a cricketer whose enthusiasm and pride in playing for Yorkshire knew no bounds.

The left-arm spinner from Settle, who went on to play for England and was later chief coach of the cricket school at Lord's, was easily the Second XI's top wicket-taker in 1958 with 61 dismissals.

On the batting side, one young man who particularly stood out was to become one of cricket's greatest celebrities after his playing days were over. Harold Denis Bird, universally known as Dickie, was the second leading run-scorer with 483 at an average of 40.25, the highlight of his season being 108 against Durham at Darlington.

Dickie had made his Yorkshire first team debut against Scotland in 1956 and his second team form in 1958 was good enough to earn him a first team place in the last four Championship matches, opening first with Stott and then in the last three outings with Sharpe.

As we shall shortly see, Bird enjoyed one memorable innings the following year but it could not save his career at Yorkshire and he moved on to Leicestershire where he was a reliable member of their side until 1964.

It was not until Dickie donned a white coat, however, that his fame spread and he became the most celebrated umpire in the world, teased and respected by the players and loved by the public at large. When he retired from the world stage in 1996 he had 'stood' in a record 66 Tests and 71 one-day internationals over a 23-year period and on his farewell in the England v India Test at Lord's the players lined up to give him a guard of honour and the whole ground rose to its feet. It goes without saying that Dickie was in tears.

Two years later he umpired his last first-class match in the Yorkshire v Warwickshire game at Headingley and once again a great fuss was made of him. Typical of Dickie, he was involved in a bizarre incident on the last day, the September sun shining so low above the scoreboard while the ground was in deep shadow that Dickie was dazzled and could not see the light meter to assess whether to bring them off for bad light.

Since then, Dickie has set up the Dickie Bird Cricket Foundation to help under-privileged young people achieve their ambitions at sport and he is a constant visitor to Headingley and Scarborough. Yorkshire has produced many greater cricketers than Dickie but nobody more famed and nobody whose biographies have been in such high demand by mums, dads, aunts, uncles and children alike.

CHAPTER TWENTY-THREE

EIGHT OUT OF TEN

And so we move on to 1959 and the start of a new golden era of Yorkshire cricket, but as winter turned into spring few felt that the emerging young side were good enough to go all the way and knock Surrey off their perch.

That doubt even rumbled through the corridors of power at Headingley and at the annual pre-season lunch for players, club officials and Press, cricket chairman Sellers said that team rebuilding would probably go on for another year or two and that Championship success was unlikely. Burnet, out of Sellers' earshot, told his players that they should "commit the unforgivable" and prove the chairman wrong.

In the event, Burnet could not have been more right or Sellers more wrong because in ten incredible seasons from 1959-1968, Yorkshire were crowned champions seven times.

In fact, their record was even better than that, more like eight out of ten, because during the same period Yorkshire also lifted the Gillette Cup, just to show that whatever private thoughts they harboured about the new fangled one-day cricket they were still pretty good at playing it. The only lean years in this time of plenty were in 1961, when they were runners-up to Hampshire in the Championship, and in 1964, when they were fourth to Worcestershire and went out of the Gillette Cup in the first round to Middlesex at Lord's. They were, however, in that year missing at various times, Boycott, Trueman, Sharpe and Taylor through Test calls for the Ashes series.

The run of Championship triumphs may have come to an end after 1968 but Yorkshire firmly set the seal on the 60s being their decade by walking off with the Gillette Cup for a second time in 1969.

Yet the turning point came not in the 60s but in 1959 when the Yorkshire team, like the weather in that year, looked pretty settled. They began their glorious summer in the Championship by beating Nottinghamshire by 194 runs at Middlesbrough, Taylor hitting a century and Trueman picking up 7-57 in the first innings, but they were brought back to earth with a bump in the Roses match at Old Trafford which Lancashire won by 179 runs, despite a classy 100 out of 188 from Padgett.

The strength-in-depth brought about by the excellent showing of the Second XI over the past couple of years was by now paying dividends and against Glamorgan at Bradford Yorkshire included five uncapped players but still won by an innings and 35 runs.

One of the five was Dickie Bird and he gave the batting performance of his life with an unbeaten 181 out of 405-8 declared after Trueman, at his most fiery, had claimed five wickets. Bird so dominated the middle for seven-and-a-quarter hours that Sharpe was the next highest scorer with 45 and Dickie sailed past his previous best innings of 62. He hit 24 boundaries and was dropped twice but Wisden commented that it was, nevertheless, "a great display of concentration" ... "with good all-round strokes".

Despite his big score, Bird was dropped for the next match upon the return of Taylor – a decision which was just as sore a point to Dickie half a century later as it was at the time – and although he had other chances that summer he never found that sort of form again. Surplus to requirements, he went on to join Willie Watson and another Yorkshire cast-off, Jackie van Geloven, at Leicestershire.

Jackie played three times for Yorkshire in 1955 before moving to Grace Road where he was a fine all-rounder and holds the distinction of being the last Yorkshire-born player to complete the double of 1,000 runs and 100 wickets in a season. Born at Guiseley, he was the landlord of a pub there and later one at Scarborough. Like Dickie, he became a first-class umpire. He was a droll man, extremely popular, and, also like Dickie, a great story teller, perhaps the funniest I have ever heard.

Not all was sweetness and light in 1959 and Vic Wilson, the senior professional, was so out of touch that he was dropped for long spells, but Padgett blazed the trail with 1,807 Championship runs, 2,158 in all, with Stott on his coat-tails and Close, Illingworth and Taylor all easily exceeding 1,000 runs.

The wrecker-in-chief was the incomparable Trueman but his old mate Bob Platt was almost his equal that season with 85 Championship wickets, only eight fewer than Fred himself who was bowling down the hill and with the wind at his back, as Platt was happy to verify.

Illingworth and Close were just as effective with the ball as with the bat, Don Wilson was good enough to snatch 53 wickets and Jimmy Binks, the players' player if ever there was one, had made the wicketkeeping position his and his alone for years to come.

No wonder Yorkshire were buoyant and increasingly confident but they were not yet the masters of every situation and seven-times champions Surrey beat them convincingly at The Oval and completed the double at Park Avenue, where Peter Loader claimed six in each innings. The young John Edrich, in breathtaking form up to now, broke a finger in this game and his absence, along with that of Peter May for much of the time, were factors in Surrey's slow decline.

Then, well into August, came the debacle at Bristol where the covered pitch had sweated overnight and Yorkshire followed up Gloucestershire's 294-8 declared by being shot out for 35, the lowest first-class score of the season and what was then the sixth lowest score in the county's history. Tony Brown took 7-11 and David Smith 3-16. The last six in the order, from Bird to Platt, all failed to score and Brian Bolus, later of Nottinghamshire, Derbyshire and England, coming in at No 5, ended unbeaten on 12. He was instructed to keep his pads on and go straight back in again. It was a shrewd move by Burnet because Bolus struck 91, which was half of Yorkshire's total, but it could not stop them suffering defeat by an innings and 77 runs.

This sort of setback would have demoralised some young teams but not Burnet's Babes who moved on to New Road for their penultimate match and overcame Worcestershire by six wickets, Stott becoming the first left-hander to carry his bat for Yorkshire with 144 out of 262 in the first innings and Close claiming eight wickets in the match and Trueman seven.

Stott was undoubtedly one of the heroes at Worcestershire and he played an even more memorable innings in the magnificent title-winning match at Hove. But he would be the first to admit that on this occasion there was not one Yorkshire hero but eleven, each member of the team thrilling the band of supporters who made the pilgrimage to Brighton and also the many thousands glued to the BBC radio commentary by Robert Hudson from after lunch on the final day.

Yorkshire went into this crucial game with Sussex knowing that the Championship title was theirs if they won but that anything less would leave their hopes depending upon how Surrey fared in their last two matches.

Burnet had built up a notorious reputation for losing the toss and he was true to form at Hove where the glorious weather and excellent pitch meant that whoever called correctly would automatically bat first.

Trueman struck early but, more surprisingly, it was then Taylor with his 'darts' that brought the next four wickets to help reduce Sussex to 67-6 before rallying to 210.

The top half of Yorkshire's batting also failed but Illingworth, gamely supported by Jackie Birkenshaw and Don Wilson, hit an admirable 122 to ensure a useful first innings lead of 97.

Sussex showed greater resilience in their second innings and as the lead approached 200 with time running out there was a feeling within the home camp that skipper Robin Marlar should declare, but he would have none of it.

Burnet threw the ball to Trueman before lunch to see if one final fling could wipe out the tail but after bowling nearly 1,000 overs that summer his legs had given up on him and he was spent. It was Close who urged Burnet to bring on Illingworth to mop up and the captain agreed. Illingworth did as instructed but now only 105 minutes remained in which to chase down 215.

As Yorkshire walked off the field, two young fans rushed up to Stott and asked: "Are we going for them"? "Yes" was the immediate reply and Stott was as good as his word.

In view of the urgency of things, the batting order was juggled and Taylor, rather than Bolus, opened with Stott, 15 coming off the first over before Taylor fell lbw to Ted Dexter.

Close joined Stott and promptly thumped a huge six into a nearby garden, the downside of this mighty blow being that four or five valuable minutes were lost searching for the ball! Then Dexter also dismissed Close to leave Yorkshire on 40-2 but now the scene was set for one of the great Yorkshire partnerships of all time.

With Marlar unsure how to set fields to the left-hand right-hand combination, Stott and Padgett found the gaps brilliantly, the young third-wicket pair racing between the wickets in such an audacious manner that Sussex soon lost their grip on the situation.

In just over an hour, Yorkshire had 150 on the board and in around the same time Stott and Padgett's partnership reached 141 before it was broken when Padgett was out for 79, Stott going on to 96 in 86 minutes. The atmosphere in the Yorkshire dressing room was electric and the bubble of built-up tension finally burst with just seven minutes remaining when Bolus glanced the winning boundary.

And so Surrey's dominance had been broken and Yorkshire again wore the crown which they regarded as rightfully theirs. They packed their bags at Hove and made off in a motley assortment of transport to Scarborough where they were due to open the Festival the following day by playing MCC.

Stott recalls: "Glorious memories will never fade of the tumultuous welcome which we received on arriving in Scarborough in small and tired groups in the early hours of the morning after our long car journeys. Scores of jubilant supporters at the Salisbury and Balmoral hotels would not go to bed until they had seen us home and heard our stories at first hand.

"Then, so few hours later, there was an unbelievable crescendo of noise and celebration as we first arrived at the ground and then as the skipper led us all on to the field. A cheering throng of families, friends, members and supporters formed a huge guard of honour leading from the dressing room to well beyond the pitch. It will come as no surprise that practically every member of this proud team had tears in his eyes by the time we reached the middle."

The celebrations continued long after the season was over and the players particularly enjoyed their invitation from president, Sir William Worsley, to a special dinner at Hovingham Hall where his daughter, the present Duchess of Kent, Yorkshire's Patroness since 1967, sat between Stott and Taylor and was hungry to feed on every morsel of information about the team's triumph.

For Burnet, life had truly begun at 40 on the field of play, but unbeknown to anyone then, it would have come to an end by the time he was 41 and something which seemed of little consequence when it occurred was to have a bearing on his sudden retirement.

After the MCC match at North Marine Road, the new Champions moved on to London to sign off for the summer by taking on The Rest of England. And because Vic Wilson had endured such a wretched season, Burnet asked the committee if he could be included in the team by way of consolation as his fine career could well be drawing to a close.

This was agreed, Wilson was drafted into the side and after top-scoring with 41 in the first innings he then guided Yorkshire to a prestigious victory with a splendid 105.

Had Burnet decided to retire at the end of 1959, Close would have been the popular choice to replace him as he had already offered a guiding hand on a regular basis to his amateur captain, but Burnet had no intention of standing down.

Sellers, however, had a plan of his own and after much discussion he persuaded Burnet that it was in the club's best interests for him to stand down. Burnet reluctantly agreed and the upshot was that Wilson became Yorkshire's first professional captain of modern times. But would Sellers have reached the same conclusion had Wilson failed at The Oval?

If there were some in the side who would have preferred Close, none questioned Wilson's right to the job through his professionalism and experience or his steadfastness in the heat of the battle. Wilson's batting technique was not perfect but it was a combination of ability and sheer determination which propelled him to a career aggregate of 20,548 runs for Yorkshire, a figure surpassed by only ten other batsmen.

Paying tribute to Wilson upon his death in June, 2008, Illingworth said: "Vic was one of those players you would want in the trenches with you. He was totally reliable, a man who gave 100 per cent and never gave up fighting. If he was beaten by five balls in a row he would lose none of his determination when facing up to the sixth."

Wilson may have lacked the natural flair as captain which Close was later to exhibit but he was a respected leader with a typically Yorkshire stubborn streak and his record can hardly be faulted. He retained the Championship title in his first year in office, took the runners-up spot in 1961 and pushed Yorkshire back to the top of the pile in his third and final term.

He had, of course, got a magnificent band of players under his wing and the nucleus of a team which would keep Yorkshire ahead of the pack throughout the 60s.

Yorkshire's one regret when Wilson retained the title in 1960 was that president and former captain, Tom Taylor, did not live to see it. He died a month or so before the season began and was replaced as president the following year by another former captain and influential figure, Sir William Worsley, who had been a vice-president since 1952.

For the first time in many years, Yorkshire took on all counties twice in 1960 and although they narrowly lost their first match to Sussex at Hove – the scene of their great triumph only a few months earlier – they immediately bounced back with six consecutive victories.

But then came the first of two big blows that season in the form of conceding the double to Lancashire for the first time in 67 years. They went down by ten wickets at Headingley, when they were beguiled by the leg-spin of Tommy Greenhough, and later on at Old Trafford in a much tighter encounter which they lost by two wickets. This time they were undone by the pace and deadly accuracy of Statham but Lancashire struggled to reach their 81 target, Mel Ryan taking 5-50.

Once again Yorkshire bounced back from adversity and they nailed the title in the penultimate match by beating Worcestershire by nine wickets at Harrogate, Trueman and Illingworth each seizing four wickets as the visitors were bowled out for 139. A violent assault from Trueman brought him a half-century in half an hour with five sixes and three fours, to set up a lead of 104, Worcestershire again being bowled out cheaply, Don Wilson this time taking four wickets along with Illingworth.

Close was the leading run-maker that year with 1,650 in the Championship, including a career-best 198 at The Oval, and Padgett and Stott also topped 1,400, but it was Trueman who was the most admired by colleagues and fans alike. He shrugged off inevitable weariness to net 175 first-class wickets in all from an amazing 1,068 overs, 150 of the wickets for Yorkshire and 132 in the Championship at 12.72 runs apiece. The remaining 25 were for England in the five-match series against South Africa, Trueman and Statham magnificent together in the 3-0 win. Roses wins bring joy and misery in equal measure but Yorkshire-Lancashire combinations in Test cricket unite the two sides of the Pennines like nothing else.

Sir William Worsley was also elected president of MCC in 1961 but he was unable to boast in the Long Room of a Yorkshire Championship hat-trick because Hampshire took the title for the first time, their lead in the table being sufficient to withstand defeat by Yorkshire in the last match at Bournemouth, where Bolus hit a century and Illingworth enjoyed figures of 12-102.

Remarkably, Bolus, Taylor, Close, Padgett, Stott and Sharpe all managed 1,000 runs and Trueman and Illingworth each secured 100 wickets but they were just short of the necessary back-up required to turn a good season into a highly successful one.

Close was in the spotlight for one of the biggest cricket stories of the season – but it was while playing for England rather than Yorkshire. His innings against Australia at Old Trafford, when he perished while persistently attempting to sweep Richie Benaud in an effort to prevent him using the rough created by Trueman's footholds, was widely condemned and the selectors took their time to forgive him.

This was one of many brushes that the future England captain was to have with the authorities in his colourful career but to include all the details of Close and also Boycott's international dealings in this book would require two volumes and not one.

Ill-health meant the summer of 61 was the last in which the faithful Cyril Turner, the former dependable all-rounder, would act as Yorkshire scorer, Ted Lester taking over to continue his long and uninterrupted service with the county.

Sharpe was undoubtedly the form batsman of 1962 when Vic Wilson brought the Championship pennant back to Headingley. In all, Sharpe managed 2,201 runs and 1,872 were in the Championship, where Close, Illingworth, Padgett and Vic Wilson also hoisted 1,000-plus with Taylor only a handful away. Trueman and Illingworth were again the principal bowlers with more than a little help from Ryan, Platt, Don Wilson and Co.

Once again, Harrogate was the scene of the decisive battle, Glamorgan being the opponents for the final match which Yorkshire needed to win in order to pip Worcestershire. The result shows that they did it comfortably enough – by seven wickets at 4.04pm on the third day – but this obscures the fact that they would not have achieved their objective without the heroic efforts of the residents of St. George's Road.

There were 10,000 excited spectators present for the first day which saw Don Wilson take 6-24 as the Welshmen were skittled for 65 before a concerted effort by their bowlers sent back Yorkshire for 101 of which Taylor, head and shoulders above the rest, contributed 67.

By close of play, Glamorgan were 13 without loss but the next day was a complete wash-out, much to the dismay of 5,000 hardy souls who sat through the rain that began as drizzle and ended in a torrential downpour which had flooded the field by tea-time.

It was not only the groundstaff who worked through the night to shift the thousands of gallons of water under which the ground was submerged. They were joined by nearby neighbours who rolled up their sleeves and gave all the help they could. Illingworth recalls that during the hours of darkness the ground was lit up by car headlights.

The reward for all this was that play started on time on the third day with even more spectators packed into the ground than on the first and they watched Illingworth and Don Wilson reduce Glamorgan to 72-7 before unexpected resistance came from Don Ward and wicketkeeper David Evans. Close appealed to his captain to be given the chance to break the deadlock and his wish was granted. He began with a long hop which was clattered for four and then cleaned up with three wickets for no runs, a Yorkshire win now being inevitable.

Four youngsters with little or no previous experience played a modest part in winning the Championship that year. They were John Hampshire, who settled in well during the second half of the season, and new bloods Richard Hutton, Tony Nicholson – and Geoffrey Boycott.

CHAPTER TWENTY-FOUR

CLOSE CALL

Some years stand out more prominently than others in the history of Yorkshire County Cricket Club and 1963 was a time of momentous events both on and off the field.

For a start, it was the centenary of the club's birth and the team marked this in the only way imaginable so far as the members and fans were concerned – and that was by retaining the Championship title.

By then, however, the club had already paid homage to its 100 years of existence with a centenary celebration dinner at the Cutlers' Hall in Sheffield, the city of its birth.

And what a grand affair it was. No roast beef and Yorkshire pud on this glittering occasion but lobster bisque, followed by fillet of sole a la mazarine, chicken Rossini, Macaroon cream, bonne bouche a la galloise and coffee, all helped down with the finest sherry, moselle, burgundy, port and brandy.

Three of Yorkshire's greatest batsmen were in the hall in Herbert Sutcliffe, Sir Leonard Hutton and Maurice Leyland while top table guests included former captains Norman Yardley and Vic Wilson. Apologies were received from Wilfred Rhodes, Cyril Turner and Percy Holmes.

The 400 members and guests stood as president Sir William Worsley proposed the toast to Her Majesty The Queen. Later, a toast to Yorkshire CCC was proposed by Viscount Monckton of Brenchley, president of Surrey CCC, and after Sir William had responded, a toast to Cricket was proposed by H.S. Altham, treasurer of MCC and president of Hampshire CCC, with cricket committee chairman Brian Sellers responding.

County cricket clubs around this time were becoming increasingly aware that they needed money to prosper – or even to stay afloat – and Sir William used the dinner as an opportunity to launch an appeal for funds to carry out improvements which that year included the building of new offices at Headingley to accommodate the staff as they moved out of their old headquarters at Old Bank Chambers, 9 Park Row, Leeds.

The new offices and dressing rooms were estimated to cost at least £21,500 and Leeds CFAC, the ground's owners, had agreed to contribute £5,000. By the end of the year, £15,610 had been raised and the club's annual report for 1964 stated rather tartly that the response to the appeal had not been as good as could be expected and the result would not enable the committee to carry out anything like the work envisaged on the various grounds. The subscription list would be kept open in the hope that many more people would respond.

From then until the present day, Yorkshire have struggled to make ends meet and there can be no doubt that never owning everything, lock, stock and barrel, at Headingley has been the root cause of their financial problems and has also meant that to some extent they have always been dependant on others.

But back to the cricket and some of the reasons why Yorkshire were able to stand and deliver in their centenary year.

The retirement during the winter of Vic Wilson had brought the captaincy to Close a little later than might otherwise have been the case and he led from the front in a courageous manner that became his hallmark and helped to establish him as one of the most inspirational captains of all time. Unlike Hawke and Sellers and all the other Yorkshire captains before him, Close had a rare, almost unique, quality of being an uncompromising leader while still remaining one of the boys. The high affection in which he was held by his team-mates never diminished and many have admitted that cricket was never as exciting or as much fun as when they played it under his command.

Another strong factor was that 1963 was the year that Geoff Boycott stopped being just the promising prospect who had scored far more Second XI runs the previous summer than anyone else and rapidly began to develop into one of the greatest batsman that Yorkshire and England have ever known. Not only that, he was also one of the most controversial cricketers in the history of the game and later on he ensured that Yorkshire cricket made the headlines of local and national sports pages even when results hardly merited it.

For all his brushes with the county club's hierarchy as the years rolled by, Boycott was entirely wrapped up in Yorkshire cricket and as a senior player he once said that his ambition was to become chairman of the club.

Since then, of course, the committee set-up which allowed for a chairman has ended but he has served on the all-powerful Management Board and has achieved his aim by being elected club president, his two-year term of office covering the 150th anniversary.

Boycott in 1963 led the way with 1,446 Championship runs, the only batsman to make it to the 1,000 mark, and two of his three centuries, including his maiden one, were in the pressure cooker atmosphere of Roses battle, early proof that here was a man who could not only withstand all that was hurled at him but also thrive on it.

By the time that Boycott took over the captaincy from Close in 1971, Yorkshire's most recent golden period had drawn to a close and the team were unable to bring the success which the increasingly frustrated fans demanded. Boycott, though, continued to stack up the runs and for many supporters this personal success compensated for the team's failure. They may not be able to see Yorkshire win very often but at least they could pay their money and be pretty sure that Boycott would make a big score.

Others took a different view, believing that concentration on personal success did little to help re-build the team and so the club became split into two camps.

But there can be no argument about Boycott's spectacular achievements as a batsman while others around him very often floundered. For England, he became Test cricket's leading run-scorer when he overtook Garry Sobers' 8,032 runs to end with 8,114, his 22 centuries also being the most for his country; for Yorkshire he amassed 32,570 first-class runs, a figure beaten only by Sutcliffe and Denton, and his 103 centuries are exceeded by Sutcliffe alone with 112 although he played in 188 more matches than Boycott; and in all first-class matches he made 48,426 runs, with 151 centuries at an average of 56.83. He remains, quite simply, one of the heaviest run-scorers that the world of cricket has ever known.

Other important factors also occurred in 1963, some of which had a bearing not only on that season but also shaped the history of the club in the years ahead.

The trio I mentioned – along with Boycott – that had begun to make an impression the previous season all went a good deal further towards establishing their careers.

John Hampshire came next to Boycott in the run-scoring stakes with 1,236 in all first-class matches, the pair of them being rewarded with their county caps at the end of the campaign along with Tony Nicholson, who took such big strides forward that he claimed 66 Championship wickets and contested with Ryan the right to be considered Trueman's second in command.

And also making satisfactory progress with bat and ball was Richard Hutton, son of Leonard, and a fine all-rounder who needed no-one to pull any strings to get him in the side which he did purely on merit.

If Boycott was the one to go on to achieve true greatness with his textbook batting and unrivalled hunger for runs, then it was Hampshire who more often than not provided rich entertainment with his powerful batting and domination of the crease.

No Yorkshire-born batsman since the war – and very few before it – have torn attacks to shreds more often than Hampshire has done when on the top of his form. Once he had overcome a certain natural reserve and fully asserted himself, he would flex his arm muscles, throw back his shoulders and assault the bowling with blistering drives. There was no finer sight for Yorkshire eyes when in full flow.

He holds tenth place in the list of the county's biggest run-getters with 21,979 and he would almost certainly have overtaken Close and Len Hutton had the politics of Yorkshire cricket not weighed him down sufficiently for him to move to Derbyshire from 1982-84.

Hampshire accepted the Yorkshire captaincy for two years after Boycott had it taken away from him at the end of the 1978 season but such were the internal tensions that had built up that it was never easy for either of them.

The only England batsman to score a century on Test debut at Lord's, Hampshire was for a decade a popular player and coach for Tasmania during the English winters and he remained fully involved in cricket at the highest level once his playing days were over. He was a first-class umpire from 1985-2005, standing in 21 Test matches and 20 one-day internationals as well on the county circuit, and upon his retirement he became one of the ECB's panel of umpiring 'referees'.

A founder member of the Yorkshire Players' Association, Hampshire has upheld the family tradition of involvement in cricket, his father, also John, a fast bowler, playing three matches for Yorkshire in 1937, and his brother, Alan, a batsman, making one appearance in 1975.

A special word, too, at this stage, about Nicholson, who was one of the best-loved players ever to step into the Yorkshire dressing room. Even though he was to die tragically young at the age of 47, he is still talked about in the fondest terms by his contemporaries and each year at Ripon, Yorkshire cricketers compete in a golf tournament in memory of 'Nick'.

Nicholson's career was coming to a close when I first started reporting on Yorkshire cricket in 1975 but I still have clear memories of his mastery of swing while playing against an International XI in a three-day match at Scarborough when he claimed 5-45 in the first innings and 2-20 in the second, his victims being Alan Jones and Graham Gooch.

It was a constant source of amazement to everyone how Yorkshire's popular physiotherapist, Colin Kaye, managed to keep Nicholson just about in one piece, but he did – and this amiable former policeman whose lack of razor-sharp fitness would not be tolerated by the back-up staff these days responded by bagging 876 wickets at just 19.74 runs apiece.

Nicholson was the only regular in the Yorkshire side around this time not to play for England but he came desperately close to it and he was selected, along with Boycott, to tour South Africa in 1964-65 but had to decline owing to health problems.

Close's own splendid form and his ability to integrate his team into a fighting force did much to make Yorkshire tick in 1963 but in one game, at least, victory came in quite an unexpected form. Against Glamorgan in Cardiff, all of the batsmen had performed creditably in a first innings score of 332-7 declared and the momentum was maintained by Wilson who took 5-33 as the home side were fired out for 88 and forced to follow on. Glamorgan offered sterner resistance this time until an inspired move by Illingworth, captaining the side in the absence of Close who was on Test duty, brought Hampshire into the attack with his occasional leg-spin which had so far earned him a solitary career wicket.

Suddenly, Hampshire was unplayable and he destroyed Glamorgan with amazing figures of 7-52, which remain the second best by a leg-spinner in Yorkshire's history and beaten only by Leadbeater's 8-83 against Worcestershire in 1950. The end came so quickly on the final morning that a cricket journalist who was covering the match for a national newspaper arrived late and found the players with their bags packed. He thought he was being set up and refused to believe them when they told him that it was John Hampshire who had gone through the opposition like a dose of salts.

There was one other feature of note about 1963 and that was the introduction of one-day cricket in the form of the Gillette Cup, although such little importance was attached to it that it was known, rather begrudgingly, as The One-Day Knock-Out Competition.

And, indeed, Yorkshire were knocked out after the first round which was played at Middlesbrough. Bolus, having left his native county for Nottinghamshire at the end of the previous season, made his former team-mates appreciate what they were missing by carrying his bat for a sparkling 100 out of 159 in the 65-overs-a-side match, Yorkshire needing 55 overs in which to reach their target. Next up were Sussex at Hove and Yorkshire lost an evenly-fought game by 22 runs, the early kings of one-day cricket going on to beat Worcestershire in the Lord's final in front of a 25,000 crowd. The public at large, if not yet the cricketing authorities, knew that this form of the game was here to stay. Not only was it here to stay but without it county cricket may well have gone bust.

Of all the years Close was captain of Yorkshire, 1964 was the most disappointing because they slipped to fifth in the table – Worcestershire taking the spoils for the first time – and were drummed out of the Gillette Cup in the first round when they lost to Middlesex at Lord's after scoring only 90.

Illingworth was as versatile as ever and he extended his double of 1,055 runs and 104 wickets in the Championship to 1,301 runs and 122 wickets in all matches for Yorkshire. There were, however, the first signs of a small decline in Trueman's powers but he still managed 75 Championship wickets at 20.82 while Nicholson had 76 at 15.69.

Yet Trueman remained a much revered figure on the world stage and he enjoyed one of the greatest and proudest moments of his career in the fifth and final Test against Australia at The Oval when Neil Hawke became his 300th Test victim.

It is appropriate at this stage in the narrative of Yorkshire's history to pose the question: "Who was Yorkshire's first overseas player?" And those who reply "Sachin Tendulkar" would be wrong.

The answer is the greatest all-round cricketer of them all – Garfield St Aubrun Sobers!

Immediately following the disappointing 1964 season, Yorkshire embarked on an unofficial tour of Bermuda and Sobers accepted an invitation to join the party. He had been in England in early September as part of Sir Frank Worrell's XI which played three matches against an England XI, including one at the Scarborough Cricket Festival, and he was happy to stop off in Bermuda on his way home.

Yorkshire had a whale of a time and so did Sobers, who stacked up the runs and wickets in each of the four matches. He rattled up 117 against St George's Cricket Club when Boycott also made a century and, opening the bowling, he helped himself to four wickets per game, his most astonishing analysis being 8-7-2-4 against the Pick of the Leagues.

Close, of course, was a great friend of Sobers and they enjoyed similar interests, horse racing being pretty high up the list. There is no doubt, according to Close, that Sobers would have jumped at the chance to join Yorkshire but the club was still resolutely against taking on outsiders in those days and the cricketing genius went on to play for Nottinghamshire from 1968-1974.

Those two impostors, Triumph and Disaster, were with Yorkshire in 1965 but, as Eric Morecambe may have pointed out, not necessarily in that order.

Disaster came at Middlesbrough in the third week in May when Yorkshire were bundled out for 121 on a dodgy pitch by Hampshire, who replied with 125. At that stage, it appeared as if Yorkshire had gone a long way towards redeeming themselves and openers Boycott and Hampshire put their side into the black before seven without loss became eight runs for six wickets and an all out total of 23, the lowest in the club's history. In the first innings, that very model of consistency, Derek Shackleton, had done much of the damage with six wickets, but this time it was David 'Butch' White who inflicted most of the pain and humiliation by returning figures of 10-7-10-6, assisted by Shackleton and Bob Cottam with two apiece.

Up to that point of the season, Yorkshire had cause for satisfaction, the first four games bringing two comfortable wins and two weather-hit draws in which they had quite comfortably gained a first innings lead. But they were unnerved by their experience at Acklam Park and as a consequence they drew five and lost two of their next seven matches.

Richard Hutton led a rally towards the end of the season when, sharing the new ball with Trueman, he took five wickets in an innings in the wins over Essex and Somerset twice, but Yorkshire still had to be content with fourth place in the table.

Triumph came in the form of the Gillette Cup – now sufficiently established for Yorkshire to refer to it by name rather than just the One Day Competition – which they won by the handsome margin of 175 runs when they pulverised Surrey at Lord's.

This was the occasion on which Boycott came so much out of his shell that he creamed 146 in what is generally considered to be one of the finest one-day innings of all time.

Prompted, perhaps even instructed, by his captain, to get a move on, Boycott played all the shots in the book while adding a dashing 192 for the second wicket with Close who made 79. The upshot was that Yorkshire reached 317-4 in their 60 overs and Surrey were never in with a sniff as Trueman and Illingworth ran through them.

Strangely, this was Boycott's sole century in a summer of such bad weather that only Hampshire could get into four figures, although Boycott, Sharpe and Padgett only just fell short. Trueman recovered much of his stamina to forge ahead of anyone else with 115 Championship wickets but Ryan played on only a couple of occasions because of business commitments and he went on to announce his retirement.

Another who called it a day for business reasons was Bradford woolman Robin Feather, who had most competently captained the second team for the four seasons since taking over from Lester. He was succeeded by former Bradford CC captain Derek Blackburn, who had played one first team game as an amateur in 1956, and whose name had once been mulled over, along with those of Burnet and Crawford, for the first team captaincy.

There was to be no change at the top at senior level – and rightly so because Close was about to lead his team to three consecutive Championship titles.

CHAPTER TWENTY-FIVE

HERO AND VILLAIN

Yorkshire were unable to repeat their Gillette Cup triumph in 1966, Somerset beating them in the first round at Taunton, but their Lord's success of the previous year did them a power of good and with Close now at the top of his form both as a captain and player they prevented Worcestershire achieving a hat-trick of Championship titles and set off on a similar mission of their own.

The season saw the introduction for the one and only time of a complicated new regulation in the County Championship. The first innings was restricted to 65 overs for the first 12 matches played by each of the 17 counties on a home and away basis. Where counties met only once in the season normal conditions prevailed as they did in the return matches.

Although some of these 'reduced' games produced exciting cricket, the experiment was not well received and it was quickly ditched but Yorkshire fared sufficiently well under the system to win the majority of their games, including the Roses clash at Headingley by ten wickets. Even the 65 overs were not required as Lancashire were sent back for 57, Trueman picking up 5-18. Three of the wickets were claimed by another of Trueman's 'back-up staff', John Waring, who stole the show in the second innings with a career-best 7-40.

Born in Ripon, the tall and well-built Waring had first appeared for Yorkshire in 1963 and he gave great service in league cricket both before and after his first-class career. An occasional rather than regular player for Yorkshire, he left at the end of 1966 and turned out once for Warwickshire the following year when he also joined the Bradford League club, Bingley. He spent four seasons at Wagon Lane and helped them to the cup and league double in 1969.

So well did Yorkshire fare, despite another season of indifferent weather, that by the end of July they appeared clear of the field but they then experienced a cold wind in August that brought three defeats while Worcestershire made a late charge.

The upshot was that St George's Road, Harrogate, once again became the national focus of attention as Yorkshire needed to beat Kent there in the last match to make sure of the title. Heavy rain had left the pitch soft and runs were hard to come by but the true value of Boycott's 80 out of 210 became more apparent as the game went on.

Trueman and Nicholson were largely responsible for sending Kent back for 119 before Derek Underwood lived up to his nickname of 'Deadly' by snatching the first seven wickets to wipe out Yorkshire for 109. In these conditions, Kent's target of 201 seemed a difficult one but Yorkshire's main concern was the return of bad weather which threatened an abandonment until a strong drying wind set in and allowed play to resume after lunch on the third day. Now it was the turn of Illingworth and Wilson to be the tormentors and Illingworth had Norman Graham caught by Padgett in the final half hour to trigger scenes of jubilation.

The runs throughout the summer had been pretty evenly distributed but the majority of the wickets had been picked up by the main new-ball pair and the two leading spinners, Nicholson taking 105 wickets to Trueman's 101, while Illingworth topped the averages with 85 at 14.51 and Wilson bagged 87 at 16.58.

Two newcomers made little impact on their debuts but both went on to have international careers ahead of them and become outstanding performers for Yorkshire. They were fast bowler Chris Old and off-spinner Geoff Cope, who would also play a prominent part in securing Yorkshire's future long after his playing days were over.

Winning the Championship was only one of Close's outstanding achievements in 1966. The other one was leading England to an innings victory over the West Indies in the final Test at The Oval after taking over the captaincy from Colin Cowdrey with England already 3-0 down in the series. As at Yorkshire, Close was absolutely fearless and had hunches which paid off, such as instructing John Snow to bowl a first ball bouncer to Sobers, who mis-hooked it into the skipper's waiting hands in the leg trap.

The wettest May since 1773 could not stop Yorkshire from going on to win the Championship again in 1967 when Close struck gold three times over. Not only did he keep Yorkshire at the top but he presided over Test match series wins over first India and then Pakistan, five of the games being won by large margins and the other drawn.

But Close continued to be drawn to controversy as a moth to a lamp and as a consequence of events which occurred during Yorkshire's Championship visit to Warwickshire in mid-August, the MCC did not offer him the captaincy for the winter tour of the West Indies – which had seemed a foregone conclusion – but gave it instead to Colin Cowdrey.

The storm at Edgbaston broke on the third day but leading up to then there had been a couple of incidents which left a sour taste in the mouth of the Yorkshire Post's respected cricket correspondent, Jim Kilburn. On the second morning he felt that Yorkshire's bowling and fielding left a lot to be desired and as the players repaired for lunch a derogatory remark was picked up by Close who, it seems, confronted an innocent spectator by mistake and immediately apologised for his error. Nothing further transpired but a newspaper later carried a report that Close had been seen to assault a spectator and the story would not go away.

The battle for first innings lead at this stage of the game was being keenly fought, Warwickshire eventually just pipping Yorkshire's 238 which contained a brilliant century from Hampshire. And because Boycott was suffering from a bruised foot he was, quite properly, substituted in the field by the agile 12th man, Taylor. But when Yorkshire faced a difficult 50 minutes batting in the evening, Boycott was sent in first, despite his earlier absence from the field, and the Edgbaston faithful felt that this went against the spirit if not actually the letter of the law. Certainly today's regulations would not have allowed it.

Not until Warwickshire chased 142 to win in 100 minutes on a wet outfield with light rain falling intermittently did events occur which were to have disastrous consequences for Close. Even though the wet ball had to be constantly dried, it was perceived that Yorkshire were employing stalling tactics and this belief was strengthened in the last 15 minutes when Warwickshire required 24 with seven wickets in hand.

An appeal against the rain was disallowed but the arrival of a heavier burst sent Yorkshire scurrying off the field. Before the umpires had reached the gate it stopped and they returned to the middle for the game to resume but with the wet ball being constantly dried only a couple more overs were possible for the loss of two wickets before time ran out.

Yorkshire, therefore, picked up two points for drawing the match but the angry Warwickshire fans believed their side had been short-changed and as the affair rumbled on a statutory report from the umpires initiated an enquiry by the Executive Committee at Lord's.

It was found unanimously that Yorkshire had used delaying tactics which constituted unfair play and were against the best interests of the game and, furthermore, that Close was entirely responsible for these tactics. The findings were conveyed to Yorkshire CCC, who acknowledged them and said steps would be taken to avoid repetition of the offence.

The outcome of the Edgbaston match was of little importance in itself but it ended Close's inspirational days as England captain, no doubt giving those powerful voices at Lord's with a Southern bias the ammunition which they needed to fire.

Close continued to defend himself fiercely, maintaining that the only reason why the over rate was so slow was because of the constant need to dry the ball but his pleas were disregarded.

Whenever Close has been asked over the last half century or so what is the most important aspect of cricket he has always insisted that the spirit of the game comes first with playing to win second. I believe he has always stood by those principles.

Less than a month after the turmoil at Edgbaston, Yorkshire found themselves in the familiar position of attempting to win the Championship in the last match of the season at Harrogate. They did so emphatically, beating Gloucestershire by an innings and 76 runs inside two days after Boycott and Sharpe had got them off to the ideal start by each making 70s and sharing in an opening stand of 127.

Illingworth also contributed a valuable 46 to the all-out score of 309 but it was his bowling which devastated Gloucestershire. His 7-58 forced them to follow on and now he trampled them underfoot with 7-6 to give him a match return of 14-64.

It was a good team effort by Yorkshire to lift the Championship despite having Boycott, Close and Illingworth often missing on Test duty, and it was an encouraging sign for the future that the emerging Chris Old and Cope should make the most of their limited opportunities, Cope's 32 wickets at 12.78 runs apiece putting him top of the bowling averages by some distance.

Losing the England captaincy was a hard blow for Close to take but he bounced back in typical whole hearted fashion in 1968 by leading Yorkshire to their hat-trick of Championship title triumphs. The club had double reason for celebration because the Second XI, now captained by Bob Platt, walked off with the Minor Counties Championship, the first time that this particular double had been achieved.

Sharpe, his slip fielding once again of the very highest quality, was the only batsman to complete 1,000 Championship runs but Boycott would undoubtedly have joined him but for Test calls and injury restricting him to 15 innings from which he scored 774 runs for an average of 77.40, over twice that of anyone else.

Illingworth and Wilson spun their magic to good effect to pick up 102 and 86 wickets respectively and they were followed by Nicholson with 80.

As usual, the Championship went right down to the wire and it was in the final game at Hull that Yorkshire made certain of keeping the crown by beating Surrey by 60 runs with only minutes to spare.

Many are the stories that have combined to make Close a legendary figure in the game but none exemplify his courage more than his role in the closing stages of this game.

Chasing 250 at around 55 an hour, Surrey plunged to 84-6 against Illingworth and Wilson but Younis Ahmed and Arnold Long settled in and the tension grew as time began to run out. Wilson then sent down a delivery to Younis which he smacked off the middle of the bat flush on to Close's shin and the ball ricocheted to Hampshire, striking him on the ankle. Blood spread out over Close's flannels and trickled into his boot but he refused to go off. Instead he moved even closer at short leg to Younis and the next ball was thwacked into the side of his body and rebounded to Binks who held on to the catch. Suddenly, Yorkshire were buzzing again. Pat Pocock was run out, Robin Jackman bagged a pair and Long was caught behind to end the match.

Every capped player did what was expected of him that season but change was just around the corner and for three of them it was the last hurrah. Trueman and Taylor both announced their retirements and Illingworth found himself forced to move to Leicestershire because of Sellers' intransigence over giving him a contract.

Cope, the young apprentice off-spinner, had once again done well in his handful of appearances, and Illingworth, perhaps perceiving a threat to his place at some later stage, wanted the insurance a longer contract would provide. It was not forthcoming, Sellers said in plain language that Illingworth could leave if he wanted to and he did exactly that, so paving the way for even greater international success after taking on the England captaincy the following year.

Trueman, a true warrior in every respect and the people's champion, laid down his arms quietly against MCC at the Scarborough Festival, bowled by Underwood for a duck in his only innings and failing to take a wicket, but already in that final season he had achieved something of which he was immensely proud until the end of his days.

Captaining the side at Bramall Lane in Close's absence, he led Yorkshire to a famous victory by an innings and 69 runs against the Australians in what was the highlight of the summer. Building on a century opening stand between Boycott and Sharpe, Yorkshire had reached 355-9 when Trueman astutely declared half-an-hour before lunch, leaving himself and Hutton sufficient time in which to dispose of Ian Redpath and Doug Walters.

In the afternoon, Trueman continued to lead from the front by holding three slip catches, running out Ian Chapple and taking the last wicket before enforcing the follow-on. He then took three more wickets, including top-scorer, Redpath, and he was assisted in the mopping up process by Illingworth, the Australians leaving Sheffield with their tail between their legs. Trueman had shown in the clearest of terms that even though Close was the undisputed leader, Yorkshire could still have prospered under his own command.

The 1960s were a happy time for Yorkshire and they waved farewell to them in 1969 by winning the Gillette Cup. But they were on the decline now and as well as slumping to 13th in the Championship, their lowest-ever position at that time, they also made little impact in the new 40-overs-a-side, John Player League, finishing in mid-table.

There were some extenuating circumstances. Close missed nine Championship matches through injury and Boycott, Sharpe and Hampshire at various times were lost to England, who were so ably captained by the 'exiled' Illingworth that they overcame both the West Indies and New Zealand, all four Yorkshiremen notching centuries at some stage or other.

Sharpe, despite playing in all the Tests, still completed 1,000 first-class runs for Yorkshire, along with the consistent Padgett, and there were 101 wickets for Wilson, while Hutton did a commendable all-round job with 734 runs and 66 wickets.

Barrie Leadbeater, one of the nicest and most amiable of Yorkshire cricketers – and one of the most technically correct at the crease – was a more than useful Championship performer that season, but it was in the final of the Gillette Cup at Lord's that he covered himself in glory.

In a career stretching from 1966-1977, Leadbeater only rarely turned his undoubted technical ability into regular run-making and it took him until his 209th Championship innings to register his first and last century.

But he was the star of the show and man of the match in the Gillette final against Derbyshire and his performance helped to gain him his county cap at the end of the season, Old already having received his in late August in recognition of polished fast bowling which brought him 57-first-class wickets at 18.61 runs apiece.

Boycott, having just fractured his left hand in the Championship match at Hove, was forced to sit out the final, but Yorkshire's problems intensified when it was discovered that Leadbeater had also broken a finger bone in the same hand and in the same game.

With a heavily strapped finger, he opened with competition newcomer, John Woodford, who, like Leadbeater, never realised his full potential, and after the pair had added a valuable 39 together, Leadbeater went on to bat into the afternoon session, his hand so swollen that he could not take off his glove during the lunch interval.

His 76 was over twice as many runs as anyone else made in a modest total of 219-8 off 60 overs, but Derbyshire had little to offer against Close and Wilson and were bowled out for 150.

It was a fairy-tale day for a dedicated Yorkshire player who was often dogged by misfortune on the field and tragedy off it but after his playing days were over he became a popular and respected first-class umpire until his retirement at 65.

Leadbeater's man-of-the-match award at Lord's and the receipt of his county cap in the autumn brought down the curtain on the Sixties. Yorkshire were about to embark on a darker era.

CHAPTER TWENTY-SIX

THE TURNING OF THE TIDE

On the face of it, 1970 appeared a pretty tranquil year in the history of Yorkshire County Cricket Club as the team lifted itself from an unacceptable 13th spot in the Championship table the previous year to challenge strongly for the title before falling back to fourth place.

But beneath the calm surface, a tsunami began to swell which would see the start of people power within the club and the end of over a century in which the establishment had reigned supreme.

Sellers at this time was still the driving force, the man whose word was law, but the departure of Illingworth had caused disquiet among the fans who were also unhappy that there seemed little Yorkshire could do to end fears that cricket at Bramall Lane was drawing to a close.

On a murky November day at the end of the season, a bombshell went off which brought the rank and file together – Close was called into the Headingley offices by Sellers and, with secretary John Nash also in the room, was told the captaincy had been taken off him and that he had ten minutes in which to decide whether to resign or be sacked. Numbed by this shock news, Close said he would resign but later rang from his Tong Park home to say that he wanted it to be known that he had been sacked. By now, however, Nash had contacted the Press even though it was still some way off 2pm, the time Close had been led to believe the announcement would be made.

During the winter months which followed, those Yorkshire members incensed by the way in which Close had been treated formed themselves into an Action Group and were successful in bringing about significant changes to the Club.

They did not get Close re-instated but they proved to have sufficient clout to be listened to and acted upon and they paved the way for the even more powerful and determined Reform Group which a few years later would fight tooth and nail for Boycott in the civil war that brought down the general committee.

There were other factors which also made 1970 a very significant season indeed. It began without the familiar face of Binks behind the stumps, the second most successful wicketkeeper in Yorkshire's history having decided to hang up the gloves which had brought him 1,044 victims, a number second only to David Hunter's 1,186, plus a sequence of 412 consecutive Championship matches

The battle to replace Binks was fought out between Neil Smith and an ebullient, larger-than-life David Bairstow, the Bradford-born teenager making headlines by sitting his GCE A levels at Hanson Grammar School at six o'clock in the morning of June 3 so that he could make his Yorkshire debut against Gloucestershire at Park Avenue later in the day.

Bairstow, of course, was to win this duel with 'Nelly' Smith, who went on to carve out a distinguished career with Essex, and 'Bluey' remained unchallenged in his role until the twilight of his playing days which saw him end with just six fewer dismissals overall than Binks but with a club record of 907 catches.

The father of current Yorkshire and England star, Jonny, David was to captain the county for three years from 1984-86, and his immediate successor in charge was another player who made his debut in that 1970 season, Phil Carrick, taker of 1,018 first-class wickets with his left-arm spin, and scorer of just six short of 10,000 runs.

With the tide bringing in younger players around this time as older ones were taken out on the ebb, another familiar face no longer around in 1970 was Chris Balderstone, one of the very last to make a distinguished professional career out of both cricket and football.

One more in the long line of notable Huddersfield-born cricketers, Balderstone was a sound technician with the bat, a useful left-arm slow bowler and an outstanding fielder. He managed 68 appearances for Yorkshire between 1961-69 and although he made several useful contributions his place was always under pressure during this time of plenty.

Balderstone decided to join Illingworth at Leicestershire and it proved to be a wise move because his career finally took off at Grace Road and he was an important member of Illingworth's re-energised side. Nothing gave him more pleasure than when Leicestershire beat Yorkshire in the 1972 Benson and Hedges Cup final and he received the man-of-the-match award for his unbeaten 41 in a low-scoring game.

He played in two Tests for England in 1976 against the mighty West Indies pace attack and his debut, appropriately enough, was at Headingley where he helped his country recover from 23-3 in the first innings with an unflinching 35 in almost three and a half hours of courageous batting. But the match was still lost and in the final Test at The Oval he was unfortunate enough to bag a pair as Michael Holding twice breached his defences with thunderbolts.

When he retired, Balderstone became a well-respected first-class umpire, officiating in two one-day internationals as well as becoming the first third umpire in televised matches, and it came as a great shock to the world of cricket and football when he died suddenly at his home in Carlisle in March, 2000, at the age of 59.

Huddersfield Town, Doncaster Rovers and Carlisle United were among his soccer clubs and it was in September, 1975, that he became the envy of practically every schoolboy in the land. Turning out for Leicestershire against Derbyshire at Chesterfield, he was unbeaten on 51 at the close of play when he dashed to Doncaster to take his place for Rovers in a League encounter with Brentford. Back on the cricket field next day, he completed a sparkling century on his way to 116.

The fact that Yorkshire were more competitive in the Championship than in one-day cricket in 1970 comes as no surprise considering that they lost their first round Gillette Cup match to Surrey in between the snow showers at Harrogate when arch-rival Robin Jackman became only the competition's third bowler to bag seven wickets, and finished a humiliating 14th in the John Player League.

Yet in the 'proper' game there were early signs of promise as Hutton scored his maiden century in the opening fixture with Derbyshire, who were beaten by an innings and 20 runs, Old taking 5-14 in helpful conditions on the first day and

Cope and Wilson doing the damage later on when the Park Avenue pitch began to assist the spinners.

But, as already hinted, it was not to be Close's year and on May 17 in the John Player League match with Glamorgan at Bradford he injured his shoulder so severely while diving for his crease that the following day he was unable to continue his brave innings of 56 out of 107-8 against the same opponents at Middlesbrough, the Welshmen going on to win by five wickets.

The injury caused Close to miss the next three matches, two of which were lost, and he was below full fitness for the remainder of the season although his return to the helm inspired a recovery which resulted in a surge up the table until falling away in mid-August.

Boycott, by now the scourge of bowlers nationwide and beyond, enjoyed a splendid season in which he headed Yorkshire's averages by some distance with 1,558, taking his aggregate in all cricket to 2,051. His tally included his career-best score of 260 not out against Essex at Colchester when he batted for seven hours almost without blemish and caressed 27 boundaries.

Close was able to declare at 450-4 and Cope then took over with match figures of 10-80, his 7-36 in the second innings including a hat-trick with the dismissals of Graham Saville, Keith Fletcher and Leeds-born Gordon Barker.

A summer of great personal satisfaction, no doubt, for Boycott, as it was for Cope, who more than doubled his haul of Championship wickets from 37 to 75 and was awarded his cap in early August before some of the icing was sliced off his cake when his bowling action was once more called into question. It was pronounced he had only a minor fault to iron out and he was not barred from playing but this was the second time so far that his action had been monitored and there was real grief in 1972 and 1978 when bans were imposed.

Nobody could possibly have fought harder than Cope to put things right, later spending countless hours with Johnny Wardle at his coaching school, and there was an opinion in the game, not without some foundation, that Cope was being picked upon by Lord's when other, much quicker bowlers, did not come under the same scrutiny. He overcame his problems sufficiently to play for England in Pakistan in 1977-78 but a question-mark always hung over him and it contributed largely to his premature retirement in 1980.

Ironically, he had to share a benefit in that season with Barrie Leadbeater who was also dogged by misfortune. Each of them surely deserved a benefit of his own because few others have come through such adversities and remained so loyal to the cause.

Another whose loyalty and commitment were beyond question was Close himself which is why he had to open his car window to be physically sick on his way home in November after Sellers had delivered a verbal blow which hurt more than any cricket ball thudding into his frame had ever done.

Close that summer had been granted a testimonial which added £6,540 to the £8,154 he had received from his benefit in 1971, a figure at the time exceeded only by Len Hutton's £9,712 in 1950. And many of the club's members who had subscribed were so unhappy with the shoddy treatment of the captain that they formed the Yorkshire Action Group, chaired by Keighley solicitor and Craven

League stalwart, Jack Mewies, a friend and adviser to Close and a friend, also, of Trueman's.

The Group openly criticised the way the club was being run, sought a vote of no confidence in the committee, demanded rule changes and called for a better relationship between selectors and players. It was the sort of people power that had never been witnessed before and this first real winter of discontent led to huge speculation as to what would happen at the club's annual meeting early in 1971.

So keen was the interest aroused that 1,500 members turned up for the meeting in Leeds Town Hall and my Yorkshire cricket predecessor at the Telegraph & Argus, David Swallow, reported that in the long history of Yorkshire CCC this was one of the biggest scenes of high drama – and that it all happened off the field.

The 'rebels', led by Mewies, successfully opposed the adoption of the committee report and statement of accounts, the vote being hailed as a great victory by the group.

Their actions led to Sellers stepping down as cricket chairman after 13 years in charge and being replaced by John Temple, who never seemed entirely comfortable in what became an increasingly hot seat. Furthermore, they brought about changes to the rules from 1972 which resulted in vice-presidents no longer being ex-officio members of the general committee or sub-committees. The general committee was to consist of not more than six elected members and 23 district members.

Having demanded and got significant changes, the Action Group stood back to allow an uneasy peace to settle on the club, but it could not have been the most comfortable of environments in which the new captain, Boycott, found himself having to work, particularly as some of the most influential players from the great side of the 60s were no longer around.

Close later said that Boycott would have been his choice to succeed him a couple of years or so down the line when he had acquired more experience but with Sharpe overlooked the club opted for Boycott who looked like churning out the runs for years to come. The certainty that Boycott would often be absent on Test duty led to Don Wilson being appointed his deputy.

With the membership and fans craving a return to the golden days of the previous decade, there was to be no honeymoon period for Boycott and with other counties increasingly looking overseas for help the pressure was on a Yorkshire of thinning resources as never before.

But things got worse rather than better and at the end of the 1971 season the club had to admit: "It is with regret that your Committee has to report that the season of 1971 was, without doubt, the worst in the history of the Club, both from a playing and financial point of view."

Positions of 13th in the Championship, next to bottom in the John Player League and a loss on the year of over £12,000 left little room for cheerfulness, the misery in the committee room never deeper than when Close renewed his acquaintanceship with Yorkshire by scoring a determined four-hour century at Taunton. Somerset went on to win by ten wickets, their cause also being helped by Tom Cartwright with nine wickets and Australian leg-spinner Kerry O'Keeffe, with seven.

There were promising centuries that season from Andrew Dalton and John Woodford, who had both shown outstanding form in youth cricket but would bow out of first-class cricket prematurely, because of business commitments in Dalton's case and school teaching in Woodford's. Hampshire again showed his class with 1,259 first-class runs for Yorkshire but way ahead by almost 1,000 was Boycott, who collected 2,221 with 11 centuries for an incredible average of 105.76.

Once again, Essex saw the width of Boycott's blade at Colchester where he scored his second double century in as many years but this time his immaculate 233 did not lead to a victory, the home side clinging on despite four wickets in each innings for Mike Bore, the left-arm bowler who became Yorkshire's and then Nottinghamshire's version of Derek Underwood.

Boycott gave clear evidence for the first time – and certainly not the last – that the weight of captaincy upon his shoulders would not in any way affect his ability to score runs. Indeed, the greater the pressures upon him personally the more he was able to push them to one side when he arrived at the crease.

This ability consistently to stack up the runs while the team as a unit failed to make any sort of impact was one of the biggest single reasons why the club was to split into pro and anti Boycott factions.

Some felt that he put self before team and was pre-occupied with his own batting to the exclusion of everything else but others saw him as being gloriously successful at a time when those around him could not match his own standards. It is true that many spectators came to matches more in the expectation that Boycott would score a century than that Yorkshire would go on to win the match.

There was a shaft of light among the gloom in that the Second XI lifted their Championship for a second time under Bob Platt in a season in which they lost only one match. Their leading wicket-takers were Howard Cooper and Arthur 'Rocker' Robinson who would both go on faithfully to front Yorkshire's attack when bowling resources were weakened partly through being starved of overseas players.

Platt retired as captain because of business pressures and another link with the past was severed when Arthur Mitchell told the committee that he wished to resign as coach because of ill-health. Their places were filled by Doug Padgett who had wanted to continue in the first team. His cause was championed by Boycott, who believed Padgett's experience and technical skills were an asset to the side, but he was overruled by the new cricket chairman, Temple.

Further signs that the old magical days were drawing to a close came in early September with the death of Percy Holmes, followed at the end of October by the retirement of John Nash after 41 years' service as secretary. He was rewarded by being elected an honorary life member and vice-president.

Now was the time for Joe Lister to step up to the plate as secretary. Little would he realise when he came back to Yorkshire from his enjoyable years at Worcestershire that he would need all his wits about him to keep the lid on the cauldron that continued to bubble over as time went on.

CHAPTER TWENTY-SEVEN

BRAMALL LANE FAREWELL

The weather in 1972 was bitter-sweet with rain ruining the first half of the season before the sun asserted itself in the second and Yorkshire also found it a summer of sharp contrasts.

A rise of three places to tenth in the Championship was of little comfort and there was a double blow in the Gillette Cup in early July as Yorkshire were again jettisoned in the first round, this time by Warwickshire, and Boycott had the middle finger of his right hand split by a brute of a ball from Bob Willis which lifted sharply on the Headingley pitch to put the captain out of action for the next five weeks.

Climbing from 16th to fourth in the John Player League was far more encouraging, however, and there was great joy that Yorkshire should reach the Lord's final of the Benson and Hedges Cup in its inaugural season, even though, without the injured Boycott, they were soundly beaten by Illingworth's Leicestershire.

Alas, this was to be Yorkshire's last appearance in a Lord's final until they won the Benson and Hedges Cup under Phil Carrick in 1987, but they were not bereft of silverware in 1972 because at the Scarborough Festival they won the Fenner Knockout Trophy, now in its second year, by outplaying Lancashire in the final, thanks to the clean-hitting Old smacking a century in 75 minutes with 15 fours and a six.

One-day cricket may have taken a time for first-class counties to feel comfortable with but Yorkshire by now were happy to trumpet any success, even if it came in a locally-organised competition.

Despite his hand injury restricting Boycott to just ten Championship matches and 17 innings he still scored 1,156 runs for an average of 96.33 but was the only one in his team to top 1,000 runs. He hit a double century and five other centuries, yet his support was so thin that there were only three other 'tons' in the entire season – two from Hampshire and one from Dalton who had just four knocks in three matches but compiled a splendid 128, followed by 49, in the win over Middlesex at Headingley. Dalton may well have achieved much more had a leg injury not kept him out until late August.

Nicholson was the leading bowler with 60 wickets but he may have been harder pressed by Cope had the off-spinner's suspect action not led to him being reported by umpires and opposing captains and consequently banned after the first eight matches in inclement weather had brought him 15 wickets. An attempt to be re-instated in August was rejected by the TCCB and although he worked tirelessly with Wardle to remodel his action it was into the second half of the following summer before he appeared again.

On a happier note, the opening combination of Boycott and Richard Lumb – the second most successful in Yorkshire's history – finally established itself in the latter part of the season.

Richard, whose grandfather founded the prestigious Joe Lumb Trophy for junior league teams around Yorkshire, had made his Yorkshire debut in August, 1970, against Worcestershire at Worcester. He batted in the middle order and in his first innings was run out for 17, a fate he was later to suffer more times than he cared to remember when opening with Boycott.

The first time the pair opened together was against Hampshire at Bournemouth in 1971, when they recorded stands of 19 and 84, and the first of their 29 century alliances followed at Edgbaston with 134 off the Warwickshire attack in the second innings.

Lumb was forced to play his cricket in the shadow of Boycott but he was a very fine player in his own right and came close to winning an England cap. Ted Lester judged him the best legside batsman since Peter May but he could still cut the spinners as late and as delicately as anyone I have seen.

A man of few words and a nice laid-back sense of humour, Lumb would have enjoyed his cricket more if happier times had prevailed but when he retired and emigrated to South Africa at the end of the 1984 season he could look back with pride on his record of 11,525 runs and 22 centuries. He was also a good slip fielder, even though his concentration could wander at times, and on one memorable occasion at Middlesbrough in 1972, the season under review, he held on to edges from five Gloucestershire batsmen in one innings, a figure exceeded only by Ellis Robinson, who pocketed six against Leicestershire at Bradford in 1938.

If the first team struggled for consistency in 1972, steady progress continued to be made by the Second XI, who were led to the summit of the Minor Counties Championship by Padgett, but they lost by three wickets at Barnsley when accepting a Championship Challenge match from second-placed Bedfordshire.

Two up-and-coming youngsters who were beginning to make their mark in the second team were Arnie Sidebottom and Graham Stevenson, both of whom had an abundance of natural talent, particularly Stevenson. The Ackworth lad was a contemporary of Ian Botham's and it would have taken a brave man in those formative years to bet on which of the two would become one of the biggest stars the game has ever known.

Stevenson scratched the surface with England, playing in two Test matches and four one-day internationals, but his all-round gifts were never fully utilised. He bowled sharply with late movement off a good length, he could hit out spectacularly, particularly high over extra cover, and he could return balls from the outfield with the speed of lightning. He became a firm favourite of Boycott, who revelled in his boyish humour and practical jokes and even encouraged him to become the team jester. Yorkshire cricket was never dull when Stevo was around.

And don't let us fail to acknowledge what an outstanding member of the team Arnie became with his mastery of seam and swing and his much under-rated efforts with the bat. He was technically equipped to bat much higher up the order than he usually did and when circumstances demanded he went in earlier he never looked out of place.

His son, Ryan, went on to much greater achievements with England than his dad, who managed only half-a-match before breaking down, but Arnie's record of 558 first-class wickets and 4,243 for Yorkshire speaks for itself. He went on to become a popular and successful coach with his native county before, unfortunately, getting squeezed out.

Memories of Yorkshire's great past and the realisation that the re-building process was proving slow and painful were very much to the fore in 1973 when three outstanding figures from an earlier age died, Bramall Lane staged its last match and the team plummeted to 14th place in the Championship table.

The well-loved and ever-cheerful Arthur Wood died on April 2, the time of year when, as a younger man, he would eagerly have been picking up his wicketkeeping gloves again; the mighty Wilfred Rhodes, perhaps mightier even than his friend and neighbour George Hirst, slipped away on July 8 at the grand old age of 95, and Col. Sir William Worsley, former captain and faithful president of the past 13 years, departed this life on December 4, having devoted 46 years to the club in various capacities.

He was succeeded as president by the amiable and kindly Sir Kenneth Parkinson, chairman of Yorkshire Post Newspapers and successful Bradford woolman. Sir Kenneth had always held a deep interest in the club and he was a calming and unbiased figurehead during his eight years in office.

It was appropriate that a short service in Rhodes' memory was conducted on the pitch by the Bishop of Wakefield at the Roses game at Sheffield in early August in what was Yorkshire's farewell appearance on the famous ground in the city of their birth. No sooner was the game over than work began on erecting a stand as the ground, the home of Sheffield United, sadly turned its attentions solely to soccer.

Yorkshire would move to Abbeydale Park the following season although this was not known at the time of the Roses farewell to 118 years of cricket at Bramall Lane, the weather having the final say in a match which fizzled out.

The only half-century of the game was struck by Sharpe with an unbeaten 62 after Yorkshire had been bowled out in their first innings for 99 by Peter Lee, who grabbed 6-43 on a damp pitch.

Yorkshire were also at Bramall Lane in their previous match against Derbyshire and the last century at the venue was scored by a Yorkshireman – but not for Yorkshire! It came from former 'old boy' Brian Bolus, now captain of the Peakites, who hammered 138 but could not prevent his current side from going down by four wickets.

The last century for Yorkshire on the ground occurred in the first of the three Sheffield fixtures that season and it was scored by middle-order batsman and brilliant cover fielder Colin Johnson, who hit 107 after Sharpe opened with 133, the pair adding 146 for the fourth wicket. It was Johnson's maiden century and he was able to compile only one further three-figure score in a total of 100 first-class matches. He never really managed the sort of scores which he showed he was capable of at second team level, yet his fielding and speed of movement were a delight to watch.

The same can be said of Peter Squires who played alongside Johnson in the Bramall Lane match. More noted for his Rugby Union and British Lions exploits in the 1970s, Squires featured in 49 first-class and 56 List A matches for Yorkshire between 1972-1976. An extrovert character with an obvious zest for life, Squires also never scaled the heights with Yorkshire but his fielding was magnificent and the team never had better men at mid-wicket and cover than when Johnson and

Squires were on patrol together.

Another England and British Lions player was partly responsible in 1973 for one of Yorkshire's most headline-grabbing humiliations of the decade – and to rub salt into the wound his much more celebrated cricketing brother was in the defeated side!

The occasion was Yorkshire's Gillette Cup first round match against Minor Counties outfit Durham at Harrogate, with Chris Old playing for the home side and his elder brother, Alan, for the opposition.

Victory should have been a formality for Yorkshire but they were pinned right back after winning the toss by Alan, whose seven new-ball overs cost only ten runs, and when captain Brian Lander stepped in with 5-15 they were swept aside for 135 in 58.4 overs.

Chris was then economic but ineffective with the new ball and Durham romped it by five wickets for Yorkshire to suffer the indignity of becoming the first county to be beaten by a junior side since the Minor Counties first entered the competition ten years earlier.

The trouncing was such a jolt to Yorkshire's ego that it was one of the reasons why the committee agreed that greater efforts must be made to develop the talents of the thousands of young cricketers spread across the largest of England's counties and they decided that from the following season they would sponsor an inter-league knockout competition confined to Yorkshire-born players under the age of 24. Thus the White Rose Trophy was born and the Bradford League's young team were to become its first winners.

Despite all the upsets of 1973, the season was not entirely without excitement and the most dramatic match in the Championship was saved right until the end when Yorkshire tied with Middlesex at Bradford to register only the second such result in their history.

The tie was a triumph for Yorkshire who overcame all sorts of obstacles, including the absence of Boycott and Old, who were both ill, and the coming and going of several players during the course of the match as they went down with a sickness bug which struck the dressing room.

Stevenson made his debut in this match and was one of those confined to his bed for a while, yet although Yorkshire at one stage were forced to field four substitutes they clung on bravely. Set 208 to win, Johnson and Bairstow both hit half-centuries and the scores were level when, in mounting tension, last man Arthur Robinson was bowled by Mike Selvey.

There was little change in Yorkshire's fortunes in 1974 and although they moved up three places in the Championship table, 11th spot could hardly be considered satisfactory. Even that position looked unlikely as Yorkshire made a poor start to the season, injuries being a factor, and it was July 17 before they gained their first success by beating Nottinghamshire by an innings at Worksop, an unusual feature being that four of their bowlers each claimed five wickets.

On what started out as a green pitch, Arthur Robinson helped himself to 5-27, including a hat-trick, to send Notts back for 94 while at the other end Holmfirth-born Dennis Schofield, in his third and final appearance for the county, captured 5-42. Later, the track took spin and Cope and Don Wilson destroyed Notts for 87. Either side of these two collapses, Hampshire batted brilliantly for his unbeaten 157 out of

250-7 declared, his boundaries made up of 20 fours and three sixes. Hampshire was in such glorious form that the very next day he powered his way to 158 against Gloucestershire at Harrogate to set Yorkshire up for another innings win.

Just as Schofield had answered Yorkshire's call in the previous match for a fast bowler to see them through an injury crisis, so did Sheffield-born Steve Oldham on this occasion and he helped wipe out Gloucestershire in their first innings for 71 by returning the remarkable figures of 4.5-3-7-3.

Had Yorkshire not been ignorant of Oldham's situation at the time they may well never have picked him and a remarkable career with the county, temporarily put on hold when he moved to Derbyshire, may never have taken place.

The fact was that Oldham was experiencing a brief spell without any cricket at all, having just left Bradford League Club Idle after an unhappy stay before returning to Barnsley. There were few signs of rustiness against Gloucestershire, however, and his success had a dramatic effect on his life.

He left for Derbyshire in time for the start of the 1980 season and gave them valuable service until 1984, when he was brought back to Yorkshire by manager Raymond Illingworth, initially to assist the younger bowlers. He was appointed second team captain for a couple of years, became assistant coach and then the club's first cricket manager in 1990. After serving in that role he continued to bring on the younger players and he earned a reputation for nurturing some of Yorkshire's greatest fast bowlers, including Darren Gough and Tim Bresnan.

Oldham was in the thick of it during many of Yorkshire's tempestuous years since the mid-70s and his great skill in developing young pacemen helped him become one of the club's great survivors until he was not retained for the 2012 season when the coaching was restructured.

On the bright side in 1974, Yorkshire enjoyed the services of Boycott for much of the time as a consequence of him losing his England place to David Lloyd for the second Test with India and not regaining it during the remainder of the summer. Inevitably, he was the leading scorer with 1,478 runs in a benefit season which raked him in a record £20,639. He received good support in the middle from Hampshire, Leadbeater and Lumb without any of that trio managing to reach the 1,000 mark. One felt for Leadbeater who, still searching for his first century, was stranded on 99 against Kent at Scarborough when the innings had to be declared at the 100 overs stage. Perhaps, with a little more urgency, he could have made it because he required only a further 17 with ten overs remaining.

Cope, too, enjoyed himself, shrugging off the ever-present worry about his action to lead the way with 77 wickets, and with Carrick chipping in with 47 the spin options looked promising, even though the old warhorse, Don Wilson, struggled, and at the end of the season announced his retirement.

Don remained one of the proudest men ever to wear a Yorkshire sweater and a spark went out with his death on July 21, 2012. Friends and former colleagues turned out in good numbers for a moving memorial service at St Chad's Church, Headingley, in September, Richard Hutton giving a splendid eulogy and Philip Sharpe reciting a poem as well as reading out tributes which included one from former Australian captain, Ian Chappell.

CHAPTER TWENTY-EIGHT

SUNSHINE AND SHADOW

Undoubtedly, the happiest times Yorkshire experienced during the 1970s occurred in 1975, my first year on the circuit, when their cricket and their mood matched the sunny weather. After four consecutive seasons of wallowing in the lower half of the Championship table they finished as runners-up, their best effort since last clinching the title in 1968.

Boycott had much to do with the revival in terms of leadership and runs and Yorkshire certainly benefited from his decision, announced just ahead of the Roses match at Old Trafford in May, that he would continue to take leave of absence from the Test side, having declined to tour Australia and New Zealand during the winter.

His long-awaited decision, which had kept everyone guessing, meant he would play no part in the Ashes series that summer or the very first World Cup, then known as the Prudential Cup.

The reasons for his temporary stepping back from England while at the summit of his career were never fully explained but the fact that Mike Denness was captain for part of that period may have had something to do with it.

Whatever the ins and outs of it, turning his back on England meant Boycott could spend a full summer with Yorkshire and although he missed out on a couple of matches through injury he still chalked up 1,891 Championship runs at 72.73 with Lumb and Hampshire also making it into four figures.

The fine weather and dry pitches made it a spinners' paradise and Cope and Carrick responded with 148 dismissals between them which was just over 47% of all Yorkshire's wickets. Cope, at last able to enjoy his cricket, had 69 victims while Carrick topped that figure by ten. Caps were not given away in those days and Carrick was bitterly disappointed when he did not receive his at the end of the season and had to wait another year.

As well as the retirement of Don Wilson, two other regulars were absent from the 1975 line-up, Sharpe moving to Derbyshire after his contract had been ended with a year to run, and Hutton writing to Lister from South Africa in the winter to say that he was retiring from first-class cricket. Both had given great service to Yorkshire and England and Sharpe had become one of the greatest of slip fielders.

Yorkshire took a while to find their rhythm in the Championship, drawing all five of their opening matches for the first time since 1928, but they went on to lose only one match all season for the first time since 1946 and by the beginning of August were top of the table and serious title challengers. Ten wins from their last 15 matches, however, was still not quite good enough.

The series of five early draws included the rain-affected match against Worcestershire at New Road when Boycott hit an unbeaten 152 out of 278-8 to complete the full set of a century against each of the 16 other first-class counties. Of all the landmarks which were to follow, I don't think any of them gave Boycott greater pleasure than this particular achievement and he celebrated in the team hotel that night by holding a party and splashing out on champagne.

Curiously, he was never able to complete a century against Oxford University, the students always denying him through stunning acts of brilliance in the field. This happened, for instance, in The Parks in 1978 when he fell for a duck to an athletic return catch by Stephen Wookey in a first innings of 468-6 declared and an even more spectacular diving effort by Roger Moulding at cover point in the second for three.

The sequence of draws was finally broken against Gloucestershire at Bristol where, ten minutes into the third day, they emerged winners by an innings and 122 runs, Cope claiming career-best figures of 8-73. Yorkshire had amassed 446-2 declared through centuries from Boycott, Lumb and Hampshire. It was the first time since 1947 that three of their batsmen had scored centuries in the same innings of a Championship match and it could so easily have been four if Leadbeater had not gone into his shell and got no further than 68 when the innings was closed.

Boycott was the first batsman in the country to reach 1,000 first-class runs, the landmark being reached at Harrogate on June 8 soon after the start of a cracking match with Somerset in which Viv Richards plundered 217 not out and put on 227 for the fifth wicket with Close (91), the biggest stand against Yorkshire in 16 years. A declaration by Boycott left Somerset to make 300 in two hours and the game ended in a thrilling climax as Cope just failed to complete a hat-trick which would have secured victory off the very last ball.

Two nerve-tingling wins in London added to Yorkshire's growing confidence. At The Oval they overcame Surrey by 35 runs. Set 267, Surrey were 228-6 but lost their last four wickets for three runs, Old and Carrick finishing with four apiece. Even this was tame stuff compared to what happened a couple of matches later at Lord's. An unbeaten double century for Boycott only resulted in a first innings lead of 51 and when Yorkshire were routed for 106 by John Emburey (6-46) it left Middlesex needing only 158. Five wickets remained with just ten needed but the second half of the batting was scythed away for four runs, the last three in the penultimate over and the game being won by Squires' direct hit on the stumps.

A new career started with the debut of Jim Love and a much-admired one ended with the retirement at the end of the season of Nicholson, his 876 wickets at 19.74 runs apiece giving him a place in the top 20 Yorkshire bowlers of all time. Nicholson had thought his grand farewell was at Scarborough but a crop of injuries brought him back for the final Championship game against Essex at Middlesbrough which Yorkshire won by 59 runs.

A crowd of fans surged in front of the pavilion at Acklam Park, acclaiming their team and calling for them to take a bow, but it never came. Boycott felt that finishing second left little to celebrate but it was a further 26 years before Yorkshire went that one step further.

Yorkshire failed to fire in either of the knockout competitions and they could not capitalise on a good start in the John Player League which saw a memorable match played out in front of a packed 15,000 crowd at Park Avenue, the biggest on the ground since the Australians were there in 1964 and a figure never to be repeated.

They watched Yorkshire win a tight match against Somerset by 12 runs but the real reason they had turned up in such large numbers was to welcome Close back on his native soil. He received a standing ovation when he came in to bat and was applauded all the way to the crease. Clearly overwhelmed by the reception, he later admitted that he was glad the first ball wasn't a straight one and he was probably still not fully composed when he edged Stevenson to Bairstow and departed for nine.

The biggest headline-making day of the season came at Headingley but it did not involve Yorkshire. In the third Ashes Test, Australia were set 445 to win and at the close of the fourth day were 55 without loss. Next morning the teams arrived to discover that the pitch had been dug up and oil poured on the strip by supporters of George Davis, who was serving a 20-year prison sentence for his part in an armed raid.

Captains Tony Greig and Ian Chappell agreed that the pitch was unplayable and there was no option but to call the match off. There would not have been a positive result, anyway, because rain soon began to fall steadily throughout the remainder of the day.

Yorkshire secretary Lister said he believed that all reasonable precautions had been taken and that one patrolling policeman would have been sufficient under normal circumstances. He admitted, however, that times were changing and that pitch security would have to come under consideration.

The improvement in Yorkshire's cricket led to a general air of optimism that the club was on its way up again, but in 1976, in one of the hottest and sunniest summers on record, the team lurked in the shadows and pressures, still below the surface, gradually continued to build.

A fall from second to eighth in the Championship, won by Middlesex for the first time since 1949, was a shock made worse by a slump from seventh to an unacceptable 15th in the John Player League with little to write home about in either the Benson and Hedges Cup or the Gillette Cup.

Some of the problems stemmed from the large amount of injuries, many of them to senior players, including Boycott who had his finger broken by Barry Wood in the JPL Roses match at Old Trafford on May 16. What was expected to be a three-week period out of action turned into one of two months as back problems set in while his finger was healing.

With Boycott unable to say exactly when he would return, tensions mounted within the cricket committee and at one stage cricket chairman John Temple had to deny to the Press that there were any plans to replace Boycott as captain because of his absence.

Old's appearances were restricted to six matches because of constant knee trouble which severely limited his bowling and Hampshire missed five games with a broken thumb but was there to lead the team when Boycott was missing. He also enjoyed top form during his benefit season and notched 1,241 runs compared to Boycott's 1,040 from five fewer appearances.

Spinners were again to the fore in the baking heat and Cope and Carrick did not shirk their duties, Cope prising out 80 batsmen in the Championship to be rewarded with a tour place to India at the end of the summer and Carrick sending back 59, sufficient to be awarded his county cap along with Arthur Robinson who toiled away manfully for his 32 victims. Cooper sweated out even more overs for his 40 wickets but the cap which should have been his by right at some stage or other in his career never materialised.

The dry spring meant that the ground was rock hard when Yorkshire raised the curtain on their Championship programme against Gloucestershire at Headingley on April 28 in a drawn match which produced six centuries, the most in any Yorkshire fixture. There were centuries for Yorkshire from Boycott, Lumb, Johnson and Hampshire and for Gloucestershire from Zaheer Abbas and Sadiq Mohammad, overseas players now spreading out more widely than ever before over the county circuit.

Three years on from the tied match with Middlesex at Bradford, the same teams nearly repeated the result at the same venue, this time Hampshire leading Yorkshire to a nail-biting victory by one run. Clive Radley, who had retired from the action after breaking a finger in the slips early on, returned to the fray with Middlesex nine down in their second innings and still requiring five to win. Batting left-handed and with his damaged arm in a black sling he managed three before stepping out of his ground to Cope and being stumped by Bairstow.

Another dramatic game occurred outside the Championship when Yorkshire met the West Indies at Sheffield and lost by 19 runs. The result might have been very different if Leadbeater, one not out at the end of the second day, had not injured himself quite badly in a car mishap on his way home and put himself out of the contest. Yorkshire were bundled out for 90 by Wayne Daniel, one of the West Indies most feared but perhaps under-rated bowlers, who returned match figures of 10-61, but the Tourists themselves had been routed in the first innings by Old with a magnificent 7-42.

Speculation continued early in the season as to whether Boycott was about to return to Test cricket and this heightened on May 8, upon Yorkshire's visit to Hove in the Benson and Hedges Cup, when England and Sussex captain Tony Greig held a secret meeting with Boycott after the match to discuss his intentions. Again, Boycott decided his loyalties would solely be to his county. Not long afterwards, Greig successfully urged the selectors to bring back Close to face up to the searing pace of the West Indies – which he did so heroically for three matches before being dropped for what would have been a home Test at Headingley.

Despite Yorkshire's failure to move forward, Padgett continued to bring on players of obvious talent in the Second XI and two of the most outstanding made their Championship debuts, one at either end of the season.

Middlesbrough-born Bill Athey, whose father followed Keith Boyce as groundsman at Acklam Park, was considered to be another Boycott in the making because of the pureness of his technique and his unruffled temperament. He first turned out against Northamptonshire at Wantage Road in May and had made just ten when he experienced at first hand the wiles of Championship cricket. Aware of Yorkshire's renowned vulnerability against leg-spin, captain Mushtaq Mohammad brought himself on for one over, trapped Athey lbw and immediately took himself off again.

Undeterred by this early lesson, Athey soon worked his way back into the team and when he was promoted to open the innings with Lumb against Sussex at Leeds in July he scored his maiden century. At 18 years, 9 months he was the second youngest centurion in Yorkshire's history, Len Hutton being 18 years, 1 month when he made 196 at Worcester in 1934.

If he never quite scaled the heights which many thought he was capable of, Athey still played in 23 Tests and was among the most prolific batsmen of his generation. Had he churned out the bulk of his 25,453 runs for Yorkshire, instead of just 6,320 of them, he would have found a place among the county's top ten batsmen of all time.

But he moved away at the end of 1983 to give incredible service to Gloucestershire and then Sussex before becoming coach at Worcestershire, where he also played one first team game and several for the Second XI.

The other youngster to take his first bow towards the end of the summer was 17-year-old Kevin Sharp, already a left-hander of precocious talent who would score a century the following season for England Under-19s v Australia Under-19s and top this in 1978 with an unbeaten 260 for his country against West Indies Under-19s.

Perhaps the fleet-footed Sharp was thrown in at the deep end before his temperament had fully developed because he rarely looked entirely at ease with himself even though he was invariably a joy to watch when exhibiting his wide range of strokes. He last played for Yorkshire in 1990 and after netting £89,770 in his benefit the following year, he played for Shropshire for a while before becoming the first coach of the Bradford-Leeds University of Cricketing Excellence. He then returned to Yorkshire as batting coach and remained as popular a figure as ever but he was unsuccessful in gaining a post when a new system of coaching came into place ahead of the 2012 season.

CHAPTER TWENTY-NINE

TESTING TIMES

At 5.50pm on August 11, 1977, with the summer shadows lengthening, Boycott reached the zenith of his astonishing career by becoming the only batsman in world cricket to complete his 100th first-class century in a Test match.

And the unique achievement was all the more memorable in that it was played out at Headingley against Australia in his first appearance in Yorkshire since returning to the England side from a self-imposed walk in the wilderness.

Boycott's name was the banner headline in newspapers all over the cricketing world and I wrote in the Telegraph & Argus at the time:

"Rarely can every run have been so frantically applauded, never can such scenes have been witnessed for hitting a century of centuries.

"It was as if Boycott wanted to see exactly 100. A scoreboard showing 101 or 102 would have spoiled the symmetry of it all.

"So, when he was 96, he on-drove Australia's Greg Chappell for a boundary which was a purist's delight and the magical figure had been reached.

"Boycott's bat was raised aloft and there was just time for congratulations from Roope and Chappell before he was swallowed up by a surging tide of boys.

"All the time, the crowd were on their feet shouting, cheering, waving, and when the tide ebbed they saw that Boycott's cap had gone with it.

"Secretary, Mr. Joe Lister, brought out another and a policeman took it to Boycott. Still the crowd were rooted to their feet, applauding wildly. This was what they had come to see and this was what they were acclaiming.

"Eventually, his original cap was returned by a repentant youth, the other was taken back and the masses sat down. It was 5.55 before he was able to receive the next ball."

Throughout this book I have generally ignored Headingley Test matches in order to concentrate more fully upon matters directly affecting Yorkshire CCC but this Test and the Botham-Willis epic four years later are exceptions to the rule, simply because they produced two of the greatest cricket stories ever told and the pages were turned on Yorkshire soil in front of thousands of ecstatic Yorkshire fans.

Even by his own impossibly high standards, Boycott never experienced a more glorious or eventful period than in the midsummer of 1977 when he was the hero of millions. However, Yorkshire's continuing failure to rediscover their halcyon days meant that the pressures were mounting on Boycott before the year was out and the divide was growing ever wider.

Who could ever have imagined at the time of Boycott's Headingley triumph that a few weeks on there would be calls from within the club for him to resign the captaincy, that the Yorkshire Reform Group would be formed to fight his corner, and that it would be announced that Raymond Illingworth would return 18 months down the line as team manager?

In the Championship at least, the season had started satisfactorily, a combination of poor weather and positive cricket combining to leave them undefeated after a dozen matches, something which had not happened since 1954.

But the rot set in immediately after the dramatic announcement on July 24 that Boycott was to return to the England side and had been selected for the third Test against Australia at Trent Bridge. Yorkshire promptly lost to Kent at Folkestone to signal the start of a run of five defeats and one win, a sequence which helped push them to a final 12th place in the table.

The news of Boycott's return to the England fold after three years outside it, however, gripped the nation at the cost of all else, and it was kept a closely guarded secret until the Test team was announced, although it was known that Boycott had been involved in behind-closed-doors talks with Alec Bedser, chairman of the England selectors.

On the day in question, Yorkshire had left their Championship match at Folkestone to take on Kent in the John Player League at Canterbury and it was in the pavilion there before the game began that I interviewed Boycott. As I was leaving, I said: "It's all set up for you now." "What is?" he replied. "Your 98th century for England at Trent Bridge, your 99th for Yorkshire at Edgbaston and your 100th for England at Headingley." He smiled back. I never thought it would happen. He did.

In the weeks leading up to all this, Boycott was already peeling off the centuries with sublime ease -139 not out v Somerset at Harrogate, 117 v Middlesex at Lord's and a sumptuous 154 v Nottinghamshire at Trent Bridge which pushed Yorkshire to the top of the table. There can be no doubt that suddenly taking leave of the side upset the rhythm and left them desperately short of his runs.

Yet his impact on the one-day game was less noticeable, Yorkshire stumbling to 15th in the John Player League, exiting the Gillette Cup in the first round, and failing once again to qualify from the zonal stages of the Benson and Hedges Cup.

Boycott occupied centre stage for a lot of the time in 1977 but not quite all of it and at Sophia Gardens in late May, Arnie Sidebottom was the star with Arthur Robinson and Stevenson playing strong supporting roles.

We were still in the days when top sportsmen could make a living out of both cricket and football and Sidebottom's season with Yorkshire had started late because of his involvement with Huddersfield Town. The Glamorgan match was his first of the summer and after the Welshmen had been bowled out for 149 Yorkshire found themselves on exactly the same score with nine down. Then last man Robinson survived long enough for his career-best score of 30 not out while Sidebottom crashed the ball to all parts on the way to his only century. The pair were four short of Yorkshire's tenth wicket record of 148, set by Lord Hawke and David Hunter in 1898, when Sidebottom was run out on 124.

The partnership was big news and raved about in the Press Box but it meant little to the two men concerned. Sidebottom confessed never to having heard of Lord Hawke and Robinson said he was not at all interested in the breaking of records which was far less important to him than the picking-up points.

Having been dazed by Sidebottom, Glamorgan were knocked out for the count by Stevenson who added career-best figures at the time of 6-82 to give him a match return of 10-137.

As predicted, tongue in cheek, Boycott constructed his 99th century at Edgbaston and Love made his second but what looked like becoming a dreary draw suddenly exploded into life as Old smashed the second fastest century in cricket history.

Rain over the first two days had dashed any hope of a positive result and as soon as the follow-on had been avoided Warwickshire declared their first innings on 204-3 and trailing by 149. Bob Willis bowled a couple of overs off three paces as Warwickshire hurried things on to improve their slow over rate but even when Old was promoted to come in at 40-3 there was little immediate sign of the carnage to follow.

His first 50 came in 28 minutes, with few taking little notice, but all that changed when Rohan Kanhai and John Whitehouse teamed up and began bowling donkey drops. Hitting the ball as clean as a whistle and often clearing the big ground, Old thrashed his whirlwind second 50 in a mere nine minutes. He had struck 13 fours and six sixes off the 73 balls he faced for his 37-minute century and had he lashed out from the start he would surely have beaten cricket's fastest century which was scored in 35 minutes by Percy Fender for Surrey in 1920.

Asked about his innings, Old replied modestly: "There was nothing much I could do but hit it around the ground. Runs were there for the taking and I took them."

It was, of course, and remains Yorkshire's fastest-ever century, and earlier in the season, another Yorkshire record was set – this time by a woman rather than a man.

Mollie Staines, from Savile Town, Dewsbury, a staunch Yorkshire follower since early childhood, became the first woman to gain a place on the general committee as the Dewsbury representative when she beat two male opponents in a by-election brought about by the death of Noel Anderson.

It was a thoroughly well-deserved victory and not before time that a woman's voice was heard on the committee. Many women have been, and continue to be, equally as passionate about Yorkshire cricket as men and they tend to stick loyally with the team through thick and thin which is more than can be said of some of their male counterparts.

The season was not long over before the first rumblings from within the club about Boycott's captaincy were voiced by Bradford woolman Don Brennan, and they were to cost the former Yorkshire and England wicketkeeper his place on the four-man selection committee.

Brennan launched a campaign to have Cope elected as captain in place of Boycott because he believed Boycott was a great batsman but not a great leader and he felt that Cope would be able to spend more time with the team in future and be prepared to put everything before his own personal achievements.

His remarks infuriated a group of Yorkshire members who immediately met in a Huddersfield hotel and formed the Yorkshire County Cricket Club Reform Group, their top priority being to petition for Brennan's removal from the cricket committee. The chairman of the Reform Group was Peter Briggs, from Davyhulme, Manchester, who continued to play a key role in later battles, and the chairman was John Featherstone, a man so dedicated to Yorkshire cricket that in future years he would give full-time assistance in the county offices on a voluntary basis.

Events were moving at quite a pace and Michael Parkinson spoke out firmly in support of Boycott at a tribute dinner in Leeds given by Yorkshire Television in association with the Variety Club of Great Britain to mark his 100 first-class centuries.

"I have no doubt that if it came to the crunch of whether Geoff Boycott should be sacked or the committee jump over a cliff they would be advised to book a bus to Scarborough," said Parkinson, Boycott's former batting partner at Barnsley.

Speculation heightened as the day approached when it was believed the cricket committee would recommend next year's captain to the general committee for approval. And shortly before the meeting began the Reform Group handed in a petition signed by 828 club members which stated they had no confidence in Brennan.

Other Yorkshire committee members had shown a greater reluctance than Brennan openly to criticise Boycott in the days leading up to the meeting and it came as no great surprise when the opening batsman was re-appointed captain.

Unknown to the public, however, the cricket committee had met in secret the previous week and had decided then to recommend that Boycott should continue to lead the side. The only dissenting voice was that of Brennan who resigned from the selection committee once the vote had been taken and the following April he failed to be re-elected to the cricket committee, his place being taken by Ronnie Burnet.

News of Boycott's re-appointment was predictable but what came like a bolt out of the blue from the same meeting was the disclosure that Illingworth had been appointed team manager from the start of the 1979 season. This move would spell the end upon his arrival for the four-man selection committee, often criticised for picking teams without attending sufficient matches – an accusation which club chairman, Arthur Connell, agreed was true.

Explaining the decision to appoint a team manager, Connell said it was felt the running of county cricket had become so commercial and highly technical that it was essential there was a full-time expert in charge.

"We had the feeling at the end of the summer that Illingworth's time as a player with Leicestershire was coming to an end and it was believed he was the right man to carry Yorkshire forward," added Connell.

An uneasy peace settled on Yorkshire for the remainder of the winter and at the club's annual meeting in Sheffield in March, Sir Kenneth Parkinson made an impassioned appeal for unity. Burnet replaced Mel Ryan on the selection committee, again chaired by John Temple, and shortly before the new season arrived, Love said he was going to wear a protective helmet with a strong plastic guard over the face when fielding close to the wicket.

Time was moving on – and storm clouds were moving in, faster than anyone could have imagined.

CHAPTER THIRTY

THE BATTLE BEGINS

With an active and hungry Press pack chasing Yorkshire around and a 23-strong committee whose members were rarely reluctant to air their views, the county club seldom kept "inner sanctum" discussions secret for long. But their decision to appoint Illingworth as team manager was the exception which proves the rule.

Who actually set the ball rolling has never been established but chairman Connell and treasurer Crawford, both vice-presidents, were doubtless among the chief instigators of the plan.

When it was finally revealed, it was well received by the members and fans although many felt that two personalities as strong as Boycott and Illingworth would find it difficult to work together without a bust-up occurring at some stage or other.

That proved to be the case but few predicted that Yorkshire would be torn apart at the seams in the season BEFORE Illingworth's return to Headingley.

Signs of tension were clearly evident in the July of 1978 when Hampshire staged what became known as his "go slow" at Northampton in apparent protest at Boycott's slow scoring and the loss of batting bonus points.

An enquiry followed but things settled down again as Yorkshire showed a moderate all-round improvement in form but then all hell broke loose on September 29 when Boycott was sacked as captain and replaced by Hampshire.

Suddenly, members and fans were divided as never before, split down the middle over whether to show allegiance to Boycott or to give full backing to the club. The Reform Group came out fighting more fiercely than ever, an extraordinary general meeting was demanded, solicitors became involved, a High Court judge gave a ruling, letters appeared in The Times, both sides flung bitter accusations at each other and Boycott waited until a deadline was upon him before saying he would continue as a player in 1979.

It was the start of two acrimonious and costly wars that the club was forced to fight, this first one over the captaincy and the next one, a few years down the line, over Boycott's sacking as a player. The club narrowly won the first and lost the second.

On both occasions the club was torn asunder. In my youth I enjoyed Clarence 'Frogman' Henry's version of the song You Always Hurt The One You Love and its theme sums up neatly the wounds that the Yorkshire committee and members inflicted on each other and their beloved club.

It makes the point that true love still does not come without its hurt and pain and says that you always take the sweetest rose and crush it till the petals fall.

Sentimental, perhaps, but the whole colourful history of Yorkshire County Cricket Club has been one of turmoil and triumph – and the White Rose has bloomed despite it all. In the Broad Acres, at least, it remains The Sweetest Rose.

Boycott and Hampshire were not only the key figures in all the political dramas in 1978, they were also the key players, each battling with the other to finish top of the Yorkshire first-class batting averages. The scrap went right to the wire with Hampshire finally heading the list with 1,596 runs at 53.20 compared to Boycott's 1,074 at 51.14. It ended a run of 15 consecutive seasons by Boycott as the county's leading batsman, an achievement without parallel.

Hampshire was in the form of his life that season, batting with great power and authority, but Boycott played in eight fewer Championship matches because of injury, although he still managed five centuries to his rival's three.

Boycott aggravated a back problem while bowling in the Benson and Hedges Cup defeat to Nottinghamshire at Trent Bridge on May 20 – when Bairstow also shed his wicketkeeping pads to send down three overs – and his misfortune did not end there because four days later he badly bruised his left thumb while fielding in England's Prudential Trophy match against Pakistan at Old Trafford, an injury which kept him out of the next game and the three-match Test series which followed. It was not until the second England v New Zealand Test at Trent Bridge from August 10-14 that Boycott was recalled.

Boycott was out of action with Yorkshire for five weeks and tensions began to mount between the player and the cricket committee because of his reluctance to give any firm indication as to when he would be able to play again. Hampshire took over the captaincy and his own sparkling form helped the team embark on a successful run of results.

The Somerset match at Taunton in late June signalled Boycott's return and he guided Yorkshire to two draws and two wins leading up to the infamous match at Northampton which was the catalyst for all that was to follow.

After Northants had declared at their 100-overs score of 280-7, Athey knocked up 114 in 210 minutes with 15 fours, putting on 202 with Boycott whose 113 took him 367 minutes, his first 53 runs coming exclusively in singles and twos. When he was out in the 90th over, Hampshire and Johnson added just 11 runs in the final ten overs and a fourth batting bonus point was missed, Hampshire taking 18 overs to make an unbeaten seven.

The sparks were quick to fly, with some blaming Boycott for his perceived slow scoring, particularly since his return to the side, and others blaming Hampshire for a seemingly deliberate action which cost a point. Here I have to confess that I did not see the day's play myself as I had succumbed to a bout of flu and returned home, a rare instance in well over 30 years of covering Yorkshire that I was not on hand to witness dramatic events unfold.

Cricket chairman Temple, who had not been on the ground either, promised that an enquiry would be held shortly to establish the cause of the "go slow" but even at this early stage it was generally accepted that Johnson was an innocent and mystified partner in what had occurred.

The promised enquiry was held a couple of days later at Park Avenue with high drama both on and off the field, the emergency meeting of the selection committee following hard on the heels of Yorkshire's one-wicket Gillette Cup-tie win over

Nottinghamshire, last man Oldham clouting the winning three runs by bisecting Derek Randall and Paul Todd in the covers with three balls remaining.

The Press, out in force, then had to wait over four hours for the meeting to end late in the night, their vigil being broken when Hampshire left for home carrying a pair of flannels over a coat hanger and declining any comment as to what was going on inside.

Around this time, Yorkshire were at their very worst in not officially divulging information to the media about practically any issue under the sun in which they were involved. This policy only served to fuel the feeling that they plodded on inefficiently rather than having the ability to sort things out quickly. It was also one of the reasons why so many committee members would talk "off the record" to the Press, whose representatives were always more than willing to listen.

Even by their own standards, Yorkshire surpassed themselves on this occasion and although the eyes of the cricketing world were on them they summed up the marathon meeting in one bald sentence which was read out by Temple. It said: "The selection committee have considered all aspects of the incident at Northampton and have conveyed their findings to the players concerned and consider the matter closed." Questions were then stonewalled.

Boycott chatted amiably to the Press afterwards without breaking an undertaking not to reveal details of the meeting and the general assumption was that he had been strongly supported and Hampshire censured.

Whether or not this was so, it was at odds with the bombshell which exploded on September 29 when it was announced that Boycott had been sacked as captain and replaced by Hampshire.

The timing was insensitive as it came while Boycott was mourning the death of his mother and still making arrangements for the funeral. In addition, his mind was partly focussed on England's tour of Australia, starting on October 24, and for which he had been overlooked as vice-captain in favour of Bob Willis.

While the Reform Group gathered names for a petition calling for a special general meeting, Burnet, who was on the cricket committee, urged members to consider the other side of the controversy and said that if Boycott were re-instated as captain it would be a victory for mob rule. The cricket committee's decision had been unanimous and among its numbers were four former captains, two former second team captains and a former first team player.

Boycott confirmed that he wanted to remain as captain and as the story gripped the nation he appeared on television on the Mike Parkinson Show, castigating the cricket committee and saying: "These are the sort of people who are running the game…they could not even wait for my mum to be buried they were that keen to get me out."

His attack brought a fierce response from the cricket committee with Temple saying that the full reasons why he had been sacked would be made public but very little was immediately forthcoming. The rift grew wider, Boycott writing a letter to The Times referring to disruptive elements within the club and his belief that he would have been sacked the previous year but for his century of centuries. Fred Trueman then used the correspondence columns of The Thunderer to say that Boycott's letter was "manifest rubbish" and that he had no divine right to the captaincy of Yorkshire.

As the autumn wore on, the Reform Group wanted their resolutions for Boycott's re-instatement and a vote of no confidence in the cricket committee to be put to a special general meeting on December 2. Yorkshire declined to do this and were putting forward their own resolution calling for a vote of confidence in the general committee's handling of the club's affairs.

The Reform Group took the matter to the Chancery Division of the High Court at Liverpool where Vice-Chancellor Blackett-Ord ruled that the Group's resolutions had to be put to a special general meeting.

As a consequence of this, Yorkshire put back the meeting for a week and reconsidered their own resolutions. Illingworth entered the fray by writing to the club to say that the players were overwhelmingly behind the club in their decision to appoint Hampshire as captain.

A fortnight before the re-arranged meeting, Yorkshire members were sent a whole batch of literature from Headingley urging their support. It contained a long report from Connell with a strong attack on Boycott which stated: "We repeat that the committee's decision has little to do with what Geoffrey Boycott has or has not done as a cricketer, but rather with what he has not achieved as a leader.

"He is too wrapped up in his own performance and record, so much so that this has frequently increased the pressure on those who follow him in order to achieve a reasonable run rate."

The tennis match between the two parties continued, each volley over the net being returned with another one, and Boycott sent an eight page statement from Australia in response to the committee's attack on him and answering Connell's criticisms in detail.

The Reform Group went from strength to strength and 400 supporters and guests were to attend their inaugural dinner in Sheffield but powerful though their campaign undoubtedly was it could do no more than give the establishment a bloody nose at the Harrogate special general meeting.

The committee resolution that the meeting had confidence in the committee of the club was passed by 4,422 votes to 3,607; the Reform Group resolution of no confidence in the cricket committee and recommending their resignation forthwith was lost by 4,216 votes to 3,346 and the Group's resolution that Boycott be reappointed captain for 1979 went down by 4,826 votes to 2,602.

Yorkshire had come out of the scrap badly shaken and the aftermath of the turmoil rumbled on because Boycott, in Australia, kept everyone on tenterhooks over whether he would remain at the club and play under Hampshire's captaincy. He was given until January 31 to provide Yorkshire with his answer and it came at 3.10am on that very day in a telegram sent to secretary Lister.

Two days earlier, I had been able exclusively to forecast in the Telegraph and Argus that his answer would be "yes." I had been told by Boycott's close friend, Bob Slicer, boss of the National Breakdown Recovery Club, that Boycott had intimated to him in a long telephone call that he would remain with Yorkshire. I reasoned that Boycott may be evasive with the Press but he would not lead a friend down a blind alley.

Trueman by now had gained a place on the Yorkshire committee as a Craven district representative following the compulsory retirement after 21 years' service of Godfrey Sellers, the younger brother of Brian. At the club's annual meeting on March 17, 1979, only one of the four Reform Group members who stood for election to the committee was returned – and that was a significant figure indeed because Reg Kirk, from Hull, would go on to become Yorkshire chairman after the general committee was brought down over the sacking of Boycott.

John Featherstone, wanting an end to the divisions within the club, resigned as Reform Group secretary, and as the season approached differences were patched up for the time being. Illingworth, Hampshire and Boycott all spoke of their keenness to work in the best interests of Yorkshire cricket and when the players reported back for training the trio even agreed to have their photographs taken together.

While all this was going on during the winter months, one member of Yorkshire's squad had his own problems to worry about. In the middle of the previous season, Cope had without warning been banned for a second time by the TCCB after they had studied secretly-taken film of his action at The Oval. He immediately returned to Wardle for help and spent the remainder of the summer and all of the close season re-modelling his delivery but it was well into 1979 before he was ready to rejoin the first team.

The sudden blow to Yorkshire of Cope's enforced withdrawal in 1978 was partly offset the following week when Harrogate off-spinner Peter Whiteley replaced his senior colleague against Glamorgan at Abbeydale Park and earned Boycott's praise with splendid Championship debut match figures of 7-88, including four wickets in 17 balls in the first innings.

And so it was all eyes on Illingworth, Boycott and Hampshire as the 1979 season got off to such a watery start that the first seven Championship matches all ended in draws but, inevitably, as time went on, Boycott grabbed the spotlight by finishing top of both the batting and bowling averages, something not achieved for Yorkshire since George Hirst in 1910.

Like Hirst, Boycott tended to bowl with his cap on and his in-ducking medium-pacers were never used to better effect than against Lancashire at Headingley when he captured 4-14 in the first innings before making 94 despite having to break off for ice-pack treatment on an ugly black eye which he had suffered when sweeping a ball from 12th man Johnson into his face in the morning nets.

Big Clive Lloyd went on to batter a century in the Lancashire second innings but the young Neil Hartley, whose only previous appearance had been over 12 months earlier, surged Yorkshire to a thrilling six-wicket win against all the odds with an unbeaten half-century when time was of the essence.

This sterling effort established Hartley as a first team player and although, by his own admission, he fell a fraction short of being in the top drawer of county players, he was a rugged and determined competitor with both bat and ball and he possessed such a sound temperament that Illingworth had no qualms about promoting him to the vice-captaincy when others around him had greater experience. As fit as a fiddle for much of his career he was a particularly fine one-day all-rounder and would have been an automatic selection had Twenty20 been on the scene.

Test calls and injuries restricted Boycott to 11 Championship outings in which he scored 1,160 runs for an amazing average of 116. He also headed the national averages with 1,538 runs at 102.53, the second time he had cruised along at over 100.

Cruising alongside him for Yorkshire was Lumb, who was also in such dynamic form that he contributed 1,465 runs for the county with five centuries as well as being the first batsman in the country to reach the 1,000 mark. The first wicket pair so dominated the crease that they were responsible for nine of Yorkshire's 11 Championship centuries and could fairly claim to be among the best opening combinations in domestic cricket.

Much improved performances in the one-day contests, coupled with the appalling weather which saw five consecutive days' play wiped out – the last two days of the Old Trafford Roses match and the whole of the Notts fixture at Sheffield – helped Hampshire take his side through to June 26 before tasting a defeat of any sort, the best unbeaten start to a season in 25 years.

But there was still little tangible to show for all of the winter ructions, a drop from fourth to seventh in the Championship being offset by taking fifth place in the John Player League and by reaching the semi-finals of the Benson & Hedges Cup and the last eight in the Gillette Cup.

The new regime functioned smoothly enough on the surface but the Reform Group, emboldened by their higher profile, were always lurking in the background. They were guilty of unnecessary interference in June after Illingworth had toyed with the idea of taking his whites out of mothballs to captain the side at Northampton if Hampshire had pulled out with a broken finger. In the event, Hampshire, as he so often did, bit the bullet and played, but Group secretary Sid Fielden despatched a letter to club chairman Connell saying it would have been wrong for Illingworth to have played and so keep Whiteley out of the side.

Fielden, from Skellow, Doncaster, at the time was a close friend of Boycott's and one who defended him to the hilt at every opportunity. A sergeant in the C.I.D. he was also a Methodist local preacher with great oratory skills and he was a leading figure in the revolution still to come. Later, he changed sides and his relationship with Boycott cooled almost to freezing point for a while. He worked tirelessly for the club in his role as public relations chairman and was generous to a fault in giving of his time to bring the elderly and infirm to matches.

Some on the committee never forgave him for his unshakeable support of Boycott and the upheaval which it caused, but others became good friends, including Appleyard and Trueman, and he gave a memorable reading of the 23rd Psalm at Trueman's funeral service. He served on the committee first as the representative for Doncaster and then in South District before being elected a vice-president when the committee was disbanded in 2003.

Although Boycott and Lumb were the principal players in 1979, others had their moments, none more so than the mercurially brilliant Stevenson who decimated Warwickshire on a rain-affected pitch at Abbeydale Park and sent them packing for 35 in 75 minutes of mayhem in which his steep bounce brought him 6-14. It was Warwickshire's joint lowest score against Yorkshire, equalling their 35 at Edgbaston in 1963 when Trueman and Ryan did the damage.

Against Warwickshire at Edgbaston a few weeks earlier, the immensely talented all-round sportsman, Alan Ramage, had made his Championship debut and had marked it in style by trapping Dennis Amiss lbw with his fifth ball.

Ramage, then spending the majority of his time playing soccer with Middlesbrough and later Derby County, had the pace and the ability to have become an England Test bowler if he had given cricket his full concentration and commitment. Like some others before him, Ramage found fitness levels for cricket even harder to attain than for soccer but he was a bowler to be feared on his day and this popular player gave cheerful service to Yorkshire.

Born in Guisborough, Ramage had been something of a boy prodigy and at the age of 12 he became the youngest ever to represent Yorkshire Schoolboys. He went on to take all ten wickets for Marske against Darlington and also had the reputation of being a formidable hitter of the ball.

Cope, having grabbed 9-27 while readjusting his action with the Second XI, returned to the first team just as quickly as he had left it by appearing against Nottinghamshire at Worksop on July 25 and there were contrasting surprises that season for Love and Bairstow.

Having won back his place, Love blasted an unbeaten 170 against Worcestershire at New Road only to be axed from the next match when Boycott returned from Test duty.

Bairstow declared himself "flabbergasted" when his dream of Test cricket finally came true with his selection for the final Test against India at The Oval and a couple of weeks later he was just as ecstatic with the news that he would tour Australia in the winter alongside Boycott. The ebullient wicketkeeper-batsman rarely featured "down under" but at least he had a close friend to keep him company when suddenly joined on the tour by Stevenson, who was flown out as a replacement for the injured Mike Hendrick.

Yorkshire suffered a shock during the 1979 season with the sudden death of Mike Fearnley, a highly respected assistant coach for several years and a leading light at Illingworth's club, Farsley, and internal changes were on the way at the end of the summer when Connell decided he would be standing down as Yorkshire chairman after serving since 1971.

The chairman's role was a particularly stressful one at this stage in Yorkshire's history and the pressure did not ease on his successor, Michael Crawford, who was unanimously elected to the hot seat. In order to focus fully on the job, Crawford resigned as club treasurer and was replaced by David Welch, the well-respected Rotherham representative on the committee.

A strong link with the past was broken in February, 1980, when Brian Sellers also announced he would not be seeking re-election to the county committee, so severing a continuous family connection which went back 77 years. A year later, Sellers died, aged 73, and Yorkshire had lost perhaps their greatest-ever captain and one of the game's most colourful characters.

Hampshire again took on the captaincy in 1980 and at the club's pre-season luncheon he made a spirited defence of Yorkshire's policy of not drawing on players from outside the county boundaries, despite the effect which was being felt from the mass influx of overseas cricketers into the domestic game.

"We have rightly and proudly made a rod for our own back and excuses cannot be tolerated. We have to stand by our decisions," he said. His words were well received but opposition to the "Yorkshire-born" policy was quietly beginning to crumble and even the private opinion of the players themselves would soon be that they were growing tired of having to come up against world class performers without having any of their own to hit back with.

Yorkshire had now embarked on a new decade but they still could not drag themselves clear of the mire into which they had sunk during the 70s and discontent continued to rumble under the surface.

A one-place rise in the Championship suggested little progress at all on that front and they slumped to joint 14th with only Glamorgan below them in the John Player League after a disastrous start which saw them lose their first six matches. They failed to get beyond the zonal stages of the B&H but some pride was salvaged in the Gillette Cup where they advanced to the semi-finals before losing out to Surrey, who had much the better of the conditions at The Oval.

The game was unable to start until 3.30pm because of bad weather and when Yorkshire were put in to bat they had to face up to the alarming speed of West Indian Sylvester Clarke in dreadful light. He began with a maiden which was packed with an assortment of ten extras after which he struck Boycott on the shoulder with one of several bouncers and then pinned him lbw before bowling Love. Half the wickets were down for 54 and Yorkshire did well to recover to 135, Sidebottom then keeping them in with a shout for a while with his own fiery bowling.

Yorkshire had acquitted themselves less well in the B&H where they were knocked back right at the start by Warwickshire who gained a surprise win by one wicket at Headingley after appearing doomed. Their last pair were at the wicket for the final over and their chances of making the ten still required appeared nil but the field was spread back and Dilip Doshi managed to dash two runs off each of the first five deliveries.

Overall, performances should have been much better than they turned out to be, even taking into account poor weather and a stack of injuries. Athey and Love both excelled with the bat to earn their caps and Boycott and Hampshire would undoubtedly have joined Lumb and Athey in making 1,000 runs but for Boycott's international calls and a broken finger for Hampshire which kept him out for five weeks. In all, nine players completed centuries, so underlining the depth of batting in the line-up.

Stevenson led the way with the ball by capturing 72 wickets, including a five-for-none spell at Trent Bridge where he returned figures of 11-74, and against Northamptonshire at Headingley he may well have become only the fourth Yorkshire bowler to take all ten if he had not squandered the opportunity. Having bagged the first eight in the order and with "rabbits" remaining in Tim Lamb and Brian Griffiths he left the field to change his wet shirt! He came back but the chance was lost and the visitors declared in a rain-hit match which they went on to win, Griffiths taking 7-52.

Stevenson had considerable back-up in Old and Sidebottom, who also received his cap, while Cope and Carrick ensured it was a well-balanced attack but things never quite went right for the team.

Boycott's future and speculation about who would be the next captain remained to the fore. When Boycott was left out of the Sunday League side against Essex in July because Illingworth insisted he wanted to run the rule over some of the younger players, word spread around that Boycott's days were numbered. But shortly afterwards he and his solicitor joined in secret talks with leading club officials, including Illingworth, and a new two-year contract was promised. It transpired that Hampshire and Old were also to be offered new deals but the rest of the team complained that all contracts should be considered together and Crawford promised that this would be the case in future.

During Hampshire's absence with a broken finger, sustained while batting in the Roses match at Headingley, Lumb was given an opportunity to captain the side along with Old as Illingworth pondered which of the two would be the next leader.

There was something of a stir when Illingworth's book was published and contained criticisms of some of the current players, notably Old, but he was sympathetic with the way Boycott had been treated at the time he lost the captaincy. Boycott himself was due to visit Buckingham Palace on July 30 to collect his OBE for services to cricket but he chose a fresh date in order not to miss a Yorkshire fixture.

Kevin Sharp scored a delightful maiden century at Lord's but some weeks later had to rest up while he sorted out the pressures that were building up on him and there was a debut at Weston-super-Mare for the likeable left-arm swing bowler Simon Dennis, nephew of Sir Leonard Hutton. On occasions, Dennis turned in some admirable performances but this popular member of the dressing room was never able to look quite as fearsome as a fast bowler should.

A season rarely ends calmly for Yorkshire and this time the waves were caused by Hampshire's sudden announcement he wanted to step down from the captaincy after two years in charge.

It also became clear towards the end that Cope's action had once again been called into question, this time by secret filming at Cheltenham, and it was, therefore, decided not to renew his contract or that of another fine servant of Yorkshire cricket, Howard Cooper.

Now was the time that Illingworth had to evaluate the qualities shown by Lumb and Old on the occasions he had put them in charge and he came down in favour of Old taking over from Hampshire. It did not prove to be a happy reign.

CHAPTER THIRTY-ONE

OLD CONFLICT...

The death of Sir Kenneth Parkinson ushered in Norman Yardley as Yorkshire president in 1981 and nobody, even in those turbulent times, could take issue with the widely-held view that he was one of the most highly-regarded and well-liked men ever to be closely associated with the county.

The quietly-spoken former Yorkshire and England captain was also the perfect gentleman and someone who intensely disliked internal rancour and dissent.

Yet such was the volatile state of Yorkshire cricket when he was elected to the presidency that conflict was bound to occur at some stage or other and in the end it resulted in him resigning from office, a sad and disillusioned man. Of all the war mongering that went on nobody was more hurt by it than Yardley and it pained him deeply to see his great club reduced to such bickering and strife.

Although Old bowled his socks off in the first few weeks of his captaincy he could not prevent it being another very ordinary season on the field and an extraordinary year off it with Yorkshire leaping into the headlines in summer and winter alike.

Old was also a part of one of the greatest cricket matches ever seen but that was with England rather than Yorkshire, although all of the action took place at his county headquarters.

The Ashes Test at Headingley remains one of the most thrilling international contests of all time and at 2.19 on the fifth afternoon England won by 18 runs a match which they seemed certain to lose by an innings only 24 hours earlier.

At that stage, England were 135-7 in their second innings and still 92 runs away from making Australia bat again. No wonder the bookies were offering 500-1 against a home victory.

But then came Botham with his unbeaten 149 with 27 fours and a six, followed next day by Willis with his demonic 8-43 and Australia had been flattened like never before.

And Old was no mere onlooker in this startling about-turn because he played two crucial roles in it. First he made 29 while partnering Botham in a ninth-wicket stand of 67 after Botham and Graham Dilley had initiated the revival with 117 in 80 minutes, and later he greatly assisted Willis by knocking out one of Allan Border's stumps before he had scored.

Back to Yorkshire and a story in May that the Reform Group had now settled their differences with the club seemed too good to be true and, indeed, that proved to be the case. Briefly, however, the Group were prepared to become solely a supporters' club and they underwent a temporary name change to the Yorkshire Cricket Supporters' Association which is what they were known as when fresh and unprecedented hostilities were to break out.

For a friendly and good-natured man, captaincy was never going to be easy for Old with two former captains now in his ranks, one having been stripped of the leadership and the other having stood down because he had grown tired of all the constant pressures. It is surprising that Old even agreed to take it on, particularly in view of some of the criticisms which Illingworth had made of him in his book the previous summer and which must have stung.

The captaincy issue became ever more complicated as the season wore on because Illingworth promoted Neil Hartley to the job when both Old and official vice-captain, Lumb, were absent, and he acquitted himself so well that he was put in charge in the John Player League in similar situations with considerable success.

But when Lumb returned to the side with Old still missing, he declined to accept the captaincy because he felt he had too often not been consulted on decision-making, patrolling the deep rather than being on hand much closer to the action.

The continuing internal wrangling should not be allowed to mask what was happening on the field and there were many great stories to report, not least Bairstow's sensational innings in the Benson and Hedges Cup match with Derbyshire at Derby which prompted Illingworth to say that he had never seen a better knock.

Chasing 203, Yorkshire looked stone dead at 123-9 at which stage debutant quick bowler, Mark Johnson, joined Bairstow, and the tenth wicket pair charged to victory with an unbroken stand of 80. To be more accurate, Bairstow charged them to victory because Johnson's share of the spoils was four while the wicketkeeper thrashed his way to 103 with nine sixes and three fours.

Johnson, a stocky 21-year-old from Sheffield, who spent the previous winter playing cricket in South Africa, had just the one season with Yorkshire after being signed mainly as a limited overs bowler. He made four Championship appearances and took seven wickets, the one to treasurer being:

I.V.A. Richards c Stevenson b Johnson 153

Many years later, meeting up with Johnson at a Players' Association function, he revealed to me the wonderful story behind that dismissal in the match with Somerset at Abbeydale Park.

Having flogged the bowling to all parts and with Somerset nearing a declaration, the megastar approached Johnson in the middle of an over and asked where he would like him to give a catch? A stunned Johnson asked what he meant and Richards said he had batted long enough and would like to give the bowler his wicket because he was most impressed with the effort he had put into his work earlier on. Sure enough, he holed out to Stevenson and Somerset went on to win by 167, which was only six runs more than the West Indian maestro's contribution to the match.

Chris Lethbridge, a 19-year-old pace bowler from Altofts, near Wakefield, made a memorable debut for Warwickshire at Edgbaston in May by getting Boycott caught at second slip by Amiss with his first ball in first-class cricket and he also helped avoid the follow-on with a courageous 69 batting at No 8.

But a Yorkshireman who was to make a far more significant first-class debut the following month was Barnsley-born Martyn Moxon, who was given his chance against Essex at Headingley and responded with a majestic 116, the highest score by a Yorkshire player on debut and only the second centurion, the other being Cec Tyson, who hit 100 not out against Hampshire at Southampton in 1921.

Tyson, who also scored an unbeaten 60 in the second innings, only played in three matches for Yorkshire because he and the club could not agree terms to satisfy both parties, but the sheer class of the 21-year-old Moxon made it certain that he would have a much longer stay.

Moxon had begun his career almost unnoticed by being selected for two Sunday matches in 1980, without either batting or bowling, and not too much attention was paid, either, to a pre-season friendly between the Yorkshire squads when Moxon contributed 47 to a century opening stand with Boycott before both batsmen retired to let others have a go.

Moxon showed his Championship century was no fluke by striking 111 in Yorkshire's next home match against Derbyshire at Sheffield and putting on 218 in an opening stand with Lumb. He became the first Yorkshire batsman ever to hit centuries in his first two home matches but in true Yorkshire fashion was then dropped for the Worcestershire fixture with the return of Boycott and Lumb.

Except for his spell in charge of coaching at Durham between 2001-07, Moxon has been a fundamental part of Yorkshire cricket for over 30 years and not only did he become one of the county's best batsmen but his engaging personality, which hid a much tougher streak as time wore on, ensured that he was an enduringly popular figure with the fans. Of all the batsmen whose careers began after the 1939-45 war, only Boycott has scored more than his South Yorkshire colleague's 41 first-class centuries for Yorkshire while Moxon's 18,973 runs place him 14th in the scoring list.

Like Boycott before him, Moxon was unable to lead Yorkshire to any of the major trophies during his six-year reign as captain from 1990. Unlike Boycott, he never featured with England as often as he should have done and it was typical of his misfortune that 99 should remain his highest score from ten Test appearances.

Another batsman attracting attention in 1981 was Love who deservedly made it into the England side for the three-match Prudential Trophy series with Australia but with only moderate success.

He and Boycott returned to Yorkshire for the fixture with champions Nottinghamshire which marked the centenary of the club's visits to Park Avenue, the first match against Kent starting exactly 100 years ago to the day – on June 13, 1881.

Civic dignitaries were invited to the game along with Bradford Met officials who had been responsible for demolishing the unsafe football stand and tidying up the ground during the winter to make sure that county cricket could continue at the famous but crumbling venue. A century from Boycott and 97 from Love saved Yorkshire from defeat on this big occasion after they had been bowled out for 78 in their first innings, New Zealand supremo Richard Hadlee taking 4-16 to go with his unbeaten 142.

Nottinghamshire's South African captain Clive Rice also made significant all-round contributions and barely a week later I became the first Yorkshire cricket journalist to urge the club to break with tradition and sign an overseas player.

Time and again I was seeing Yorkshire yielding to teams strengthened by imported stars and the breaking point for me came with the defeat by Somerset in the quarter-final of the Benson and Hedges Cup at Headingley. Botham, incidentally, made a nil contribution on this occasion by failing to claim a wicket and then being bowled for a duck by Neil Hartley, and the difference between the two sides was due to West Indian giant Joe Garner who took three wickets, and Viv Richards, who struck 47.

"Is it not better to swallow some pride in order to see the side compete on equal terms with others?" I wrote. "It seems to me that Yorkshire can no longer go on choosing solely from their own stock when all other counties have the whole cricketing world to go at."

The article drew a swift response from Yorkshire, secretary Lister saying: "Having regard to certain speculative comments, the cricket management committee wish to re-emphasise that it will stick fully to the policy of playing only Yorkshire-born cricketers."

Yet the idea was gaining ground, however reluctantly, and in the Spring of 1982, Yorkshire held their first referendum on the subject in order to test the waters. Out of 5,032 votes – 41 per cent of the membership – 4,493 were against any change, an 89 per cent majority. Significantly, though, only 241 of the 4,493 opposed to a break in tradition threatened to resign if such a move went ahead and, indeed, there was no rebellion when the barriers finally came down in 1992 with the signing of India's little master, Sachin Tendulkar.

The whiff of rebellion, however, continued to be in the air in 1981 and Boycott's legion of supporters began to grow suspicious when Illingworth started leaving their man and Hampshire out of the Sunday League side in order to take a closer look at some of the youngsters.

One of young 'uns was Paul Jarvis, from Redcar, who gained his first senior outing in the Sunday League Roses match at Headingley and a couple of weeks later, at 16 years and 75 days, became the youngest cricketer ever to play for Yorkshire in a first-class match, beating by some distance the previous record-holder who was his county coach Padgett, at 16 years and 321 days.

Jarvis may never quite have fulfilled his abundant early promise but on his day he could still be a mighty fine performer who could turn on a genuine burst of speed that disturbed the best of batsmen. As with so many of his fellow fast bowlers, Jarvis broke down far more often than was good for him and with a better fitness record he should have played for England in more than nine Tests and 16 one-day internationals.

In 138 first-class matches for Yorkshire he took 449 wickets at 26.70 while in one-day matches he collected 209 victims at 21.88, statistics which show he was a prominent figure in the side until his release at the end of 1993. He saw out the remainder of his career with Sussex and Somerset and ended up with 654 first-class wickets.

In early September, the resurgent Reform Group demanded that Yorkshire sack Illingworth because of disappointing results but Crawford retorted that the club refused to have a pistol held to its head.

Then, at Scarborough on September 9, open warfare broke out as Illingworth showed Boycott the dressing room door before the start of the Northamptonshire match and banned him from this fixture and the final Championship game against Sussex at Hove.

About 90 minutes before the game began at North Marine Road, I had approached the pavilion with John Callaghan, my opposite number from the Yorkshire Evening Post, with a view to acquiring the Yorkshire team from Illingworth.

Then we saw Boycott coming out of the dressing room door carrying his cricket coffin and looking shaken. When asked what was happening, Boycott said: "You had better go and ask Raymond."

Illingworth issued a brief statement which said: "Geoff Boycott is suspended for the remainder of the season because of comments he has made on the radio, TV and in the newspapers."

The final straw for Illingworth, apparently, came the previous evening when Boycott said on a local TV station that when the season ended he would seek a meeting with the committee to find out why he had not played in several matches.

The effect of Boycott's suspension was immediate. Within minutes, Reform Group secretary Fielden had started a petition calling for an extraordinary meeting to discuss a resolution of no confidence in Illingworth. Members queued to sign it and within an hour over 200 names were on the sheet.

The furore continued day after day with fresh revelations that only added to the feeling that Yorkshire gained more publicity from what they did off the cricket field rather than on it.

When Illingworth returned to Yorkshire he had set up a deal which saw Berger Paints become the club's main sponsors but now they threatened to pull out of a new package worth £300,000 if he were sacked. He wasn't, but neither was Boycott, and the deal still never went through, Home Charm Paints coming to the rescue.

Intense discussion in committee led to Yorkshire agreeing to try and keep the pair of them to ward off further trouble but this news was coolly received by Illingworth who felt the committee were not backing him as they should and were failing to grasp the nettle.

No sooner was the season over than Hampshire dropped a further bombshell by saying he was leaving Yorkshire and about to sign a contract with Derbyshire. The mayhem had proved too much and he wanted to see out the remainder of his playing days in a more peaceful environment.

Old expressed regret at Hampshire's departure and agreed to stay on as captain for another season but he might have had second thoughts had he been able to foresee how things would turn out.

Some of the sting was temporarily removed from the situation with Yorkshire's announcement that they had set up an in-depth investigation into all aspects of the running of the club and that this was being chaired by an independent chairman in Peter Dobson, a 64-year-old retired chartered accountant from Wetherby. The seven other members of the committee were Reg Kirk, Tim Reed, Philip Sharpe, John Temple, Julian Vallance, David Welch and Don Brennan.

Their deliberations, including confidential interviews with a wide variety of people connected with Yorkshire, lasted well into the New Year, but before the old one was out Fielden gained an overwhelming majority in a by-election in Doncaster district which had been called through the resignation from the general committee in September of Eric Baines in protest at the club's decision to reveal details of a players' poll which claimed they did not want Boycott in their side.

Fielden romped home by claiming 77.70 per cent of the vote and his presence on the committee meant an increase in support for Boycott, who had returned home from India unwell in early January soon after breaking Sir Garry Sobers' record of 8,032 Test runs and taking his own final tally to 8,114. He was seen upon his arrival by Fielden who cited Boycott's concern over his future with Yorkshire as a likely contributory factor in the breakdown of his health.

An interim report from the investigation sub-committee came out in late January, with several recommendations concerning the running of the club, but these caused little more than a ripple and the real storm broke a month down the line when it was leaked that the sub-committee had recommended that Boycott should go once his contract expired at the end of the 1982 season.

To complicate matters still further, a few days later Boycott went on the England rebel tour of South Africa accompanied by his new Yorkshire captain, Old, with Arnie Sidebottom joining them later, but Boycott's future with Yorkshire remained the hot topic in the Broad Acres.

Boycott was not long into the tour when he learned that a six-hour meeting of the Yorkshire committee had accepted the recommendation that he should stay at Headingley that summer, along with Illingworth. He also received a letter in Cape Town from secretary Lister, instructing him to not to say anything on the issue, a similar missive being sent through the post to the team and committee representatives.

Another consequence of the in-depth investigation was the setting-up of a three-man peace-keeping sub-committee to rule on any disputes which may arise between Boycott and Illingworth. It was chaired by Burnet with Trueman and Billy Sutcliffe the two other members.

Once again, a reprieve for Boycott had taken the immediate heat out of the situation but so intense was the interest in Yorkshire's affairs that the police were called to the club's annual meeting in Sheffield on March 20 when the doors had to be shut with all 522 seats taken and 100 members locked out. One of those who could not gain admission was the Reform Group's chairman, Peter Briggs, who had contacted the police in an attempt to get the meeting called off if fire regulations had been breached but they hadn't.

An undeniable fact about Yorkshire's most controversial years is that nothing that was said or done off the field did much to improve performances on it and this was pretty much the case in 1982 when they remained in tenth position in the Championship and never recovered from a disastrous start in the John Player League, where they finished 16th with only Warwickshire below them.

They failed to get beyond the zonal stages of the Benson and Hedges Cup and suffered humiliation in their final game against Derbyshire when their former captain, Hampshire, struck a six to win it by seven wickets for his new team and also pick up the man-of-the-match award for his unbeaten 66.

The only redeeming factor was that they had a couple of outstanding wins in the NatWest Trophy – now in its second season after replacing the Gillette Cup – to reach the semi-finals, only to lose to Warwickshire at Edgbaston. By this time,

REVERED AND RESPECTED: No player in Yorkshire's (or England's) history has won the admiration of this cricketing nation to a greater degree than Len Hutton. Knighted after becoming England's first professional captain and leading his country to Ashes glory, Len (or Leonard as he was invariably referred to by his awestruck contemporary team-mates) will for ever be remembered for his record-breaking 364 against Australia at The Oval in 1938. Here he is pictured going out to bat and, below, striding to the middle with Arthur Mitchell.

ALL-ROUND SKILLS: Hutton batting in the Victory Test at Sheffield in 1945; a rare picture of him bowling his leg-breaks, and receiving congratulations during his epic 364.

WHAT A PICTURE: The portrait of Len Hutton, owned by sons Richard and John, which hangs at Lord's, a copy of which is displayed in the Headingley museum. Right, recalling "the good old days" with Godfrey Evans, Alec Bedser and Denis Compton, and pouring a drink at Headingley for Fred Trueman (right) and Yorkshire-born England captains, Norman Yardley and Raymond Illingworth, both of whom, unlike Hutton, also captained their native county.

LAST CALL: The great Yorkshire team of 1939 – and a more confident set of young men it is hard to imagine. By the end of the summer, war clouds were gathering and the team would never assemble again. Pictured from left, back: Arthur Mitchell, Bright Heyhirst (masseur), Hedley Verity, Bill Bowes, Frank Smailes, Len Hutton, William Ringrove (scorer); middle: Herbert Sutcliffe, Norman Yardley, Brian Sellers, Maurice Leyland; front, Ellis Robinson, Arthur Wood, Wilf Barber.

RED LETTER DAY: Brian Close and Fred Trueman, two of the greatest figures in Yorkshire's history, both made their county debuts against Cambridge University at Fenner's on May 11, 1949, along with another future Yorkshire and England player, Frank Lowson. Although Close and Trueman each held firm, unshakeable opinions they had the highest regard for each other and were the best of friends and unyielding competitors, Close leading Yorkshire to four Championship titles under his command and remaining England's youngest cricketer, and Trueman becoming the first bowler in Test history to claim 300 wickets.

CLOSE FRIENDS: Sir Ian Botham puts a friendly arm round Close who was captain of Somerset when Botham made his first team debut in 1973. Like Close, Botham went on to captain England and he had no hesitation in agreeing to front a Yorkshire dinner in honour of one of the bravest and most popular cricketers of all time.

PRACTICE MAKES PERFECT: Trueman warms up at Bradford Park Avenue, the favourite ground of both himself and Close – and many other top Yorkshire players.

SOLE MEMBER OF 200 CLUB: Bob Appleyard, seen in action, was among the finest bowlers ever to play for either Yorkshire or England and he remains the only bowler ever to take 200 first-class wickets in his first full season. Appleyard, Yorkshire president from 2006-2008, is also pictured at Headingley with his old England team-mate, Frank Tyson, the pair no doubt reminiscing over the parts they played in helping to retain the Ashes on Hutton's tour of Australia in 1954-1955.

PIPE DREAM COMES TRUE: Ronnie Burnet, Yorkshire's last amateur captain, was put in charge in 1958 at the age of 39 and the following year led them to glory.

HOVE HEROES: Bryan Stott (left) and Doug Padgett, whose dynamic partnership rushed Yorkshire towards their win at Hove in 1959 which clinched the Championship title and led to a decade of outstanding success. Here they are seen going out to bat at Scarborough. Padgett, who at 16 years and 321 days, became Yorkshire's youngest player, later took over as second team captain and club coach, while Stott went on to become the first chairman of the Yorkshire Players' Association.

HIGH FLYING BIRD: Harold 'Dickie' Bird made his Yorkshire debut during the 1959 Championship winning season – and was dropped after scoring a century – but it was later on as a Test umpire that he acquired world fame. He went on to be awarded the MBE and the OBE and this statue of him was erected near his birthplace in Barnsley.

TOP FLIGHT: Raymond Illingworth, classic off-spinner and batsman, who tasted Championship glory with Yorkshire, led England to Ashes triumph, and returned from Leicestershire to manage and captain his home county before finally becoming President Pictured opening in his younger days with Vic Wilson at Scarborough and, much later, coming out to bat at Harrogate.

TEAM TALK: Illingworth, on his return as manager in 1979, chats to new captain, John Hampshire, and the previous leader, Geoff Boycott.

OPEN FOR BUSINESS: President Illingworth shakes hands with the Duke of Gloucester who officially opened the new Headingley Carnegie Pavilion on July 21, 2010.

MAN OF MANY PARTS: Over the past 50 years or so, Geoff Boycott has been to the fore of Yorkshire cricket in a variety of ways, making him one of the highest profile and most controversial figures in the Club's history. He established himself in the side in the Championship-winning Centenary year of 1963 and half-a-century on he is Club President in the 150th year. He is pictured right with his wife, Rachael, who arranged the official launch of the celebrations to mark the occasion.

1973 – BRAMALL LANE FAREWELL: Yorkshire captain, Boycott, and Lancashire skipper, David Lloyd, leave the field together during the final Championship match on the famous Sheffield ground.

1977 – 100 HUNDREDS: Boycott completes his 100th first-class century by on-driving Greg Chappell to the boundary during the Ashes Test at Headingley.

1977 – MEETING OF THE MASTERS: Boycott is congratulated on his achievement at the Headingley Test by two other great Yorkshire and England openers from an earlier age who also topped 100 first-class centuries, Herbert Sutcliffe and Len Hutton.

1985 – READY TO FIRE: Boycott and Martyn Moxon go out to bat at Worcester in 1985 when they put on 351 together, then Yorkshire's highest partnership since Holmes' and Sutcliffe's 555 in 1932 and the Club's fourth highest.

2002 – ALL SMILES: Past differences were put aside when this quartet of Yorkshire and England heroes joined forces to open the new East Stand at Headingley. From left: Brian Close CBE, Raymond Illingworth CBE, Geoffrey Boycott OBE and Fred Trueman OBE.

View from the boundary edge by John Blakey painting (by permission of Barry Cox).

COPING NICELY: Nobody in the Club's history has shown greater passion for Yorkshire cricket than Illingworth's off-spin successor, Geoff Cope, who captured 630 first-class wickets and would have had many more but for the allegations of throwing which led to his premature retirement. His allegiance to Yorkshire never faltered and after serving on the committee he became one of the Gang of Four which took over the management of the club.

OLD MATE: Popular Yorkshire and England fast bowler, Chris Old, who claimed 647 first-class wickets for his county and also smashed what was then the second fastest first-class century in history. Left for Warwickshire at the end of the season in which he was removed as captain.

CUP CONQUERORS: Phil Carrick marked the first year of his captaincy in 1987 by lifting the Benson & Hedges Cup, thanks to a match-winning batting effort by gold award winner, Jim Love.

however, a lot more water had swept under the bridge, taking with it Old's captaincy and leaving Illingworth to assume command 15 days after his 50th birthday.

The first real indication that Illingworth could be thinking of resuming active service came two days after his 50th when he agreed to lead Yorkshire in their one-day match against Zimbabwe at Sheffield, which also saw the debut of Ashley Metcalfe, Illingworth's future son-in-law, who would go on to link up with Moxon as among the most exciting pair to watch of Yorkshire's great opening partnerships.

Illingworth and Metcalfe already had a lot in common, each of them being born in Farsley, each of them playing for their local club in the Bradford League, and each of them making their Yorkshire debut at the age of 18.

The reason for Illingworth's participation was put down to the long injury list and he refuted any suggestions that it was the start of a comeback, even though he had found his golden touch immediately by dismissing opener Jack Heron with his first ball, and finishing with figures of 9-1-29-1.

Boycott also played a prominent part in the three-wicket win, scoring an unbeaten 98 and putting on 77 in 17 overs with Metcalfe, but the colt was to enjoy an even more remarkable partnership with Boycott on his Championship debut the following season.

Despite Illingworth's protestations at the time, the Zimbabwe match must have sown the seed for his take over and, once implanted, it grew so rapidly that within a fortnight Old was disposed of and the former England captain was officially installed as his native county's captain for the first time.

Had results improved during the interim period, Old might have survived but by the time of the Northamptonshire encounter at Middlesbrough on June 19, 21 and 22 Yorkshire's only victory in a competitive one-day match had been against the Minor Counties in the B&H. In fairness to Old, it should be mentioned that the Sunday League match against Nottinghamshire at Hull had ended in a tie and some of the other one-day games had been closely fought while in the Championship, five of the six games leading up to Middlesbrough had been drawn and the other won.

Northants have been Yorkshire's opponents on many occasions of high drama and the meeting at Acklam Park proved to be no exception. Old's first mistake on the Saturday was to put the opposition in to bat and he then looked on helplessly as he and Stevenson and Sidebottom were hammered to all parts by Middlesbrough-born Geoff Cook (112 not out) and Wayne Larkins (186) in an opening stand of 278, leading to a declaration at 383-3 in 81.4 overs. At the close on Saturday, the visitors were 302-1 and there was to be no respite on Sunday because on the same ground Northants plundered 282-4 in the John Player League on their way to a 55-run win.

Speculation intensified as the Championship game went on that Old's removal was imminent and it came around lunchtime on the rain-lashed third day, when a Press conference was hastily arranged outside the dressing rooms. In a statement Burnet said: "We sincerely hope that Chris Old will continue to be the valuable member of the side which he undoubtedly is, and we apologise to him for having lumbered him with a job which was clearly not his forte."

Burnet also disclosed that on two previous occasions that season long discussions had been held with Old concerning his captaincy and he had been told that it was essential there should be a considerable improvement, particularly in one-day matches, in his tactical approach and in his ability to lift the side when things were not going well.

One had the greatest respect for the dignified and uncomplaining way in which Old took his removal from a job which was never easy due to all that was going on around him. But it must have been a relief for him at the end of the season when he was released and he was able to find a happier environment at Warwickshire with whom, inevitably, he was able to exact no small measure of revenge over Yorkshire.

So Illingworth, Old and Co drove away from a drenched Middlesbrough and through pouring rain all the way to Ilford where Illingworth's first game in charge was ruined by further bad weather. There was just enough cricket for Old to show that he could still get the best of them out by flattening Graham Gooch's off-stump.

Results did improve under Illingworth and one of the most amazing wins was against Worcestershire at Headingley where Yorkshire came back from the dead in the NatWest Trophy to register one of the most sensational victories in one-day cricket. Replying to 286-5, Yorkshire were 40-4 in 16 overs when rain pushed the game into a second day and few turned up for what everyone thought was a lost cause. Everyone, that is, apart from the middle-order batsmen who tore the bowling to shreds, man-of-the-match Bairstow smacking 92 and Neil Hartley and Old weighing in with half-centuries. The impetus was maintained by Stevenson, who hit his first ball for four and belted consecutive sixes off John Inchmore, the four-wicket villain of the previous day. There were three balls remaining when Old drove the winning boundary and soon afterwards there was a two-fingered salute to a contrite Press Box from Bairstow for having written them off.

Through all the twists and turns of this incredible summer, Boycott stood head and shoulders above the rest of the batsmen and continued to reach new milestones. In the Championship curtain-raiser at Northampton he accumulated his 100th first-class century in England, 79 of them for Yorkshire, and against Worcestershire at Sheffield he drew level with Hutton's tally of 129 first-class centuries before overtaking it at Headingley against Warwickshire where he was on the field for the whole of the match, thanks to unbeaten knocks of 152 and 24.

This was Yorkshire's first Championship win under Illingworth and in being on the field for the entire match Boycott was only repeating what he had done against the same opponents at Edgbaston in May when he and Stevenson had combined to set a record Yorkshire batting partnership for the first time in 50 years.

The pair achieved what Sidebottom and Robinson had so narrowly failed to do in 1975 and that was overtake, by one run, the 148 by Lord Hawke and Hunter for the tenth wicket in 1898. On this occasion, Boycott was quite happy to let his partner take most of the acclaim for his 115 not out, the highest unbeaten score ever assembled by a No 11 batsman.

Boycott was 50 when Stevenson came in at 143-9 and he eked out a further 29 before being bowled attempting to sweep Asif Din. Stevenson's innings contained 15 fours and three sixes and Boycott managed just two fours, neither of them while

Stevenson was in.

In the dressing room, Boycott told me: "I coaxed him every ball and told him to get his head down and play sensibly until the fast bowlers tired. I did not know we were getting close to a record until David Bairstow came out with a message. It was a marvellous piece of cricket to be involved in and it turned Yorkshire from a losing position into a winning one."

The margin of victory for Yorkshire was nine wickets, the same as they went on to beat Warwickshire by at Headingley when Dennis lifted his game to collect 5-42 and a match return of 8-109 in his first appearance of the season.

Nick Taylor, the 19-year-old son of the multi-talented Ken, made his Yorkshire debut in 1982 and was with the club until the end of the following season without making the sort of progress Illingworth had hoped for upon first seeing him. An energetic fast bowler, he was as keen as mustard, so much so that his dad admitted that had he shown the same level of keenness for his cricket then he would have played far more matches for England than he did.

Come September, another record-breaker was Bairstow, who became the first Yorkshire wicketkeeper to dismiss seven batsmen in an innings in the match against Derbyshire at Scarborough. He followed up with four in the second innings to equal the world record of 11 catches in a match, the two other 'keepers being Arnold Long for Surrey in 1964 and Rodney Marsh for Western Australia in 1975-76.

The final game of the season was at The Oval when Boycott's 37 was sufficient to make it his third most successful summer for Yorkshire. He was offered a new one-year contract, which he accepted, but any hopes that harmony would finally descend upon Headingley proved to be misguided.

CHAPTER THIRTY-TWO

NEW BATTLES

Throughout the whole of Yorkshire's history, no two years have been as turbulent as 1983 and 1984 when the club was torn apart and put back together again but some of the wounds in this internecine war would never heal.

Yorkshire cricket ruled the front pages and the back of the county's newspapers with readers eager to soak up the day-to-day episodes which made even the long-running soap, Dallas, seem tame by comparison.

People who no-one had barely heard of in cricketing circles before assumed positions of power while others with glowing reputations within the game were tossed aside.

But throughout it all the adversaries stuck to their guns and to their principles and if Yorkshire cricket itself was relatively weak during this period those who fought its battles were not to be cowed. They were determined and resolute and stubborn and courageous and unwilling to give an inch.

And during the summer of 1983, while tensions continued to build, both Illingworth and Boycott were each deserving of the greatest admiration for what they managed to achieve personally.

There was no hiding the shame of Yorkshire finishing bottom of the Championship table for the first time in their history and if winning the John Player League title did not compensate for this, one still had to marvel that Illingworth, at 51, was chief architect of the success, not only as leader but as one of the two main bowlers. Stevenson claimed 22 wickets but they cost him 18.95 runs apiece whereas Illingworth's 20 victims came at 12.95. The pair controlled the middle to such an extent that no other bowler managed more than nine wickets.

Once again, the continual worry for Boycott about his future did not impair his ability to make runs and, as events would show, he remained the people's favourite. In the Championship he surged on to 1,941 runs, with a double century and six centuries, and in the Sunday League he contributed 341 runs after briefly being dropped because he had not been scoring quickly enough. He also helped Yorkshire sustain their JPL challenge by opening the bowling in the later matches because Illingworth could rely on him more than his regular pacemen to keep the runs down.

Neither Boycott's runs, nor the 1000-plus from Bairstow and Sharp, could prevent the disastrous showing in the Championship where the bowlers too often disappointed and were too often injured, the best efforts coming from Carrick and Dennis who was rewarded with his cap.

Clutching at straws, the Yorkshire committee tried to console members by saying that only five matches had been lost, the same number of defeats as champions Essex, but they failed to add that for the first time since 1866 – when they played just three fixtures – Yorkshire had won only one match.

By Yorkshire's standards, there was relative calm in the early part of 1983 and Close was honoured at the annual meeting by being given honorary life membership. The club were, in effect, saying 'sorry' for how they had treated him in the past, even though almost half of the committee who endorsed the move were in office at the time he was sacked.

In April, Illingworth indicated he might be prepared to stand down as captain later in the summer in order to give his successor first-hand experience of leadership and just before the season began his recommendation was approved that Neil Hartley be appointed vice-captain. Illingworth's intention never materialised, one of the reasons being that Hartley's form dropped away and he had to spend a time in the second team rediscovering it.

A welcome reminder of Yorkshire's glorious past occurred in early May when Sir Leonard Hutton opened the new £130,000 bar situated in the centre of the main stand and named after the great batsman. Jointly financed by Yorkshire CCC and Leeds CFAC, the bar looked directly on to the cricket field and also had direct access to the rugby stadium. It certainly improved facilities on a ground woefully short of them but some felt it was inappropriate for it to take Sir Leonard's name because drinking was not one of his chief recreations.

The start of the season was the wettest of the century. Four of the first six Championship days were completely washed out and there were only four hours' play out of a possible 38 but wins in the first two Sunday League matches got Yorkshire on the right track in the 40-overs competition. The second of these positive results was against Middlesex at Hull and Illingworth showed he was still a master of his craft by exploiting a helpful pitch to claim 4-6 in eight overs, figures which rival off-spinner, John Emburey, could not match, well though he bowled.

Old's name cropped up again when he was fined £1,000 by Warwickshire for having said in a newspaper article that Yorkshire would never be a success again until they "booted out" both Boycott and Illingworth. He may have been in breach of contract for saying what he did and Yorkshire wanted the matter to be taken further but one could hardly blame him for taking a pop at the set-up he had left behind.

Boycott was in the news again in early July because when he had reached 16 in the match with Leicestershire at Harrogate it gave him 42,720 runs and put him in the chart of the top ten scorers of all time. Shortly afterwards, Yorkshire acceded to his request to be given a testimonial for 1984 but this apparently charitable action proved to be a millstone around their necks because no new contract came with the testimonial. It made for an absurd situation when he was sacked and the club's attempt to compromise by offering to let him play in certain home matches was widely ridiculed.

After a patchy start, partly due to the bad weather, Boycott was soon into his rhythm and against Derbyshire at Sheffield he played one of his technically finest innings, carrying his bat for 112 out of 233 on a sub-standard pitch on which 37 wickets fell on the first two days, the problem believed to have been caused by a faulty top dressing put down by the unfortunate and hard-working groundsman, John Fulford. If there was a criticism of Boycott it was that he did not dominate sufficiently on the final morning and Yorkshire went down by 22 runs, their first defeat by Derbyshire in 26 years.

Boycott recorded the tenth double century of his career by hitting an unbeaten 214 in the draw with Nottinghamshire at Worksop but only a week later in that month of August came the match against Gloucestershire at Cheltenham, the aftermath of which brought the club to its knees.

Once again, the nub of the matter was what was perceived to be Boycott's slow scoring, for although he made an unbeaten 140 out of 344-5 declared, Yorkshire still missed out on a vital batting bonus point.

Sharp, coming in at 50-2, quickened up after a careful start to score his first Championship century in three years and by the time he was run out accepting Boycott's call for a single to mid-wicket he had reached 121 to his partner's 113 and had batted for 22 fewer overs.

Boycott's 140 spanned the full day of 375 minutes. He faced 347 balls, which was slightly more than half of the 115 overs sent down. He was 53 out of 87-2 at lunch; 95 out of 210-2 at tea and 120 out of 299-4 in 100 overs, scoring a further 20 runs in the final 15 overs.

Well before close of play on that first day, I was aware that Illingworth was incensed by what he regarded as Boycott's ultra-slow progress and that some form of disciplinary action was likely to follow. I prepared a story for Monday's paper on these lines and was accused by a furious Sid Fielden of having been tipped off by Illingworth that action would be taken, an allegation which he later withdrew unreservedly.

The truth of the matter was that I happened to be walking to the other side of the players' balcony at some stage in late afternoon and could not help but overhear the rumpus that was going on. It seemed obvious to me that this was a matter which could find its way to the 'peacekeeping' sub-committee trio of Burnet, Trueman and Billy Sutcliffe. I asked Illingworth if he was likely to take the matter any further and, always honest with his answers, he said he was considering it. That was sufficient reason for me to realise that the sparks were ready to fly, particularly as members of the currently dormant Reform Group were up in arms at the thought of Boycott being censured.

By Monday morning, news of a Boycott-Illingworth clash had spread like wildfire and the national Press were out in force at Cheltenham although they were not sure at the time exactly what was going on.

The mystery deepened even further on the Monday morning when Boycott was not at the ground for start of play. Upset by this latest drama he had spent a couple of sleepless nights and Illingworth had allowed him to return to the team hotel for a while. "He said that he was extremely tired and that he hoped to get in a few hours' sleep," said Illingworth.

Gloucestershire went on to declare their first innings 37 runs behind and Boycott responded to his captain's request for quick runs by making smooth progress to 97 before falling to David Graveney. Illingworth declared at 239-8, setting the home team a 277 target in 190 minutes and they made it by virtue of a century from Chris Broad and a gem of an innings of 75 from Zaheer Abbas.

Over the next few days, Illingworth handed in a written statement to Burnet giving his account of the Cheltenham affair and after Boycott had spent an hour and three-quarters explaining his side of the story to the peacemakers they decided he had batted too slowly and reprimanded him.

Burnet stressed that the matter was now closed and he did not think it would have much bearing on the considerations for a new contract but in a statement explaining their decision the sub-committee said: "We are satisfied that in this instance his batting was not in the best interests of the side and he has been told again that he must at all times play the sort of innings the side needs, irrespective of his own personal ambitions."

Boycott's almost unbelievable response to this challenge was to score a century in each innings in the very next match against Nottinghamshire at Park Avenue to become the only Yorkshire batsman ever to score a century in each innings twice off the same opponents. To cap it all, his second innings 141 not out included 103 runs in the morning session.

Even Boycott was forced to share the headlines in this game, however, because it also marked the first-class debut of his young opening partner, Ashley Metcalfe, who signed on with a fine 122, the highest score by a Yorkshire debutant. He also managed it at a younger age than the other two – Tyson and Moxon.

The glut of runs in late August did nothing to quell the turbulence that was building up over Boycott's censure and Illingworth was outraged when he learned that Fielden had put in a written request to Yorkshire that the general committee should meet to discuss the whole affair, Fielden now being additionally angry that Burnet had said Boycott batted well at Bradford which, he believed, suggested that he had scored unusually quickly in response to the reprimand.

It was myself and John Callaghan, cricket correspondent of the Yorkshire Evening Post, who passed on this information to Illingworth when he came into the team hotel at Scarborough one evening and he was so incensed by what he considered to be the building-up of aggravation to an intolerable degree that he retorted that he was prepared to quit both as captain and team manager.

"If Yorkshire will pay me out on my contract, which has about 18 months to run, I will leave the club now," he fumed. "I don't see why I should be playing first-class cricket at the age of 51 to try to help Yorkshire, and at the same time having to put up with a constant barrage of attacks from Boycott supporters on how I am handling the game."

The ever-thickening cloud that was enveloping the club could not distract Illingworth and his team from vigorously pursuing the John Player League title and they were kept in the hunt in the penultimate match by an innings of outstanding bravery from Athey. The game, against Derbyshire at Park Avenue, came the day after Athey and Moxon had been involved in a car crash the previous night as they returned home from Chesterfield following the first day of the Championship match.

Both men received severe bruising to ribs and stomach from the seatbelts as they were flung forward but Athey still took his place in the side at Park Avenue and opened the batting with Boycott in the chase towards a 169 target. After playing just one ball from West Indian pace merchant Michael Holding, however, Athey doubled up in pain and had to be assisted off the field by the physiotherapist, Eric Brailsford.

Wickets fell at regular intervals and when Carrick departed Yorkshire were 131-7, at which stage Athey agreed to return to the middle with Neil Hartley as his runner, and in great discomfort he proceeded to take the attack to the opposition with some brave strokes. He was on 21 with two wickets remaining in the final over when Dennis drove a straight six into the sightscreen to win the match and keep Yorkshire two points ahead of Somerset.

Athey's courage was duly rewarded a fortnight later when Yorkshire lifted the trophy at Chelmsford, despite pouring rain preventing a ball being bowled. The two points Yorkshire got from the 3.30pm abandonment made sure of the title and although Somerset's victory left them level on points they only had nine wins to Yorkshire's ten.

It was a particularly happy moment for Illingworth when he was able to hold the trophy aloft on the players' balcony and listen to the cheers of scores of bedraggled travelling fans, the loudest of them being reserved for Boycott. Then it was realised no-one had ordered champagne so Bairstow dashed out and assailed a startled Essex official with the earnest and voluble request: "Get us some champagne, any sort of champagne." Soon it was being sprayed around in time-honoured fashion.

On the same ground two days later, Yorkshire came down to earth with a bump, their draw with Essex leaving them on the bottom of the Championship table for the first time. All the celebrations were in the home camp now as the stalemate left Essex as the new title-holders. Rain ended the game early after Illingworth had been last out in the second innings, bowled by Norbert Phillip. It was not known then but he was taking his final bow and would be swept away before the start of next season. The date was September 13.

*   *   *

The crunch meeting of Yorkshire's general committee was held on the afternoon and evening of October 4 and after hours of heated debate it was agreed by 18 votes to seven to approve the recommendation of the cricket sub-committee to appoint Bairstow as captain and to sack Boycott or, as they put it, not to renew his contract.

Bairstow's appointment was well-received and he bustled into the T&A newsroom to see me the following morning with all the energy and drive that he always showed on the field of play. He was "up for it" in a way which few if any of his colleagues could have matched given the circumstances.

A message was sent to Boycott, who was in South Africa, informing him of the club's decision, and within minutes of the news breaking the inevitable fight to have him re-instated had started, Fielden's first reaction being that the whole of the cricket committee should resign. "The decision to dismiss Boycott after 22 seasons is awful. We are full of sympathy for a man who has served the club so loyally over the years," he said.

One of the early casualties of all the blood letting was Athey, who could not be persuaded to stay on, and the day after D-day he signed a three-year contract with Gloucestershire.

A protest meeting chaired by Peter Briggs at The Post House at Ossett – the hotel which was to become the rebels' headquarters – sent out an ultimatum to Yorkshire: Offer Boycott a one-year contract or face a special general meeting at a cost of several thousand pounds. Fielden, Kirk and Slicer were among the many eloquent and impassioned speakers and there was only one voice of dissent, Ken Harvey, from Leeds, urging everyone not to take action which would destroy the club.

An emergency meeting of Yorkshire's executive sub-committee did, indeed, discuss the ultimatum and it was agreed that because feeling was running so high, they should convene meetings of the cricket sub-committee and the general committee to reconsider the decisions over Boycott.

Optimism rose of a swift end to hostilities but quickly turned to pessimism because the same decision was reached again, this time with an 18-8 majority.

Now the gloves were off, Burnet insisting that Athey's departure was only the tip of an iceberg and that others may follow him, and the former Reform Group reconstituting itself as Yorkshire Members 1984 at another meeting at Ossett at which Briggs was elected chairman and Slicer treasurer. Fielden turned down appeals for him to become secretary because he felt it would not be right for a Yorkshire committee member to serve in an official capacity on the group. Without any difficulty, the meeting acquired the 240 signatures which were needed to call a special general meeting of Yorkshire.

The day after Slicer had handed in the petition, Yorkshire set the date of the meeting as December 3 at the Harrogate Conference Centre, although this was later changed to January 21 after Judge Blackett-Ord refused to make an order in the Chancery Division of the High Court in Leeds compelling Yorkshire to stick to the original date.

The application to the High Court was made by five members of Yorkshire Members 1984, who objected to Yorkshire cancelling the December 3 meeting when it was discovered that 684 members who hadn't paid the current year's subscriptions were entitled to vote but hadn't received their papers.

In the meantime, significant other developments had taken place with the thrusting into prominence of businessman Tony Vann and Bob Appleyard.

Vann, who owned a petrol filling station in Bradford and was an out-match playing member of MCC, took over as secretary of Yorkshire Members 1984 and announced that he would be standing as a candidate for Leeds district in the forthcoming elections. He, Briggs and Kirk formed a formidable trio of officers for the Group which also had the strong backing of Fielden and Brian Walsh QC, who would in time become Yorkshire chairman after Kirk. Vann, duly elected, served for a while on the cricket committee and had a spell as its chairman in less than harmonious circumstances. Many years later he was elected a Yorkshire vice-president in recognition of his services to the club.

Appleyard, now a self-employed businessman living in Ilkley with a business postal address in Bradford, was able to find sufficient time to pitch himself headlong into the debate and his continuing close involvement with Yorkshire CCC led to him being elected President in 2006-2008.

He opened up another front by spearheading a campaign which became known as "The Appleyard Initiative" and which asked for Boycott to be given a one-year contract within the framework of a three-year plan that would include raising £500,000 to build an indoor cricket school with chief coach and administrative staff.

The "Initiative" was debated by Yorkshire and rejected a few days before the January special general meeting but by then Appleyard had announced his intentions of standing in Bradford when the next elections took place. Robin

Feather, one of the current trio of Bradford representatives, made it clear that he would stand down immediately if Boycott were given a new contract and when this happened Appleyard was returned unopposed with the blessing at the time of the 1984 group.

While all this was going on, a saddened Yardley said he would quit as president if the membership supported the 1984 group motions of no confidence in the cricket and general committees and chairman Crawford hinted that he would follow suit.

As claim and counter-claim continued on an almost daily basis, the next piece of stunning news came in late December when Boycott revealed he was about to hand in his nomination papers to stand as a candidate for Wakefield district where he would oppose the retiring member, Dr. John Turner, one of the eight committee members who had voted in favour of Boycott being given a new contract. Boycott had no real wish to oppose Turner but his home at Pear Tree Farm, Woolley, was within the boundaries of the Wakefield district and he could not stand elsewhere. He said it had been his wish for some time to serve on the committee and if he had waited for three years to try to get on he may still have had to oppose Dr. Turner.

With the new date set for the special general meeting, the club's members were bombarded with literature from both sides and playing a prominent part in spelling out the club's official line was one of the committee's rising stars, Julian Vallance, who earlier in the year had taken over from Trueman as chairman of the public relations committee.

"I am working hard for the club to win at the special general meeting but I in no way welcome it or wish it was taking place," said Vallance, a former captain of Harrogate CC who had on occasions captained Vann, the Yorkshire 1984 secretary, in MCC matches.

Snow threatened on a cold winter's day when the special general meeting finally took place in front of 1,700 Yorkshire members who packed themselves into the Harrogate Conference Centre

What followed was pure theatre as leading figures from Yorkshire CCC and Yorkshire Members 1984 marched up to the microphone at the side of the stage and argued vociferously either for or against the three resolutions: 1 – that Boycott be offered a new contract; 2 – no confidence in the general committee; 3 – no confidence in the cricket committee.

History shows that the club won the day on the postal vote but the hall was swayed by the superior rhetoric of the rebels, who were articulate, concise and well-rehearsed. Their speakers generally got through what they had to say within the allotted time span whereas too many of the establishment advocates got bogged down in detail and were howled down when their time expired.

The hall erupted when the outcome of the voting was announced and it became clear that the revolution had succeeded. Members voted by a majority of 1,006 for Boycott's re-instatement as a player and by a majority of 788 in no confidence in the cricket committee.

But what brought the house tumbling down was the slender 31 majority given to the resolution calling for a vote of no confidence in the general committee. Had that resolution failed, the government of the club could have continued but now it became obvious that the general committee had little option but to concede defeat and resign when they met on the Monday.

The day was still far from over, however, because the 1984 group arranged a Press conference for Boycott that night at the Post House at Ossett and even though snow was now falling heavily it did not deter the whole media army from turning up.

Arriving 90 minutes after the scheduled starting time, Boycott had to hold two Press conferences because the small room was not big enough to accommodate the battery of reporters and photographers all in one go.

"I want you to know what I feel and I have always felt," said Boycott. "I want you to know that I accept the members' offer to me with joy and humility and I will do my best to be worthy of the confidence and affection that the members have shown towards me."

Many people had assumed Boycott would stand down as a candidate at the elections if retained as a player but he scotched this suggestion.

"I am a nominee and will ask the members of Wakefield to elect me," he said. "I have already indicated that should there be any conflict then playing for the club comes first, although there is no secret about my wanting to serve Yorkshire on the committee."

Even the weather was no friend of the Yorkshire committee and they had to battle through blizzards on the Monday to reach Headingley for their meeting, which acknowledged defeat and agreed to new elections across the board.

Chairman Crawford and president Yardley resigned their positions immediately and Bradford district members Feather and Brennan decided to call it a day and not seek re-election to the new committee, Vallance later following suit. Burnet announced he would stand again and if elected would support a one-year contract for Boycott to run alongside his testimonial.

Illingworth said he was prepared to continue as manager but would never play cricket for Yorkshire again, "because I have taken enough of the shouting and bawling which went on last season and is likely to continue".

The former players on the committee who were seen to have been opposed to Boycott may have been held in low esteem by the membership at large but Close had not been part of the warfare and when he announced he would stand in Bradford the news was warmly received. He may have been pushed into it by ex-players and friends but once the scent of Yorkshire cricket was in his nostrils once again there was no holding him back.

No general election campaign ever attracted more interest in Yorkshire than these elections did and throughout the whole of February candidates in the various districts held members' meetings and sent out through the post their election addresses.

The results were due to be announced at the annual meeting in Sheffield on March 3 but news began to leak out after the votes had been counted the previous day, the rebels being unable to contain their excitement at their landslide victory.

The biggest sensation was in Craven, where Trueman was quite heavily defeated by Keighley printing firm boss Peter Fretwell, who gained 70.18 per cent of the votes. It was a bouncer which Trueman never really saw coming and, upset and disillusioned, he kept his distance from Yorkshire cricket from that point on.

Boycott took up his dual role by winning Wakefield from Turner, Burnet was unseated by a mere four votes in Harrogate by British Telecom engineer Roy

Ickringill, and Vann easily overturned Billy Sutcliffe in Leeds where Brian Walsh, who had summed up for the opposition at the Harrogate special general meeting, was also elected by a comfortable margin

Another former player was axed in Huddersfield, where Platt narrowly fell to Tony Ramsden, but Bryan Stott just withheld the challenge from Harold Lister in Wharfedale and Sharpe held on in York, beating Ian Connell by seven votes.

Close romped home in Bradford and within a week emerged as the new strong man in the club by becoming cricket chairman. Also in Bradford, Raymond Clegg, a trustee of Bradford Cricket Club, had an easy win against postman Dennis Pratchett, who had delivered, unstamped and in his own time, 900 of his election addresses, while Appleyard was returned unopposed.

Philip Akroyd beat Mollie Staines in Dewsbury but Jack Sokell, founder of the Wombwell Cricket Lovers' Society, was much too strong for his 1984 Group opponent, Mike Helliwell in Barnsley, proving that one did not necessarily need to have been a top player to be the people's choice, although being one of the original eight to have voted for a Boycott contract obviously stood Sokell in good stead.

Establishment figures Tim Reed and the county's former fast bowler, Ted Burgin, came to grief in Sheffield against Tony Boot and Terry Jarvis, and in North Riding the outspoken anti-Boycott member, Captain Desmond Bailey, was ousted by Peter Quinn.

Kirk was given a closer run than he would have expected in Hull by Geoff Denton, who gained a committee seat at a later stage, but so prominent had Kirk been in Boycott's campaign that he was the natural choice to be voted in as Yorkshire's new chairman.

Finding a new president was to prove more difficult and something of an embarrassment because no-one would take it on over the coming months. Huddersfield-born Lord Hanson, chairman of the multi-national industrial management group, Hanson Trust Ltd., and a life member of Yorkshire CCC, was approached but after some consideration turned it down.

The aftershocks of the winter earthquake still rumbled on, Welch resigning as club treasurer through "being out of sympathy with the aims and objectives of the new committee". And then on March 21 Illingworth was contacted in Spain by Kirk to say that his contract had been terminated forthwith. Perhaps his removal was inevitable but it only came after a plea from Close fell on deaf ears.

Close had also spoken out strongly for Appleyard to become part of his cricket committee team but Ickringill objected to this and after a long discussion and ballot, Appleyard was replaced by Vann.

Suddenly, spring was in the air. Close gave a rallying call at the pre-season lunch where the John Player Special League Trophy was handed over to the club and new captain Bairstow said the fact that they had won it seemed to have been lost over the winter. Boycott was back on the top table as the senior professional but Yardley, Crawford, Trueman and Burnet were among the familiar faces which were missing.

CHAPTER THIRTY-THREE

FALSE DAWN

Bairstow's three years in office as Yorkshire captain may have brought little overall improvement in results but his enthusiasm, energy and drive in the build-up to each season rubbed off on to his players, who invariably managed a promising start before fading away in the latter part of the programme.

After the trauma of the winter months, everyone was relieved to turn their attentions to the cricket in the April of 1984 but trouble continued to bubble away underneath the surface and at the end of the season a bizarre situation led to further uproar and resignations.

Several months before that, however, the first match was eagerly awaited at Taunton, where Bairstow and Ian Botham were captaining their teams for the first time on an official basis, and there was endless speculation as to which of these two great competitors would outwit the other.

It was a bitter-sweet experience for Bairstow who began his reign by losing the toss and then having to watch Peter Roebuck and Julian Wyatt put on 242 in 95 overs to set Somerset's third highest opening stand. Much of it was like watching paint dry but the tempo gradually livened up and on the final day Botham challenged Yorkshire to score 306 in 78 overs.

The gauntlet was firmly picked up by Bairstow who allowed himself to be persuaded by Carrick to promote himself to No 4 to compensate for a slow start. A brief consultation with Boycott when he got to the middle left no-one in any doubt as to the changed tactics. They added 32 in five overs before Boycott fell to Vic Marks for 60 and Bairstow continued his assault with Love so effectively that the tide turned and Sidebottom hit the winning boundary with 11 balls remaining to bring Yorkshire their first win on the opening day since 1972.

Come June 30, Yorkshire were the only unbeaten team in the Championship but they then suffered defeat by an innings and 153 runs to Essex at Headingley, courtesy of eight wickets in the match for John Lever and seven for Norbert Phillip, plus centuries from Graham Gooch and Keith Fletcher. Confidence began to drain away and they slipped to 14th place.

Once again, Boycott was the leader of the pack with 1,567 runs at an average of 62.68. Sharp also enjoyed himself with 1,445 runs and Moxon, in his first full season, continued his rapid development with 1,016. He was due to make his England debut against the West Indies in the Second Test at Lord's on June 28 but had to pull out with a cracked rib, the legacy of a blow from Northamptonshire's Rupert Hanley the previous Saturday which proved more serious than first thought. Moxon had to wait until January 23 of the following year for his international debut in the fourth one-day international between England and India at Nagpur and although England lost by three wickets, Moxon top-scored with a solid 70.

Arnie Sidebottom was the best of Yorkshire's bowlers with 63 wickets at a respectable 20.07 but several of the other pacemen had long spells out with injuries and all proved too expensive when they did play.

One of Illingworth's last acts before his sacking had been to bring back Steve Oldham after four fruitful years at Derbyshire. His main brief was to develop the young bowlers – something which was always his forte – but injuries soon saw his return to action and he was reliable in the Championship and outstanding in one-day matches. Who would ever have imagined that, 27 years on, both Sharp and Oldham would be nudged out of their coaching jobs in a big shake-up of the backroom staff following a disappointing season?

Making his senior debut in 1984 was Keighley-born Phil Robinson, whose batting style was uncomplicated with no frills attached but it could not have served him better because he enjoyed one of the best runs by any Yorkshire batsman in his initial season, including Boycott.

Robinson had unbeaten scores of 74 and 32 on his maiden appearance against Derbyshire at Harrogate in mid-June and in 15 Championship games he totalled 756 runs, with six half-centuries, to finish next to Boycott in the averages. Few players gain such a high number of regular matches in the earliest stages of their careers.

Off-spinner Ian Swallow and left-armer Paul Booth showed genuine signs of promise but it was Yorkshire's overall inability to bowl sides out which lay behind the slump down the table.

The poor showing in three-day cricket came as a shock to the system of the new regime but they were able to draw a degree of comfort from the Second XI, who, under captain Colin Johnson and coach Doug Padgett, won their Championship after finishing as runners-up the previous year.

Yorkshire's most humiliating display of the season was reserved for the first round of the NatWest Trophy when they lost to Shropshire at Telford by 37 runs, beaten in the main by the versatility of their old adversary, Mushtaq Mohammad, who scored 80 and then destroyed the middle order with his leg-spin, which brought him 3-26.

Major disappointments, too, in the John Player Special League where they were unable to reproduce the form under Illingworth that had brought them the title and they were forced to share 13th place along with three other sides.

But redemption of a sort came in the Benson and Hedges Cup which saw them get to within four runs of making it into the Lord's final. Their stumbling block was Warwickshire who twice beat them in thrillers – by seven runs in the zonal stages at Edgbaston and by three runs in an exhilarating semi-final at Headingley.

In the first encounter, Neil Hartley scooped the gold award for shrugging off an arm injury and plundering an unbeaten 65 but the task of scoring 13 off the final over from Bob Willis was asking just a little too much. Willis, bowling with fervour usually reserved for country rather than county, had already pegged Yorkshire back with an exceptionally quick opening spell that gave away only two runs in seven overs and included the wicket of Boycott. Both Moxon, just capped, and Sharp weathered the storm with gritty half-centuries but progress was slow and only Hartley's late blast got them close.

Yorkshire's target had been 255 and at Headingley it was a much stiffer 279 but they were almost at the winning line in front of a packed 15,000 house when victory was most cruelly snatched from their grasp. The flailing bats of Bairstow and Stevenson brought 71 in ten overs for the sixth wicket and seemed to have knocked the stuffing out of Warwickshire but in the penultimate over both fell in the space of three balls from Gladstone Small. Bairstow was out to one of the most spectacular catches I have ever seen, his 60-yard pile-driver skimming a couple of feet over the turf to within inches of the cover boundary where Paul Smith came from nowhere to cling on in a frantic dive.

The batsmen having crossed, then Stevenson gave a high catch to Willis at fly slip and the ball would have only brushed the outstretched fingers of a smaller man. Still Yorkshire pressed forward and Oldham needed to hit the last ball of the match from Willis for six but the miracle did not happen.

Bairstow's man-of-the-match award was of little consolation. "If you want it bluntly, I am as sick as the proverbial pig," he said, immediately after the heat of the battle. "We did everything right but still lost and we did not deserve to lose."

Lancashire went on to claim the cup but one-day cricket came as close as it has ever been to a Roses final at Lord's, the showdown which the players, the fans and the media have always craved but has never so far happened.

Bairstow finally caught the England selectors' eye again in late May when he was chosen for the Texaco one-day series against the West Indies. Yorkshire, against Sussex at Abbeydale, were led by Boycott who had just missed the Roses match because of a hamstring injury. The absence of Bairstow resulted in Bradford-born wicketkeeper Steve Rhodes being brought in for his Championship debut. His only previous first team appearance had been on the same ground three years earlier when he was included against Sri Lanka but rain set in before he could bat and he never actually set foot on the field.

Rhodes would undoubtedly have enjoyed a long and successful Yorkshire career if events at the end of the season had not resulted in his move to Worcestershire, where he has given distinguished service ever since as player, captain, coach and director of cricket.

Another youngster to make an impact that season was 20-year-old Chris Shaw who bagged 5-41 in only his second Sunday match. He was one of the lower-profile but extremely useful and highly-committed fast bowlers who helped Yorkshire out around this time, another being Chris Pickles, whose debut arrived the following summer.

As the season went into decline, Yorkshire were pushed further on the downhill path by Old who achieved the most prolific bowling performance ever recorded by an exiled Yorkshireman against his native county, his match figures of 11-99 at Headingley guiding Warwickshire to victory by 191 runs. He became the only bowler to take ten wickets in a match both for and against Yorkshire and he also aided Warwickshire's cause by scoring 52 and 13 not out.

"I am still a Yorkshireman at heart, so it isn't really the sort of record I would have wanted to set," he said modestly, adding: "To be honest I would still rather be playing for Yorkshire but that isn't to be. And, anyway, I am enjoying my cricket with Warwickshire."

The realisation that another season was moving towards failure caused old sores to be re-opened and Captain Desmond Bailey, defeated in North Riding at the elections, threatened another extraordinary meeting if Boycott stayed on as a player, his gripe being that his members had only voted for the batsman to be given a contract in his testimonial year.

The build-up of pressure brought a remarkable outburst from club chairman Kirk who strongly attacked the Press, saying it was time to stop such reports and concentrate more on Yorkshire's promising team. It seemed mildly amusing that Press coverage should get so deeply under the skin of a man whose own words had produced so much of the publicity which had helped get rid of the old committee and put himself into a position of power.

If Kirk feared further upheavals he was right to do so because before the autumn was out, Close resigned from the cricket committee and soon afterwards gave up his seat on the general committee – and all because Boycott had been given a further year's contract and had NOT been made captain, even though Boycott himself did not want the job!

Close's dilemma came about because he, as chairman of the cricket committee, and his ex-player colleague, Sharpe, had opposed a new contract for Boycott but had been outvoted by the three others on the cricket committee in Yorkshire historian Tony Woodhouse, Sokell and Vann.

The majority decision was endorsed by the general committee but Close persuaded the club to hold back on re-appointing Bairstow as captain because he believed that it was impossible for Bairstow to be an effective leader with Boycott in the team and wielding the additional power of being on the committee. Therefore, he urged Boycott be made captain in view of him being given a contract.

After much further discussion the cricket committee offered the captaincy to Bairstow on condition that he gave up the wicketkeeping gloves in order to concentrate fully on his leadership. But when Bairstow refused point black to do this, Close had to back down and Bairstow was given the job in any case – a move which quickly led to Rhodes leaving for Worcestershire because he did not want to be the wicketkeeping understudy for any longer.

Sharpe also stood down from the cricket committee but remained on the general committee as York's representative whereas Close said he would stand for re-election in the spring to see if he had a fresh mandate to restore Yorkshire's fortunes.

It was all crazy stuff but at the same time that Boycott was given a new contract it was announced that the presidency would be filled by Viscount Mountgarret, of South Stainton, Harrogate. Amidst all the confusion and turmoil this proved to be an even better move than it appeared at the time because his Lordship, with a loftier perspective than others, favoured no particular faction above any other and he brought considerable energy and drive in his honest and sometimes eccentric endeavours to restore peace and harmony.

Resignations were coming thick and fast and the next to go, voluntarily but only temporarily, was Fretwell, the Keighley printing boss who had ousted Trueman. He said he was doing so because he had broken the rule of speaking to the Press but had felt compelled to do so. "I believe the character assassination of Boycott is nothing short of a disaster and I don't agree that he is a bad influence on the committee," he said. "I did not know him from Adam but I quickly found him to be extremely perceptive in committee and he has conducted himself in a very accurate way."

Generally, however, the pressure was increasing on Boycott over his dual role and it was the start of a major rift between himself and, until now, his closest ally, Fielden, who spoke out strongly against Boycott continuing on the committee while still a player. So far apart did they become that Fielden on one occasion said: "He is a very great cricketer. I wish I had never met him."

And opposition to the new pro-Boycott committee became even more organised with the formation of the Yorkshire Cricket Devotees, who soon recruited Close to their numbers which also included Bob Platt. They handed in to Yorkshire a whole string of resolutions for the annual meeting, the most notable being one of no-confidence in the general committee and another which sought the ending of current players serving on the committee.

Among the Devotees other leading figures were their chairman, David Brooks, chairman of Modern Maintenance Products who were long-time sponsors of Yorkshire CCC and the White Rose Competition; David Hall, chairman of Hepworths; insurance broker, Derek Blackburn, the former Bradford Cricket Club president and captain and former captain of Yorkshire Seconds; David Brawn, senior partner in a firm of Harrogate solicitors; and former Yorkshire committee members Julian Vallance and Desmond Bailey.

Close's resignation had resulted in Appleyard being moved on to the cricket committee but he proved to be even more outspoken than his predecessor and he particularly went gunning for what he believed was chairman Kirk's ineffective running of the club. He also lashed the plan to build nine hospitality boxes on top of the winter shed at Headingley at a cost of £200,000 but these were well-received when erected and were the first purpose-built boxes of their type on the ground.

The New Year brought little relief to the heated debates which continued to rage but cricket got a look-in with the news that Appleyard had arranged for Wilf Paish, of Carnegie College, to organise a special training programme for Yorkshire's bowlers. Paish had coached Tessa Sanderson to an Olympic gold medal in the javelin the previous year and Appleyard felt that bowlers would benefit from similar training but its success proved to be limited.

Back to the politics and Appleyard urged members to vote for the no confidence resolution, even though he realised it would mean him losing his seat, also. "I will be happy to stand for re-election in Bradford on getting cricket priorities right," he said.

But Vann, given the task of putting the club's case in the run-up to the annual meeting, responded: "It doesn't follow that ex-players make good committee men, particularly when they have been out of the game for 25 years, as in Appleyard's case."

The annual meeting, when it arrived on March 2, proved to be the longest and most complicated in the club's history, but throughout its seven hours of heated debate it was brilliantly chaired by Mountgarret, who drew rapturous applause when he used a Churchill phrase in appealing to the factions to bury the hatchet.

"If this can be done this club will move forward into broad sunlit uplands but should it fail we will sink into the abyss of a new dark-age, never to recover," he thundered.

The committee narrowly survived the motion of no-confidence but got into an almighty tangle because of its own resolution to remit a whole raft of rule change proposals to a special sub-committee. This was carried by a small majority of 143, despite counsel's opinion already obtained that the resolutions had a legal right to be heard, and as a consequence a special general meeting was arranged to be held on March 30 at Harrogate at a cost to the club's members of around £4,000-£5,000.

Again, Mountgarret earned huge praise for working out a plan which allowed the meeting to be cancelled and replaced by a referendum over the rule changes, so saving Yorkshire money they could ill-afford to squander.

Close was returned in Bradford after being given a good run for his money by licensee Peter Baren who polled 184 votes to his opponent's 248, yet the squabbling continued as Close was denied a place on the cricket committee and Fielden was sacked as public relations chairman because of his outspoken attacks on Boycott.

Kirk, challenged for his post as Yorkshire chairman by Brian Walsh, came through by an 11-8 vote and Vann was elected cricket chairman by the narrowest of margins, 9-8, Appleyard by the time of the vote having left the meeting to coach players at the indoor nets while Sharpe was absent. With the four ex-players, plus Boycott, declining to serve on the cricket committee, Vann was in a difficult position but the situation eased for him when he was able to announce that the team that season would be chosen by himself, Boycott and Bairstow.

Shortly before the season got underway, the results of the rule change resolutions which had gone to a referendum were revealed and they showed that Boycott's dual role had received a massive vote of disapproval – 2,595 votes against it continuing and 560 in favour. Boycott remained on the committee, however, because the referendum was neither retrospective nor legally binding.

CHAPTER THIRTY-FOUR

STILL SEARCHING

The second year of Bairstow's captaincy was very much like the first with Yorkshire failing to show their full potential, despite some thrilling matches, and finishing with little to show for their efforts.

Although the final table is no indicator, Yorkshire were at their most dangerous for much of the time in the John Player Special League. They lit the blue touch paper early on but the fireworks fizzled out when they lost their last three matches in tight contests and had to settle for eighth place, which was still a vast improvement on the previous year.

Yorkshire failed to qualify for the knockout stages of the Benson and Hedges Cup and got no further than the second round of the NatWest Trophy but again the biggest disappointment was in the Championship. A rise of three places to 11th in the table was neither here nor there and the less-than-mediocre effort was largely due to persistent injuries to their leading fast bowlers – a talented bunch but of no use whatsoever when sitting on the sidelines.

Against this backcloth, Yorkshire should be grateful that they had sufficient strength in reserve to be able to call up Peter Hartley, Chris Shaw and Chris Pickles to fill some of the gaps and as a result each of these willing pacemen were awarded first team contracts for the 1986 season.

Hartley was one of three significant figures to make their first team debuts in 1985, the others being Richard Blakey and David Byas, the latter just scratching the surface with a couple of one-day outings.

The most remarkable story concerning the three debutants belonged to Hartley, whose Yorkshire career seemed at first to be over before it had even begun and then over again soon after it had started.

The Keighley-born fast bowler and hard-hitting lower-order batsman, who was so good at golf that he once turned down the chance of going pro so that he could concentrate on his cricket, had failed to make an impact during a couple of seasons with the Second XI at the start of the decade.

He moved on to Warwickshire in 1982 and played in three Championship matches, including an appearance at Headingley when he dismissed Lumb and Bairstow, but was not offered a new contract.

Still keen to prove his worth, Hartley wrote to Yorkshire coach Doug Padgett pleading to be given a second chance and when Padgett agreed, his faith in the young bowler was amply rewarded. Unfortunately, Hartley had no sooner established himself than he went down with a back injury which was so severe that he thought it would rule him out of the game permanently.

With other treatment having failed, he agreed to an injection as a last resort and from that point on he never looked back, becoming one of Yorkshire's most consistent and successful bowlers, taking 579 first-class wickets for the White Rose until he was deemed surplus to requirements at the end of 1997 and moved to

Hampshire to see out the remainder of his active career before becoming an umpire of international standing.

The 18-year-old Blakey, who had already staked his claim by being the Second XI's heaviest scorer in 1984 with 922 runs, made an unexpected debut in an incident-packed match against Middlesex which opened the home season at Headingley.

He got his chance because of an injury to Boycott and although he started the game as a batsman he ended it as a wicketkeeper because of a hamstring injury to Bairstow. At the time it seemed quite incidental that the Huddersfield-born teenager had agreed to deputise behind the stumps but he calmly pouched four second innings catches in an atmosphere of increasing tension as Yorkshire won by just two runs with four balls remaining, Jarvis wiping out the tail to capitalise on good work by Sidebottom.

Blakey, through a twist of fate, was now looked upon not so much as a genuine wicketkeeper but as someone who could assist in an emergency, and the day would arrive when he would answer the call on a permanent basis and become one of the top six wicketkeepers in Yorkshire's history with 824 dismissals at an average of 2.43 per match, the best of any of his predecessors.

The downside of this additional duty, willingly undertaken, was that it most probably contributed significantly to Blakey not becoming the world-class batsman that had seemed probable but his 14,150 runs for Yorkshire with 12 centuries, two of them doubles, rank him high in the list of the county's greatest achievers.

Byas, the farmer's lad from Kilham, near Driffield, barely rated a mention in 1985 and it was only when he was thinking of quitting the game and going back full-time on the land that he became an indispensible part of the side. Strong from knowing the true meaning of hard work, Byas was honest and straight both as a batsman and person, and wretchedly unlucky not to get the England cap he deserved. Here was the man who, in 2001, would go on to lead Yorkshire to their first Championship triumph in 33 years and then serve as their director of cricket before becoming not the first and certainly not the last to be forced out of the club.

To an outsider, it may seem strange that a sportsman well into his 40s could still be such a power in the game and a topic of conversation on and off the field, but, of course, they would not know Boycott who made a mockery of his years by again leading the way with 1,545 Championship runs and notching six centuries and nine half-centuries. Some of his runs seemed to be scored more slowly than ever and his stance was more crouched, yet his batting was unarguable testimony to his superb fitness and unique concentration.

At Edgbaston on August 6, Boycott completed his 100th first-class century for Yorkshire – exactly five days short of eight years since his 100th century in all first-class cricket against Australia at Headingley – and in the final home match of the season his unbeaten 125 off Nottinghamshire's attack at Scarborough brought him level on all first-class centuries (149) with Herbert Sutcliffe, a figure not reached by any other Yorkshireman.

Boycott and Moxon combined at Worcester to put on 351 together, the highest Yorkshire partnership since the last war and the fourth highest ever, but it was a depressing feature of the season that most of the centuries came from opposing batsmen who thrived on the weakened bowling resources. There were 20 in all, Lancashire's Neil Fairbrother and Surrey's Monte Lynch scoring them home and away, and there were 17 from the last 15 matches while Yorkshire were scoring only five.

One of the century-makers, it almost goes without saying, was Athey, whose 101 in Gloucestershire's eight-wicket win at Gloucester followed directly on the heels of his 52 and 114 not out the previous season in their similar win at Park Avenue. How these exiles love to rub it in!

New bowling sensation David Lawrence caused the damage at Gloucester with 5-50 in 11.3 blistering overs as Yorkshire were sent packing for 83 in their second innings and he later admitted he had been motivated by the racist abuse he had suffered while fielding on the boundary edge at Scarborough the previous year when bananas were also hurled from the crowd. It was not the first time or the last that groups of drunken yobs were to cause problems during Sunday matches at North Marine Road but in recent years trouble has been snuffed out by swift intervention before it could get a grip.

Allegations of crowd racism were not confined to Scarborough in 1985 and Ian Botham branded Yorkshire fans as racist over their remarks when they booed Viv Richards during a remarkable incident in the NatWest Trophy match at Headingley.

Somerset were chasing 209 and Richards was on ten when he tucked his bat under his arm, peeled off a glove and headed for the pavilion after a vociferous appeal for a catch behind off Shaw. Umpire John Jameson did not react and Richards walked back to the crease to pulverise the bowling with an unbeaten 87 in the four-wicket win.

Botham said that Yorkshire crowds seemed to think that because Richards was black they could give him some stick and added: "I don't particularly want to come back here when you get comments like these from idiots in the crowd."

Not everyone agreed that there had been racist chants, however, and the allegations were not supported by Somerset skipper Peter Roebuck but the row rumbled on and chairman Kirk's handling of the affair caused problems for him which culminated in him quitting his post at the end of the year. Kirk had said Botham's views were totally unfounded, an opinion which was shared by many others, but president Mountgarret was furious that Kirk involved the TCCB in the matter rather than trying to smooth things out quietly between the two counties involved in the rumpus.

It was while Sidebottom was travelling from Gloucester to Maidstone in Love's car that the radio was switched on and Sidebottom discovered he had been drafted into the England squad for the third Test against Australia at Trent Bridge the following day, surprise news which prompted an unexpected train journey back to his Huddersfield home and then more travelling on to Nottingham.

Sidebottom got his chance through a late injury to Neil Foster but he was already suffering toe problems and his only Test appearance ended when he was forced to limp off after 18.4 increasingly painful overs had brought him the wicket of leg-spinner Bob Holland. A brief international career it may have been but most can only dream of walking out for England against the Aussies.

A Yorkshire paceman with somewhat happier memories from around that time was Jarvis who, at just turned 20, became the youngest bowler to bag a hat-trick for the county on a day when little else went right at picturesque Queen's Park, Chesterfield, his victims being Rajesh Sharma, Bruce Roberts and Paul Newman. In the same over that he began his hat-trick, Jarvis also dismissed century-maker Kim Barnett, to give him four wickets for no runs in seven balls.

A shaft of light at Park Avenue pierced the general gloom of another disappointing season and, appropriately, it was Bradford League products Bairstow and Carrick who did most to achieve victory in what was to be the last regular Championship match on the decaying ground. Bairstow smacked an unbeaten 122 and Carrick had an overall return of 10-105 in the innings and 24 runs win over Derbyshire. County cricket was to return to Bradford a few years down the line but, despite the brave efforts of the Friends of Park Avenue, its days were numbered.

Come September and Kirk's earlier actions over Botham's remarks were causing the Yorkshire committee to split right down the middle once again and Mountgarret ratcheted up the tension by calling for Kirk to resign. Yet when Kirk faced a motion of censure brought by Stott and Walsh at a three-hour meeting it was Mountgarret who saved his neck by declining to give the casting vote after 11 were in favour and 11 against, Kirk having declared he would go if the vote went against him.

It was only a temporary reprieve for Kirk, however, because he came under fire again from Mountgarret over his opposition to a new package of rules being presented to the annual meeting in February, feeling that insufficient time had been given to the recommendations of members in the referendum.

But Mountgarret had worked tirelessly on the framework of the new rules and was furious at Kirk's refusal to support them. The two most important members of the club's committee were at loggerheads and it was obvious that they could not work together in harmony. The strain proved too much for Kirk, who resigned on New Year's Eve, and Mountgarret commented: "It is no surprise to me. The only surprise is that Mr. Kirk – and others like him – can feel able to continue on the committee when they cannot accept democratically-taken decisions."

Mountgarret took over the chair until the annual meeting but the forthcoming district elections were as contentious as ever. In Bradford, Close was fighting his third election in as many years, Baren once again being his opponent, while 1984 group chairman Peter Briggs announced he would stand in Craven. Although living in Manchester, Briggs had a new business address in Keighley. He said he did not really agree with the validity of business addresses and would stand down if others who had been similarly elected would do the same. In the event, his nomination was not accepted because he had not notified Yorkshire of his business address beforehand.

The mayhem continued on another front as a group of members put forward an alternative set of rules for the annual meeting to sit alongside officially sanctioned rule proposal changes. There were calls for the four committee men who seconded the alternative rules, proposed by Tony St. Quintin, to resign but they stayed firm and when Yorkshire took the resolution off the agenda there were threats of a High Court injunction to stop the annual meeting taking place. But this never materialised.

On the eve of the February 22 annual meeting, Kirk wrote out his resignation from the committee after already having discovered the hard way that being prime minister is much more difficult than leader of the opposition.

And law and order seemed to return to the club with the approval of the new set of rules by 3,370 votes to 310 which represented a massive vote of confidence in Mountgarret.

As expected, Close was re-elected to the committee and a couple of days later he was back in the hot seat of cricket chairman with Walsh being voted in as club chairman in place of the vanquished Kirk. But it was Mountgarret who chaired the new management committee which was to be responsible for the running of the club.

During all the committee upheaval, another drama was being played out concerning Bradford Park Avenue, whose bleak future took a critical turn for the worse on February 18 when Bradford Cricket Club officials delivered an ultimatum to the Bradford Metropolitan Council: "Take over Park Avenue or we will close it down."

The Council had for three years given an annual £15,000 grant towards the upkeep of Park Avenue but this was only a quarter of what was required for maintenance.

In the 1970s, Yorkshire had been offered the ground free of charge by Bradford CC to develop as their own but they had rejected the idea. Had they taken it up then, Bradford rather than Headingley could have become their headquarters at a fraction of the cost but, most probably, without Test cricket.

Bradford Council was not in a position to respond positively to the ultimatum and the ground was closed for the coming season, despite passionate appeals from Trueman for it to continue functioning, so ending Yorkshire's involvement in cricket in Bradford going back to 1881.

Worse was to follow when the council ordered the closure of the ornate Victorian pavilion until money could be spent on making the roof structure safe and this decision brought about the closure of the thriving White Rose Banqueting Suite which had existed there for 12 years and had 117 functions already booked stretching into 1989.

Business plans to re-develop Park Avenue on a massive scale had also just fallen through and it looked as if all lifelines had now drifted away, but the end was not nigh just yet, even though all seemed at this stage to be dead and buried.

The changes brought about at the annual meeting gave Yorkshire a more stable look and while Bairstow and his squad were busy making their preparations for the 1986 season the club were able to announce a development which showed that things were moving in the right direction.

Largely through the behind-the-scenes efforts of Vann, they had purchased a disused warehouse in St. Michael's Lane at Headingley, just opposite the Herbert Sutcliffe gates, and plans were in hand to convert it into a cricket school at a cost of around half a million pounds.

The building was the first piece of fabric actually to be owned by Yorkshire but they were working in close co-operation with Leeds City Council who contributed

£115,000 towards the cost and would install their cricket development officer, Ralph Middlebrook, in an office in the building, the school to be run jointly by Yorkshire and the Council. A grant of £110,000 had also been received from West Yorkshire County Council before it went out of existence and the Sports Council had agreed to donate at least £30,000. Work on constructing the indoor school went on throughout the year and 1987 was declared a benefit year for the club with proceeds going into the running of the school.

Although Appleyard had campaigned unsuccessfully for the school to be built at Bradford he later approached Paul Getty to see if he could help with the construction costs at Headingley and the oil tycoon's response was to donate £10,000 – a gesture which was to bring him honorary life membership of the club.

Just before the season began, the death occurred on April 24 of Jim Laker, the greatest Yorkshire-born cricketer never to play for Yorkshire and also a true Yorkshireman to the tip of his boots. Yorkshire never discarded Laker, they just regarded him in his formative years as simply not being good enough and Laker admitted they were right to do so. But the change came when Laker experimented with off-spin and Surrey's request to Yorkshire to sign him on special registration in 1946 was the start of his long and loyal career with the London club.

But Laker still reserved one of his greatest bowling achievements for Park Avenue, just three or four miles away from Frizinghall where he was born. In the Test Trial in 1950, bowling for England against The Rest, he took 8-2 in 14 overs, a forerunner of his unique capture of 19 wickets against Australia at Old Trafford six years later.

As we have seen, Yorkshire were straight out of the traps in the first two of Bairstow's three seasons in charge but this time they appeared unstoppable after winning their first five matches in all competitions and their first four in the John Player Special League for the first time.

Once again, however, they were unable to keep the impetus going once injuries and self-doubt set in but it is still to Bairstow's great credit that he got what he did out of the team in three of the club's most difficult years. No fault of his in 1986 that Boycott should miss out on a good deal of cricket early on with hamstring and hand problems or that Sidebottom, Jarvis and Sharp should all break down for substantial periods. But there was compensation in the emergence of Peter Hartley as a genuine all-rounder and the flashing blade of the young Metcalfe who was the only batsman to complete 1,000 Championship runs on his way to 1,582, his cavalier approach suiting him – and the crowds – very well.

An incredible two-handed catch at full-stretch on the long-on boundary by Peter Hartley gave Yorkshire's season a fairytale start with a five runs win off the last ball of their Championship opener at Taunton and over the next few weeks Hartley and Jarvis did much to maintain the momentum with both bat and ball.

The pair saw Yorkshire home in their next Championship match against Sussex at Headingley by putting on an unbeaten 32 for the last wicket in a finish equally as exciting as the one at Taunton and it took them to the top of the table.

They also led the way in the Sunday League and nothing which had gone before was more palpably exciting than what Sidebottom did at Sheffield to make it four straight wins and end Essex's record of 16 consecutive one-day triumphs. Chasing

163, Yorkshire were 102-8 when Jarvis joined Sidebottom to launch a last-ditch assault which looked to have fallen just short with ten still wanted from three balls. Foster then sent down a no-ball off which Sidebottom failed to score but he swept the penultimate ball for four, leaving him requiring a four off the final delivery to tie or six to win it. Sidebottom's response was to step down the pitch to the England man and drive him gloriously for six and into the ecstatic crowd.

Injury had marred the start for Boycott but when Yorkshire went to Lord's in June he managed to reach two milestones and narrowly miss out on a third. It was his 600th match, his second knock was his 1,000th innings and he required a century to become the only Yorkshire batsman to hit 150 first-class centuries. He did manage 100 runs, but only from 69 in the first innings and 31 in the second, and his batting drew criticism for its overall slowness. He was vindicated when Jarvis roared in to grab 6-47 and complete match figures of 11-92 in Yorkshire's first win at cricket's headquarters since 1975.

Metcalfe, batting at No 3, confirmed his pedigree as Boycott's likely successor by hitting a sparkling 108 at Worcester, and in the next game against Northamptonshire at Luton he opened with Boycott in Moxon's absence and scored 151.

The spotlight was soon back on Boycott, who reached his record 150th first-class century against Leicestershire at Middlesbrough in June to leave Jack Hobbs (197), Patsy Hendren (170), Wally Hammond (167) and Phil Mead (153) as the only batsmen in the history of the game ahead of him.

Unknown at the time, Boycott had a bone broken in his left hand by Phil DeFreitas during this match but when an X-ray revealed the fracture it meant another lengthy spell out and he was unable to return to first team action until the final match at Scarborough.

Away from the Championship, Moxon found much improved form to become the only Yorkshire batsman ever to make a century in each innings of a match against a touring side, but his 123 and 112 not out against India at Scarborough was insufficient to prevent the tourists from winning their first game in 13 encounters with Yorkshire.

Metcalfe continued to go from strength to strength and was awarded his cap in August, a month in which groundsman Keith Boyce dug up and re-laid the Test strip at Headingley after the pitch was heavily criticised in the Test against India and Yorkshire's NatWest Trophy tie with Sussex.

As the season drew to a close, it did not take a genius to work out that the odds were stacked against Boycott getting a new contract. He was approaching 46, had endured two spells out with injury and the balance of power on the committee was likely to work against him.

All this was still speculation as Yorkshire's last Championship game against Northamptonshire at Scarborough drew nearer and Boycott earned his recall following his hand injury by making 81 for Close's International XI on the same ground and then underlining his fitness by turning out for Yorkshire Seconds and hitting 121 at Edgbaston.

Boycott set out in determined fashion to notch the 152nd century of his amazing career but it was slow stuff and he took eight overs to get off the mark. He moved to 61 in as many overs before being run out, a mode of dismissal he had more often witnessed from the other end. Looking for his first run, new batsman Love steered a stroke to third man and sent Boycott back when the pair turned for a second run but Boycott could not beat Alan Walker's accurate throw to the wicketkeeper.

Love atoned for any error on his part by hitting his first century in over two years while Boycott's misery was compounded by falling just eight runs short of 1,000 for the season.

A fortnight later, Boycott's playing career was finally over, his fate decided in two meetings which ran for a total of six hours. The six-man cricket committee voted 4-1 against a contract, with chairman Close not needing to exercise his vote, and their recommendation was supported 12-9 by the general committee.

Boycott, who was at the meeting, had nothing to say to reporters afterwards, but the man who had made 48,426 first-class runs – more than any other batsman since the war – was to remain one of the most powerful forces in Yorkshire cricket there has ever been.

Predictably, Stevenson was also released by Yorkshire, his recent attendance record through injury and loss of form not meriting another contract and he moved to Northamptonshire for a couple of seasons but could not reproduce the form that had made him one of the most exciting players in the country to watch.

The captaincy was not discussed at this meeting but it was evident that Close and his cricket committee favoured a change, one of their reasons being that they felt Bairstow's wicketkeeping had declined over the past season or so.

Bairstow was hurt by the moves which were taking shape to replace him but he was unable to stop them. He refused to resign and in mid-November he was "relieved of his duties" and replaced by Carrick, Close believing that the left-arm spinner's in-depth knowledge of bowling would be of enormous benefit to a team which needed a boost in that direction.

Despite general sympathy over Bairstow's situation, the year managed to end on a more harmonious note than for some time. Over 400 members packed into the Old Swan Hotel at Harrogate to mingle with HRH The Duchess of Kent, Yorkshire's patroness, at the club's triennial dinner; Boycott showed his allegiance by rejecting the offer of a two-year contract at Derbyshire, and the larger-than-Lord's indoor cricket school at Headingley neared its completion.

CHAPTER THIRTY-FIVE

MY SWEET LORD'S

For three years Bairstow's sheer energy had galvanised Yorkshire into making good starts to the season but even he could not scale the heights which Carrick managed to achieve in the first half of 1987.

Triumph followed triumph right from the start as Yorkshire topped the Championship table and they also won six games out of six in the Benson and Hedges Cup on their unstoppable march to Lord's, where they beat Northamptonshire in a pulsating final.

But Carrick then felt the same despair as his predecessor as the second half of the season collapsed around him, so much adrenalin having been pumped into Lord's that there was nothing left afterwards – apart from the golden memories and a conviction that they could now compete with anyone.

Preparations for the new campaign were boosted by being able to use the new indoor school for the first time at its Press launch in late January, Carrick expressing himself delighted with how the eight lanes played. Further good news arrived when Bassett Foods of Sheffield the liquorice allsorts people, signed a year's sponsorship deal worth around £25,000, the company's chairman and chief executive, Bev Stokes, being a genuine cricket fan who went on to give outstanding service as chairman of the Sheffield Cricket Lovers' Association.

Boycott again beat Dr. Turner in Wakefield to stay on the general committee but he was not given a place on the cricket committee which continued to be led by Close and included other former players in Appleyard, Stott and Sharpe as well as Vann and Woodhouse.

For once, off-the-field stories and gossip paled into insignificance as Carrick got Yorkshire off to their best-ever start with a run of nine consecutive wins in all competitions. Everything that he touched turned to gold and the victory over Derbyshire at Harrogate in June took them to the top of the Championship table at a time when they were already through to the B&H semi-finals and performing strongly in the Sunday League.

Carrick himself had played a crucial role in the Derbyshire match by recording astonishing figures in the innings and 169 runs win after centuries from Moxon and a revitalised Bairstow. The skipper was virtually unplayable as his match figures of 26.1-20-10-5 so clearly show. Verity would have been proud of him – and also delighted that his fellow left-armer had just been named the country's player-of-the-month for May.

Proud though the fans were that Yorkshire led the Championship, it was making it through to the semi-finals of the B&H that caused genuine excitement because it opened up the prospect of a first Lord's appearance since 1972 and the first chance of cup glory since 1969.

Yorkshire had won all four of their games in the qualifying stages, Moxon and Metcalfe getting things moving with an unbroken 211 stand against Warwickshire, the club's highest for any wicket in one-day cricket, and Metcalfe continued to dominate to such an extent that he scooped three of the four man-of-the-match gold awards before receiving another 'gong' for his unbeaten 93 in the quarter-final overpowering of Hampshire.

In the semi-final, Moxon got the gold award for his unflinching 97 that steered Yorkshire to a modest 238-7. Sidebottom stepped in with two early wickets and also the last, opener Grahame Clinton for a stubborn 69, but it was undemonstrative medium-pacer Stuart Fletcher who clinched it with three wickets in a 12-ball spell which gave away only four runs.

Yorkshire by now were on cloud nine but a lot more cricket remained before the final on July 11, not least the Roses clash at Old Trafford when Yorkshire clung on for a tense draw before pandemonium broke out as a consequence of Lancashire veteran Jack Simmons strongly attacking Fletcher in the Press for not walking.

Blakey, having firmly established himself as a batsman of prodigious talent, was the only one who seemed capable of settling down after Yorkshire had been set 320 in 79 overs in the rain-hit match. A thrashing seemed likely at 185-9 with 17 overs remaining but last man Fletcher calmly stayed put while Blakey went to his century and then the tail-ender valiantly saw it through to stumps after standing his ground at one stage when Ian Folley claimed a close-in catch off Simmons, the appeal failing to impress umpire David Evans.

The chuntering from Lancashire was to be expected and it was like water off a duck's back to Fletcher but Simmons's lashing attack afterwards caused the affair to rumble on, despite Lancashire's immediate apology and a three-match ban for the off-spinner.

An angry Simmons, under stress from the death of his 88-year-old mother, said: "He was definitely out – it was not debatable. I cannot understand how a player could stay in such a situation and I cannot understand David Evans for not giving him out. I am feeling absolutely disgusted. We wanted to play cricket and Yorkshire didn't."

Yorkshire rightly came to Fletcher's defence and the issue was only settled and quickly forgotten when Simmons gave a full written apology to the club and to the players, particularly Fletcher.

County Champions Essex were steamrollered into submission by nine wickets at Headingley, and irrepressible Yorkshire next turned their attentions to the NatWest Trophy, crushing Wiltshire by 129 runs at Trowbridge where Moxon and Metcalfe again led the way with a club record opening stand in the competition of 161, Moxon's 74 giving him 611 runs from his last seven innings.

Suddenly, one or two results showed that Yorkshire were not infallible and they were rocked by Championship losses to Northants and Nottinghamshire, who spun them to defeat inside two days at Trent Bridge.

But they bounced back in the second round of the NatWest Trophy by annihilating Glamorgan at Headingley by nine wickets, the indisputable man-of-the-match being Sidebottom who sent the Welshmen reeling to 24-5, claiming all five wickets for seven runs in 6.1 overs.

This was exactly the result Yorkshire wanted in their build-up to the B&H Cup final against Northants which was blessed with glorious weather as well as great cricket. On the eve of the big game, Yorkshire practised at Lord's and were encouraged in their preparations by Raymond Illingworth and Don Wilson, who had popped over from the indoor school where he was in charge.

Also prowling around and just as nervous as the players was another great Yorkshireman, Dickie Bird, who was keenly anticipating officiating in his 20th final at Lord's. "Naturally, I am strictly impartial in the middle, but I am looking forward immensely to being in charge with Yorkshire here," he said.

Dickie would have been even more jittery than usual had he known he was about to be involved in one of the finest cup finals ever to grace the hallowed turf and one which Carrick would describe as the greatest cricket match in which he had ever played.

The thriller, in front of a packed house, went right down to the wire and ended with the scores level on 244 but Yorkshire winning by virtue of losing fewer wickets – six to their opponents seven.

I had said in print that I thought Love was looking in the sort of nick that could see him playing a big part in the final and, for once, I backed the right horse because his innings was the rock which held firm while Northants did all in their power to cause a landslide. He ended up with an unbeaten 75 that brought him the gold award and some of the most magical moments of his career.

Love walked in to ecstatic applause and great rejoicing among Yorkshire's success-starved fans but it had by no means been a one-man show. Jarvis was the pick of the bowlers with an inspired 4-43 even though it was Peter Hartley who ended the best innings of the match by clean bowling David Capel for 97. And after Moxon and Metcalfe had got Yorkshire off to a predictably good start with a stand of 97, Sharp, Bairstow and Carrick all chipped in with valuable runs.

Carrick even sacrificed his wicket when he saw that otherwise Love would have been run out amidst the confusion over a second run and when the last over was called Love and Sidebottom needed to score five off Winston Davis. Singles came off the first two balls, Love played back the third and took one off the fourth. The fifth ball Sidebottom drove towards mid-on and Rob Bailey, dashing in missed the stumps with an underarm throw from a few feet away to leave the scores level. Realising that Yorkshire would win if they did not lose a wicket off the final delivery, Love dug one out of his blockhole and dashed for the sanctuary of the pavilion.

The next moment Carrick and Love were holding the Cup aloft on the Lord's balcony and the first of the many messages of congratulations which Yorkshire had showered upon them came from Prince Andrew, Duke of York, and a keen follower of the team's fortunes.

Sidebottom's unconfined joy was short-lived because seconds after reaching the dressing room he learned from his sister that their father, Jack, had been rushed to hospital from the ground at lunchtime with angina but it had been agreed to hold the news back from Arnie until after the match.

The pair went straight to hospital to visit him and he was comfortable enough for Sidebottom to return to Lord's and travel with Yorkshire on the team bus to Selby for their overnight stop before moving on to Scarborough for their Refuge Assurance League fixture with Middlesex.

Mike Gatting cadged a lift north on the coach which set off after Don Wilson had organised a private celebration at his home and it was a tired but happy crew which chugged into the car park of their Selby hotel in the early hours of Sunday morning.

The celebrations continued at North Marine Road a few hours later and the 10,000 crowd who turned up to cheer their heroes were not disappointed by what they saw. Love was given a standing ovation all the way to the crease and he joked later that it was so loud and so prolonged that he thought Boycott must be shadowing him to the wicket!

Yorkshire repaid the fans by entertaining on a grand scale, Metcalfe, middling practically everything, hitting 51 with seven fours and a six, and Bairstow clubbing 54 with four fours and three sixes. All five bowlers picked up wickets in the 33-run win.

And that really was that. After the Lord Mayor's Show, they slid away alarmingly and did not win another Sunday match, a sequence of five defeats and three no-results sending them spiralling to 13th in the table. They made a disappointing exit in the quarter-finals of the NatWest Trophy, losing by 36 runs to Leicestershire, and although they never dropped out of the top three of the Championship until September they were generally off the pace and finished eighth.

Nothing, however, could undo what had been done earlier, and all things considered, it was Yorkshire's most celebrated season until they ended their Championship famine in 2001.

Two young players in opposing teams that season gave Yorkshire a good deal of trouble without having the remotest idea that they would later become part of the White Rose fabric themselves.

At Canterbury, Kent's 19-year-old wicketkeeper Paul Farbrace struck an unbeaten 75 in only his second Championship match but it did not quite prevent Yorkshire from gaining a heart-stopping two-wicket win. Over 24 years later, Farbrace came to Headingley as second team coach, one of several new appointments which were made at the end of the 2011 season.

At Taunton in August, a gritty unbeaten 48 from Richard Harden on his 22nd birthday saw Somerset beat Yorkshire by five wickets with one ball remaining in the Refuge Assurance League and in the drawn Championship match which followed he made 58 not out and 35. He was rather surprisingly signed by Yorkshire in 1999 to shore up the batting and he stayed for two years without ever contributing in the way he consistently did for Somerset during his prime years.

The chance of first-class cricket returning to Park Avenue flickered to life with Bradford Central League side Fields gaining permission from the ground's owners, Bradford Council, to use it as their home base, and the pressure for Yorkshire to return there at some future stage was firmly applied by the increasingly influential Friends of Park Avenue group, whose chairman was wealthy Bradford businessman Bruce Moss and included among its numbers the likes of Close, Appleyard, Trueman and Stott.

Everyone seemed agreed when 1988 was ushered in that Yorkshire's committee were working together more positively than for many years and everyone seemed agreed, also, that the team were poised to add more silverware to the Benson and Hedges Cup which was currently in their possession.

Everyone may have been right on the first point but they were way off beam on the second and in the two seasons that Carrick was to remain in charge he never again experienced the delights that 1987 brought, although he was to have the satisfaction of changing the course of the club's history by bravely standing up and making the first official call for overseas players.

The record start of nine consecutive wins in all competitions the previous summer was quickly forgotten in 1988 as the team failed miserably to put it all together and now they set another record they could happily have done without by losing their first three matches in the Championship programme. Their next five matches produced two further defeats and three draws and it was not until June 29 that they won a game, beating Sussex by three wickets at Hove.

Four-day cricket was slipped into the Championship format for the first time, two games being played at the beginning of the season and four towards the end, but neither of Yorkshire's two opening fixtures needed a fourth day because they succumbed in three both to Derbyshire at Headingley and Warwickshire at Edgbaston.

Neither could Yorkshire do anything to suggest that they would keep a tight hold on the Benson and Hedges Cup but their failure to qualify for the knockout stages was partly due to the atrocious weather which virtually washed away their first two matches. They overcame Minor Counties easily enough but got hammered at New Road where Worcestershire captain Phil Neale launched a violent assault on Peter Hartley and Ian Botham forced Yorkshire into submission with his best B&H figures of 5-41.

The relief of winning their first Championship match at Worcestershire was offset by a serious back injury to their sharpest paceman, Jarvis, who was out for the remainder of the season, and Yorkshire were not helped by an uncertainty over selection that resulted in several players being dropped and then recalled at various stages.

One so affected was Bairstow who was first struck down by injury and then left out of the side – and all at a time when he was stuck on 999 wicketkeeping dismissals and just one away from becoming the only Yorkshire player to do the double of 10,000 runs and 1,000 victims behind the stumps.

Bairstow found himself on 999 when he caught Chris Scott at Abbeydale Park on August 5 shortly before Nottinghamshire followed on. He looked certain to reach the magical figure in the second innings until he had to drag himself off the field with a back injury, the pain of which was so intense that this toughest of men could not resume, even after intensive treatment from Yorkshire physiotherapist Wayne Morton.

Blakey, who had been dropped for a while himself, once again found himself entrusted with the gloves and he fitted into them so well that Yorkshire were reluctant for the eager Bairstow to return and he was told in a phone call from Close that he had been dropped from the Somerset match at Scarborough in order to give Blakey an extended run.

Desperate to get back, Bairstow accepted an invitation to play for a World XI against Yorkshire at the Scarborough Cricket Festival and not only finished up on the losing side but was distraught by the mode of his dismissal. Coming in at 98-6, he suddenly saw Carrick turn to the rarely-used spin of Love, who bowled his old team-mate before he had scored.

Bairstow was down but not out and a century for the Second XI helped him to win back his place for the final match of the season against Nottinghamshire at Trent Bridge – and what a cracking finale it turned out to be and how Bairstow distinguished himself.

His magic moment came when Paul Johnson, another doughty fighter, got an edge off Sidebottom and Bairstow held the catch, tossed the ball high into the air and was besieged by team-mates eager to congratulate him on his 1,000th victim.

Truly fired up by now, Bairstow scored a rugged unbeaten 94 which allowed Yorkshire to declare on 340-8 and enabled them to go on to chalk up their first win in a four-day match, aided by four further catches from the ecstatic wicketkeeper.

Hero that he was, Bairstow's performance could not match up to that of Nottinghamshire's all-rounder Franklyn Stephenson, the West Indian giant plundering a century in each innings as well as taking 11 wickets in the match, statistics previously enjoyed only by George Hirst for Yorkshire against Somerset at Bath in 1906, when his scores of 111 and 117 were identical to Stephenson's.

One consolation for Stephenson was that he became the only player in four years to complete the double and the last one ever to do so.

Both Sidebottom and Love also had cause to remember the epic match, Sidebottom's first innings haul of 7-89 being the second best of his career and Love's 38 in the second innings leaving him stranded over the winter months on a career tally of 9,999 first-class runs.

Away from the cricket, the Yorkshire committee earned bouquets rather than the more customary brickbats for the wonderful way that they and Pudsey St Lawrence Cricket Club jointly organised a dinner at Headingley to mark the 50th anniversary of Len Hutton's 364 for England at The Oval.

That great occasion was recalled time and again as a host of celebrities from the past came to raise their glasses to Sir Leonard on a memorable evening which followed the first day's play in the Headingley Test between England and the West Indies.

Sir Leonard was in his element swapping stories with Trueman, Denis Compton, Alec Bedser and Godfrey Evans, but even more honoured that his old adversaries Ray Lindwall and Neil Harvey should fly over from Australia especially for the event.

Illness was the only reason why Sir Donald Bradman did not make the trip from the other side of the world but he sent an emotional message which included the following:

The passage of time has taken from our midst many of Len's pals and mine from the two teams but happily Len is still with us dispensing appropriate words of wisdom.

I salute him as one of the great craftsmen of all time whose skill and style was the envy of us all.

Congratulations Len on the 50th anniversary of your never to be forgotten performance and I'm proud to remember I was the first to shake you by the hand.

The dinner helped to hide Yorkshire's embarrassment from earlier in the day when the Test match got underway 50 minutes late due to mopping up operations and then slid to a quick halt soon after the start of the England innings. Much to the consternation of umpires Dickie Bird and David Shepherd, water began to well up mysteriously from the bowler's run up at the football end and the players were forced to leave the field while the groundstaff came on to investigate.

It was discovered that water from heavy overnight rain had worked its way back up the drainage system as a result of the drains being blocked, with Yorkshire's approval, a few days earlier, in order to stop the pitch cracking and becoming dangerous.

Coming at a time when the Headingley Test pitch was suffering all sorts of problems it did nothing to improve the ground's reputation at Lord's. The result was also a disaster because England received a ten-wicket caning in Christopher Cowdrey's only match as captain to go down 3-0 in the series with only one to play – and they lost that, as well.

CHAPTER THIRTY-SIX

ANCIENT AND MODERN

The four seasons from 1989-92 inclusive saw Yorkshire in the grip of their bleakest period in the history of the Championship, never once rising higher than tenth place and wallowing much lower in the table on the other occasions.

Yet this was also a time of much significant change with Yorkshire beginning to realise that they could not go on living in the past and that they must modernise their image as they went into the final decade of the 20th century.

The greatest of these changes included the casting aside of tradition in 1992 by signing India's teenage batting wonder, Sachin Tendulkar, as the club's first overseas player, and the setting-up in 1989 of the Yorkshire Academy of Cricket at Bradford Park Avenue.

Sir Lawrence Byford, Yorkshire president from 1991-99, was the man who dared to end the club's longstanding policy of playing only those cricketers born within the county. And he did so without going to the membership for approval, knowing that if he did so a majority would not give their approval because they preferred to live in the past and would go on hoping that the golden days of yesteryear were just around the corner.

Surprisingly, there was very little vocal opposition or adverse reaction when the die was cast but that was not the case when the subject of overseas players was given its first official airing in 1989 by Carrick in the final year of his captaincy.

Besieged by injuries and increasingly handicapped through being unable to fight fire with fire by not having their own overseas player, Yorkshire suffered a mighty loss of confidence that season as they plunged to the penultimate spot in the Championship, dipped to 11th in the Refuge Assurance League, failed to qualify in the Benson and Hedges Cup and lost to Surrey by just one run in the second round of the NatWest Trophy.

I had known from private discussions on the subject with Carrick that he favoured the introduction of overseas players in order to fight on a level playing field and in late August he showed the courage of his convictions by writing a letter to each member of the general committee urging them to bring about the change.

When Yorkshire played Derbyshire at Chesterfield on August 24-26, I agreed to draft out the letter for Carrick, knowing the points he wished to make, and after vetting it and making some minor changes he went ahead and delivered it. His decision to act at that particular moment was probably influenced by events in the previous game when Yorkshire had been hammered by 181 runs by Lancashire at Old Trafford. The 21-year-old Michael Atherton had celebrated receiving his county cap by hitting an unbeaten 115 in the first innings but what had really stuck in Yorkshire's throat was a match return of 10-95 by Wasim Akram (5-44 and 5-51) and a second innings century from Gehan Mendis.

Most representatives of the Yorkshire committee had over the years strongly opposed opening up the boundaries, knowing that to support such revolutionary ideas would be to commit political suicide. It was no surprise, therefore, that Carrick's letter should be coolly received and although he was perceived to have been replaced as captain at the end of the season by Moxon because of poor results, there is no doubt that breaking the ice on the overseas players issue was a factor in him losing his job.

Well before being confronted with Carrick's letter the committee had already had a lengthy discussion on the overseas player issue because at the turn of the year Viv Richards had made it known upon leaving Somerset that he would like to play for Yorkshire.

The publicity gained from such a deal would have been truly tremendous but it was a step too far for Yorkshire to take at that time and when the approach was rejected on January 5, chairman Walsh said: "The general committee has considered the offer and thanks Mr Richards for his interest but has decided not to accept."

At the same time as the overseas aid debate raged, the argument over whether the proposed new Academy of Cricket should be sited at Bradford or Leeds also rocked the committee boat before it harboured at Park Avenue for a while. And Yorkshire's entry into the modern world was given a further hefty push by the introduction of two iconic players during these crucial years.

First came the debut early in the 1989 season of a certain Darren Gough, who went on to become Yorkshire's greatest showman of the modern era, and further down the line came the signing at the Academy of Salford-born Michael Vaughan who would earn the tag of England's most successful captain.

Not only did this dynamic pair raise Yorkshire's image at a time when marketing demanded high-profile faces but they were also among the best at their respective trades that England have ever produced. Indeed, the overall records of Gough and Vaughan for Yorkshire were relatively modest compared to some of the county's other great names but for England they were players par excellence.

Throughout the winter leading up to the 1989 season, the pressure was on Yorkshire – from within and elsewhere – to agree to build their Academy at Park Avenue, the main purpose of the Academy being to nurture home-grown talent regardless of overseas player issues.

The front man of this campaign was Appleyard, who pressed his case both as a member of the cricket committee and as a leading light among the Friends of Park Avenue, both bodies also having Close among their numbers.

The "sweetener" that was placed in front of Yorkshire by the Friends was the promise of substantial financial help if the club agreed to take over the running of Park Avenue free of charge with a commitment to build the Academy there and also to consider a return to first-class cricket on the ground at some stage.

Furthermore, Yorkshire were known to be keen to map out some of their future away from Headingley where relations continued to be strained with the venue's owners, Leeds Cricket, Football and Athletic Company, despite the Company's announcement that they were to give the complex a £2.7m facelift which was intended to turn the stadium into one of the most prestigious sporting arenas in the country for cricket and football.

The decision to site the Academy at Park Avenue was still not a simple one to take because another group on the committee, led by Vann and Boycott, preferred it to be build at Headingley, their reasoning being that it would run alongside the indoor cricket school and that the general ground facilities would be much more comfortable than at Bradford where decay continued and vandalism could not be easily stopped.

The trump card for the Bradford faction was that all of the ex-players, Boycott apart, strongly supported its case, and Yorkshire's officials could hardly ignore the repeatedly stated claim that no ground in the country had a better cricketing surface than Park Avenue.

Negotiations continued throughout the autumn of 1989 and into the New Year and the situation became extremely tense again in March when Vann asked Yorkshire to have a re-think and give serious consideration to offers of financial assistance from Leeds City Council and Leeds CFAC if the Academy were to come to Headingley.

Out of step with his other cricket committee colleagues, Vann did the honourable thing and resigned from that group, his departure indicating that much of the power of the pro-Boycott faction was beginning to wane now that their man was no longer a player and president Mountgarret and chairman Walsh were starting to tighten their control at the top.

Speculation that Headingley was gaining the upper hand was ended on March 23, 1989, when Yorkshire finally agreed on Park Avenue and the Friends were able to work their fingers to the bone in order to get the ground as shipshape as possible for the Academy's opening on May 15.

The official opening took place on June 7, the eve of the First Ashes Test at Headingley, and part of the celebrations included England chairman Ted Dexter naming a 125 class locomotive "Yorkshire Academy of Cricket" at a ceremony at Leeds City station.

Scores of guests invited to the launch, sponsored by British Rail InterCity, were transported to Leeds from all parts of the country and after the naming ceremony they were given lunch and taken on a tour of West Yorkshire by a special train, before ending up in Bradford and being escorted to Park Avenue for the grand opening.

A week before the Academy was started, Yorkshire chose the 11 young cricketers, aged between 17 and 19, who would attend – and seven of them came from the Bradford League. They were:

Colin Bartle (Saltaire CC)
Jeremy Batty (Bradford and Bingley)
Richard Benson (Castleford)
Stephen Bethel (Barnsley)
Colin Chapman (Pudsey Congs)
Matthew Doidge (Bowling Old Lane)
James Goldthorp (Pudsey St Lawrence)
Darren Gough (Barnsley)
Paul Grayson (Yorkshire Bank)
Stuart Milburn (Killinghall)
Bradley Parker (East Bierley).

Of this group, seven went on to play first-class cricket for Yorkshire, but even though Gough was marked down as one of the original intake it would be stretching it a bit to say he was one of their graduates. Just before the Academy opened its doors, Gough made his Yorkshire first team debut and then went down with a serious back injury but his reputation was already such that when he returned to action in August he was straight into the second team. His progress continued at such a pace that he was never at the Academy for any length of time.

The Academy launch was deemed a great success but the run-up to the 1989 season had not been without the odd hiccup or two, including the embarrassment of having to call off the February 13 annual meeting at the very last minute and re-schedule it for March 18 because notices of the original date were sent out from Headingley to Yorkshire's 10,000 members by second class post and arrived too late to meet the deadline.

Secretary Lister apologised for the gaff but he was not entirely to blame because all of the literature which accompanied the notices was not ready for distribution until a late hour.

In the first of Carrick's three seasons in charge, Yorkshire had got off to a dream start in all competitions but, two years on, the preparations for 1989 turned into a nightmare for him as the injury list grew and grew. Peter Hartley was unfit with a back injury sustained while playing for Orange Free State in February; Shaw was to be out for the whole season with a serious neck problem; Fletcher was missing with a swollen elbow, and new vice-captain Moxon in early April broke a bone in his left forearm while training with weights.

Jarvis was fit again after lengthy back trouble but Yorkshire knew that they would have to travel to Lord's for the opening match against Middlesex with Sidebottom the only paceman to have played in the Championship since the previous June.

The crisis was so acute that Oldham, now assistant coach, was asked if he would consider joining the squad, but the 40-year-old said he would prefer younger players to be given their chance at first-class level.

And so it came about that the unknown 18-year-old, Darren Gough, who was attached to Yorkshire on the Government's Youth Training Scheme, was called up to make his debut at cricket's headquarters on the strength of 44 overs and four wickets for the Second XI the previous season.

Unknown he may have been and raw he certainly was, but from the moment he stepped on to the hallowed turf it was apparent that this slightly overweight youngster had a sprinkling of stardust upon him.

There was also an element of sadness about the occasion because Middlesex were without their popular opening batsman Wilf Slack, who had died over the winter months. Slack had been an old friend and formidable opponent of Yorkshire's, two years earlier making 84 and 28 in the corresponding fixture and in the following year hitting 144 at Lord's and 75 and 83 at Headingley.

Rain ruled out any chance of a positive result and only 24.4 overs were possible on the first day when Middlesex struggled to 36-2 but by then Gough had already acquired his first scalp. Replacing Sidebottom, the Barnsley lad almost had Paul Downton lbw first ball and it took him only a further seven deliveries to get his man, who edged to first slip where Sidebottom held on to a splendid low catch.

Keith Brown and Norman Cowans, both pouched by Bairstow, were Gough's other first innings victims in a commendable return of 3-44 while Jarvis strengthened his Test claims with 5-77.

The greatest prize was still to come for Gough, however, because after breaking the Middlesex opening stand in the second innings by dismissing John Carr he then bounced no less a personage than former England captain Mike Gatting, who mistimed his stroke and was caught by Blakey.

Gough aggravated a bad back with all the effort he put into this first appearance and he did not re-appear until the penultimate match of the season. It would be quite some time yet before he achieved star status but at least everyone knew he had arrived, even though few could have predicted that he would go on to capture 229 wickets for England, collecting nine hauls of five wickets or more on the way as well as a hat-trick against Australia.

So acute remained Yorkshire's bowling woes that Oldham was pressed into service in one-day matches and Bradford League fast bowler Ian Priestley came in for his debut in the first home Championship match against Nottinghamshire, turning in a maiden performance which was the equal of Gough's. He began by fastening on to a stunning slip catch offered by skipper Tim Robinson and then came on to dismiss Chris Broad before adding a further three wickets as Nottinghamshire were skittled for 86 in reply to Yorkshire's 92, seven of their batsmen perishing to Franklyn Stephenson at a cost of 38 runs.

The West Indian tormented Yorkshire a second time with 6-32 and Nottinghamshire cruised home by ten wickets, Stephenson's match figures of 13-75 being the best for the county since Bruce Dooland's 15-193 against Kent at Gravesend in 1956 and the best recorded by Notts against Yorkshire since Fred Morley's 14-94 at Trent Bridge in 1878.

This early heavy reversal for Yorkshire was a sign of things to come and the catalogue of injuries to bowlers coupled with the dismal form of the batsmen soon began to take a toll of the team's confidence and pile up the pressure on Carrick.

One good piece of news was the spirited bowling of Jarvis who overcame the disappointment of being included in the England squad for the Texaco Trophy one-day series against Australia without ever getting selected by making the starting line for two of the six Ashes Tests.

Moxon, too, did little wrong once back from his pre-season training injury and he chalked up 659 runs in his first eight Championship matches, the most consistent form of his career leading to his England recall for the Fifth Test. Like his country that summer, Moxon experienced little joy, out fourth ball in the first innings in sharp contrast to the start made earlier for Australia by Geoff Marsh and Mark Taylor who put on 329 together.

The Yorkshire slide continued and Jarvis was in the headlines again in early August when it was learned he was one of a party of 16 top England players who had agreed to make up a rebel tour of South Africa. Yorkshire failed in their attempt to make Jarvis change his mind and he had to face anti-apartheid demonstrations during matches at Sheffield and Scarborough.

Love, Swallow and Booth were not offered new contracts at the beginning of

September – and Bairstow would have gone also if cricket chairman Close had not pleaded for him to be retained – but the story took second billing to the sensation caused by Carrick's letter to committee members pleading for Yorkshire to end its unwritten rule of picking only Yorkshire-born players.

In his letter, Carrick included the passages:

The plain truth is that, even with a full squad of players, we just about compete with other more progressive counties, as 1987 proved. Any injury at all to key players proves that with our 'Yorkshire Born' policy we do not compete on level terms and always have our backs to the wall.

The other 16 counties either import overseas players or sign English cricketers who will complement their existing staff.

Whether we like it or not, sponsorship is the lifeblood of cricket these days and we will not add to our list of sponsors, or retain existing ones, unless we are seen to be successful and progressing. Repeated failure cannot be the right image for companies who put their marketing and advertising budget into our club. They obviously want to be associated with success.

There is nothing that I and the other Yorkshire players would like more than Yorkshire to win competitions with a team composed solely of Yorkshiremen. But, realistically, this is not going to happen and I believe the time has come for the committee to take stock of the situation and relax its Yorkshire-born only policy.

May I suggest that you should decide in future that we play a minimum of eight Yorkshire-born players and allow three outside signings to complement our existing players. There are players of the highest quality around who would strengthen our team and could bring some refreshing ideas into Yorkshire cricket.

The publishing of Carrick's letter brought an instant response from former cricketers, members and fans, some strongly in favour of admitting overseas players and others vehemently against.

Trueman, an honorary life member, said he would rip up his membership ticket if there was a change in policy and his Test Match Special colleague Don Mosey, a diehard Yorkshireman himself, said he was shocked beyond his wildest belief that a Yorkshire captain could make such a stand.

But Boycott came out in support of Carrick by saying he did not think Yorkshire would win anything without an overseas player and there was plenty of support, also, from the local cricket journalists who had so often witnessed at first hand the failure of Yorkshire to compete on equal terms.

It was against this controversial background that Yorkshire's miserable season drew to a miserable close, Lancashire overpowering them by 184 runs at Scarborough, despite a fine century from Phil Robinson and a successful debut for off-spinner Jeremy Batty, who claimed 5-118 in the second innings to give him eight wickets in the match.

Batty's maiden appearance contained more happy memories than had been experienced by Simon Kellett when he made his debut against Hampshire at Southampton in June. Kellett, regarded as one of the finest batsmen ever produced by the Bradford League, began his first-class-career with a duck, but it came as some comfort to know that county colleague Byas had made an exactly similar start while Len Hutton had registered ducks on his first and second team debuts for Yorkshire and also for England.

The season was not long finished before Yorkshire overwhelmingly rejected bringing in an overseas player at a stormy meeting at which Boycott walked out after being at loggerheads with Close and the cricket committee over how the team should be run and the reasons for its poor showing.

One person who sought out the view of the players themselves was the club's Patroness, the Duchess of Kent, who delayed her departure from the triennial dinner in Sheffield by wandering over to their table to listen to their problems.

"It was marvellous of the Duchess to demonstrate her concern for the team in this way," said one player. "She said she really cared about the side and takes a close interest in our matches."

Yorkshire's internal bickering over the right way forward continued until a decision was reached to appoint assistant coach Oldham as cricket manager for a trial two-year period. One of Oldham's first recommendations was that Moxon should replace Carrick as captain and this was approved unanimously by the committee a fortnight before Christmas.

Carrick described it as his "blackest day" upon receiving the news but he still had sufficient bottle to attend a special benefit lunch for Love in York when he marched up to the top table and in an impromptu speech proposed a champagne toast to Moxon and the future of Yorkshire cricket.

The ending of Carrick's three years in charge took few by surprise, unlike the sudden ousting of Mountgarret as president in January, 1990, when many held the view that he had been shabbily treated. At a general committee meeting chaired by Close in the absence of Walsh, it was generally expected that Mountgarret would be nominated for a new term, but there was a view among some of those present that he should become a figurehead president stripped of any decision-taking powers.

Mountgarret, not unreasonably, rejected such requests and he was made to stand outside for 45 minutes before being called in and told that he would not be nominated. Furious, he walked out of the meeting and made for home, but later agreed to stay in office until the annual meeting in February.

Yorkshire were in danger of facing another long period without a president but they were saved from that embarrassment when Sir Leonard Hutton agreed to be nominated. His acceptance was warmly received, for Hutton was every Yorkshireman's hero, and it came as something of a shock at the annual meeting in Sheffield when 201 members voted against the nomination and only 140 in favour.

Hutton was in no real danger because the proxy vote, already counted but not yet disclosed, would show 1,402 in favour and only 132 against. The reason for the large 'no' vote in the hall was because many members were upset at the way Mountgarret had been treated and asked to stand down. They demanded and got a full discussion on the issue and Mountgarret left the room ahead of the debate to rapturous applause, Walsh taking over the chair and explaining that a majority on the committee felt the club should have a president with a more "hands off role" than in the last few years. But he accepted that the president's role should have been an item on the agenda.

Had anyone other than Hutton been nominated to take over from Mountgarret the result might have been very different but the popularity of his Lordship was never in any doubt and he was deeply moved by the affection in which he was held.

Once Mountgarret had made his exit from office, Yorkshire were united in their conviction that no other person was as suited to the presidency as Sir Leonard. It was to be a sweet but tragically short reign because he was to die before the season had been completed.

If the committee were surprised at the strength of feeling at the annual meeting over the Mountgarret issue, so was Leeds Labour MP Derek Fatchett when he stood up and condemned Jarvis's visit to South Africa on a rebel tour which had just ended early and in chaos. He wanted to know what action Yorkshire would take against Jarvis if he went on another rebel tour but he was howled down, members siding strongly with Mountgarret when he told Fatchett that the meeting was not a political forum.

Members were united with the club on one other hot subject, the committee receiving massive support for their firm stance in favour of retaining three-day Championship cricket. A referendum showed 2,283 in favour of its retention and only 286 against. Asked if they supported the Test and County Cricket Board's desire to have a 16-match four-day programme they voted 326 in favour and 2,103 against.

With the annual meeting out of the way, thoughts turned increasingly to the 1990 season and two appointments were made, Metcalfe being named as vice-captain and former Yorkshire player Mike Bore moving back from his job as youth cricket development officer at Trent Bridge to take charge of the Academy

Even more significant in the changing face of Yorkshire cricket was the arrival from Australia in time for the new season of 20-year-old Craig White, who was Morley-born but had moved 'down under' with his family as a seven-year-old.

White, a member of the ground-breaking Australian Academy in Adelaide, had already played for Australia at Under 17s and Under 19s level and was in New Zealand with the Academy when a deal was struck for him to widen his experience by coming to Yorkshire in the English summer.

Appleyard was the prime mover and his interest was sparked after White had been mentioned to him in a conversation with Australian Academy official, Jack Potter.

Keen to see if this Yorkshire-born 'Aussie' was good enough to represent his native county, Appleyard persuaded the club's main sponsors, Tetley's, to pay his air fare while Yorkshire Bank agreed to stump up £5,000 to cover the cost of an intended season at the Academy at Park Avenue.

Like Gough, however, White was to have little to do with the Academy because it was soon discovered that he could be of immediate value to the first team. Arriving in England on April 17, he was greeted by his grandmother and other close relatives from Pudsey before meeting up at Headingley with Oldham, who threw him in at the deep end by including him in the opening fixture, a Refuge

Assurance League clash with Nottinghamshire at Trent Bridge.

Despite having less than a week in which to adapt to English conditions, White looked the part from the start, scoring a brisk unbeaten 26 in Yorkshire's 161-7 and putting on an unbroken 54 with Jarvis to stage a recovery from 107-7. That was still not a sufficient total to worry Derek Randall, who scored an unbeaten half-century as Notts won by five wickets, White not being asked to bowl the off-breaks he had cultivated in Australia.

White had done enough to be given a run of matches in all competitions and he was proud to become the first Yorkshire player since Fred Trueman to earn a Championship place before even appearing for the Second XI. He was not an instant success at first-class level but his various talents were such that once he ditched off-spin for fast bowling he became one of Yorkshire's leading all-rounders and he also proved Raymond Illingworth right in his claim that White was an England player in the making.

In his first season at Yorkshire, White was still seen as progressing towards a Test place with Australia and his summer of county cricket was cut short in July when he was chosen for Young Australia's tour of the West Indies. It was later on that he declared his allegiance to England.

There could sometimes be an inconsistency in White's batting and bowling and his career was also affected by too many injuries, but on his day there was no Yorkshire batsman with greater style and no bowler with the same deceptive pace and bounce off the pitch.

Constant back problems ended his first team days in 2007, by which time he had scored 10,376 first-class runs for Yorkshire with 19 centuries and taken 276 wickets as well as having become the county's best one-day all-rounder with 6,376 runs and 246 wickets. He went on to captain the Second XI for a while and was deputy director of cricket for a couple of years before deciding in late 2011 not to apply for one of the new coaching posts, preferring instead to join Hampshire as bowling coach and at the same time work towards becoming a first-class umpire.

Much was expected in 1990 of the new combination of Oldham as cricket manager and Moxon as captain but genuine success once again eluded Yorkshire and it continued to do so throughout Moxon's six years of leadership, a particularly upsetting fact in view of his popularity and his own unquestionable desire to make his team the best in the country.

Moxon never had to struggle to become recognised as one of Yorkshire's greatest batsmen but luck was rarely on his side in other areas and he soon had reason to believe the fates were against him. A severely bruised toe in the Refuge opener at Trent Bridge caused him to miss the first Championship game against Northamptonshire at Headingley and when he returned for the next match at Edgbaston he spent part of his 30th birthday in the casualty department of a Birmingham hospital waiting for stitches to be inserted into the split webbing of his right hand, the price he paid for dropping a catch at second slip.

In some respects, Moxon would not have been too sorry to drop out of the Northants encounter because Yorkshire lost by an innings and 50 runs after Allan Lamb and Alan Fordham had plundered double centuries and featured in a 393 stand for the third wicket, the second highest partnership for any wicket against

Yorkshire. To make matters worse, it was the third consecutive match between the sides that Northants had produced a double century stand.

The emphatic defeat was the first of four Championship reverses for Yorkshire from the start of the season and it brought about the worst sequence of results in the club's history – 11 defeats from their last 13 matches with the other two being drawn.

Late consolation came in the form of handsome victories in the last two matches of the season, these September successes being largely due to the phenomenal form of Metcalfe who hit 150 not out and 32 against Derbyshire at Scarborough and followed up with an unbeaten 194 and 107 off Nottinghamshire's attack at Trent Bridge, where even an unbeaten 220 from home skipper Tim Robinson could not save his side.

This late burst of 483 runs in four innings left Metcalfe top of the Championship averages with 1,854 runs at a little in excess of 50 and in all first-class matches for Yorkshire he boasted 2,047, with six centuries and seven half-centuries, making him the first batsman since Boycott in 1971 to top the 2,000 mark.

Moxon and Phil Robinson made it well into four figures and Blakey found himself only seven runs short but Yorkshire could still only rise from 16th in the table to tenth which represented another failure. Their bowling was often too weak without Sidebottom, who was restricted to two Championship matches because of a knee injury, and for the first time in the competition no bowler made it to 50 wickets. The best was Peter Hartley, now fully recovered from the back injury which had threatened to shorten his career, and he headed the list with 48 wickets.

Sixth in the Refuge Assurance League represented an improvement of sorts but once again there was a failure to qualify in the Benson and Hedges Cup and one of the more remarkable statistics of the season occurred in the NatWest Trophy where Yorkshire became the first team ever to reach the quarter-finals without losing a wicket.

The reason for this was the unconquerable spirit of Moxon and Metcalfe who could not be shifted in either of the first two matches, knocking off the 105 required to beat Norfolk at Headingley and then, on the same ground, making a century apiece to overtake holders Warwickshire's much more competitive 241-9. Their 242 was a record opening stand in the competition.

They were unable to continue their dominance at Southampton, where there was a packed house for the televised quarter-final match, Hampshire cantering home by 111 runs. Chasing a gettable 230, Moxon was run out in the first over, Malcolm Marshall sent back Metcalfe and Kellett in the space of three hostile balls and at 9-3 Yorkshire had much too steep a hill to climb, despite a plucky 52 from Peter Hartley who had earlier grabbed 5-46 and went on to snatch the man-of-the-match award.

By this time, a familiar face had all but departed the Yorkshire scene and it should come as no surprise to learn that David Bairstow, in his testimonial season, did not go quietly. He reacted with fury to his axing from the side to meet Warwickshire at Sheffield in June, the reason given by Oldham being that his wicketkeeping had fallen below its usual high standard – a charge which Bairstow not unexpectedly denied.

Approaching 39, Bairstow was not the dynamic force of old and, with runs also drying up, it was difficult to keep him in a side which contained such a capable deputy as Blakey with another up-and-coming wicketkeeper/batsman in Colin Chapman waiting in the wings.

Ironically, Yorkshire would have won by one run the last Championship match in which Bairstow played had his shy at the stumps found its target. Needing two to win off the final ball from Jarvis at Harrogate, Surrey's last pair frantically scurried for a bye and Bairstow's desperate throw was just inches away from running out Waqar Younis. The previous ball had seen Bairstow run out Martin Bicknell in identical circumstances.

Bairstow was carpeted for his outspoken comments upon being dropped but this great Yorkshire warrior was brought back for a special farewell appearance in the Festival Trophy game against Essex at Scarborough on September 1. He stumped John Stephenson and top-scored with 36 but Yorkshire still went down by 36 runs.

The most poignant moment of an incident-packed season came at Eastbourne on August 8 when the Yorkshire and Sussex teams lined up for a minute's silence in memory of local MP Ian Gow who had been assassinated by the IRA and whose funeral was to take place later that day.

Yorkshire were most appropriately led out by their new president, Sir Leonard Hutton, who was attending the match each day with his old friend and neighbour from Pudsey, Keith Moss, himself destined to play a big part in Yorkshire's affairs.

Sir Leonard thoroughly enjoyed his three days at the cricket, chatting to the players and gently giving advice whenever it was sought, and his welcome presence made the shock all the greater when he died almost exactly a month later following a heart attack.

His time as president had been all too short but his county club did him proud in organising a moving memorial service at York Minster which was attended by 1,000 people from all backgrounds.

Assisting in conducting the service was the Bishop of Liverpool, the Right Reverend David Sheppard, who played for England when Hutton captained the side in the early 1950s.

Sir Leonard's widow, Dorothy, was present along with their sons, Richard and John, who both took part in the service, John reciting a passage from Ecclesiasticus and Richard reading a passage from his father's biography by Gerald Howat.

A host of cricketers, past and present, paid their respects, including England contemporaries such as Brian Close, Bob Appleyard, Fred Trueman, Trevor Bailey, Denis Compton, Godfrey Evans, Tom Graveney, Brian Statham and Cyril Washbrook. Apologies were received from Alec Bedser, Colin Cowdrey, John Murray, Frank Tyson and Peter Richardson.

Another link with Yorkshire's great and nostalgic past had ended and soon it would be Sir Lawrence Byford's presidency which guided the White Rose club into a new and much different future.

CHAPTER THIRTY-SEVEN

NO LOOKING BACK

Yorkshire's on-going inability to add significant silverware to their trophy cupboard increased the pressure to sign an overseas player, even though a second members' referendum had again flatly rejected such a move.

Yet everyone felt that change was in the air and the fans were also aware that shortly after Carrick's letter to the committee, a similar missive had been sent to chairman Walsh and signed by all but three of the capped players.

A shift towards opening up the boundaries occurred in November, 1990, when the committee voted 18-1 in favour of relaxing the home-grown policy and making eligible those who, though not born in Yorkshire, had grown up there.

A resolution to sign an overseas player fell 15-5 and resulted in Yorkshire no longer discussing Australia Test batsman Dean Jones's offer to join the Headingley playing staff, but the club did at least admit they had earlier made a tentative approach to Jones in case the policy was about to change suddenly.

The committee would still not tolerate open debate on the issue and Paul Jarvis's outspoken remarks that he would consider leaving Yorkshire if they did not go ahead and sign an overseas player led to a reprimand. Jarvis asked for his release, which was rejected, but injury was to ruin his season in 1991.

Yorkshire were reluctant to give precise details of their conversations with Jarvis and they then started to try to shift the blame by claiming the Press was responsible for all the adverse publicity and that the Jarvis problem would not have surfaced if the committee and players had stopped discussing such sensitive issues with the media.

I responded in print by saying: "Yorkshire's latest attempt to blame the Press for their own shortcomings is pathetic and hopefully will be treated with contempt by the members...

"It is because of Yorkshire's reluctance to bring things into the open that the Jarvis affair has caused such a furore.

"The club are angry that he spelled out so clearly his support for an overseas cricketer – a view held by almost every other player on the Yorkshire staff."

So strong was the wish to control Press leaks that a resolution was placed before the annual meeting aimed at suspending members who spoke out of turn to the media and this was squeezed through, despite strong opposition from the hall and further dissenting voices in the form of committee members Boycott, Appleyard, Vann and Tony Cawdry, the likeable Halifax district representative who it was impossible to gag.

At the same meeting that the committee eased the qualification policy, they also agreed unanimously to nominate Sir Lawrence Byford as club president and, as he would also take on the role of general committee chairman, he quickly became a powerful figure.

Having joined the West Riding Police Force in 1947 and going on to become

Chief Constable of Lincoln, he worked his way even higher to become Her Majesty's Chief Inspector of Constabulary in 1983. By the time of his retirement in 1987 he was the principal professional adviser on police matters to the Home Secretary and other Ministers. With such a background, it was hardly surprising that Sir Lawrence should lead from the front and get things done with a speed which Yorkshire had rarely experienced before.

It was also very much in his favour that he was passionate about cricket, particularly Yorkshire cricket, and that for many years before his presidency he had been among the club's keenest followers, particularly at Scarborough where he and Lady Muriel were members of a longstanding and friendly group of supporters who adopted a section of the seating on the balcony above the players' dressing rooms.

Big changes were to take place after Sir Lawrence's election as president at February's annual meeting but before the old year was out, the willingness of Yorkshire to widen their search was evident in December, 1990, when they signed Hull-born fast bowler Mark Robinson from Northamptonshire, beating several other counties for his signature.

Robinson served Yorkshire honestly for five seasons, occasionally turning in an outstanding analysis and always bringing a consistency and steadiness to the pace bowling which had often been lacking, but it was only upon moving to Sussex that his career really took off and he became one of the most successful cricket coaches in the country.

Just as Sir Leonard Hutton's death in September was to lead to a hands-on type of presidency – despite Mountgarret having been forced out earlier for being exactly that – another death that rocked the club just four months later also led to a different more modern style of government.

Joe Lister, Yorkshire's conscientious secretary for the past 20 years, had gone into Harrogate District Hospital and it was widely assumed that he was recovering from his operation but he died suddenly while still in hospital.

Lister, who had been much admired in 1975 for working on during a busy period despite losing one of his sons, Richard, in a tractor accident, had skilfully and without fuss guided Yorkshire calmly through extremely testing periods over the past decade and more.

David Ryder, his popular and efficient assistant, took over from Lister as secretary, but it was a post which would never hold the same authority with the decision soon afterwards to appoint a chief executive.

In the days leading up to Lister's death, there was speculation that Walsh was thinking of quitting the committee because of mounting pressures on his family and professional life, but these were ended when he confirmed that he would be standing for re-election because he had unfinished business in wanting to negotiate a new sponsorship deal with Tetley's and to continue the talks with Leeds CFAC over ground development.

As Sir Lawrence's election as president drew ever closer, however, there was increasing support from within for him to take over as chairman also. Walsh, duly returned to the committee, said he would stand down from the hot seat if there were any other nominations for the committee to consider at their meeting a couple of days after the annual meeting, at which Sir Lawrence received a massive vote of confidence. His popularity was such that a resolution to restrict the president's term of office to three years was heavily defeated.

Mindful of public opinion, Sir Lawrence was voted in as chairman with hardly a dissenting voice among his colleagues. At that first committee meeting, a future hands-on chairman was also welcomed to the fold, Keith Moss, a lifelong friend of Sir Leonard's, winning a seat in Bradford district where Raymond Clegg had retired after 21 years of continuous service. Moss, who would become a long-serving president of the Bradford League as well as Pudsey St Lawrence, was immediately given the important job of deciding, with Byford and treasurer Peter Townend, on the most suitable type of appointment to replace Lister.

Not only the committee were making important decisions at this time. Rank and file members had their say as never before at the annual meeting when they changed the course of the club's history by pressing to reduce the size of the committee from 23 to 12 by 1993, a resolution to that effect being put forward by Tony Chalk and Brenda Smith, an avid follower of Yorkshire along with her husband, John.

Finances became an even greater worry for all counties in the early part of the 90s and Yorkshire were relieved in March, 1991, that the prospect of watching Viv Richards at Headingley in the first Test between England and the West Indies in the coming June had already resulted in advance ticket sales of £100,000.

But treasurer Townend was still worried that ticket sales remained lower than at some of the other Test venues and it was an open secret that the TCCB would like to play two Tests at Lord's at the expense of one from the provinces.

Townend warned that if Test cricket were taken away from Headingley, the ground's owners would lose a substantial amount of their advertising income and it was because of this fear that Leeds CF&AC had embarked on a ten-year plan to improve facilities at Headingley and bring them up to the required standard. Improvements costing £1.2m had already been completed to the main stand, including new changing rooms for RL matches. These would soon be used by Yorkshire's players also but it was never a completely satisfactory arrangement because the facilities were out of sight of the cricket and, therefore, very inconvenient.

Yorkshire wasted no time in advertising for a chief executive at a salary of about £30,000 with appropriate benefits and Sir Lawrence stressed that the successful applicant would have more powers than the secretary ever had and would have day-to-day control of the running of the club.

Within days of the post being advertised it was revealed that England's Rugby Union supremo Geoff Cooke who lived in Shipley and had just masterminded his country's Grand Slam triumph, had applied for the job as well as putting in an application for a similar new post at Lancashire.

But the leaking of this information was a severe embarrassment to Cooke who immediately withdrew his two cricket applications and underlined that he was looking forward to leading England on tour to Australia in July and in the World Cup in October and November.

Whether Cooke would have joined Yorkshire we shall never know but the new season was barely underway when it was announced that Yorkshire had persuaded Lancashire's dynamic secretary Chris Hassell to cross the Pennines and take charge at Headingley.

Born in Surrey, Hassell had spent the past 13 years at Old Trafford, turning Lancashire into one of the most profitable clubs in county cricket, and his link-up with Sir Lawrence at Headingley formed an exciting new partnership which was keen to move Yorkshire into the future rather than letting them languish in the past.

Hassell came to Yorkshire with a wealth of experience in both cricket and football administration. A former Football League referee, he had worked as assistant secretary with Arsenal and then as secretary with Crystal Palace, Everton and Preston North End.

Unlike Nash and Lister, who both showed a natural reluctance to expose Yorkshire to the glare of publicity regarding internal matters, Hassell was outwardly enthusiastic about his role and determined to take measures to improve finances, which had shown a loss of £80,000 the previous year compared to Lancashire's profit of £107,000 in 1990 and £306,000 in 1989.

By the time that Hassell had placed his feet under the table at Headingley, Yorkshire had already got off to a poor start after their promising preparations had included a two-day draw against Durham at Scarborough in some of the bleakest and coldest conditions in which I have ever watched cricket.

Durham had by now received the news that they would join the first-class scene in 1992 and they had looked forward immensely to this 'friendly' battle with Yorkshire but perhaps the most important thing they learned was how essential it is to maintain concentration in the grimmest of early season weather. All of Yorkshire's batsmen managed to thaw out sufficiently to make some runs, apart from Colin Chapman, and Byas struck an unbeaten 65 on his home ground, his farming background helping him to come to terms with the cruel conditions better than most of the others. This was the season in which Byas ended any lingering doubts about his ability to become a front line batsman and promotion in the order brought sufficient runs for him to be awarded his first team cap.

To kick off with four consecutive Refuge Assurance League defeats and then reach July without a Championship win was clear evidence for the new brooms that they were not going to sweep Yorkshire to success overnight and Sir Lawrence wasted no time in saying that a star overseas player would have to be signed within two years if results did not improve.

In the end, Yorkshire could manage no better than 14th in the Championship – a slump of four places – and even though they improved in the Sunday League they were way off the pace in seventh spot.

During the disappointing start, the club showed that bad or unsporting behaviour would not be tolerated by fining Jarvis £300 and severely reprimanding him for a bat-throwing incident when he was run out in the final over of the RAL match with Warwickshire at Headingley which the visitors won by two runs. Jarvis responded by apologising to the umpires and all concerned and promised that there would be no repeat.

The defeat was Yorkshire's third in a row in the competition and a fourth followed against Leicestershire at Grace Road, despite Sunday-best scores for two emerging top-drawer players in Byas and Gough, the unlikely combination adding 129 in 18 overs for the seventh wicket. Byas smacked 74 off 92 balls with five fours and a six while the 20-year-old Gough played his part with 72 from 73 deliveries with six fours and two sixes.

The RAL rot was stopped in the next match against Northamptonshire at Headingley and it was the start of a record run of six consecutive victories which concluded with a splendid win over Middlesex at Lord's when Metcalfe slammed 116 and added 167 for the first wicket with Moxon.

Good though Metcalfe's innings was, it could not compare with that of Moxon's unbeaten 129 at The Oval a fortnight later, an innings of poetry in motion which saw Yorkshire to their 228 target with eight wickets in hand and 23 balls to spare.

Despite this welcome revival, Yorkshire in 1991 were at their best in the Benson and Hedges Cup and after losing their first match to Nottinghamshire at Trent Bridge they won their next three to top their group as they made it through to the quarter-finals.

In the last of the zonal games, Moxon blitzed 141 not out at Sophia Gardens and put on 213 for the first wicket with Metcalfe (84), a county record for any wicket in the competition. So dominant were the openers that Glamorgan were crushed by eight wickets in spite of skipper Alan Butcher's brilliant 127 for the Welshmen.

Moxon took the gold award as he was to do in the quarter-final encounter with Warwickshire at Headingley but on the later occasion he was the star bowler with a career-best 5-31. He entered the attack as the sixth bowler and only then because Sidebottom had left the field with a groin injury and Jarvis was struggling with hamstring trouble and may not have been able to complete his spell.

The semi-final saw Yorkshire in a Roses battle at Old Trafford and there was a near-capacity 20,000 shoe-horned in for the match but, as so often in one-day tussles with their old enemy, Yorkshire were to come off second best, even though Metcalfe walked away with the gold award for his 114 out of 200 in reply to Lancashire's 268.

There was some ill-feeling in the match and the flashpoint came when a ball from DeFreitas clearly – in my view through binoculars – deflected off Moxon's shoulder to Paul Allott at first slip.

Moxon was given not out by umpire Kevin Lyons, whereupon several Lancashire players seemed unwilling to accept the verdict and Allott walked over to Moxon to ask where the ball had hit him. Moxon replied "just below the shoulder" and asked Allott if he wanted to see the mark left by the ball.

"Lancashire were fired up and they can be very aggressive on the field. If that is how they want to play their cricket that's fine, but it's not what I want from my team," said Moxon.

As Yorkshire's season moved into midsummer, two momentous landmarks were reached although neither would have any impact on current happenings on the field.

First, on June 24, Yorkshire finally threw tradition out of the window by signing 16-year-old Lancashire-born batsman and off-spinner Michael Vaughan, initially on a two-year contract at the Academy, and on July 10 they voted to open up the boundaries completely and sign an overseas player. Nine days later it was announced that Australian pace bowler, Craig McDermott, would join them in 1992 for three years, the deal being possible through sponsorship of around £100,000 obtained by Sir Lawrence from Yorkshire Television.

Several months down the line, while Yorkshire were on a history-making pre-season tour of South Africa, it emerged that McDermott would not be fit to take up his engagement because of injury, and he was replaced by India's young batting prince, Sachin Tendulkar. A change of name and a batsman instead of a bowler but still the ending of a tradition going back to the very start in 1863, despite all those 29 non-Yorkshiremen turning out for the county at various stages and for various reasons. And the most notable of all these, of course, Lord Hawke himself!

At the time, the signing of Vaughan was a big story only because it broke the age-old custom but it did not take long before it became obvious that the lad first spotted by Doug Padgett playing on the outfield during a tea interval at Abbeydale Park was a truly outstanding prospect, with an alert young mind always on the lookout for personal betterment.

The signing took place in the Abbeydale secretary's office before start of play on the final day of Yorkshire's Championship match with Middlesex – and the day after Michael had helped Sheffield Collegiate to an eight run win over East Bierley in the NCA National Club Championship.

Michael's hugely supportive parents, Graham and Dee – his mother being related to the famous Lancashire cricket family of Tyldesleys – were present at the signing ceremony, along with Hassell and Oldham, the latter, at least, being able to boast a Yorkshire pedigree.

Yorkshire had acted swiftly to sign Vaughan, who had already received an approach from Northamptonshire and was attracting the interest of Lancashire through their monitoring of his impressive form with Collegiate.

Vaughan's very first words to the Press upon committing himself to the White Rose showed diplomacy beyond his years and were an indicator of his ability to think ahead and map out his future.

"I am delighted to be given this chance to make cricket my career and would be extremely proud if I became the first player in recent years to play for Yorkshire who was not actually born inside the county," he said.

"Although I was born in Manchester and lived there until I was eight I feel very much a Yorkshire lad at heart. I have learned my cricket here and I already know a lot of the boys who I will be joining at the Academy of Cricket."

Just two days later, Vaughan was up and running, scoring an unbeaten 76 for the Academy against York University at Park Avenue and sharing a fifth-wicket stand of 164 with Stephen Bethel. It was not obvious then, but this was his first significant stride towards the England captaincy and Ashes glory.

Meanwhile, on another important front, the move towards signing an overseas player was gathering pace and Halifax committee member Cawdry went public and said he would support such radical action when it was due for discussion by the general committee in July.

Although cricket chairman Close remained opposed to looking abroad to strengthen, he said he would abide by the majority decision rather than resign, and the most powerful argument in favour came from Sir Lawrence, who stressed that the club would be bankrupt within four years unless an overseas player were signed and other measures taken. He said that Yorkshire were budgeting to lose £100,000 that year (in the end it was much less) and their liquid assets were only around £420,000.

He was also able to sweeten the pill for some of the ex-player representatives by giving strong support to the principle of redeveloping Bradford Park Avenue and returning Yorkshire to one of their favourite grounds with a view to owning it if possible.

Not only did the general committee vote in favour of an overseas player on July 10 but they also agreed to open up the boundaries entirely and compete on exactly the same terms as other counties. The cricket committee resolution had simply sought to sign an overseas bowler but Boycott and Vann successfully put forward another resolution to unblock the boundaries altogether and Sir Lawrence's words were heeded when he urged that this was the way forward.

Even before the official search began for an overseas player, Yorkshire are believed to have made behind-the-scenes enquiries about South African paceman Richard Snell but nothing materialised on this front. When a shortlist was drawn up, the West Indies and Hampshire dynamo Malcolm Marshall's name was near the top as was Australia's McDermott, who soon confirmed that he had spoken to Yorkshire.

Marshall was pressed hard to come to Headingley but in the end Yorkshire opted for the younger McDermott, an official approach to the Queenslander being made in a telephone call by Oldham after the bowler's name – and others from 'down under' – had been supplied to the club by Australian-born journalist David Frith, then editor of the Wisden Cricket monthly.

"Craig made it quite clear that he was not coming here on a holiday but on business," said Oldham, who was impressed by the Aussie's no-nonsense attitude.

Yorkshire were playing Surrey at Guildford when McDermott signed a three-year contract via a satellite link with Brisbane and one faithful follower summed up the general feeling with the comment: "I would like Yorkshire to be good enough to win the Championship with their own boys, but we have to be realistic and move with the times."

Without exception, the senior Yorkshire players were happy with the news and Carrick said wryly: "I have a little smile at times when I see the speed with which things have happened and it disappointed me two years ago when I was not listened to."

And so Yorkshire moved surprisingly smoothly towards a new era – but it would not be McDermott who was the man to lead them into it.

That honour, as we shall soon discover, went to teenage sensation Tendulkar, but thousands of Yorkshire's pioneering floodlit cricket fans had an early glimpse of India's idol in the unlikely setting of the Don Valley Stadium at Sheffield in July, 1991.

Promoter Don Robinson ploughed over £100,000 into putting on two limited overs matches between Yorkshire and an International XI at the Stadium on July 14 and 15 and the balmy evening weather, more reminiscent of the Canaries than

Sheffield, ensured that this early experiment in floodlit cricket was a resounding success.

Yorkshire were led on these two occasions by Metcalfe because Moxon over this period had been chosen to captain England A against Sri Lanka at Old Trafford.

In the first game, Kapil Dev stole the show by slamming the white ball to all parts of the ground while dashing up 91 with Derek Randall, but in the second encounter he shared centre stage with Tendulkar, who thrashed four sixes in his unbeaten 32 off 19 balls in a match-winning stand of 73.

The first match, which ended almost at midnight, was watched by a shirt-sleeved crowd of 15,668 and the second attracted 8,134 but the weather reverted to type for the following year's event and the time was not yet quite right for cricket under lights to take a real hold.

Now that Yorkshire were soon to work on an equal footing with the other 17 counties (Durham about to become first-class), the new Yorkshire regime were ever eager to show greater savvy than the rest and there was even discussion about bidding for Botham's services upon his release from Worcestershire. Close was keen on signing his Somerset prodigy but Sir Lawrence and others in the hierarchy were less enthusiastic and the great all-rounder eventually went to give Durham a helping hand.

With so much going on off the field in 1991, Yorkshire were at least grateful that they avoided the bottom three places in the Championship table and they were, indeed, often better than their lowly position would suggest.

Byas was first in the camp to reach 1,000 runs and Robinson and Metcalfe also got there but none of them could match Moxon's aggregate of 1,669, boosted by his 200 against Essex at Colchester in late August when he batted imperiously throughout the first day and was out to the first ball of the second.

Kellett also did himself proud with 1,266 first-class runs and Blakey fell only 59 short of four figures but the most significant 1,000 of the season was nothing to do with runs and everything to do with wickets, Carrick choosing the Roses match at Old Trafford to snap up his 1,000th victim in all first-class cricket.

The moment arrived when he bowled DeFreitas to join Botham, Marshall, Eddie Hemmings and John Emburey as the only current players to make it to the 1,000 mark. It was a fitting and utterly praiseworthy achievement for a dedicated county cricketer who never quite made it into England colours but at least it placed him alongside other Yorkshire legends.

Carrick went on to experience further joy 63 wickets down the line by which time he had captured 1,000 solely for Yorkshire but he was desperately sad to see his career close in 1993 when just six runs shy of 10,000. He was fading out of the picture in that final summer and he just could not make it over the line when his limited opportunities arose.

He was still a force to be reckoned with in 1991, however, and he was Yorkshire's top Championship bowler with 61 dismissals, often ably assisted at the other end by up-and-coming off-spinner Jeremy Batty whose brother, Gareth, had an even more successful first-class future ahead of him. The two brothers were a chip off the old block because their father David, or George as he was more commonly known, was a top-notch leg-spinner who played for Yorkshire Seconds and broke bowling records in the Bradford League.

Yorkshire had the small consolation of ending the season by winning the Joshua Tetley Festival Trophy at Scarborough but the biggest prize was snared by the Second XI who were led to the Championship title by Neil Hartley after the side had finished bottom the previous year.

This great achievement could not save Hartley who was awarded a benefit the following year but not retained, the axe falling on both himself and the under-rated Fletcher as Yorkshire sought to save £70,000 on their cricket budget.

Off-spinner Phil Berry, denied a regular place, was released from his contract to join Durham, but the biggest loss turned out to be Phil Robinson who could not settle differences with the club regarding off-the-field matters, despite top level talks, and eventually informed them that he did not wish to accept the offer of a further engagement. His departure was a blow to both parties, particularly after making 189 and 79 not out in the penultimate match against Lancashire at Scarborough, a rousing contest in which Ian Austin scared the pants off Yorkshire with a breathtaking unbeaten 101 batting at No 9. Had the tea interval not allowed Moxon's men to pull themselves together, Lancashire may well have pulled off one of the greatest shocks of all time but in the end Austin ran out of support and Yorkshire were mightily relieved to win by 48 runs.

There was still time in this headline-making year for the committee to agree a return to Bradford in 1992, much to the joy of Appleyard and Close and other active members of the Friends of Park Avenue. But anyone who thought that quieter times were just around the corner was mistaken.

CHAPTER THIRTY-EIGHT

OUT OF AFRICA...

Out of Africa came Sachin Tendulkar – or at least that is where the Yorkshire team and their top officials were when the frantic search began to find a replacement for Craig McDermott.

The bombshell that McDermott would not be joining them because surgery was required on a serious groin injury hit the party only a few days into their tour of Cape Town.

They had left England on March 13 eager to make a good impression as the first team of cricketers to visit South Africa since the international ban imposed by the cricket authorities 24 years earlier and now lifted with the imminent ending of all forms of apartheid.

Yorkshire were acutely aware that they were in South Africa at a most crucial period in the country's history with more than three million whites taking part in a referendum on March 17 over whether to bring in power sharing and so continue the sweeping social reforms which were taking place.

It made for an extremely tense situation because nobody knew what the outcome would be if there were a *No* vote but everyone was able to relax when the size of the *Yes* vote was revealed to be 68.6 per cent, a majority greater than anyone had dared to predict.

Covering the tour for the Telegraph & Argus and its sister papers, The York Evening Press and Northern Echo, I spoke to many ex-pats who were ready to pack up and head for home if the vote had gone the other way.

One who was greatly concerned by the situation was Warwickshire director of cricket Bob Woolmer, the former England batsman who lived in Cape Town during the winter months with his South African wife and who, in mysterious and tragic circumstances, would exactly 15 years later die in his hotel room in Jamaica hours after Pakistan, the team he coached, had been knocked out of the 2007 World Cup by Ireland.

Woolmer, who also went on to earn even wider fame as South Africa's coach, told me at the time: "Had the No vote won then the government would have collapsed and a general election would have followed.

"A new government committed to turning the clock back to the old days of white rule and repression would have been elected. South Africa would be in isolation, the economy would have collapsed and violence would have spread like wildfire. This would not be a country you would want to live in. I would have been on the first available plane out."

Happily, this scenario was not realised, but even while the votes were being counted news filtered through to Yorkshire about McDermott's injury, which still allowed him to play with a pain-killing injection in Australia's final World Cup game against the West Indies in Melbourne.

Sir Lawrence and Hassell went public with the news at a hastily-arranged Press

Conference in the Yorkshire team's hotel in Cape Town and said that the operation would mean McDermott missing the first few weeks of the English season with the added possibility of him having to return to Australia before the end of the Championship for Test match preparations.

It was quickly decided, therefore, that Yorkshire had little option but to look elsewhere and the offices of the Western Province Cricket Association at Newlands, where Yorkshire were playing on the Test ground, became the nerve centre of the operation, telephone calls going out to Headingley, to Boycott in Australia and to cricket chairman Close at his Baildon home in an attempt to pinpoint their man.

With cricket committee members Philip Sharpe and Bob Platt also in South Africa, along with newly-appointed finance chairman Keith Moss there was no shortage of club officials present for on-the-spot top level talks and this group were often in deep debate with Sir Lawrence and Hassell.

To add to the excitement, Sharpe's travel firm, Travel Friends, had taken a party of around 75 of Yorkshire's keenest followers on the tour and the air was rife with speculation as to who would replace McDermott.

Several names were discussed but the main ones were Tendulkar and Western Province's own Brian McMillan, once with Warwickshire and at the time of the inquiry a key member of South Africa's World Cup team, whose progress in the competition was the nation's only talking point, apart from the referendum.

While talks were proceeding, Western Province's fast bowler Craig Matthews was ripping out six Yorkshire wickets without any trouble at all but his name was not up for discussion because he had already rejected an offer to play for Surrey and wanted to take a break from the game to rest a slight shoulder strain.

Tendulkar got strong backing in England from Solly Adam, the captain of Bradford League club, Spen Victoria. He had extensive cricketing contacts in India and had already fixed up Tendulkar's World Cup colleagues Vinod Kambli and Praveen Amre with Spen Victoria and East Bierley respectively for the coming season.

Adam contacted Close about Tendulkar and even spoke on the telephone to the teenage idol as well as ringing his mentor, Sunil Gavaskar, asking if he could persuade Tendulkar to sign.

While most of the Yorkshire party were relaxing on their last full day in Cape Town, Sir Lawrence himself was on the phone to Tendulkar in Bombay, Yorkshire having previously also contacted Gavaskar for his advice.

The deal was almost done and dusted on this telephone call but it was at the cricket committee meeting at Headingley on April 3, just days after Yorkshire had returned home, that it was announced that Hassell was already in Bombay with a contract for Tendulkar to sign.

Boycott attended that cricket committee meeting, having accepted an invitation to serve under Close, and Sir Lawrence had spoken to the general committee in advance to get their approval for whatever the cricket committee might recommend.

So, Hassell acquired the signature he wanted during a local cricket match in Bombay, in which Tendulkar scored a century, and a dashing young man still 20 days short of his 19th birthday had become Yorkshire's first overseas player.

That Yorkshire had initially taken on a world class bowler and had ended up with a batting prodigy instead does not alter the fact that they could not have made a made a better signing in their first foray into the overseas market.

Sachin, with his youthful looks and impeccable manners, not to mention his genius with the blade, quickly became a resounding success with the fans, not least the women members, many of whom would have adopted him on the spot, given half a chance.

He arrived in England during Yorkshire's first Championship match at The Oval and was ushered to the ground for a Press conference just before which he was incongruously photographed with a flat cap on his head and a pint of beer in his hand, an image which neither he nor the new-look Yorkshire really wanted. But he was too much of a statesman and diplomat to object.

Tendulkar faced the media with astonishing maturity and he had done his homework thoroughly, swotting up on the Yorkshire traditions and the famous players and stressing that, above all else, he would love to help the club win the Championship.

"They say that when Yorkshire have a great side so do England and I am looking forward to the challenge," he said.

"When I toured England with India two years ago, I played against several counties and it was my dream to join one. To have been signed by Yorkshire is very satisfying because they are a great club."

The composure which Tendulkar has shown throughout his glittering career surfaced in his first innings for Yorkshire when he was bizarrely run out for seven in the Benson and Hedges Cup zonal match against Kent at Headingley. Leaning on his bat at the non-striker's end he saw Byas drive powerfully back to Richard Ellison who attempted a right-handed catch but could only parry the ball into the stumps with Tendulkar fractionally out of his ground.

Despite an early return to India which caused him to miss the last four Championship matches, Tendulkar still oozed class without ever making a really big score. His only century in the competition – exactly 100 – came against newcomers Durham at the University ground and it helped Yorkshire to win a thriller after they had trailed by 106 on the first innings when Botham and Simon Hughes bowled them out for 108.

Tendulkar in that innings became the first Yorkshire batsman of the season to top 1,000 runs and he was followed to that mark by Moxon, Blakey and Kellett. He also played some memorable one-day innings, none better than his 107 in the Sunday League Roses game at Headingley which Yorkshire still lost by four runs.

Over 20 overseas players have since followed Tendulkar on the trail to Yorkshire, some of them inspired choices and others less so – and most of them batsmen, even though bowlers may more often have been needed.

The most successful of all turned out to be Darren Lehmann, the Australian batting dynamo never having been equalled or bettered when equating runs with the number of innings played, but South African Jacques Rudolph also churned out the runs and was hugely admired both inside and outside the dressing room, as was Pakistan's Younus Khan. Australian Phil Jaques had two splendid seasons in 2004-2005 and returned to bolster the batting last year; New Zealand's leader

Stephen Fleming did well in his half-season at Headingley, and Australians Matthew Elliott and Damien Martyn dazzled during short stays. Australia's Greg Blewett and India's Yuvraj Singh, however, both struggled and Pakistan's Inzamam-ul-Haq did not fire during his brief stay.

Michael Bevan was an Australian with a natural Yorkshire approach to the game who did all that was asked of him, while former West Indies captain, Richie Richardson, was greatly respected and tried his heart out but he had to battle uncomplainingly with a fatigue syndrome and was not at his best – and neither was Aussie Simon Katich in his brief spell.

Remarkably, it was 2004 before Yorkshire, with one-day cricket in mind, signed a true-all rounder in Australian Ian Harvey and not until the following year did they engage a genuine pace bowler in South African Deon Kruis, who came on a Kolpak contract and excelled with 64 wickets in his first season without reaching such heights again, though not through lack of effort.

Now back at Headingley as first team coach, Jason Gillespie, one of Australia's greatest fast bowlers, worked tirelessly in 2006-2007 without quite recapturing his glory days, but Pakistan's Rana Naved-ul-Hasan was plagued by injuries and never really settled. South Africa's Morne Morkel went down injured in what turned out to be his only match; Pakistan-born globe trotting leg-spinner, Imran Tahir had one disastrous game, and Australian paceman Mark Cleary performed modestly on a short contract while South African Herschelle Gibbs stacked up the runs on a Twenty20 engagement.

On balance, Yorkshire have shown shrewdness in their overseas signings and they can always claim that it was Tendulkar's time in a Yorkshire cap which added the finishing touches to his mastery in all conditions.

CHAPTER THIRTY-NINE

THE STARS PEEP OUT...

One tradition which Yorkshire did not wish to shed was the general acceptance that they were the best club in the land with a pedigree second to none but as they opened up their boundaries so the pressure increased on them to get back to those winning ways not consistently seen since the 1960s.

Yet it soon became apparent that Tendulkar alone would not be the panacea for all of Yorkshire's ills and the team even went back rather than forward in 1992, slipping from 14th to 16th in the Championship and from a middling seventh to a disastrous 15th in the Sunday League, the consequence of finishing the season with a record seven consecutive defeats.

Lean though this long period was in terms of trophies, Yorkshire still proved to be a fertile breeding ground for top quality performers, two of whom would rank among the greatest ever produced anywhere.

The pre-season tour to South Africa brought harmony to the players but shortly before Yorkshire flew out there was further discord within the committee – a tradition which would not go away quite as easily as some may have thought.

The recommendation from the club's members the previous year that the committee should be reduced in size from 1993 was honoured in the form of two resolutions drafted for the 1992 annual meeting, one aimed at cutting it from 23 elected representatives to 12 and the other that the old districts be abolished and replaced by four new ones, each with three members, only one of whom could be an ex-player.

This proviso particularly vexed Appleyard and Close because they would have to oppose each other in Central District if they decided to seek re-election. Appleyard saw it as a snub to the ex-players and vowed he would not stand against Close but the resolution was welcomed by Boycott as well as by a majority of the non-ex-players on the committee.

And the members at large were on the same wavelength because they voted over 70 per cent in favour of the changes, yet some of the ex-players were shocked by the size of the majority and issued a warning that the new set-up would greatly diminish the chance of Park Avenue being fully developed because two of its three staunchest backers in Appleyard, Close and Stott would not be allowed to keep their committee places. There would be an even more unexpected consequence of the changes but these matters were still a year down the line.

The winter months had not been kind to Moxon who had been delighted to be appointed captain of England A on their tour of Bermuda and the West Indies. But the fates once again conspired against him and the squad had barely arrived in Bermuda when he broke his left thumb attempting a catch in a hastily-arranged 20-over knockout match.

Moxon's immediate chances of enhancing his England claims had been shattered and he was forced to return home, the break being expected to take six weeks to heal. The tour, in February and March, had meant that Moxon would not be able to lead Yorkshire in South Africa and now he travelled with the team for gentle net practices once the injury began to mend.

Fit for the start of the season, Moxon's woes were soon to continue because while hitting a brilliant 141 in the Championship opener at The Oval he was struck on his right index finger by a ball from Surrey's South African paceman Rudi Bryson and the fracture sidelined him for a further five weeks.

That was not the end of it because Jarvis went down with a hamstring strain in the same game. On the brighter side Gough was a constant worry while capturing four first innings wickets with the new ball and Carrick scored the four runs he needed to give him 10,000 first-class runs and 1,000 wickets, only Botham among current players having achieved a similar distinguished double.

Failure to make the qualifying stages of the Benson and Hedges Cup and an early exit in the NatWest Trophy added to the gloom. It lifted a little with five consecutive Sunday wins, which contained centuries for Kellett and Blakey, but descended again as all form deserted the team in early July in the 40-over contest and they did not win another match.

Moxon's early injury gave Kellett his chance to open and he performed with such style that he held on to the role when his captain returned, Metcalfe surprisingly being axed as a result of poor form.

Once again, Yorkshire relied heavily on Peter Hartley, who was to the fore with 56 Championship wickets, but he received solid support from Mark Robinson who would be capped, along with Kellett. Blakey did well enough to attract the attention of the England selectors and make his debut in the Texaco Trophy one-day international against Pakistan at Lord's.

Carrick continued to be a force to be reckoned with and on his 40th birthday he was swept by Warwickshire's Roger Twose into Blakey's gloves to give the veteran left-armer his 1,000th first-class dismissal for Yorkshire. Strangely for a spinner, his first and 1,000th victims were both openers, Peter Robinson of Somerset initiating his account. Of all the opposition counties, Derbyshire succumbed the most readily to his skills, losing 127 wickets compared to his second favourite bunnies, Northamptonshire (85).

The abysmal run of Sunday League failures could not sully one of the most fascinating duels of the season when Tendulkar refused to be bullied by Courtney Walsh at Cheltenham. Struck on the helmet by a vicious delivery, Tendulkar responded by pulling the West Indian for six on his way to his first half-century in 14 one-day knocks since joining Yorkshire.

His gallant 63 enabled Yorkshire to reach 200 but an early assault from Athey and a ferocious 41 off 21 balls, with five fours and a six, from Jack Russell, who had earlier snapped up his 100th Sunday League catch, brought Gloucestershire victory with three balls remaining.

Tendulkar was responsible, but only in part, for Yorkshire being handed the biggest trophy in sport, the Durham Light Infantry Cup, upon beating Durham in the Championship at the University ground.

The trustees of the Regiment had agreed that the splendid four foot high piece of silverware, originally known as the Lahore Trades Cup, should be competed for annually in Championship matches between the two Northern sides to commemorate the Regiment's links with both counties.

Tendulkar, of course, stroked his one and only Championship century but Yorkshire may well have lost the game but for his restorative fifth-wicket stand of 130 with Carrick and ten wickets in the match for Robinson.

Neither Tendulkar nor Carrick was in Yorkshire's side for the much awaited return after an absence of seven years to Park Avenue, Tendulkar having gone home early and Carrick being omitted to allow his potential successor, Paul Grayson, a run of matches.

The ground did not look quite the same with the grand old Victorian pavilion having been pulled down and the football stand long since gone, but, uncharacteristically, the sun shone at least for the start of the game and the 3,000 crowd was able to enjoy a fascinating contest and one of high drama. The only thing wrong was the result, Surrey's last pair of Neil Kendrick and James Boiling eking out the 21 runs still required and passing the 302 target with just two balls to spare.

Kevin Sharp, now second team captain, was not re-engaged at the end of the season, Chris Pickles also being among those to go, but before the last ball had been bowled another controversy had sprung up over the unexpected signing of 30-year-old West Indies captain Richie Richardson to replace Tendulkar, who was not available for a sufficiently large part of the 1993 summer to be considered.

A majority on the cricket committee felt it was in the club's greater interests to go for a fast bowler and West Indian Anderson Cummins featured prominently in their deliberations. But Hassell said that the cricket committee had then felt none of the three 'quicks' they had pondered over was up to standard so it had been decided to sign a world-class batsman instead.

Raymond Illingworth added fuel to the flames by suggesting that Yorkshire had been influenced in their choice by Yorkshire Television, who were sponsoring the overseas player, but this was strongly refuted by Sir Lawrence who said he had scoured the world for a fast bowler of international repute but there just wasn't one available.

Unaware of this latest wrangle, Richardson, who at the time was playing for Blackpool in the Northern League, said it had always been his ambition to play county cricket and being with Yorkshire should help him develop his skills still further. In the event, he was often too exhausted for this regularly to happen but he was to become an inspiration to the players and even partly responsible for Gough's rise to international status.

During the summer of 1992, Castleford-born fast bowler Chris Silverwood had begun to show promise in the Second XI and this most pleasant-natured of pacemen was chosen by Oldham, now with the title of director of cricket, to fill a vacancy with Cape Town side Wellington, who play at Stellenbosch. Also joining him in South Africa was another developing quick bowler, Harrogate-born Stuart Milburn.

Oldham had been able to arrange these trips as a consequence of the club's initial pre-season tour to South Africa when he had met up with his old Derbyshire team-mate and friend Andy Watts, who played and coached in that country.

Preparations for the new season were well-advanced even before the old year was out and in November Oldham signed Worcestershire's 24-year-old left-arm spinner Richard Stemp on a three-year contract.

Stemp had one of the smoothest actions I have ever seen a spinner possess and he went on to claim 241 first-class wickets for Yorkshire over the next six seasons and 100 in one-day matches, so he did make a telling contribution.

But young left-armers Paul Grayson and Gary Keedy had just taken 33 and 29 wickets respectively in the Second XI Championship and Yorkshire had another potentially top-drawer spinner in 15-year-old off-break bowler Gareth Batty, who had been selected to go to South Africa with England Under 15s in January and was soon to be awarded a scholarship by his county club. Some were left to wonder if the arrival of Stemp were really necessary. Keedy could not make it into the first team until the last Championship game of 1994 and lack of opportunities made him decide to leave and join Lancashire where he went on to enjoy a sparkling career.

The decision to call on Stemp was partly influenced by the impending introduction of a full programme of four-day Championship matches, a move that was considered would help spinners come into their own.

The prospect of constant four-day cricket and the increasing use of computerised scoring rather than with pen and paper was all too much for 69-year-old Ted Lester, who announced his retirement in January and so severed a continuous link with Yorkshire going back half a century. For the previous four seasons, Lester had cut down on travelling to away matches where his seat had been filled by John Potter, from Beverley, who now snatched the chance to become full-time scorer. The new age of scoring suited Potter down to the ground and he is without peer in his field. The intricacies of the Duckworth-Lewis system for calculating rain-hit matches are beyond the ability of most people to fathom, but not Potter, who is eagerly sought out by umpires when the weather turns inclement.

Another aspect of the approaching season guaranteed to make Lester's teeth stand on edge was the introduction of coloured clothing for the increasingly hyped up one-day game but winter was not over yet and March brought one of the club's biggest upsets.

The long-awaited annual meeting with its election of 12 committee members in four new districts – North, West, South and Central – duly arrived and to everyone's amazement Boycott had his stumps sent flying in West District. He was pushed into fourth place by former fast bowler Bob Platt, who polled just three more votes, sufficient to have him elected along with Akroyd and Cawdry in what had been an eight-horse race with Mollie Staines and Dr John Turner among the other runners.

A year earlier, Platt had shrewdly observed that if a year were a long time in politics it was even longer in Yorkshire cricket and once again he was to have an outstanding day when all eyes were looking in the other direction – don't forget he used to open the bowling with Fred Trueman!

Boycott learned the news of his demise in a telephone call to Hassell from India, where he had been commentating on England's Test tour, but he was calm and magnanimous in defeat, saying that he had helped to put in place the streamlining of the committee from 23 elected members to 12 and he fully accepted what had been a democratic vote.

Sharpe topped the poll in North District, where Eric Houseman lost his seat, and other familiar faces missing from the new regime because they did not stand were club chairman Walsh, Appleyard, Stott, Anthony Roberts and statistician and historian Tony Woodhouse, who had not fully recovered after his road accident in Oxford the previous summer.

Two increasingly important posts went to Keith Moss as finance chairman and Fielden as public relations and membership chairman, both of them putting untold hours of work into their jobs.

Yorkshire were streamlined and running more efficiently than ever but money spent and decisions taken still could not turn things round on the field and Moxon's men endured another season of mediocrity, the only stand-out feature as a unit being their progress through to the quarter-finals of the NatWest Trophy, where they lost to Warwickshire by 21 runs.

This year, Yorkshire had got off to a great start by thrashing Champions Essex by a whopping 239 runs at Chelmsford, Jarvis holding the tiller in the absence of Moxon because of the birth of his son, Jonathan.

Moxon's unavailability enabled Jarvis to push Byas into the No 3 batting spot and he produced one of the greatest innings of his distinguished career by driving his way with awesome power to 156 off 267 balls, with 23 fours and three sixes, to record Yorkshire's highest individual score on the ground, easily overtaking Boycott's 121 in 1972.

Gough boosted the final score to 397 by scoring all 38 runs in a last-wicket stand with Mark Robinson and he went on to snaffle three wickets but it was an inspired Jarvis who kept Yorkshire in control. Working up a searing pace he bowled Paul Prichard and flattened Salim Malik's off-stump with a slower one before running out Mike Garnham. But his moment of true glory came in the second innings when he fired out four of the top six, including Graham Gooch whose off-stump cartwheeled several yards.

It was Yorkshire's biggest runs win for 30 years and their biggest against Essex in 70 years. In addition, it was achieved without either Moxon or Richardson but it proved to be a standard of cricket which they could simply not sustain.

Richardson arrived in time to make his debut against Northamptonshire at Headingley in the Benson and Hedges Cup and although he scored a solid 52 he blamed himself for the 34 runs defeat, saying if he had not got out he thought Yorkshire would have gone on to win.

The West Indies captain failed on his first Championship match at Bradford, where bad weather could not prevent Robinson from achieving a career-best 7-47, but even this fine effort paled into insignificance at Harrogate in July when, on a damp and helpful pitch, he grabbed 9-37 against his former county Northants, the best Yorkshire analysis since Johnny Wardle's 9-25 at Old Trafford in 1954 and the best by one of their fast bowlers since Emmott Robinson's 9-36, also against Lancashire, in 1920.

Dropped from the previous match at Edgbaston and undergoing treatment for a foot injury, Robinson only got his chance when Jarvis temporarily left the field and he was virtually unplayable, dropping the ball on the exact spot where it would do most damage. Shot out for 97, Northants did better second time around but, in a hair-raising climax, White's boundary brought Yorkshire victory off the last ball of the match.

Yorkshire had a ten-day wait for their next Championship match but their triumph over Somerset contained a far more significant bowling performance than Robinson's at Harrogate and it ended a run of six consecutive wins for the home side at Taunton.

The team were very much under a cloud in mid-season and had received a rocket from Close for their insipid general form. Gough had been left out at Harrogate but he replaced the injured Jarvis against Somerset and dramatically came of age with dynamic bowling which spelled out in no uncertain terms his ability to be a world-class operator.

Gough's chest seemed to expand in size as he grew in confidence to visibly disturb the batsmen and his second innings career-best Championship figures of 7-42 gave him a match return of 10-96. He had taken to heart Richardson's advice not to let chatter from the crease upset him, especially from opponents nowhere near his class, and Gough's newly-found bravado never deserted him throughout the remainder of his career.

His Yorkshire cap followed in early September, when he was selected for England's A tour of South Africa and he was on the road to international stardom. He was just beaten by a matter of weeks to his county cap by White, who was also mapping out an England career, having decided to make it big in the country of his birth rather than in Australia where he was reared.

Also scratching his way to the surface was 17-year-old Anthony McGrath, who had joined the Academy with another Bradford boy, Alex Wharf, but their time was still to come, unlike Vaughan who lived up to all expectations on his Yorkshire debut, appropriately enough against Lancashire at Old Trafford, where the future England captain opened the innings and his account with a cultured 64 in 46 overs while five wickets fell around him.

Vaughan finally succumbed to Pakistan's supremo Wasim Akram, who enjoyed his best Lancashire match figures of 12-125, but the youngster showed further promise in the second innings and Yorkshire went on to win a thriller by 19 runs, due in the end to another outstanding effort from Robinson, who took 6-62.

Not all eventful debuts were the catalyst for an outstanding career, however, and when Michael Foster and Silverwood strode out together for their first senior appearances against Hampshire at Southampton it was Foster who looked to have more going for him.

The solidly-built all-rounder began with a wicket in the opening over in each of his first two spells to claim his side's best figures of 3-39 and then his only scoring shot was a mighty six. In the Sunday League game at Grace Road in September he smashed his way to a memorable 118 batting at No 6, smiting eight sixes and seven fours and putting on 190 with Blakey. But he never scaled such heights again and after one more season he moved on to Northamptonshire and then Durham.

There was much sadness in the Press box towards the end of August with the death of Jim Kilburn, aged 84, the finest of Yorkshire cricket writers and a man who had covered the team's fortunes from 1934-73 for the Yorkshire Post. He had been in failing health for some time but two years earlier had made a magnificent speech while unveiling a plaque to mark the opening of the Press box in the football stand and it remained in use until the move into the new Headingley Carnegie pavilion at the Kirkstall Lane end of the ground in 2010.

Sadness, also, for Carrick as the season drew to a close. It looked as if his career was about to end just 20 runs short of becoming only the fifth all-rounder in Yorkshire's history to complete 10,000 runs and 1,000 wickets but pressure from Sir Lawrence and Hassell resulted in him being recalled for the last match against Surrey at The Oval to give him the chance of reaching the magical milestone.

In a match decimated by bad weather, Surrey made 359-7 declared in 100.2 overs and Carrick was allowed to go in first late on the third evening, but although Surrey generously gave him every opportunity to make the runs he could hardly hit the ball off the square and at the close was unbeaten on 14.

Theoretically, he still had a possible two chances to make a further six runs on the final day – or he did until the rain set in and washed away any chance of a resumption. Carrick had the consolation of being awarded a testimonial the following season but his playing days were over, leaving him a mere handful of runs short of emulating Rhodes, Hirst, Haigh and Illingworth.

Once again, Yorkshire's stock had risen higher off the field than on it and there was another red-letter day for the club in June with the completion of the refurbished Bass Headingley pavilion at a cost of £2.2m. As promised the work had been completed in time for the Ashes Test in July and it was officially opened during the match by Yorkshire's Patroness, HRH The Duchess of Kent.

Yorkshire and the ground's owners, Leeds CFAC, had worked in harmony on the project but goodwill between the two parties was often in short supply and the days were approaching when the relationship would reach its lowest ebb.

TOP OF THE BILL: Martyn Moxon and Ashley Metcalfe who formed one of Yorkshire's most successful and most entertaining opening partnerships together. Moxon, of course, went on to captain and coach Yorkshire and later returned to Headingley from Durham as Director of Professional Cricket. They are also pictured in action.

LIKE FATHER, LIKE SON: Among the distinguished fathers and sons who have played first team cricket for Yorkshire are, pictured: Herbert Sutcliffe and son, Billy; Len Hutton and son Richard (in same side); Richard Lumb and son, Michael; Arnie Sidebottom and son, Ryan; David Bairstow, celebrating his 1,000th first-class dismissal behind the stumps, and son, Jonny, keeping wicket.

SWpix.com

SWpix.com

SWpix.com

THE DAZZLER: No English-born cricketer of the modern era gained a higher media profile than Darren Gough who particularly triumphed at Test level with 239 wickets to place himself among his country's top ten wicket-takers of all time. He is pictured above in 2007 returning to captain Yorkshire for two seasons after a spell at Essex. *SWpix.com*

ACTION MAN: Few words to say for himself, Matthew Hoggard let his bowling do the talking by becoming England's sixth most successful bowler with 248 Test wickets before being nudged down a place by Jimmy Anderson. Only Fred Trueman among Yorkshiremen has more England scalps than Hoggard who left Headingley to captain Leicestershire in 2011. *SWpix.com*

PRESIDENTIAL POWER: Viscount Mountgarret stepped into the lion's den as President following the resignation of Norman Yardley, and Sir Lawrence Byford came to the fore by accepting the Presidency following the shock death of Sir Leonard Hutton. Sir Lawrence is pictured at Newlands Test ground on one of Yorkshire's pre-season tours of South Africa and it was he who brought an end to the "Yorkshire only" policy and was responsible for gaining sponsorship for the Club's first overseas player, Sachin Tendulkar.

A STAR IS VAUGHAN: History was made at Abbeydale Park, Sheffield, on June 24, 1991, when 16-year-old Michael Vaughan, pictured with Yorkshire cricket manager, Steve Oldham, and chief executive, Chris Hassell, was given a two-year contract at the Yorkshire Academy of Cricket, so becoming the first non-Yorkshire-born player in modern times to be taken on by the White Rose county. Vaughan went on to become not only one of England's record-breaking batsmen but also one of his country's greatest captains, no moment in his career being sweeter than when he was able to kiss the Ashes urn at The Oval in 2005.

SWpix.com

TEENAGE WONDER: Sachin Tendulkar was only 19 when he became Yorkshire's first overseas player in 1992 but he was already an international star and he quickly stole the hearts of the Yorkshire fans. He never lost his love and affection for Headingley and here he is pictured on his way to a brilliant 193 on the ground in the 2002 Test match which India won by an innings and 46 runs. *SWpix.com*

PIONEERING PAIR: Ajmal Shahzad became the first Yorkshire-born player from an ethnic background to play for the county when he made his Sunday League debut against Worcestershire at Headingley in May, 2004, and here he is seen in the players' viewing gallery calmly waiting to go in to bat. Later that summer, wicketkeeper-batsman Ismail Dawood, who had attended the Academy before playing county cricket elsewhere, returned to become the first Yorkshire-born player from an ethnic background to play first-class cricket for the county. He is pictured on his debut against Somerset at Scarborough appealing unsuccessfully against Rickie Ponting who went on to make 112. *SWpix.com*

SIMPLY THE BEST: No Yorkshire batsman has entertained on such a lavish scale as Australian Darren Lehmann who, by the time he said farewell to the county, had lashed 8,871 first-class runs at an average of 68.76. In his final innings against Durham at Headingley in September, 2006, he scored an epic 339 which was only three runs short of beating George Hirst's record 341. The three pictures show him attacking the bowling, acknowledging the applause on reaching 300 and responding to the standing ovation he received at the end of his innings. *SWpix.com*

BACK WHERE IT BELONGS: Captain, David Byas, admires the County Championship Trophy which he and his team brought back to Yorkshire in 2001 after a 33-year wait. Success was all the sweeter for Byas because it came in the match against Glamorgan on his home ground at Scarborough and he also scored a century as well as taking the winning catch. The other pictures show a moment's quiet contemplation for Byas in the Scarborough dressing room before the balcony celebrations begin, and coach Wayne Clark, the former Aussie Test cricketer, who helped guide Yorkshire to their triumph in his first season at Headingley. *SWpix.com*

JUMPING FOR JOY: Never one to hide his emotions, Steve Kirby celebrates wildly after the umpire raises his finger. Kirby's sudden arrival at Headingley was a major factor in Yorkshire lifting the Championship title and also in raising the level of entertainment. *SWpix.com*

BLAKEY'S HEROES: Richard Blakey holds aloft the Cheltenham and Gloucester Trophy after captaining the side to victory over Somerset in the Lord's final in 2002. Man-of-the-match was their short-term signing, Australian left-hander, Matthew Elliott, who plundered an unbeaten 128. *SWpix.com*

LONG SERVICE: Bradford-born Anthony McGrath was Yorkshire's longest serving player in 2012 as the club entered its final season before its 150th anniversary. Captain in 2003 and again in 2009, McGrath established himself as one of Yorkshire's best batsmen since the war and he also represented England at Test and one-day level. *SWpix.com*

RARE COMMODITY: Leg-spinner, Adil Rashid, is cheered off the field after his sensational Yorkshire debut against Warwickshire at Scarborough in 2006 when he captured 6-67, so setting out on the path to becoming the most successful bowler of his type in Yorkshire's history. *SWpix.com*

CHIEFS OF STAFF: Chris Hassell (top left) became Yorkshire's first chief executive in 1991. Colin Graves (centre) took over from 2002-2005 and officially held the job again from 2012, and Stewart Regan (right) was in the post from 2006-2010 during years of great change.

GANG OF FOUR: With the abolition of the old committee system in 2002, the new Management Board was originally comprised of, pictured together, Robin Smith, Colin Graves (chairman) and Brian Bouttell, along with Geoff Cope. *SWpix.com*

THE CHANGING FACE: The new Headingley Carnegie pavilion and the Yorkshire Cricket Museum which was opened on the ground floor of the East stand in 2011. *SWpix.com*

FOREVER YOUNG: Brian Close, who at 18 years and 149 days became the youngest England Test cricketer in 1949, met up at Headingley in 2012 with wicketkeeper-batsman, Barney Gibson, who the previous year became the youngest ever to play English first-class cricket when he made his debut for Yorkshire against Durham MCCU at 15 years and 27 days. *SWpix.com*

G-FORCE: Captain Andrew Gale and newly appointed first team coach, Jason Gillespie, were fully focussed in 2012 on trying to make Yorkshire the best team in the land once again. *SWpix.com*

YORKSHIRE 2012: Back, left to right: Gurman Randhawa, Alex Lilley, Alex Lees, James Wainman, Callum Geldart, Dan Hodgson. Middle: Iain Wardlaw, Azeem Rafiq, Adam Lyth, Steve Patterson, Oliver Hannon-Dalby, Joe Root. Gary Ballance, Moin Ashraf. Front: Richard Pyrah, Adil Rashid, Anthony McGrath, Joe Sayers (vice-captain), Andrew Gale (captain), Ryan Sidebottom, Gerard Brophy, Ajmal Shahzad, Jonny Bairstow. Tim Bresnan was on England duty and Australian fast bowler, Mitchell Starc, and South African batsman, David Miller, joined the squad later on. *SWpix.com*

DOUBLE TON-UP BOYS: The soggy summer of 2012 still could not prevent Joe Root and Adam Lyth from rapping out double centuries in the space of three rain-hit Championship matches. Root was first there with an unbeaten 222 against Hampshire at the Rose Bowl and Lyth followed with 248 not out against Leicestershire at Grace Road to become the only Yorkshire batsman to carry his bat with a double century. *SWpix.com*

MILLER MAGIC: Yorkshire's South African batsman, David Miller, hits out during his splendid unbeaten 72 against Hampshire in the Friends Life t20 final at Cardiff in August. *SWpix.com*

HOW'S THAT? Ryan Sidebottom is in no doubt that he has got his man in the final of the Friends Life t20 at Cardiff. *SWpix.com*

CHAPTER FORTY

THE SUN STAYS IN

The pressures were beginning to mount on Moxon as he prepared for his fifth season in charge, the membership growing increasingly impatient for all the changes in the running of the club to be converted into better results.

That Yorkshire had oceans of young talent working its way up from the Academy was an undeniable fact, the truth of which could be seen at the 1993 Scarborough Festival when eight colt players were included in the home team which beat full-strength Durham by seven wickets to win the Northern Electric Trophy.

But although the likes of Vaughan, particularly, and Grayson, Silverwood and Bradley Parker all continued to advance in 1994, Yorkshire still lacked something of the 'wow' factor and were unable to motivate themselves sufficiently as a unit to reach the required heights.

After enjoying three first-class friendly victories, they could not repeat that sort of form in the Championship and dropped back a place to 13th while moving up four spots to ninth in the AXA Sunday League. They floundered in the knockout competitions and just made it home in the final over against Minor Counties' Devon at Exmouth where White's unbeaten 65 guided them to 246-6.

Yorkshire were without Jarvis, who had some harsh words to say about being offered his release from contract before opting to go to Sussex, one of a number of clubs hot on his trail. Having already taken 449 first-class wickets for Yorkshire he bagged a further 133 for his new employers and went on to complete his career at Somerset.

Metcalfe, pressed hard first by Kellett and then the rapidly-emerging Vaughan, was also invited to end his contract but he decided to hang around for a further two seasons and, with hindsight, no doubt wished he had packed his bags and gone to Nottinghamshire sooner than he did. After some resistance within the club, however, it was agreed to give him a benefit in 1995 which was no less than he deserved for all the entertainment he had given.

Moxon, Blakey and Byas each made 1,000 Championship runs and Vaughan and Grayson got there in first-class matches for the county but the early return home of the clearly exhausted Richardson left everyone in the doldrums and it required strong words from Moxon to boost morale in the closing weeks of the season and avoid the wooden spoon.

Hartley shrugged off knee problems to earn 61 wickets, 57 of them in the Championship, and Yorkshire at last had real firepower to launch at the enemy in Gough as well as White, who had discarded his off-spin for genuine pace to become a seriously good all-rounder.

The pair of them were quick to attract the eye of Raymond Illingworth, England's new chairman of selectors, and Gough's status as national hero and adventurer was sealed the moment he dismissed New Zealand's Martin Crowe with his sixth ball on his international debut in the Texaco Trophy match at Edgbaston.

The regular call-ups of Gough and White were good news for Yorkshire's prestige but bad from the point of view of actually winning matches and it was a problem which was set to get progressively worse over the years as selection for England meant hardly ever playing for one's county again until a player's best days were behind him.

Stemp, too, twice made the England squad against New Zealand before being omitted and returning to Yorkshire. Had he played he would have joined Close in gaining a cap for his country before his county.

At least Stemp's misfortune meant that Yorkshire were able to hold on to him but the left-arm spinner did not always make the headlines for the right reasons. Against Somerset at Bradford, he was reported to Lord's by David Constant for reacting angrily to the umpire's decision not to give Mark Lathwell out caught behind the wicket.

Although Yorkshire had previously wasted little time in fining a couple of players for unacceptable conduct, Hassell on this occasion blew his top that the incident had been reported in the Press and said that the club would strongly defend Stemp when he appeared in front of a disciplinary hearing. It made no difference because he was fined £500 for using "crude and abusive language" and he paid up without going to appeal.

Richardson arrived at Headingley in early May but it was soon obvious that misfortune, indifferent form and mental and physical tiredness would continue to shadow him.

The previous season he had returned to the Caribbean for a while upon the sudden death of his mother and three weeks after his arrival this time he had to make haste home for a fortnight because his seven-year-old son, Ari, had been seriously injured in a car accident.

Back in Yorkshire, he then missed a further short period with an attack of gout but there was a brief brighter spell when he kept his side in the thick of the Sunday League fray by slamming an unbeaten 39 off 26 balls against Leicestershire at Scarborough and hitting the winning boundary off the last ball of the match.

Richardson continued to struggle with his energy levels and after extensive medical tests had shown him to be suffering from acute fatigue syndrome he agreed to take a six-month break from cricket, Yorkshire acceding to his request to be released from his contract. His last match was against Gloucestershire at Cheltenham where he bade farewell to his colleagues and still found time to sign autographs before driving out of the car park.

Richardson's departure in late July focussed Yorkshire's attention on seeking out an overseas player for 1995 but it was not until well into September that they finally agreed on another batsman in up-and-coming Australian, Michael Bevan, after running the rule over several fast bowlers first, including South Africans Craig Matthews, Brian McMillan and Fanie de Villiers, plus New Zealand's Dion Nash. They also showed interest in ace Australian batsman, Mark Waugh, but Essex got in first.

Well before Richardson's departure another West Indian had been very much part of the Yorkshire scene, the county having assisted in the arrangements for bringing over from Montserrat for trials an athletic 19-year-old fast bowler of boundless enthusiasm in Lesroy Weekes.

Impressing Oldham with his early prowess for Thongsbridge in the Huddersfield League, Weekes was quickly given a Second XI Championship game and responded with six wickets. He was ineligible for first team Championship cricket because of Richardson's presence but he was able to make his senior debut against the New Zealand tourists and he caused a flutter of excitement by taking four wickets.

There was a very real hope for a while that Weekes could develop sufficiently to become Yorkshire's overseas player. Things did not quite work out that way but Weekes went on to enjoy a successful career at league level and has remained a popular figure in the county.

A young Scot was also attracting the attention of more than just Oldham and Moxon as they continued the search for a winning formula. Academy and second team fast bowler Gavin Hamilton, born in Broxburn, West Lothian, was called up by his country for their Benson and Hedges Cup game with Sussex at Hove in April and a couple of months later Yorkshire brought him in for a Championship debut against Kent at Maidstone.

Hamilton had a sunny nature which it was impossible to dislike and three wickets in the match, plus scores of 48 and 18, made him an instant favourite with the fans. He went on, of course, to enjoy great success with Yorkshire and play one Test for England but his Headingley days were ended far too prematurely by a mental block that made it impossible for him to bowl straight and put him under great stress.

Attempts to rectify the problem failed but he moved on to Durham, who used him almost exclusively as a batsman, and he also gave long and distinguished service to Scotland as their captain.

Other Academy products to find their feet were fast bowler Alex Wharf, who made his first team debut along with Parker, while McGrath was starting to make a name for himself at Second XI level. He and Keedy were pencilled in by England Under 19s for a three-day trial match against Sussex at Hove but Oldham put a block on it because he wanted them available for the first team if necessary.

Parker scored a splendid maiden century against Surrey at Scarborough but it did not contain a moment quite as memorable as that enjoyed by Wharf at North Marine Road a couple of weeks earlier. His first – and only – wicket of the match against Warwickshire was that of West Indian genius Brian Lara, the holder of the world record score of 501, flashing outside off-stump to be caught by Blakey for 21.

Having taken a while to establish himself, Byas was dominant in all forms of cricket in 1994 and his 702 runs in the Sunday League set a record for a Yorkshire batsman. Significantly, he coped well under pressure at Bradford in June when he found himself in charge for the Somerset game in the absence of both Moxon and Richardson. The side were further weakened through being without the injured Gough but Byas took the attack to his opponents by putting on 216 in 53 overs with Vaughan, the second highest for the second wicket in nine years. Both batsmen hit centuries and in the second innings Byas racked up 62 with 12 fours and a six to show he could really step on the pedal if the situation required it.

Byas also plundered a century in the Roses match at Headingley in mid-August but he could not save Yorkshire from a seven-wicket defeat which left them next-to-bottom of the table and in real danger of propping everyone else up.

But Moxon's rallying call was answered with two consecutive victories and the captain himself was at the top of his game, especially at New Road where he plundered a career-best 274 not out, exceeding Lowson's previous best against Worcestershire of 259 not out and overtaking Len Hutton's unbeaten 270 off Hampshire in 1947 to post Yorkshire's highest individual innings since the war.

The late burst of activity probably saved Moxon's neck for another year because in September he was appointed captain for a sixth successive season but it was the end of the line for fast bowling prospect Mark Broadhurst, who had not made sufficient strides since showing such early promise as one of the crop of young pacemen nurtured by Olympic coach Wilf Paish. Foster was not retained, either, and Keedy and Jeremy Batty both sought new pastures and greater opportunities.

There had been an outcry from Friends of Park Avenue supporters before the start of the season upon hearing the news that the Academy team were to join the Yorkshire League, the fear being that they would feature less prominently at the Bradford ground, but it was understandable that Yorkshire wanted them to enjoy generally better facilities than at their base and gain experience from playing at bigger venues.

Headingley was the home base for these League matches and although Close was passionate about Park Avenue, the prospect of truly competitive matches stirred his blood and, at the age of 63, he could not resist taking his whites out of mothballs and leading the side on four occasions. It was an unforgettable experience for the youngsters and in one game I watched they tried hard not to smile as he dived full-length to make his crease. It did not take long for him to win their admiration and respect.

The youngest member of this Academy team was Ryan Sidebottom who was showing distinct signs of following in his father's footsteps. Up to now, Arnie had been ever willing to leave the young lad's development to Oldham and others but from February, 1995, he was compelled to take a more active interest with his appointment as Academy coach, his predecessor, Bore, becoming the club's development officer and schools' coach.

Since retiring from Yorkshire, Arnie had been employed by Leeds City Council as a senior cricket coach, working in schools as well as at the indoor centre at Headingley, and the council now agreed to release him during the summer months so that he could become the Academy supremo.

The New Year had begun in a blaze of publicity for both Yorkshire and Gough who had just become a world superstar in Australia with 20 wickets from the first three Tests. He was at his peak in the third match at Sydney when he first scythed his way to a half-century which revitalised the England innings and then smashed Australia to smithereens with 6-49 as they slumped to 116 all out. In the end only an eighth-wicket stand between Shane Warne and Tim May saved Australia but Gough had restored England's pride following their battering in the first two Tests and everyone back home was eager for the Yorkshireman to inflict more damage.

But misfortune struck as Gough fractured his left foot while running in to bowl against Australia in the World Series Cup and suddenly his triumphal tour was over. Two days later his Ossett home was besieged by photographers, all eager to picture him with his wife, Anna, and their two month old son, Liam, who Gough was seeing for the first time.

The same frenzy took place at Headingley when Gough and his family turned up for a Press Conference where he was treated more like a Hollywood movie star than a cricketer. Gough was now the game's hottest property since Botham was topping the bill and Yorkshire had certainly known nothing like it since the days of Boycott.

The immediate rub-off was the interest sparked in the first Test at Headingley between England and the West Indies, scheduled to start on June 8, and secretary Ryder was able to report that advance ticket sales already topped £250,000, easily a record for late January.

While Gough was knocking 'em over in Australia, from where White was also destined to make an early return with injury, McGrath was making a name for himself with England Under 19s in the West Indies and earning a reputation as one of his country's best young prospects. He scored 133 and 79 in two of the Youth Tests and 170 against Trinidad, which led tour manager David 'Bumble' Lloyd to say he felt McGrath had advanced even further than Marcus Trescothick.

McGrath's only real ambition at the moment was to go on scoring sufficient runs to win a first team place with Yorkshire and his wish came true in the summer. There was to be many a time when he looked at least as good a player as Vaughan and although he was unable to capitalise on a promising start with England, through little fault of his own, he perhaps achieved more over a longer period with Yorkshire, including two spells as captain.

Yet another teenager with a big international future ahead of him took his first step towards stardom in February, Pudsey Congs fast bowler Matthew Hoggard being added to the Academy staff. Hoggard's rise came as no surprise to Bradford League officials but he was known to a lesser degree elsewhere because he had not trod the usual path of coming through the Yorkshire Schools' system.

Moxon knew he had earned one last chance to prove himself a winning captain and spirits were high as Yorkshire departed for their pre-season tour to Cape Town, where they were joined by Bevan and later on by Gough for net sessions once he had been told his foot had recovered well enough for him to build up his bowling.

But before their first match had begun, Yorkshire suffered two serious setbacks to their plans, Colin Chapman collapsing into a swimming pool and being saved from drowning by a local man and Kellett also having his tour ruined by an accidental beamer which broke a bone in his left hand during net practice.

Hospital tests showed that Chapman had passed out with an epileptic fit and, sadly, the illness eventually brought about his premature retirement from first-class cricket. He showed great spirit and carried on for as long as he could but he was never going to scale the heights that this positive wicketkeeper-batsman may otherwise have done.

Kellett's misfortune was the latest in a catalogue of incidents which went back to the time he was awarded his cap in 1993 and had prevented him from re-establishing himself in the first team. Until he was capped he had been practically injury free but then a bad groin strain, a pulled hamstring and a broken index finger had all held him back.

The latest damage had been done by another great Yorkshire prospect who would be touched by personal tragedy, Jamie Hood. The 18-year-old Academy graduate was playing club cricket in Cape Town that winter and he had joined Yorkshire for nets and some matches. An engaging young man with a flair for cricket and a zest for life, Hood was so seriously injured in a car accident in South Africa a few years later that he was paralysed from the neck down and forced to be attached to a ventilator.

The coming summer, however, he would score a Second XI Championship century against Worcestershire at Park Avenue and the Saltburn-player never forgot his ties to Yorkshire. He was not forgotten, either, and in 2011 he was made an honorary life member of the Yorkshire Players' Association.

At last Yorkshire had something to be cheerful about in South Africa when they were joined by Bevan at the end of his 20-hour journey from Sydney. The first question asked by White's former team-mate at Australia's Academy of Cricket was: "What are the net facilities like here and how soon can I get playing?"

The answers were "very good" and "very soon" and Bevan's response three days later was to mark his debut with 95 runs and two wickets in a one-day success over Western Province CC. Hood also made a good first team debut, scoring 12 not out and capturing a wicket with his very first ball, and Bevan went on to show his early form was no fluke by making his maiden Yorkshire century in the three-day encounter with a Western Province XI.

After an encouraging tour, Bevan kept the runs flowing in a great start to the 1995 season which suggested that Moxon and his men were capable, at last, of lifting a trophy or two.

The Australian followed up an unbeaten 113 against Cambridge University at Fenner's with 108 in the four-day friendly against Lancashire at Headingley but he still could not match the firepower of fellow left-hander Byas who helped himself to 181 against Cambridge and 193 off the Red Rose, who blushed even deeper as Gough finished them off with career-best figures of 7-28.

Encouraged by a victory margin of 219 runs over the old enemy, Yorkshire romped home in their first three Championship matches for the first time since 1962 and it was Hartley who shattered the opposition in these matches with an astonishing 25 wickets at an average of 9.36. Gough may have been the name on everyone's lips but his tally over the same period was a mere 12 wickets at 24.91.

During this rampage, Hartley had figures of 20-12-19-5 against Leicestershire, a career-best 9-41 against Derbyshire, when he completed the hat-trick and had a spell of five wickets in nine balls without conceding a run, and 6-64 against Glamorgan when he wiped out the first six in the order.

Hartley calmed down a bit from then on but still finished streets ahead of everyone else with 71 Championship wickets and 81 first-class, the most since Cope's 87 in 1976. It was an appropriate way to acknowledge the benefit he had been granted for the following season.

Although the start to the 1995 season could hardly have been better, there were some moments of concern, not least when Moxon broke a thumb while batting in the Derbyshire game and missed the next three Championship matches.

He then made up for his time off the field by spending the whole of the Kent game at Headingley on it, making an unbeaten 203 in the first innings and 65 not out in the second. Further injuries restricted Moxon to ten Championship matches, yet he still topped the averages and one can only wonder how many more runs this fine batsman would have accumulated during his career had he not been so injury prone.

Having been straight out of the traps, there was no holding Byas who was the first in the country to reach 1,000 runs. In all first-class matches for Yorkshire he thrashed 1,913 runs and was attracting the attention of England but the Test debut he deserved never came and the nearest he got to wearing the three lions was a call-up into the squad as cover without actually playing.

Whereas the previous season Yorkshire had recovered some of their dignity after a poor start the reverse was true this time and four defeats in five matches marked the beginning of a decline accentuated by the last nine fixtures producing a win only in the Roses match at Old Trafford and also containing a one-run defeat by Surrey at The Oval.

Only on three previous occasions had Yorkshire lost by the narrowest of margins and such a result looked unlikely after Silverwood's 5-62 had given him an eight wicket bag. But the second half of the batting disintegrated and it was all over when last man Mark Robinson was taken in the slips. Umpire Peter Willey had given him not out to what he thought was an lbw appeal but changed his mind upon Robinson's naïve admission to the close-in field that he had actually snicked the ball on to his pad.

Easing their way through the zonal stages of the Benson and Hedges Cup, Yorkshire came to grief in the quarter-finals at Headingley where they were skittled for 88 by Worcestershire on a rain-affected pitch which grew easier as the game went on.

They went even further in the NatWest Trophy, reaching the semi-finals before being out-batted by Northamptonshire who won by 87 runs. Once again, Headingley was the venue for their downfall but they had enjoyed a heart-stopping victory on their home ground over Lancashire by two wickets in the quarter-finals, a capacity crowd of 18,500 proving that Roses cricket had lost none of its pulling power.

A worrying factor in these Headingley matches was the bad behaviour in the Western Terrace with the worst of it surfacing in the Northants game. It prompted Sir Lawrence and Hassell to launch a lengthy inquiry and led to much stricter rules on drink being imposed. The unacceptable antics at the ground were becoming a matter of concern at Lord's and Yorkshire knew they needed to act to safeguard Test cricket.

Yorkshire slipped seven places to 12th in the Sunday League, despite Bevan's aggregate of 704 runs which broke by two runs the record set for his side by Byas only 12 months earlier. They won their last three matches but this could not compensate for five consecutive defeats, including a mauling at Edgbaston by South African Allan Donald, who captured six for 15 as they capsized to their worst-ever score in the competition of 56.

There were extenuating circumstances for this abject display – in addition to Donald's brilliance – because the Yorkshire party were going down like flies with a sickness bug picked up in the team hotel. Blakey, sick on the field, was unable to bat, others were distinctly unwell and the sick list grew as the week went on. The fact that Yorkshire had just succumbed to Warwickshire by an innings and 168 runs inside three days in the Championship, with Moxon breaking his thumb, only added to the general feeling of nausea.

The see-saw nature of Yorkshire's cricket around this period was difficult to comprehend in view of the steady trickle into the first team of youngsters who seemed destined to have big futures ahead of them. One of them was 18-year-old all-rounder Alex Morris, who Ted Lester, a shrewd assessor of young talent, thought was one of the best players Yorkshire had produced in a long while.

Well thought of at England Under 19s level, Morris made his Championship debut against Hampshire at Southampton and he also helped Yorkshire pull off a tremendous one-day win over Young Australia at Headingley with figures of 5-32, his victims including Justin Langer, Stuart Law and Adam Gilchrist.

His career never really took off at Yorkshire, however, and in 1998 he moved to Hampshire where he gave good service until the end of 2003, scoring 1,030 first-class runs and picking up 147 wickets. Yet he never truly fulfilled his promise and neither did his younger brother, Zac, who also left Yorkshire for Hampshire where he played in a handful of matches.

One who did go from strength to strength in his early days was McGrath, who sharpened his profile in September by excelling at the Scarborough Festival. He scooped the man-of-the-match award for his sparkling 106 against the West Indians in the McCain Challenge, when Hamilton claimed Lara as one of his three victims, and held centre stage with a sparkling 72 on his Sunday League debut after Moxon had stepped down to give the teenager his chance.

Not only youth enjoyed its fling at Scarborough because Metcalfe, rarely called upon these days, found sufficient late season form to be included in the three-day match against the West Indians and he rediscovered his Midas touch to make exactly 100, with 12 fours and three sixes, to register his first century since his unbeaten 133 off Cambridge University in the opening game of 1993.

It turned out to be Metcalfe's last first-class match for Yorkshire and so he gained the distinction of both raising the curtain and lowering it with centuries. He was offered a new two-year contract but decided he had been pushed into the shade too often and, instead, moved to continue his career at Nottinghamshire.

Grayson, Kellett and Milburn were all released and so was Parker but he was reprieved because he had been unable to find another county. Grayson, of course, forged out a fantastic career at Essex, where he went on to be put in charge of cricket, Milburn had two seasons with Hampshire, and Kellett began a long association as player-coach with Dunnington CC of the York Senior League, where Costcutter Supermarket founder and future Yorkshire CCC chairman and chief executive, Colin Graves, played his cricket for nearly 30 years. Kellett also worked for Costcutter as part of his contract but he still found time for Minor Counties' cricket and Yorkshire came up against him in 2003 when they played Cambridgeshire at March in the Cheltenham and Gloucester Trophy.

Before Yorkshire could debate whether to continue with Moxon as captain in 1996, the player made the decision for them by announcing he was standing down and at the same time Close said he was finishing as cricket chairman.

By the first week in October, Byas had been proclaimed as the new captain with Platt confirmed as Close's successor. Oldham's title was changed from Director of Cricket to Director of Development as the club combed the world for a manager-coach and a winter of discontent set in between Yorkshire and Leeds CFAC.

CHAPTER FORTY-ONE

GROUNDS FOR CONCERN

The time was fast approaching when county involvement on the outgrounds, so much a part of Yorkshire's rich heritage, would be no more – apart from North Marine Road at Scarborough.

By now, both Hull and Huddersfield had ceased to stage even Sunday League fixtures and those venues which survived had a double battle on their hands as they tried to preserve their status.

Maintaining facilities to the standard required for just one or two first-class matches a year put finances under a severe strain, particularly as Yorkshire no longer paid clubs for the privilege of taking games to their grounds but, instead, wanted a sum for going there.

The constant shrinking of the Championship programme meant there were also fewer fixtures to distribute and Yorkshire were only too well aware that major sponsors expected most of the matches to be staged at Headingley.

But what really sounded the death knell for the outposts was Yorkshire's desire to own a ground of their own and profit from its income sources rather than seeing the bulk of the cash go to their various landlords.

Once Yorkshire had agreed in principle to buying a ground and becoming independent they soon decided that the only games away from their Headingley headquarters would be at Scarborough, which always attracted big gates and had the largest capacity of all of the non-Test playing grounds in the country.

And so the 1996 season proved to be the last time that Yorkshire would journey into the sticks and bring first-class cricket to the populace of Sheffield, Bradford, Middlesbrough and Harrogate.

Sheffield, the city where it all began for Yorkshire CCC, had staged matches regularly since the club's inception in 1863, first at Bramall Lane and then at Abbeydale Park from 1974. Bramall Lane put on 391 first-class matches of which Yorkshire won 163 and lost 78, while 41 games were played at Abbeydale Park with eight wins and 11 defeats.

Park Avenue had hosted 306 matches since 1881 with Yorkshire generally in the ascendancy, with 145 wins compared to 41 losses but the ground with the biggest percentage of home victories was Harrogate where Yorkshire came out on top in 50 of their 91 contests from 1894, losing on just eight occasions.

The newest of the venues was Middlesbrough's Acklam Park which had first entertained Yorkshire in 1956, the White Rose being successful 21 times and losing just eight of the 45 encounters.

Ten other grounds around the county, in addition to Hull (88 games) and Huddersfield (72) had also acted as hosts to Yorkshire at various times down the years, the greatest number being 49 at Savile Town, Dewsbury.

The vexed question of where Yorkshire should play their cricket in future was discussed mainly in private by the committee during the summer of 1995 and it was during a match at Scarborough that Sir Lawrence first mooted the idea of buying their own ground.

Relations with Leeds CFAC had become increasingly strained over the past few months and the rift grew wider with the landlord's decision not to go ahead in the winter with work on a new £1.8m stand for Yorkshire members which was to have been sited on the bowling green, where temporary stands were erected for Test matches.

In mid-November the news broke that Yorkshire were holding crisis talks with Headingley's owners over a possible new development deal for the cricket ground and that if these talks reached stalemate then Yorkshire might push ahead with plans of their own to build new headquarters where Test cricket could be staged.

The news sent shock waves reverberating around the county. And from then on Yorkshire and Leeds CFAC were locked in a public battle which resulted in Yorkshire saying they had decided to leave Headingley for a new £42m ground of their own, to be built for them by Wakefield Metropolitan District Council on a 140-acre greenfield site just off Junction 39 of the M1 at Durkar.

Yorkshire organised a Press Conference to make this sensational announcement but it turned out to be too premature, chiefly because they had not reckoned on Leeds CFAC's new and determined chairman, Paul Caddick, demanding compensation if they broke their lease – which still had 84 of its 99 years to run. They also hit trouble in the shape of a Public Inquiry into the plan, ordered in February, 1998, by John Prescott, Secretary of State for Environment, Transport and Regions, to look into building in the green belt and access for public transport.

By this time, however, Wakefield Council were saying that the scheme had further been held up through Yorkshire entering into new discussions with Caddick over the development of Headingley. All energy seemed to drain away from the proposed move, which had been announced with such drive, and in September the plan was virtually ditched by Wakefield, who blamed its collapse on the prolonged Headingley talks.

The breakdown was a bitter disappointment for Sir Lawrence and Hassell, who had both sold the scheme so enthusiastically to the club's general committee and a majority of the membership, but not all were in favour by any means and the Headingley is Home action group sprang up and attracted considerable support.

Before their formation, however, it looked for a while as if nothing could stop Yorkshire's move and the wish to leave Headingley grew even stronger in March, 1996, with the Sports Council's decision to defer National Lottery funding for ground developments by three other county clubs.

Several sites around the Leeds area were considered but it was Wakefield Council which came up with the first concrete offer of providing at Durkar Yorkshire's first ground of their own in 133 years.

The scheme was on an immense scale and included a railway station, parking for 1,400 cars, hotels, business park and a riverside restaurant as well as state-of-the-art cricket facilities. Yorkshire members were provided by the council with a comprehensive document of the plan at their annual meeting in Sheffield and Sir Lawrence made an impassioned speech in favour of its implementation which received excited approval.

Leeds CFAC's immediate response was to say that Yorkshire could buy the cricket ground for £6m but Sir Lawrence said he had been advised it was worth well below that amount and he re-iterated that they wanted to move to a ground with facilities for community use in keeping with the club's cricket heritage.

In October, Yorkshire confirmed the move to Durkar and pledged to make their home into the world's best stadium but then Caddick personally entered the debate for the first time, saying he did not think the plan was "a goer" and urging cricket fans to put pressure on Sir Lawrence to reconsider.

The call was heard by the newly-formed Headingley is Home action group who arranged a meeting of Yorkshire members on November 14 to debate the issue. On a show of hands all but about four of the 350-strong audience voted for the move to be put on ice until members had been given the chance to vote on it and Yorkshire gave an assurance that it would not be steamrollered through.

Although still adamant they would move to Wakefield, Yorkshire were pressured into opening up new talks with Caddick, but come January, 1997, they remained as keen as ever to quit Headingley and were further encouraged by Wakefield Council leader Colin Croxall who said the authority had no intention of going back on their word and would soon be applying for National Lottery funding.

Boycott and Trueman both strongly backed the Wakefield plan but Close revealed at a meeting of Bradford members that he was against it, saying that the ground would quickly become a white elephant.

Caddick came out with a fresh plea and gave details of a plan for a £30m redevelopment at Headingley, at the same time warning that if Yorkshire broke the terms of the lease he would claim compensation of several millions of pounds.

Still the debate raged on and opposition increased on another front as members aired their displeasure at the loss of the outgrounds. At the annual meeting in Leeds Town Hall, a resolution to retain the outgrounds received 47 per cent of the poll but, in another vote, 75 per cent were in favour of Durkar.

Despite this vote of confidence, other factors began to go against Yorkshire and soon after the start of the 1997 season it was reported that Wakefield Council were not expected to submit their application for £20m of lottery cash until Yorkshire had secured an agreement at Headingley over breaking the terms of their lease. The project was now budgeted at £42m and the hope remained that the money would be received by October with Yorkshire still optimistic they would be in their new headquarters by 2000.

The talks with Caddick dragged on throughout the summer, with little if any headway being made and the row escalated on September 9 when Leeds CFAC issued writs against Yorkshire and Wakefield Council for £17m in damages because of the proposed move.

Hassell hit back by saying Yorkshire would "vigorously defend" any court action but it was becoming increasingly obvious to those following events closely that the battle with Caddick to be freed from the lease was being lost.

There was an unstated acceptance that a deal over Yorkshire staying at Headingley would have to be done and in order to make this easier Sir Lawrence and Caddick both stepped away from the negotiating table.

An uneasy peace settled on the two parties and Wakefield was gradually pushed on to the back burner. With Yorkshire reluctantly staying put, yet still as keen as ever to own their home ground, talks with Leeds CFAC rumbled on but there was a long way to go before Yorkshire would be in charge of their own destiny at Headingley.

Their determination to centralise operations also led Yorkshire, in July, 1996, deciding to switch the Academy from Park Avenue to Headingley the following year, the belief being that it would be based at Durkar from 2000. Crumbling facilities at Bradford and increasing problems with vandalism also made the transfer inevitable but it still came as a double blow to the Friends of Park Avenue who had already seen Yorkshire play their last match on the ground.

CHAPTER FORTY-TWO

SEMI-FINAL BLUES

Headingley's fate and that of the satellite grounds may have occupied the minds of the top officials in 1996 but these issues were of little immediate concern to the team, who gave their all for new captain Byas and new cricket chairman Platt.

They won nothing in the end – apart from two trophies at Scarborough -but they could so easily have won everything if the rub of the green had gone for them a little more often.

In the Championship they competed strongly to finish sixth, 48 points behind title-holders Leicestershire, and it was three consecutive defeats in the second half of the season that robbed them of a 15-point lead at the top of the table.

Similarly, in the AXA Equity and Law Sunday League they often dominated events, showing sufficient power to rattle up eight wins in nine matches, but a couple of narrow defeats – by five runs to Warwickshire and two runs to Somerset – left them in third place, just six points behind champions Surrey.

Even greater success beckoned in the two knockout competitions but having reached the semi-finals of both the Benson and Hedges Cup and the NatWest Trophy they were twice mortified to be denied trips to Lord's by Lancashire at Old Trafford.

It reflected great credit on Byas's mental toughness that he managed to hold his side together after both matches had been plucked from their grasp and a lesser captain may well have wilted under the strain.

The B&H semi-final was first up and two days of high drama led to one of the most pulsating finishes of all time, Lancashire winning by one wicket off the last ball of an incredible contest. Never have I seen a Yorkshire side looked more shell-shocked or utterly drained than in the few minutes after this epic confrontation ended.

Yorkshire decided at the last minute to include senior professional Moxon, who had just reported fit after being out for a month with a broken thumb, but heavy rain meant he and Byas had to hang around until 4.30pm before they could open the innings. It was a bad toss for Byas to lose because the forecast was for an improvement in the weather on the following day.

Only Bevan of the top-order batsmen really settled and at 83-5 Yorkshire were in big trouble but Blakey then entered to play a marvellous innings alongside the Australian and they took the score to 198-5 in 48 overs by the close.

Next morning they continued where they left off but with even greater urgency, piling up a further 51 off the four remaining overs to advance their stand to 167, a competition record for the sixth wicket, Bevan making 95 and Blakey 80.

A score of 250-5 left Yorkshire thinking they could now win the match, a belief which was strengthened as Lancashire slumped to 97-5. Fairbrother rallied the Red Rose with a half-century before becoming the third run-out victim of the innings but at 174-7 with 77 wanted off the last seven overs Yorkshire had more than one foot in the final.

But Warren Hegg, who had made a nervous start in his 64 stand with Fairbrother, suddenly got the bit between his teeth and laced into White with a series of searing strokes over and through extra cover. White appeared to have redeemed the situation by bowling the wicketkeeper for 81 when 11 were wanted off 13 balls.

Gary Yates had played an active part in his eighth-wicket stand of 66 with Hegg but three runs later he was run out, leaving last man Peter Martin to enter the cauldron. Eight were wanted off the last over, which began with Glen Chapple smacking White for a boundary, and a wide and a single meant there were three balls off which to score two runs. Martin twice failed to make contact but squeezed the last delivery down to third man. He knew he had to go for two, come hell or high water, and he was just into his crease as Vaughan's throw reached Blakey.

One could not begrudge Lancashire their victory or going on to beat Northamptonshire in the final but the thought of another semi-final Roses defeat just two months later was more than any Yorkshire stomach could take.

Once bitten, twice shy, maybe, but Yorkshire were again badly stung by Lancashire although this time there was none of the stunned disbelief that followed their last-ball exit in the Benson and Hedges Cup. The margin of 19 runs may have appeared slender on paper but in truth Lancashire controlled the game, apart from when Bevan was working his way steadily to 85 before becoming one of three victims in nine balls for Gold Award winner Ian Austin, who tore out the middle order.

Bevan then said a dramatic farewell to Yorkshire in James Bond style, racing to a waiting helicopter which whizzed him to Heathrow for the night flight to Brisbane ahead of joining up with Australia for a triangular knockout tournament. Lancashire were too occupied with their own thoughts to pay much attention. All that mattered to them was that they had conquered Yorkshire again and were off to Lord's to gather up more silverware.

Despite having to leave Yorkshire with over a month of the season still remaining, Bevan had again given splendid service in what turned out to be his second and final year. He rarely put a foot wrong in limited overs cricket and in a dozen Championship matches he piled up 1,225 runs, with three centuries and eight half-centuries, for an average of 64.47. Hard to believe that an even greater Aussie run-scorer would follow in his tracks to Headingley.

Vaughan was the only other batsman to make it to the 1,000 mark but the runs still flowed because Yorkshire had nine centurions in all, with Peter Hartley also chipping in with unbeaten scores of 88 and 89. Of the other regulars, only Silverwood and Stemp were not ton-up men.

One of the centuries came from Sheffield-born Richard Kettleborough, who had made his first team debut two years back, and it was to rank as one of the finest in its context in Yorkshire's history.

It was the end of August and whereas Yorkshire's form had slipped back, Essex on their visit to Headingley were going great guns and were serious Championship contenders. With Paul Grayson now in their side and opening the batting with Graham Gooch they enjoyed a first innings lead of 82 and looked set for an easy win as Yorkshire folded to 91-5.

But they had reckoned without the courageous spirit of Kettleborough who dug in deep to complete his maiden century, his doughty 108 chiselled out of five hours and 20 minutes of crease occupation.

Hamilton celebrated his belated return to the side with a career-best 61 and the innings was stretched to 329 which left Essex to make 248. But they were demoralised by the unexpected turn of events and no match for the guile of Stemp who grabbed 5-38 to bowl them out for 149.

Byas said of Kettleborough: "It was a brilliant contribution to the team effort and words cannot adequately convey how good an innings it was. I have no doubt at all that it was the best rearguard action I have seen during my time in the Yorkshire side."

Kettleborough came from a fine sporting family – his uncle Keith played soccer for Sheffield United and four other Football League clubs – and it was regrettable that he was given relatively few further chances by Yorkshire to secure a regular place in the side. He moved to Middlesex in 1998 for a couple of seasons but failed to make any real impact opening the batting. Taking up umpiring, his calm authority saw him rise to the very top and in 2011 he joined the ICC elite panel of umpires.

Turning the tables on Essex came late in the summer but the Championship season had also got off to a memorable start with a 43-run win over Glamorgan at Cardiff after Moxon and Vaughan had set the ball rolling with an opening stand of 362, the fourth highest partnership for the county. Moxon made 213 and Vaughan 183 but the Welshmen hit back with a double century and a century of their own, Hugh Morris scoring an unbeaten 202 and Matthew Maynard 136, their third wicket stand being worth 228.

Yorkshire did well enough throughout 1996 to suggest that the committee had got it right before the start of the season when they ditched plans to sign a manager-coach.

Sir Lawrence had Australia's former captain Allan Border very much in mind when the post was advertised but he did not apply. There were 14 who did, including five former Yorkshire captains in Close, Hampshire, Old, Bairstow and Carrick, plus ex-Test players in Nick Cook (Leicestershire and Northants) and Bob Cottam (Hampshire and Northants). None of them, however, seemed to fit the bill exactly and in the end it was decided not to go ahead and so save at least £30,000 a year which such an appointment would have cost.

One person who was settling in well at Headingley while the manager-coach venture was being debated was new groundsman Andy Fogarty, who had arrived from Old Trafford towards the end of the 1995 season.

Fogarty had learned his trade at Lancashire under head groundsman Peter Marron and he replaced the loyal and hard-working Keith Boyce, who was to look after the rugby ground on a full-time basis.

Yorkshire have not been in the habit of making "signings" from the other side of the Pennines but their judgment on this occasion could not be faulted. From then until now, Fogarty has done a brilliant job in his quiet, unassuming manner and, aided by improved equipment and a new draining system, he gets matches underway almost as soon as the rain stops falling.

Also settling in at Headingley in 1996 was the new marketing director, Mark Newton. He was appointed upon the departure of the popular marketing manager,

Dorothy Betts, who had taken up a post with a Sheffield advertising agency. Newton did much to sharpen up Yorkshire's image and was particularly conscious of the need to attract a younger audience to the Sunday League scene with its coloured clothing and various side attractions.

Silverwood's rapid rise to prominence and the awarding of his cap resulted in the release of Robinson, who had not made a senior appearance in 1996, but he left with a creditable record of 218 first-class wickets from 90 games and was quick to revitalise his career at Sussex, where he could do no wrong.

No senior Yorkshire bowler could rest easily at around this time because of the conveyor belt of young pacemen which Oldham was chiefly responsible for producing and Silverwood's rise had been so swift that he was included in the England party for Zimbabwe and New Zealand along with Gough.

As plans began to take shape for the 1997 season it was confirmed in January that Yorkshire wanted Bevan back for a third year but there was justifiable concern that his rising status back home would lead to him being named in the Ashes party to tour England in the summer.

Platt said in view of that possibility six other players from the southern hemisphere were being monitored just in case and at the club's annual meeting on March 8 members were somewhat surprised to hear that Yorkshire had pre-empted the situation by signing Australian opener Michael Slater.

Yorkshire were proved right about Bevan but embarrassingly wrong about Slater who was also named in Australia's Ashes squad. The cricket committee had thought he was on the Test scrapheap after being snubbed and not included on the tour to South Africa but the Aussie selectors underwent a late change of mind.

So sure were Yorkshire that Slater would be with them that Slater mugs and other items bearing his features were soon on display in the club shop in readiness for the new season.

Full credit to the club, though, for springing into action once they knew for sure that Slater would not be joining them. Their earlier contingency plans had included the name of Darren Lehmann and within a few days this largely unknown figure was on his way over.

He did not remain unknown for long because he took Yorkshire by storm and continued to do so in the five seasons over the next six years that he was with them, only missing out through unavailability in 1999 when fellow countryman Greg Blewett replaced him.

Circumstances conspired against him in his first few days with Yorkshire but the fans need not have worried in the slightest about minor hiccups upsetting him. He was due to meet up with his new colleagues at Oxford on April 25, the last day of his team's match against Oxford University, but he first had to endure a gruelling stop-start drive to the destination with coach Doug Padgett because the motorway network had been paralysed by the IRA and Padgett had no option but to choose a much slower route.

The journey was a wasted one because rain washed out the chance of any play and the weather continued to be so abysmal that Lehmann had still not picked up a bat by the following Monday when he was due to play in the Benson and Hedges Roses match at Old Trafford.

The truth was that he had been out of action since early March, when he broke his left thumb while playing in South Australia's last domestic match of the season, and Byas wisely decided to leave him out of the Lancashire match and give him a little more time to prepare. He was replaced by Parker who had been in phenomenal form, plundering 259 runs for once out in Yorkshire's two first-class curtain-raising friendlies, and Byas's decision was vindicated because he was able to lead them to a comfortable win.

Lehmann's debut was also disappointingly low key. In the next B&H zonal match he scored only nine before being bowled by Gold Award winner Phil Newport, whose four wickets saw Worcestershire home by 12 runs, but from then on it was plain sailing all the way.

He was soon endearing himself to fans whenever they saw him, whether at home or away. Inside his first month in a Yorkshire sweater he had tamed Warwickshire's previously unmanageable South African Allan Donald in the B&H Cup, lashing him for two fours and carving him for six over third man on his way to 67 off 65 balls, and he had compiled a glorious maiden Championship century at Taunton before steaming on to 177 – two match-winning innings that were just a taste of what was to come.

But the season as a whole only served to remind Yorkshire once again that a genius at work is no guarantee of success, even when well supported by other great individual players. In fact, come September and the club were forced to concede that the team had gone back a step rather than forward.

After staking a claim in the Championship race for much of the time they could only hold on to sixth spot again, while the two knockout competitions saw them disappear in the quarter-finals rather than the semis and they dived from third to tenth in the AXA Sunday League.

They should have cantered into the last four of the NatWest Trophy as a result of a superlative century from Lehmann on a soft pitch and outfield at Cardiff. He teased the Glamorgan bowlers, Waqar Younis included, with delicate back foot cuts and sweeps, but the Pakistan paceman still claimed the Gold Award – for his batting rather than his bowling. Coming in at 174-6 in the chase for 238, he should have been out before scoring but was badly dropped at mid-off by Vaughan. Two wickets fell at the other end but Waqar and Dean Cosker put on an unbroken 28 for the last wicket to win it with two balls remaining.

There was plenty of competitive cricket in the Championship and no harder fought contest than at Valentine's Park, Ilford, where Yorkshire beat Essex by two wickets. At the close of the third day, Yorkshire needed just six to win with two wickets remaining and the teams had to sweat it out on Sunday before the game resumed. There were no late scares and Yorkshire were on their way home with 23 points in the bag after five minutes.

Byas said the game was the best he had ever played in and he considered Vaughan's 161 so good that he felt he could not be far away from a Test place. By now, there was no doubt at all that he oozed class and had an exceptional temperament and 'feel' for the game but obstacles still lay ahead. In the next match, against Gloucestershire at Headingley, he broke a bone in his left wrist when a ball lifted sharply off a length from Dewsbury-born Mike Smith and was sidelined for seven weeks.

Upon his return, Vaughan scored his maiden Roses century at Old Trafford and whether it would have contributed to a Yorkshire victory we shall never know. At the close of the third day, Yorkshire were 176-5 with a lead of 318 and Byas was intent on pressing on for a win which would have enhanced their title chances.

But he was whipped into a fury upon arriving at the ground on the Saturday morning to discover that heavy rain during the night had flooded on to the pitch at the Warwick Road end because of inadequate covering and had left it a mud heap.

He was first alerted to the problem in a phone call to his hotel from Lancashire groundsman Peter Marron and as soon as he saw the state of the pitch he knew that the abandonment was a mere formality.

A distraught Byas said: "I cannot think of a word strong enough to describe my feelings. I am destroyed, gutted and devastated. If this costs us the Championship at the end of the season I will be very unhappy indeed."

Unarguably the most remarkable performances of the summer belonged to 20-year-old Paul Hutchison, who was vying with Ryan Sidebottom for the left-arm fast bowler's role. Sidebottom gave an excellent account of himself in the one-day match with the President's XI at Scarborough in July by taking 5-27 but when Hutchison's turn came he was simply stunning.

Both players had missed most of the 1996 campaign with stress fractures of the back and Hutchison had still not been fit for the pre-season tour to Anguilla but now he roared in with the greatest sequence ever recorded for the county by a young bowler.

Sprinting in and swinging the ball late, he pole-axed a startled Pakistan A side in the four-day match at Headingley with figures of 11-102 on his debut first-class appearance on home soil, his two other games being well over a year earlier on the pre-season tour of Zimbabwe.

He retained his place for the clash with Hampshire at Portsmouth and celebrated with first innings figures of 7-50, the second best on a Yorkshire Championship debut and surpassed only by the great Wilfred Rhodes, who had 7-24 against Somerset at Bath in 1898. Another five-wicket haul followed against Sussex at Scarborough and he was well on his way to 23 wickets at 16.21 runs apiece from his first four Championship matches.

A continuation of this sort of form would undoubtedly have brought Hutchison an international career at least on a par with that of his friend and rival, Sidebottom, but his spindly frame could not withstand the hammering it took and he was plagued by back problems. An attempt was made to remodel his action but he was never comfortable with it and was more at ease when he reverted to type.

He was still fit enough in 1998 to hold the attack together with 57 Championship wickets at 24.50 and although injuries intervened far more often after that it was very fitting that he should still be around to play a small part in the title-winning triumph of 2001.

By then, Sidebottom had won the duel for the left-armer's slot and Hutchison was released at the end of the season having collected 143 wickets at 22.68, figures which clearly show his value to the side. His heady days with Yorkshire were never repeated at either Sussex or Middlesex but when his county career ended after 2005 he continued to make his mark in league cricket.

Hutchison was not by himself in terrorising batsmen in 1997, Silverwood grabbing 7-37 against Kent at Headingley and then picking up the first five batsmen to fall in the second. His career-best match figures of 12-148 were also the best by a Yorkshire bowler in four years but they were to no avail, the visitors' sixth-wicket pair of Mark Ealham and Matthew Fleming clinging on for the last 48 overs.

Hutchison bowled splendidly without reward while Gough was off the field with a hamstring tear but he was on full throttle earlier in the season in the NatWest Trophy first round tie with Ireland when his 7-27 included a hat-trick and displaced Trueman's 6-14 against Somerset at Taunton in 1965 as Yorkshire's best return in this form of cricket.

The Pakistan A contest in which Hutchison played such a spectacular part also contained a monumental innings of 155 from Moxon and, although nobody realised it at the time, it was almost his swansong. His marathon effort seriously exacerbated his troublesome back and his only innings after that was a duck at Portsmouth before he was forced to rest up.

Towards the end of November, Moxon was appointed director of coaching on a three-year contract. He still had a year left to run on his playing contract but in the March he decided his back was not up to the rigours of constant cricket and announced his retirement from active service.

It had been a busy summer and when Lehmann left for home he said of his first season with Yorkshire: "I have had an absolute ball." He certainly meant it because midway through he expressed his wish to return next year and he signed a new contract on August 20. There were some hard words from Bevan, who felt that Yorkshire had reneged on an agreement to have him back in 1998, but officials had found it hard to pin him down during the Ashes tour to finalise any deal.

The surge of young bowling talent and the need to reduce the size of the playing staff resulted in Platt and the cricket committee deciding to release Hartley who saw out his days at Hampshire and, almost inevitably, gave Yorkshire good cause to realise what they were now missing. His departure angered Byas, who wanted the old stager around in case of injuries, and there were certainly times when he was missed.

Yorkshire also thought they would be missing Sir Lawrence Byford, who made it known in September that he intended to stand down as president and chairman at the 1998 annual meeting because of the pressure of other commitments.

Playwright Sir Alan Ayckbourn, former Labour minister Roy Hattersley, lyricist Sir Tim Rice and the Earl of Harewood were all on a celebrity list of candidates to be considered for the presidency but before any action could be taken Sir Lawrence was persuaded to stay on in the post. His nomination was unanimously approved by the committee but Sidney Fielden had sufficient reservations to resign his seat – which he won back at the first time of asking.

Sir Lawrence did step down as chairman and the most important role in the club was to be taken on by Keith Moss who, as finance chairman, had been able to announce a profit in 1997 of over £100,000. It was a rapid rise to the top for Moss and he would oversee essential improvements to the Headingley facilities before the committee was dissolved and a Board of Directors took over the running of the club.

CHAPTER FORTY-THREE

ON FULL CHARGE

The production line churning out fast bowlers, so expertly overseen by Oldham, was working at full capacity in 1998 and perhaps never before or since have Yorkshire had so many outstanding pace prospects coming through the mill.

Gough, White and Silverwood were past the apprentice stages by now, of course, but learning their trade quickly were Hutchison, Hamilton and young Sidebottom, and the six of them all played an active part in making it Yorkshire's best Championship season in 23 years.

They finished in third place, the highest since coming second in 1975, and had they managed to put a little more substance into the middle part of the season they would have grasped the title.

Yorkshire were successful in their first two matches – the first time they had opened their programme with a home win since 1972 – and they were on such a good roll later on that they flattened the opposition in each of their last five fixtures, the longest sequence of wins since a similar run in 1967.

Hutchison, in his final summer of peak fitness, bowled far more overs than anyone else and just pipped Hamilton in the Championship although the pair of them shared top place in all first-class matches with 59 victims apiece.

But it was the Scot who was really flying in 1998, turning in almost unbelievable performances with both bat and ball. And he combined his talents to the full at Cardiff where he was cheered off the field by Yorkshire fans after taking 5-69 and 5-43 and scoring 79 and 70, the only superior all-round effort in the club's history coming from Hirst in 1906 with 6-70 and 5-45 and scores of 111 and 117 not out against Somerset at Bath.

As Hamilton headed for the dressing room upon completion of the 114-runs win, even the Glamorgan public address operator was sufficiently moved to announce that the player's middle initial of M must stand for Midas because everything he had touched had turned to gold.

Now Hamilton was a hot name in both the England and Scotland camps and although his one England appearance was to end in failure he carved out such an illustrious career with his native country, which he captained with distinction, that in 2012 he was inducted into Scotland's cricketing hall of fame. That his bowling should suddenly and cruelly fall apart was so unfortunate.

Hamilton had placed his credentials on view right at the start of the season with four wickets in six balls on his Benson and Hedges Cup debut against Worcestershire at Headingley when he lifted the Gold Award, but his fellow pacemen never allowed him to hog all the limelight.

Gough, out of action since the previous July with injury, warmed up nicely on Yorkshire's pre-season tour of South Africa by claiming a hat-trick in the floodlight one-dayer against Western Province and promptly said he was fit for an England return. He reiterated this point by pocketing five wickets for two runs in 11 deliveries against Surrey in the AXA League in May and was duly chosen for the Texaco series with South Africa. But in the first Test which followed his right index finger was broken by Donald. Nevertheless, Gough had the last laugh and on his home patch at Headingley he fired out last man Makhaya Ntini, aided by a dubious lbw decision, to clinch the Test series 2-1 for England.

The Barnsley boy's career-best Test figures of 6-42 from 23 hostile overs were richly deserved and hugely appreciated by the fifth day crowd of 10,000 which had been admitted free to discover whether England would take the two wickets or if South Africa could knock off the 34 runs they still required. The thrilling win by 23 runs gave England their first positive result at Headingley since beating Pakistan in 1992 and their first major home series win since taking the Ashes 3-1 in 1985.

Gough loosened up for this memorable encounter by claiming 5-36 in the innings and 160-run victory over Worcestershire at New Road. Hamilton with 4-17 assisted him in routing the home side for 94 but they had earlier been unnerved by Lehmann's first double century for Yorkshire.

The Australian put on 236 with Matthew Wood to set up a new county record against Worcestershire for the third wicket. The young Huddersfield batsman was proving to be the find of the season, making 52 on his Championship debut against Somerset and in the next match scoring a wonderful century off Derbyshire's attack. Both matches were at Headingley and Wood's knocks were much admired by the fans who were quickly charmed by his cheery nature. They were just as delighted when he finished the season with 1,080 first-class runs and they went on to be just as upset when he experienced low points in a career which was full of peaks and troughs.

Sidebottom showed himself to be a chip off the old block by attracting early attention with 3-25 in the AXA League opener with Somerset and 6-40 against Glamorgan, including four wickets in five balls, but Hoggard's Championship debut at Gloucester provided him with an early lesson in the gulf between second team and first-class cricket. Opening the bowling with Hutchison he was on the receiving end of a ferocious blast from Gregor MacMillan and altogether travelled for 69 from 15 overs.

He demonstrated what he was made of by taking three second innings wickets but the bowling performance of the match already belonged to White for his career-best 8-55, which included a hat-trick and was Yorkshire's best analysis in three years. Despite this, and nightwatchman Hutchison batting throughout a morning session, Gloucestershire's far superior team effort gained them a thumping win by 300 runs.

Like Hamilton, Hutchison enjoyed a particularly fine end to the season and the pair received their caps during the match with Essex at Scarborough. They went on to win the match for their side but not in the way that most envisaged.

Hamilton's 6-50 in the first innings and Hoggard's 5-57 in the second left Yorkshire needing only 148 to win but defeat seemed inevitable as they slumped to 81-8. Then the two new caps batted out of their skin in a nerve-tingling ninth-wicket stand of 61 in 21 which tamed the rampant Mark Ilott and Ronnie Irani. Only six were needed when Hutchison fell lbw and the cheers could be heard way out at sea when Hoggard, cool as a cucumber, stroked the winning boundary.

The only batsman to outscore Wood that summer was Vaughan, whose stunning 177 at Riverside oozed class and was the highest individual score yet recorded on the ground. It saved Yorkshire from the possibility of following on and when he was last out the first innings deficit was only 18. Hutchison, Stemp and Sidebottom destroyed Durham for 74 and Vaughan managed an unbeaten 36 before Yorkshire strolled it by nine wickets.

But for the Roses defeat at Headingley, Yorkshire would have gone on to end the season with seven straight wins, yet it was the circumstances behind the drawn match with Nottinghamshire at Scarborough in July which really stuck in Byas's throat.

The North Marine Road crowd had purred with delight over Lehmann's first home century – his previous five had all been away – and Yorkshire may well have beaten both the weather and Nottinghamshire if the waterhog had not broken down at a crucial stage in the mopping-up operations. A replacement machine despatched from Headingley arrived after too much time had been wasted and Byas described the whole episode as "amateurish".

A further bitter disappointment for Byas and the team was yet another semi-final defeat, the fourth they had experienced in four years. They had cruised into the last four of the Benson and Hedges Cup with five wins out of five but were no match for Essex at Headingley, Nasser Hussain top-scoring with a captain's innings of 78 in the visitors' 95 runs success.

There was an enforced retirement late in the season when Dickie Bird, now 66 and of pensionable age, reluctantly had to hang up his white coat.

His last match in charge was Yorkshire's Championship fixture with Warwickshire at Headingley, starting on September 9. A shade ironically, Dickie, never renowned for sending a batsman on his way when his pads were in front, ended the match and his career by shooting up a finger to give Ed Giddins out lbw.

The teams afforded him a guard of honour for his final appearance and he received a portrait of himself painted by artist George Sharp, Kevin's father, and presented to him on behalf of Yorkshire by Sir Lawrence.

"It is exactly 50 years ago that I first came to Headingley as a schoolboy to practise in the Yorkshire nets and it is most appropriate that I should end my career here," he reminisced.

Yorkshire had fought back well in 1998 after the early months of the year had been marked by tragedy. On January 5, cricket had been shocked by the death, at the age of 46, of David Bairstow, who had been found hanged by his wife, Janet, at the family home in Marton-cum-Grafton, North Yorkshire.

Nobody but those closest to him had any idea of the depression which had descended on this most ebullient of sportsmen once his playing days were over and had he lived I feel sure that cricket could once again have become a big part of his life at some future stage.

In the months leading up to his death, David had been an almost lone voice among former Yorkshire cricketers in actively championing the cause of staying put at Headingley and developing the ground. He supported Caddick in his attempt to dissuade Yorkshire from moving to Durkar and once the dust had settled on this affair he may have found himself with a valuable role to fill. Certainly no-one could have brought more passion than he to any task which involved taking Yorkshire into battle.

St Andrew's Church in the picturesque village of Aldborough was packed for his funeral service on a sombre day of drenching rain and there was no more poignant moment than when the ancient arched door to the church slowly opened and the coffin was borne in by six of the men who had shared many of Bairstow's greatest moments of glory – Phil Carrick, John Hampshire, Barrie Leadbeater, Geoff Cope, Arnie Sidebottom and Peter Hartley.

Followed by his widow, Janet, and their two children, Jonathan and Rebecca, and David's son by his first marriage, Andrew, the procession towards the altar was watched closely and sadly by two great captains who both had a big influence on Bairstow's career – Brian Close and Raymond Illingworth.

They turned up in great numbers, too, for Bairstow's memorial service in Ripon Cathedral on February 27 when His Honour Judge Brian Walsh QC, the club's former chairman, gave an eloquent address, and all 400 tickets were sold for a tribute dinner the following Monday at Elland Road, the home of Leeds United.

But before these events could be held, Yorkshire were also mourning the passing of one of their greatest stalwarts and most faithful supporters in John Featherstone, the founding editor in 1983 of the club's White Rose magazine.

As this history has already recorded, Featherstone became a familiar figure in the Reform Group but this was only a passing phase in his close association with the cricket side of Headingley. For a time he was an administration officer with the Women's Cricket Association and after that he did various invaluable jobs for Yorkshire while operating from a temporary unit at the cricket ground.

Among other voluntary duties, he drove the Academy minibus on match days, acted as the club's photographer and took on the role of public address announcer. As a gesture of thanks, Yorkshire took him on their 1995 pre-season tour to Cape Town where he was in his element snapping the players in their unfamiliar surroundings.

At around this time, I had left the staff of the Telegraph and Argus and was continuing to cover the cricket for them home and away on a freelance basis. I also took on for a couple of years the role of Yorkshire liaison officer and was assisting Featherstone in developing the White Rose magazine when he so unexpectedly died in Dover, where he had gone to follow the fortunes of his other great sporting passion, Halifax Town.

James Greenfield took over the editorship of the magazine with great enthusiasm and he also continued as production editor of the Yorkshire Yearbook when I succeeded Derek Hodgson as editor in 2009.

Featherstone's untimely death further resulted in retired languages teacher and lecturer Tony Loffill taking over as public address announcer for Yorkshire matches at Headingley and Scarborough, and he played no small part in the general camaraderie of the media centre when it was based in the grandstand at headquarters.

The two deaths inevitably brought a feeling of sadness to the start of 1998 but on a more cheerful note, Yorkshire Tea were unveiled in a three-year deal as the club's main sponsors after Tetley's brewery's 11-year association drew to a close.

In some years, Tetley's had ploughed in around £100,000 and that was the amount which finance chairman Keith Moss had warned would be the increase in the players' wages bill that season, despite seven having been released.

The committee elections in March, 2008, saw Close's committee days come to an end. He was beaten by Vann, who a couple of years earlier had been ousted by David Storr. In 2009, Storr himself was unseated by Cope, the ex-off-spinner going straight on to the cricket committee and later playing a crucial role when the Management Board came into existence. Fielden, standing again following his earlier resignation, came out on top against Stuart Anderson.

Yorkshire's inaugural day-night match at Headingley had been held in August, 1998, in front of an ecstatic 10,000 crowd who roared their delight when Gough achieved the hat-trick against Lancashire. They so enjoyed the occasion that even when Chapple skittled Yorkshire for 81, with figures of 6-25 to complete a comprehensive Red Rose victory in the AXA League fixture, they still went home happy enough.

If it seemed the fans were willing to embrace coloured clothing cricket, floodlights and all the other razzmatazz features of the modern one-day game, they were shown to be far more reluctant to support plans for the team to become known as Yorkshire Phoenix in the National League from the start of the 1999 season.

Marketing director Mark Newton had to withstand so much flak when he gave details of Yorkshire's new identity at the annual meeting that Sir Lawrence promised the committee would review their decision. They stuck with it – and the new range of orange coloured clothing – and the fuss quickly subsided, although few tears were shed when Phoenix eventually failed to return from the ashes and the team became known as Carnegie.

Yorkshire's well-documented failures to so far make it through to a Lord's Cup showdown under Byas melted away in 1999 when they reached the one and only final of the much-maligned Benson and Hedges Super Cup but their joy was short-lived because they were crushed by 124 runs with ten overs remaining by Gloucestershire – on Yorkshire Day of all days!

The Glorious Glosters were not so glorious in Yorkshire's eyes that summer because they dished out three morale-sapping defeats which were all the harder to bear because the West Country side finished up as Championship wooden spoonists and were generally considered an inferior side to the White Rose.

A fortnight after the B&H battle, Gloucestershire had, by the skin of their teeth, beaten Yorkshire in the semi-final of the NatWest Trophy and earlier on they had whipped them by 128 runs at Cheltenham at a time when the visitors were top of Division One of the CGU National League. This reverse affected Yorkshire so badly that it signalled the start of a run of seven consecutive defeats and a slide to an eventual fifth place in the table – hardly a position they expected after opening up with five consecutive wins.

Yorkshire had qualified for the new B&H Super Cup by virtue of finishing in the top eight of the Championship the previous season and although some were of the opinion that to get to Lord's on the strength of only two wins was no great shakes, Byas rightly pointed out that they had had to compete strongly throughout

1998 even to make it to the starting line.

Hampshire and Warwickshire were despatched with ease on the way to the final but Gloucestershire never allowed them a sniff, captain Mark Alleyne's dashing 112 earning him the Gold Award and ensuring his side a 50-overs score of 291 which was way beyond Yorkshire's reach.

The Super Cup format was heavily criticised but this did not lessen Yorkshire's disappointment at not becoming its only winners, the Benson and Hedges Cup reverting to its more familiar guise in 2000.

Up to the Lord's debacle, Yorkshire were still in with a shout on all four fronts and spirits were never higher than when they saw off Lancashire by 55 runs at Old Trafford in the quarter-finals of the NatWest Trophy. Their unlikely hero in this home World Cup summer was Lehmann's replacement Greg Blewett, who generally made little impact with the bat, apart from one occasion in the Championship.

At Old Trafford, he was suddenly called upon to bowl his medium pacers at a time when Lancashire looked on top of the task of making the required 264 and his introduction proved to be an inspired move by Byas. His first delivery clean bowled Mike Atherton for a cultured 61 and in the same over he pinned Andy Flintoff lbw. He went on to snatch 4-18 in 5.4 overs as Lancashire panicked but he was somewhat cruelly denied the man-of-the-match award which went to White for his 43 and economic figures of 2-24.

Yorkshire got so near at Bristol but in the end lost by six runs. After Kim Barnett's 98 had enabled Gloucestershire to reach a respectable 240-7, Vaughan made a laboured 54 but Byas kept plugging away and a furious late assault from Gary Fellows in the penultimate over brought him 19 of the 20 runs which Michael Cawdron conceded.

Australian all-rounder Ian Harvey, who would become a familiar figure at Headingley, bowled the last over with 12 wanted. Byas ran two off the second and crashed the third into the stumps at the other end to deny himself a boundary, the second time that this misfortune had happened to him in his innings. He only managed a single and Fellows was bowled aiming to cover for a rousing 27 off 15 deliveries.

It was a splendid first full season for Halifax-born Fellows, who was a capable all-rounder and a fielder right out of the top drawer. He was particularly useful in one-day matches and a good team member but when Yorkshire released him at the end of 2003 they had not got out of him all that they should.

A momentous milestone was reached at Trent Bridge on August 26 when Yorkshire, thanks to a late blast from Silverwood, beat Nottinghamshire by three wickets to record their 1,000th Championship win since 1900.

Yorkshire had been one of the first counties to push for a two-divisional Championship and the ECB introduced it in 2000, meaning that it was imperative for them to gain a place in the top flight by finishing in the upper half of the table in 1999.

The consistency of their play meant they were always likely to achieve their ambition and they were optimistic about securing second place to runaway leaders Surrey after Vaughan had celebrated his inclusion on England's tour of South Africa by batting all day for 123 against Kent at Scarborough and going on to reach 153, Yorkshire winning by five wickets after a further 50 from the future England captain.

But they were deflated in their penultimate match by Glamorgan, who beat them by an innings and 52 runs at Headingley after a mammoth 186 from captain Matthew Maynard, and they rounded off with a draw against Surrey to settle for sixth place and the first time in their history that no batsman had made it to 1000 runs.

Although Vaughan, by his own admission, had performed only moderately for much of the season, he did star in a remarkable game at Chelmsford where both he (100 and 151) and Stuart Law (159 and 113) scored centuries in each innings, the only instance of this happening in a Yorkshire match. A Yorkshire win was made possible on the final day by left-arm spinner Ian Fisher, who destroyed Essex with his career-best figures of 5-73 for the county.

The decision not to re-engage Stemp that year resulted in greater opportunities for Fisher while the development in the second team of off-spinning all-rounder James Middlebrook, son of Ralph, and Richard Dawson, suggested Yorkshire were not short of slow bowling prospects.

Dawson advanced so effectively that he quickly elevated to England status and also received his Yorkshire cap before going into a sad decline. Middlebrook and Fisher were to move on to Essex and Gloucestershire respectively and one was again left to feel that Yorkshire had not got sufficient out of a long line of spinners going back several years.

Joining Yorkshire with Blewett that summer was Somerset batsman Richard Harden and neither of them set the scene alight. Harden, 33, had invariably done well against Yorkshire over the years, enjoying a Championship average of 51.46, but he was unable to provide the same service in return, injury and fading form taking their toll.

Blewett just had one of those bad seasons which every cricketer, no matter how talented, has to endure, but at least his class flared brilliant bright against Northamptonshire at North Marine Road when he plundered 98 and 190, almost 300 of his 655 runs, therefore, coming in one of his 12 matches. The Northants game was also a special one for McGrath, who received his county cap and was by now well on the way to a long and distinguished career which still had its ups and downs.

It had been something of a surprise in 1998 when Peter Hartley had made little impact for Hampshire against his old team-mates but he made up for it now upon Yorkshire's visit to Basingstoke, bowling with all his old fire to claim 8-65 and match figures of 11-117. Chasing 139, Yorkshire would have struggled to get there if Byas had not resisted stoically with a rugged 95 but Hartley still denied his former skipper a century by trapping him lbw.

England's early exit from the World Cup left Gough available sooner than Yorkshire expected but he was badly hit by injuries and only just shook off his calf strain in time to make his country's tour of South Africa and Zimbabwe along with Vaughan and Hamilton and later Silverwood and White.

The tour was the making of Vaughan as an England player but the end for

Hamilton – Scotland's hero months earlier in the World Cup – who had a miserable time in his only Test. Silverwood, coming out as cover for the injured Dean Headley, excelled at Cape Town with his best Test figures of 5-91, and White, joining the party for Zimbabwe, turned in what were then England's third-best one-day figures of 5-21 at Bulawayo.

At the other end of the scale, Yorkshire's Academy had switched from vandal-hit Park Avenue to Headingley in 1999 and they were given a helping hand by Bradford City chairman Geoffrey Richmond, who was also chairman of New Rover CC on the Leeds ring road at Adel.

Richmond had bought a farmer's cornfield, which he had developed into New Rover's new ground, and he readily agreed to Moxon's request for the Academy to play midweek fixtures at the venue which was now lovingly cared for by Keith Boyce, whose groundsman's house was situated there.

Park Avenue was thrown a lifeline, however, with the news that Bradford-Leeds Universities were to become one of the six ECB Centres of Cricketing Excellence which would begin operating in 2001. Leeds-Bradford used it as their headquarters for a few years before moving to Weetwood and Kevin Sharp became their first director of cricket.

Almost half a century of continuous professional service to Yorkshire drew to a close at the end of 1999 with the retirement of coach Doug Padgett, who way back in 1951 had become the club's youngest debutant at 16 years and 321 days. His first match was against Somerset at Taunton, and he received his first delivery from former Yorkshire off-spinner, Ellis Robinson. Yorkshire blood was not quite thick enough for Robinson to allow the youngster a single to get off the mark and Padgett would have thought him soft if he had.

Bradford has never had a more loyal son than Padgett, who was born in the city's St Luke's Hospital and has always lived within the district's boundaries. Yorkshire cricket was his profession but Bradford City was where he could let his guard down and become, purely and simply, a true fan.

CHAPTER FORTY-FOUR

THE MILLENNIUM

Part One Challenging

Yorkshire entered the Millennium safe in the knowledge that they had secured their place in the top flight of the newly constructed Championship as well as staying in Division One of the Norwich Union National League.

They would dearly have loved to open the 21st century in exactly the same style as they did the 20th, by winning the Championship, and they might well have succeeded but for handing over more than a third of their regular team to the England Test side and also seeing three of them gain central contracts which reduced their county appearances still further.

In the circumstances they did well to maintain an effective challenge all season and they ended a creditable third but Yorkshire were still left seething with anger at the events which cost them second place and robbed them of £50,000 in prize money.

Championship leaders Surrey were already looking set fair to retain the title when they came to Scarborough on August 30 but Yorkshire were only 18 points behind the Brownhats and a home victory would have stirred things up.

Byas returned to lead the side after a month out with a knee injury and he had no hesitation in asking Surrey to bat first on an emerald green pitch which had obviously been prepared to suit Yorkshire's pace attack.

Surrey did well to recover from 197-7 to 356 all out and after pitch liaison officer Mike Denness had watched the first day's play he called in colleague Alan Fordham, ECB Cricket Operations Manager, and ECB Pitches Consultant Chris Wood.

Yorkshire, rightly or wrongly, felt that they had been set up and that Surrey had tipped off the pitch inspectors in advance and their mood was not lightened by being bowled out for 158 in easing conditions. Surrey, rather too cockily, did not enforce the follow-on, despite leading by 198, and their decision backfired when long stoppages for rain on the third and fourth days worked to their disadvantage.

Relations between the two sides came under even greater strain during the match when it was revealed that Yorkshire would have eight points docked because it was felt that too much grass had been left on the pitch, causing undue seam movement and unevenness of bounce on the first day. Moxon was particularly incensed by events and Yorkshire chose to have their meals served in the privacy of their dressing room rather than joining Surrey in the restaurant area.

By taking only seven points out of the draw, Yorkshire were one point worse off than before the start of the match and to add insult to injury they finished the season five points behind Lancashire, who took second place and picked up the

£50,000 which would have gone to Yorkshire but for the pitch inspectors' intervention.

Yorkshire's quick decision not to appeal suggested they knew they were technically in the wrong, even though they gained no benefit from their actions and there was little lateral movement.

As a consequence of what happened, the offending pitch and another one were dug up and replaced, the first work of this kind at North Marine Road since 1872, and it was planned to replace the remaining 11 pitches later on.

A big disappointment entirely of Yorkshire's own making came in their final National League match under the Canterbury lights when victory over Kent would have given them their sixth win in a row and clinched the title. Sadly, they fell apart and lost by 64 runs to finish two points adrift of one-day specialists Gloucestershire Gladiators.

A below-par performance also surfaced when least needed against Northamptonshire at Wantage Road in the NatWest Trophy but their exit from the Benson and Hedges Cup was the consequence of a much more thrilling affair against Surrey at Headingley, which they lost by seven runs with one ball remaining, Alec Stewart surviving an early lethal blast from Hoggard to make an unbeaten 97 and leave his bowlers confident they could defend a modest score of 198-6. They did not let him down, despite half-centuries from Lehmann and Wood.

Lehmann once again dominated the batting and was head and shoulders above the rest, rapping out 1,477 Championship runs at an average of 67.13, with four centuries and nine 50s, and picking up the Walter Lawrence Trophy for the fastest century of the season – off 89 balls – against Kent at Canterbury. His nearest rival was the best young English batting prospect, Vaughan, who had 697 runs from only nine outings, but the gap between first and second clearly indicated the lack of solid support for the Australian.

The same applied on the bowling front to Hoggard who was rapidly making a name for himself. He led the field with 46 Championship wickets at 26.43 apiece while in the National League he topped the list with 37 wickets, a club record which still stands.

This achievement made nonsense of the theory which later took hold with England that Hoggard was not a great performer in one-day cricket but perhaps he partly contributed to this belief by sometimes giving the impression that he was not too concerned whether he played or didn't.

Not only did Yorkshire feel the strain of losing key players to England but they were hit with an unprecedented number of injuries which led to ten youngsters making their first team debuts during the season.

Among the first on the casualty list was Vaughan in the opening Championship match of the season. He had made 155 against Derbyshire with an elegance and freedom which would have delighted England coach Duncan Fletcher ahead of the first Test with Zimbabwe, but then had a bone broken in the back of his left hand by a bouncer from Matthew Cassar and was sidelined for five weeks.

The consolation for Yorkshire was they won this curtain-raiser by an innings and 79 runs and in the next match, also at Headingley, they were even stronger, beating Hampshire by an innings and 100 runs. There was plenty in this match for the home fans to revel in, not least Hamilton's maiden century and the sight of Shane Warne bagging a pair – his second in consecutive matches! In the first innings he was bamboozled and bowled by Middlebrook who was making his first Championship appearance in two years.

Middlebrook had the temperament of a first-class cricketer right from the start and looked a solid performer with both bat and ball. He only played in nine Championship matches but his 27 wickets placed him second to Hoggard and gave him the edge over his left-arm colleague, Fisher.

The young off-spinner also achieved the rare distinction of outbowling Warne in the final fixture to be staged at Hampshire's Northlands Road ground, Middlebrook enjoying match figures of 10-170 and Yorkshire winning off the very last ball of the season by 72 runs. In an intriguing twist, Hartley was taking his bow for Hampshire and he and another former Yorkshire player, Alex Morris, were the last pair at the wicket and making a desperate attempt to salvage a draw for their adopted side. They seemed to have succeeded until Morris played Fisher into Hamilton's waiting hands.

Hartley's distinguished career then entered a new phase. He gave some specialist bowling coaching the following spring to the newly-formed Bradford-Leeds Universities' Centre of Cricketing Excellence and began to work his way up to the top of the umpiring ladder.

Mirfield-born Gary Ramsden, 17 years old in March, became one of Yorkshire's youngest fast bowlers upon his debut at Derby in May, and later that month another apprentice with a familiar surname showed off his obvious skills on his first-class debut against Zimbabwe.

Michael Lumb, 21, the left-handed son of Richard, was born in South Africa and had represented his country in the Under 19s World Cup before deciding to try and make his way in England. Successful trials with Yorkshire Seconds in 1999 led to him being given a contract but he was ineligible for Championship cricket until 2001.

Lumb's relaxed style and his silky strokeplay were soon on show in the second innings of the Zimbabwe match when he came in at 13-4 and struck 66 off 120 balls with a dozen boundaries before running out of partners.

Also qualifying to play Championship cricket the following season was Lesroy Weekes, the Caribbean-born fast bowler who Oldham had first spotted on Yorkshire's pre-season tour of the Leeward Islands in 1994, and he, too, created plenty of excitement when called up in an emergency for the match against the West Indians. Yorkshire were crushed inside two days but Weekes still emerged with superb figures of 6-56 as the tourists were bowled out for 209 and he was not to blame for his side's weak batting in both innings.

Weekes' figures turned out to be the second best of the season and in the autumn Yorkshire pondered over signing him as a stand-in during Test calls but they were beaten to his signature by Northamptonshire who were looking for a replacement for Devon Malcolm. The West Indian played for them in one first-class and 12 A List matches in 2001 before returning to the leagues.

Two bouts of injury restricted Sidebottom's Championship season to six matches but they were sufficient for him to win his battle for supremacy with

Hutchison and set him on the road towards an international career. The swing bowler went down with a groin injury after the first match and did not return until the Kent game at Headingley in mid-June when he was dynamite. Five wickets in the first innings and six in the second gave him final figures of 11-43 to make him only the 13th bowler in Yorkshire's history to claim that number of wickets for fewer than 50 runs. The feat had been achieved on 17 occasions, Macaulay being the only one to do it three times.

Encouraged by this success, Sidebottom picked up five wickets in the next home game against Durham and then another five at The Oval, leaving him with a total of 22 in four matches as he moved on to Scarborough, where he was due to be capped during the Somerset fixture.

The plan was for Byas to cap both Sidebottom and Hoggard at an appropriate moment but this was scuppered because Sidebottom had to be stretchered off in agony after collapsing with a torn hip muscle while running up to bowl only his fourth over.

Hoggard received his cap in due course and responded with a career-best match return of 8-97, the paceman already having been capped by England when he made his debut against the West Indies in the 100th Test to be staged at Lord's, playing alongside his Yorkshire colleagues Vaughan (only chosen because of a late injury to Nasser Hussain), White and Gough. In a contest befitting the occasion, England squeezed home by two wickets, Gough striking six times.

Vaughan, White and Gough, all put on new ECB six-month contracts in March – Yorkshire receiving total compensation of £150,000 – each went on to play a massive part in the fourth Test at Headingley which dripped drama from the very first ball and was all over in two days, England winning by an innings and 39 runs. White grabbed five wickets and Gough three as the West Indies were dismissed for 172 and Vaughan top-scored with 76 out of England's 272. Gough then completely demoralised the visitors with four quick wickets, leaving Andrew Caddick to clean up with five of his own, the innings folding on 61 in 26.2 overs.

White had already enjoyed a moment of glory for Yorkshire at Headingley when he completed the hat-trick over Kent in the Sunday League by sending back Matthew Fleming, Min Patel and David Masters. But it was a poor summer for Blakey, who was axed at the start of August. His place behind the stumps was taken by the acrobatic Simon Guy who turned in some eye catching performances and looked a fine prospect. He was also a good attacking batsman but without the concentration to build the big innings that were required of him. Nevertheless, he was a valuable player to call upon and it was extremely sad that a brain tumour, successfully operated upon, should bring his first-class career to a halt in 2008 after exemplary service for both the first and second teams.

The new millennium proved eventful for Yorkshire both on and off the field but no sooner had 2000 dawned than Yorkshire were struck by a death just as shocking as that of Bairstow almost exactly two years earlier.

Carrick, who had succeeded his great friend as captain in 1987, had battled with leukaemia in 1999 and it was a fight he seemed to be winning when he came out of hospital in time to drive me down to the Benson and Hedges Super Cup final, where he was summarising for the Test Match Special team.

By now, Carrick was on the first-class umpires reserve list and looking forward greatly to making a career of it. During his trip to Lord's he also took the opportunity to speak to Alan Fordham and impress upon him that he did not intend his illness to get in the way of his ambitions.

Sadly, he was struck down again early in the New Year and died in Airedale General Hospital on January 11, aged 47. He was among the last of those players who showed an avid interest in Yorkshire's history and he also had a great concern for the future as his brave support for opening up the boundaries had shown to his personal cost.

His funeral service was held in a packed Bradford Cathedral and was attended by cricketers past and present from all over the country. England chairman David Graveney was there along with three former Test captains in Gatting, Gooch and Emburey – an indication of the respect in which he was held.

All the surviving members of his 1987 Benson and Hedges Cup-winning side were present and his pall-bearers were Geoff Cope, Barrie Leadbeater, David Byas, Arnie Sidebottom, Steve Rhodes, and Jonathan Smith of the Headingley groundstaff.

Happier times were ahead at the annual meeting in March when Robin Smith took over as club president in place of Sir Lawrence Byford, who had let it be known in the winter that he would be standing down and had received a revolving mahogany bookcase in appreciation of his services at a tribute dinner organised by the committee.

It was the start of a close association with Yorkshire which remains firmly in place up to this day and without Smith's deep involvement the club would not have made the advances it has done over the past decade. As a member of the Gang of Four, of which we will hear more later, he would work tirelessly on getting Yorkshire out of their difficulties and since he first took on the presidency no-one has shown more concern for the members or listened more attentively to their grievances.

But Smith was no actual newcomer to the Yorkshire scene in 2000 for he was a consultant and former senior partner with the law firm of Dibb Lupton Alsop, who had been Yorkshire's legal advisers for a number of years and had grown into one of the largest law firms in the UK.

Smith had worked in a legal capacity for Yorkshire since the early 1980s and one of the reasons why he was nominated for the presidency was because of the expertise he would be able to offer if the club went ahead with a £10m plan for the redevelopment of Headingley.

Hassell, Moss and Smith all appreciated the urgency in redeveloping the decaying headquarters if Headingley were to hold on to its status as a Test match venue and they were acutely aware of the growing threat from Durham's new ground at Riverside.

Yorkshire worked fast enough to arrange for the plans to go before an extraordinary annual meeting on September 20 and fears that they would be strongly opposed did not materialise, 92.7 per cent of the proxy vote being in favour as well as a large majority in the hall.

Work on the new West Stand, formerly the notorious Western Terrace, was able to start in November but a delay in agreeing the final details of the project meant that the building of the new north stand would not commence until after the Ashes Test at Headingley in August, 2001. At least Yorkshire were moving decisively forward but the downside for members and fans as a consequence of this and later work was that the ground would resemble a building site for the next seven or eight years.

Just as Yorkshire had been shaken at the start of 2000 by the death of Bairstow, so they found themselves in mourning again in November with the passing of Brian Walsh QC at the age of 65. Although one of the country's top criminal silks, leader of the North Eastern Circuit, and, until his death, Recorder of Leeds, Walsh always gave unsparingly of his time whenever it was needed by Yorkshire and he was chiefly responsible for bringing harmony to the club during his years as chairman from 1986-1991. It was particularly sad that he should not live to see the team's Championship revival which was just around the corner.

Part Two **Winning**

At 12.13pm on August 24, 2001, Vesuvius metamorphosed to North Marine Road and wave after wave of emotional lava erupted over the ground as Byas held on to the catch that brought Yorkshire their first Championship title in 33 years.

What Rugby Union is to the Welsh and what soccer is to Merseyside and Tyneside, so cricket is to Yorkshire and Byas's catch released a pent-up mass of joy that swiftly spread to all parts of the Broad Acres.

The location for this renaissance of Yorkshire cricket could not have been more perfect. The venue was the cricketing home of Byas, who had scored a century as well as setting his seal on the win, and the seaside resort already had a precedent for saluting its heroes.

In 1959, when Yorkshire had ended a similar famine by securing the title at Hove, the team had arrived in Scarborough in the middle of the night and crowds were lining the darkened roads to give them a rapturous welcome.

Now the fans were just as ecstatic because the rousing victory by an innings and 112 runs over Glamorgan – achieved just before rain set in – not only made sure of the CricInfo Championship and £105,000 in prize-money but did so with two clear rounds to go. It was a knockout well before the final bell.

Yorkshire's brilliant success was not entirely unexpected in view of the positive way in which they had acquitted themselves in 2000 but the twists and turns and some of the personnel involved could never have been imagined at the commencement of the year.

The 12 days of Christmas were still with us when Moxon dropped a bombshell by handing in his resignation as Director of Coaching in order to take over as first team coach at Durham.

The news came like a bolt from the blue and it was a shock to the membership, who had grown extremely fond of Moxon during his 20 eventful years on the staff.

He still had three years of his contract to run but he was reluctantly released from it at a specially convened meeting of the general committee.

"His departure is imminent and he will leave as soon as he has tidied up his desk," said Hassell, the terseness of his remarks adding to the speculation that relations between the pair had become strained in recent months.

Finance was seen to be one of the possible issues. Moxon had become an increasingly important part of the England set-up, travelling to Kenya, Pakistan and Sri Lanka in the autumn as assistant coach to England boss Duncan Fletcher for the one-day internationals, and Hassell may have felt Yorkshire were having to bear too much of the overall costs. Whatever the ins and outs of the situation, Moxon was deeply affected by it and felt he had no option but to move on.

Yorkshire, for once, wasted no time in seeking a replacement and applications came whizzing in from home and abroad. Within a matter of days they had conducted a video-link interview with former Australia Test paceman Wayne Clark and given him the job on a three-year contract. He was also to be put in charge of cricket strategy for all of the club's representative teams.

Clark, the 47-year-old coach of Western Australia, had been strongly recommended by Lehmann and, like their star overseas batsman himself, his was not a name that the Yorkshire fans were widely familiar with from the off.

He had made his debut for Australia against India at Brisbane in 1977, when he claimed four wickets in each innings to establish himself as Jeff Thomson's new-ball partner, and he went on to play in ten Test matches in all, capturing 44 wickets at 28.75 runs apiece. Since taking over as coach of Western Australia five years back, the State side had enjoyed several trophy successes both at first-class and one-day level.

Byas had been unhappy with the events surrounding Moxon's departure but he welcomed the appointment of Clark and the pair were to work extremely well together. In many ways they were not unalike, both of them being unfussy individuals with a quiet manner and a strong belief in hard graft. They rarely clashed – at least not until the title was in the bag – and each let the other get on with things.

As Byas shrewdly observed, Clark came with no baggage and little intimate knowledge of Yorkshire's history. It sounds too much like a soccer cliché, but one of the most important things he did was to convince the players they should stop building up unnecessary pressure over trying to win the Championship and just (I hate to say it) take each game as it came along.

Clark familiarised himself with the team by going on their pre-season tour of South Africa, where McGrath attracted his attention with three centuries while Hamilton, Michael Lumb and budding off-spinner Richard Dawson also caught his eye.

Before the season was under way, another change took place at Headingley which was to have wide-reaching consequences, although these were not apparent at the time. Marketing director Mark Newton left to take over from the retiring Mike Vockins as chief executive of Worcestershire CCC, and he was replaced as commercial director by Tony Panaro, a man with a vast amount of ideas on how to transform Yorkshire into a cash rich club.

Panaro was hailed as a financial saviour and everything he did received wide support from the committee. But Yorkshire allowed themselves to take their eye off the ball to some extent and the time would come when he had to bear the brunt of the criticism for the disastrous failure of the club shop and other marketing ventures. He was certainly a man of big ideas and with closer control some of these may have brought in the cash but he was forced to leave under a cloud when the full scale of Yorkshire's parlous financial situation was finally dragged into the open.

If Clark was an unknown quantity when he joined Yorkshire then even more so was 23-year-old Steven Kirby, who came from nowhere to have a remarkable bearing on the successful Championship challenge.

The greatest asset which Byas had at his command in 2001 was the number of fast bowlers he could call upon but the supply was not inexhaustible and injuries and Test calls tended to have a thinning effect on resources. In the first Test against Pakistan at Lord's, for instance, Vaughan was joined in the side by Gough and Sidebottom while White and Hoggard were both out of contention because of injuries.

Hoggard bowled well enough to take 4-48 on the first day of the Championship match against Kent at Headingley on June 6 but when he was then spirited away to join the England squad Yorkshire were left with a hole to fill.

Without a moment's hesitation they contacted Kirby at his home in Leicester, hurried him over to Headingley and registered him in time for him to replace Hoggard on the second day. There was a good deal of general scepticism about the wisdom of this move and over whether Yorkshire were guilty of a misjudgment but they were vindicated in the second innings when Kirby roared in like an unchained tiger to grab 7-50, including the last five wickets for nine runs in 29 balls.

Kirby thus shared with Hutchison the distinction of turning in the second best bowling figures ever recorded on a Yorkshire Championship debut and it was the manner in which he picked up his wickets which established him from the onset as one of Yorkshire's most eccentric and likeable characters.

His very first ball to David Fulton was an audacious bouncer and after beating the batsman with his next two deliveries he trotted down the pitch to stare his adversary in the face.

The last ball of the over, a maiden, beat Fulton over the stumps and Kirby was dancing around in anguish, his team-mates amused and impressed in equal measure.

Then in his second spell he wrecked the stumps of Rob Key and celebrated with a frenzied jig as he was showered with congratulations. And that is how he continued to amuse and entertain throughout the summer, at the end of which he topped the bowling chart by some distance with 47 wickets at 20.85 runs apiece.

Kirby rapidly endeared himself to the hearts of Yorkshire folk, who even forgave him for being born in Lancashire, and they were only grateful that the fiery redhead was released by Leicestershire the previous season following a back injury.

He had played for Leicestershire Seconds from 1995-99 and upon his release he wrote to Oldham asking for a trial. Oldham was immediately impressed and invited him to winter nets, after which he made two second team appearances, taking 5-24 against Durham Seconds at Middlesbrough for match figures of 8-58.

Kirby was not long in making Leicestershire pay for the error of their ways. In only his third game he collected 6-46 against them in the first innings at Headingley before surpassing this with 6-26 for match figures of 12-72, the best on the ground since Ron Aspinall's 13-100 off Somerset's bowling in 1937 and Yorkshire's best against Leicestershire since Trueman's 12-58 at Bramall Lane in 1961.

The game also brought a maiden century from Lumb and with Wood and Lehmann also contributing tons the margin of victory was by an innings and 227 runs. It was the first time three Yorkshire batsmen had scored a century in the same innings since Michael's dad, Richard, did so along with Boycott and Hampshire at Bristol in 1975, and it was the highpoint of Michael's season because a cartilage operation would soon put him out for the second half of the summer.

Without the coolness of Clark and the heat of Kirby, who bagged 25 wickets in his first four matches at 11.45 runs apiece, Yorkshire may not have marched towards the title with such a sense of purpose in their step but other factors also helped them become the team to be feared.

Lehmann once again was awesome, his 1,416 runs including an unbeaten record 252 against Lancashire at Headingley which he made look ridiculously easy. On practically every occasion – and there were many of them – that Lancashire made a field change in an attempt to staunch the flow of runs, Lehmann would play the ball into where a new gap had appeared. Umpire Jeremy Lloyds told me it had been a privilege to be stationed in the middle for such an innings and he got it about right when he commented: "He seemed to be taking the p*** out of them."

Wood came good after two lean seasons to top 1,000 runs for the first time and receive his cap on the way. He also helped to rub it in against Lancashire, who conceded the double. Soon after Lehmann's epic at Headingley, Wood and White each scored centuries in an opening stand of 309 at Old Trafford, the second highest in Roses cricket but topped the following year by McGrath and Lehmann who posted 317 for the third wicket.

Byas, as well as captaining with a ruthless streak that showed no mercy to opponents, also toughed it out with four centuries; Dawson shot to prominence with 30 wickets and Fellows, in that quiet way of his, was useful in whatever he did. Vaughan's contributions should not go unmentioned because he figured in only seven matches due to England calls and a knee operation but scored 673 runs.

One young man who did not quite make the Championship side that season but was given four outings in the Sunday League was an up-and-coming fast bowler called Tim Bresnan from Pontefract. Unpretentious and efficient, Bresnan would progress step by steady step to become one of England's most hard-working and dependable bowlers, emerging as one of Wisden's Five Cricketers of the Year in the 2012 edition.

In retrospect, it hardly seemed to matter in view of the Championship triumph that Yorkshire did not get beyond the quarter-final stages of the Cheltenham and Gloucester Trophy or that they could finish no higher than sixth in Division One of the Norwich Union League. But it rankled sorely that the Benson and Hedges Cup should see them lose yet another semi-final and that Gloucestershire should once again be the team to outplay them, this time by 97 runs at Headingley.

Throughout much of the season, Byas and Clark worked in great harmony together but a rift opened up at Scarborough almost immediately upon lifting the Championship.

Clark said that with the title in the bag, he had agreed to rest Lehmann for the remaining two matches against Surrey at The Oval and Essex at Scarborough so that he could be re-energised on his return home.

Byas was furious at this decision, which meant him taking a weakened team to London. Surrey were struggling in the table and Byas wanted to help make sure they would be relegated so that the two old rivals would not have to square up to each other next summer.

Surrey made Yorkshire pay for their generosity by beating them by an innings and 46 runs and in the first match of 2002 they thrashed them by an innings and 168 runs at Headingley. Bottom club Essex were the visitors to Scarborough and they diluted the celebrations by winning by 51 runs, Grayson finishing Yorkshire off with 5-20, his first five wicket haul.

Permission for Lehmann to put his feet up did not extend to the Sunday League, however, and two days after the win over Glamorgan he thrilled the North Marine Road crowd with one of the greatest exhibitions of batting ever witnessed in a one-day match, flogging the Nottinghamshire attack for an almost unbelievable 191 out of 352-6 in 45 overs, with 24 fours and 11 sixes. His lavish display set all sorts of new records in the competition and the neighbouring guest houses and hotels were under a constant bombardment from his booming bat.

So ended a season packed with thrills and spills but before September was out another bombshell went off with the totally unexpected announcement from Byas that he was retiring from first-class cricket.

The official reason he gave was that he wanted to go out at the top while memories were still fresh of the fantastic season which he and Yorkshire had just enjoyed. And that now was the time to catch up on his duties back at the family farm.

But it later emerged that Clark had wanted Lehmann to take over the captaincy in 2002, even while Byas was leading his men to the title, and the Yorkshireman understandably felt retirement was preferable to being asked to stand down.

Lehmann had never made any secret of his wish to captain Yorkshire at some stage and with Byas's departure he stepped straight into the job. The reasons given by Byas for his retirement may never have been questioned if he had not agreed the following March to move over the Pennines and play for Lancashire. It is true, however, that he never showed any resentment when he left Yorkshire and, in any case, his absence from Headingley proved only temporary.

Off the field in 2001, Yorkshire officially opened the new West Stand on August 15, the day before the fourth Ashes Test at Headingley, but there was considerable embarrassment for the club leading up to the event.

Former Prime Minister John Major had accepted an invitation to open the stand but then diplomatically turned it down in the face of opposition from some of Yorkshire's ex-England players who felt it inappropriate that the president of Surrey CCC had been chosen for the job.

Yorkshire were forced to embark on a damage limitation exercise by inviting president Robin Smith to perform the task but before the ceremony could take place they were embroiled in another controversy.

Bob Appleyard had queried why Asian women were portrayed in one of the friezes on the new Sir Leonard Hutton Gates at the Kirkstall Lane end of the ground, which were due to be opened by Lady Dorothy Hutton at the same time as the opening of the West Stand.

Appleyard was puzzled because Asian women had not generally attended Headingley to watch Hutton bat but he was outraged when a Press release put out by the Yorkshire office accused him of "racist implications" in his remarks.

An urgently arranged meeting between Appleyard, Smith and Richard Hutton resulted in Yorkshire issuing a full and frank apology to Appleyard.

It said: "The Club deplores the inference, which it acknowledges the Press release contains, that Bob Appleyard's criticism of the design was racially motivated and wishes to apologise unreservedly to him and to his wife and family for the distress which it caused.

"Throughout his career and down to the present day, Bob Appleyard has been an exemplary supporter of Yorkshire cricket and cricket development for youngsters throughout the county, irrespective of race, colour or creed."

England commitments limited Gough to two Championship matches in 2001, his benefit season, and late in the summer Essex chief executive David East played down speculation that England's star bowler was poised to join the club. The move did not happen then, but it did in 2004.

Gough was going through an unhappy period with Yorkshire at the time and not everyone wanted him to stay, including Trueman, but he was urged to do so by new captain Lehmann, who assured him in a message from Australia that he would have the full support of the players and committee as well as the fans. It took a while to convince Gough to stay but worsening problems with his knee meant he was rarely seen in action in 2002.

So many Yorkshire players made major steps forward in 2001 that seven of them were selected for various England tours in the winter but money was becoming so tight at Headingley that six got their marching orders, Middlebrook, Fisher, Hutchison, batsman Simon Widdup and bowlers Tom Baker and Greg Lambert all being told they were no longer required.

Towards the end of December, commercial director Panaro predicted that Yorkshire could expect to generate sales of at least half-a-million pounds as a direct result of winning the Championship. But any suggestion that cash-laden days were looming could not have been further from the truth.

Part Three **Rags to Riches**

Never in the field of Yorkshire conflict, both on and off the pitch, has so much happened in so short a time as it did in 2002. To marry into the narrative the playing side of events with the political would mean full justice could not be done to either, so we will conclude this chapter with the cricket and start the next one by looking elsewhere, always mindful that the general upheaval within the club had a bearing on the team itself.

Although the fans had been puzzled by Byas's sudden departure they had no reason to believe that their revitalised side would do anything other than continue to make their mark in the Championship under Lehmann.

But the much-revered Australian found it impossible to inject the magic that was in his bat into the captaincy and Yorkshire hit rock bottom in the table from mid-June and remained embedded there for the rest of the summer.

The season would have been a complete disaster but for the good old-fashioned virtues of vice-captain Blakey, who topped 1,000 runs batting mainly at No 7 and took over the reins when Lehmann went home early.

Up to that point, Yorkshire had not won a Championship match but they broke their duck under Blakey with victories at Old Trafford and Southampton before he marched them on to Lord's where they lifted the Cheltenham and Gloucester Trophy with a cracking display against much-fancied Somerset.

The figure 33 had worked in Yorkshire's favour once again. The previous year they had ended a 33-year barren run in the Championship and now they brought to a close a similar period of failure in the premier one-day competition. Even this late spoonful of honey, however, could not take away the bitter taste caused by finishing bottom of Division One of the Championship and not winning a home match all season for the first time since 1983. On that occasion they had also been bottom – but of 17 teams rather than nine.

In addition to Blakey's guiding hand, Yorkshire's late, late show was achieved largely through the brilliance of Australian Matthew Elliott, captain of Victoria, who was signed in mid-August to replace the departing Lehmann. He piled up the runs at a crucial stage, in sharp contrast to fellow Australian Simon Katich, whose short spell filling in for Lehmann much earlier on had failed to ignite.

Although Lehmann did not find the Midas touch with his captaincy, his batting was once again beyond reproach and he stacked up 1,136 Championship runs in only ten matches, at one stage enjoying a sequence of seven consecutive knocks of 50 or more.

Lehmann and Blakey received reasonable support from several other batsmen but the main weakness was in the bowling department which Sidebottom led with only 41 wickets, followed by Dawson with 39.

In March, Gough had undergone a cartilage operation after damaging his right knee in England's final one-day international against New Zealand but hopes that he would make a quick recovery were soon dashed and he missed virtually the whole of the season, during which he had a second operation.

Also shortly before the campaign began, club chairman Moss vented his fury at the ECB first-class Forum's plan to introduce the new fangled Twenty20 tournament from 2003 while at the same time throwing the Benson and Hedges Cup competition on to the scrapheap.

"It is absolute madness and I cannot understand the thinking behind it," he raged. "Neither can the vast majority of Yorkshire members who were almost unanimous at the annual meeting in their disapproval of this proposed new form of the game."

Moss and many others at the club continued to pour scorn on Twenty20, and some refused to watch it, and still do, but they were wrong in thinking that it would be a dead duck rather than a golden goose.

The annual meeting to which Moss referred had been held in Yorkshire's reconstructed indoor cricket school which had now become the first piece of property they actually owned and was the first stage of the club becoming masters of their own destiny.

Fears that Lehmann would miss the start of the season evaporated with the calling-off of Australia's tour of Zimbabwe but Yorkshire soon realised how often they would be without their leading players when Vaughan, Hoggard and Gough were all put on central contracts, although White missed out this time.

England declined to allow Vaughan and Hoggard to play in Yorkshire's opening Championship match or in any of their first three B&H games and the season began on a calamitous note as Surrey mauled them by an innings and 168 runs at Headingley.

Things went from bad to worse in the Championship with defeats following at Taunton and Canterbury, the Aussie combination of Lehmann and Clark being unable to turn the tide. Lehmann's tactics even came under scrutiny against Somerset when they lost control of the match through a robust century from Ian Blackwell, who clearly relished the plan of Hoggard constantly bowling short to him.

There was a sigh of relief at Headingley on May 27 when Kirby made easily his highest score of 57 to secure a draw against Hampshire and so end a run of five consecutive Championship reverses since clinching the title at Scarborough the previous August.

But it was only a temporary lifting of the gloom because they immediately lost to Leicestershire and Sussex, who then clung on for a draw at Arundel in the second of the back-to-back matches between the sides. Old boy Bevan had helped thrash them at Grace Road with scores of 142 and 76 not out, and now it was Mark Robinson who added to the anguish by saving Sussex with the bat!

Lehmann's explosive 216 in the second innings appeared to have condemned Sussex to defeat until last man, Robinson, held out for the final 26 balls with Matt Prior to force a draw. To be denied victory by the man with the worst batting reputation in the country was the last straw. In 93 innings for Yorkshire, including 36 not-outs, Robinson had averaged 4.21, but his bat was broad enough on this occasion.

In Sussex's innings win at Headingley, Katich had come in for the absent Lehmann, making only 21 and 16 in a generally weak batting display, but of far greater concern to Yorkshire was the complete disintegration with the ball of Hamilton, who had to be pulled out of the attack after his solitary over contained 12 balls and cost him 17 runs.

Hamilton was hardly able to let the ball leave his hand and when it did, it was hopelessly wide of the mark. This sudden breakdown led to him trying desperately to remedy the situation in the second team but when he reappeared the problems remained and ended his career as an all-rounder.

And so Yorkshire's misery continued, with occasional brighter interludes like when Lehmann (187) and McGrath (165) posted 317 together in the Roses match at Headingley, the highest partnership by a Yorkshire pair on the ground. Alec Swann, formerly of Northants and brother of Graeme, then ensured stalemate with his maiden Roses century.

Swann also registered a century in the return fixture at Old Trafford but could not prevent Yorkshire from breaking their duck under Blakey, Lehmann having departed these shores to link up with Australia again. Elliott, making his White Rose debut, along with 17-year-old fast bowler Nick Thornicroft, introduced himself with a fluent 87, but Fellows' maiden century gave Yorkshire the edge and Dawson finally destroyed Lancashire with 5-42.

Emboldened by this win, Yorkshire moved on to the Rose Bowl where they disposed of Hampshire inside three days, Elliott making 92 and 52 not out and being well supported by the young Harrogate batsman Vic Craven. But a draw and two defeats from their last three matches meant there was no avoiding the wooden spoon.

The season would have been a total disaster but for the two knockout competitions, even though there were still moments Yorkshire would prefer to forget in the Benson and Hedges Cup, the most humiliating of them being in the home zonal clash with Lancashire.

Byas was making his first visit to Headingley since his abdication (or execution) and he would have primed Lancashire on his former side's weaknesses but he could never have envisaged that they would crash to 81 all out in 27.2 overs, their lowest score in the competition, with Flintoff taking 4-11. Then he had the satisfaction of being at the crease when the runs were knocked off in a mere 10.5 overs.

Despite their humiliation, Yorkshire had already done enough to qualify for the quarter-finals but they were walloped by Essex at Cheltenham, where England captain Nasser Hussain treated Hoggard with contempt. Hussain's murderous onslaught brought him an unbeaten 136 off 144 balls with 14 fours and a six, nine of the fours at the expense of Hoggard whose ten overs cost him 65 runs.

Happily, both Hoggard and Yorkshire gained ample revenge over Hussain and Essex on the same ground in the Cheltenham and Gloucester Trophy and at the same quarter-final stage but only after a real humdinger of a match. It began with Hoggard dismissing Hussain for only seven but Andy Flower's cautious 75 left Yorkshire chasing a competitive 283 off their 50 overs.

Very much down and out at 155-5 in 32 overs, Yorkshire hit back in great style through a record unbroken stand for the sixth wicket of 128 between McGrath (72) and Fellows (68) which left the scores level at the end, the visitors winning by virtue of losing only five wickets to their opponents' nine.

The semi-final at Headingley was just as exhilarating but in a different way. Bad weather prevented play on any of the three scheduled days and the game should have been decided on a bowl-out but Lord's relaxed the rules and allowed the match to be staged on the following Sunday when both Yorkshire and Surrey had a free day.

White's 4-35 restricted Surrey to 173-8 in their 48 overs on a tricky pitch but it was his sheer brilliance with the bat that was the decisive factor. In one of the finest one-day innings I have ever seen, he scored exactly 100 not out while Wood supported him with 57, the openers requiring only 24.1 overs to see their side reach the revised Duckworth-Lewis total of 167 and glide into the final.

When White came off the field to a standing ovation he had plundered 16 fours and a six and received just 78 balls.

And so on to Lord's, where Elliott was the hero and the man-of-the-match but where others also pulled out all the stops to ensure a memorable day with victory achieved by six wickets with two overs remaining.

A stunning catch falling backwards at short cover by Vaughan cut short a violent assault from Marcus Trescothick, the first of five victims for Hoggard whose figures somewhat flattered him. Chasing 257, Yorkshire were up against it at 64-3, all the wickets having fallen to the swing of Richard Johnson, but Vaughan and Elliott rebuilt with a partnership of 93 before Vaughan went for 31, an innings of great care which did not contain a boundary.

An acceleration was now required and Elliott and McGrath supplied it in style with an unbroken 103 together, the Australian finishing on 128 off 125 balls with 16 fours. Never before or since have Yorkshire got such great value out of an end-of-term signing and it was certainly money well spent because without Elliott, the trophy would most likely not have found its way into the silverware cupboard at Headingley.

CHAPTER FORTY-FIVE

UNDER NEW MANAGEMENT

If 2002 is remembered for the team floundering in the Championship before rising to the top in the C&G Trophy, history will also show that the club itself could have gone out of existence but for the formation of a Management Board which got to grips with a financial situation that was haemorrhaging money.

That Yorkshire were on the slippery slope to ruin became apparent at the annual meeting in March when treasurer Peter Townend issued a dramatic apology over the club's "abysmal failure to conduct business successfully" during the past year.

Townend remarked it was ironic that winning the County Championship in 2001 had coincided with a substantial accounting loss. He added that the deficit on the year of over £46,000 would have been much higher but for a profit of over £150,000 from selling from the portfolio fund.

The most startling slump was in shop and merchandise income, which dropped from £32,422 the previous year to just £460, and Townend said that a full and comprehensive review of the procedures and accountability of their retail operation had been carried out at his request by two members of the committee.

"This has highlighted several serious deficiencies in the system and appropriate action is being taken with new practices in the operation of the shop having begun this month.

"The new measures will bring satisfactory control over staff but we owe you a very great apology," Townend told members, while also warning that cricket expenditure must be slashed by £250,000 in the coming year.

All this dire news was still being digested early the following week when Hassell walked into the office and told the surprised staff that he intended to stand down on his 60th birthday in November.

Hassell admitted that the stresses of the job over recent years had taken their toll and he believed the end of the season would be an appropriate time to make way for a younger person to move the club forward into the next stage of its development.

By now, Hassell was the longest-serving chief executive in county cricket, having joined Yorkshire in 1991 after spending 13 years with Lancashire. He had worked in tandem with Sir Lawrence Byford on updating and rebranding Yorkshire's image and had overseen the initial redevelopment of Headingley but deep down he was always sorry that the move to Durkar had never come off.

The inefficient running of the shop was viewed so seriously that in April Yorkshire called in the police to investigate the substantial shortfall in the belief that up to £50,000 in either cash or merchandise or both could be unaccounted for.

A West Yorkshire Police spokesman confirmed that the fraud squad "had received an allegation of certain financial irregularities and was looking into the matter" but nothing ever came of their investigation.

President Smith and chairman Moss busied themselves with finding a new chief executive and in late July it was announced that 37-year-old Alex Keay, Manchester Rugby Union Club's supremo for the last six-and-a-half years and a former captain of Saracens, would take over from Hassell.

But such was the general chaotic situation that only a fortnight later Yorkshire said they had put Keay's appointment on ice because they believed the club's bankers may insist on having more influence over the way cricket was administered if they were to agree to Yorkshire's request for increased borrowing.

This was needed because of the spiralling costs of the Headingley re-development, which was £2m overspent, and Yorkshire made arrangements for an extraordinary annual meeting on August 29 to approve an increase in the borrowing limit from £5m to £10m in order to avoid bankruptcy.

The power in the club was rapidly shifting from the general committee to a small group of people who believed that the only way to get to grips with the crippling financial situation was by introducing a new management structure.

The general committee were persuaded to request Moss to stand down as club chairman and to put the running of the club into the hands of a "Gang of Four" headed by Robin Smith and also comprising Geoff Cope, Colin Graves, chairman and managing director of Costcutter Supermarkets Group, and Middlesbrough-born chartered accountant Brian Bouttell, a former senior partner with KPMG who had been responsible for establishing KPMG China as a stand-alone practice.

Cope had played a prominent part in bringing in Graves, who agreed to replace Hassell as chief executive. From then until the present time, Graves has kept Yorkshire afloat with his unwavering financial generosity and without his guarantees the banks would not have gone on lending as Yorkshire went about buying Headingley from Leeds CFAC.

Moss left this last meeting of the general committee after he had been stripped of office and the new management group unanimously voted in – although several members voiced their support for him before he insisted on standing down.

It was a harsh blow for Moss to take but at least he had the satisfaction of knowing that the redevelopment of the West Stand and the new East Stand, including the Long Room, had ensured that Test cricket would remain at Headingley when it could so easily have been taken away if immediate improvements had not been made.

Cope succeeded Moss as club chairman during this temporary period of the new regime and in 2003 he was director of cricket, his role changing to director of operations the following year.

Days after losing office, Moss saw the official opening of the East Stand by four Yorkshire greats in Boycott, Illingworth, Close and Trueman. The ceremony took place on the eve of the third Test between England and India, and Sachin Tendulkar, Yorkshire's favourite adopted son, made a point of breaking off from batting practice to attend the event.

Tendulkar had one of the 36 hospitality boxes named in his honour. "Yorkshire was home from home for me for four-and-a-half months and now I am back on my home ground," he said. "I am really honoured that a box has been named after me." To underline his love of Headingley, Tendulkar amassed 193 in the Test which India won by an innings and 46 runs.

While Yorkshire were in the process of bringing about these great changes, mystery surrounded the whereabouts of Panaro who had not been at Headingley in the second half of July. He was first rumoured to be on holiday and then off sick but whatever the real reason, Yorkshire were seeking a settlement at the time and he was never to be seen again.

The biggest sweeping change in Yorkshire's history occurred in December when a special general meeting voted overwhelmingly in favour of officially abolishing the committee and replacing it with the Management Board, members being only too well aware that if they failed to do so then the club would most definitely be plunged into administration with a millstone of debts totalling around £6m.

The deed having been done, Graves talked about his wish to turn Headingley into the "Lord's of the North" and he referred to the closer co-operation which now existed between Yorkshire and Leeds CFAC. The negotiations had begun for Yorkshire to buy Headingley cricket ground at long last and although both parties found plenty of obstacles on the difficult path ahead they walked it together, if not hand in hand at least side by side.

They began their journey by agreeing that from now on Yorkshire would be responsible for the selling of all corporate cricket hospitality at the venue, whether for Tests or county games, a move which Graves believed could increase the club's revenue from this source from £50,000 a year to £250,000.

One of Cope's final pronouncements before the old year was out was that England should make Vaughan their next captain after he had scored more runs in 2002 than any other international batsman – 1,481 in 14 matches, a figure only ever topped by Viv Richards with 1,710 in 11 outings in 1976. Vaughan duly became captain the following summer, first in one-day matches and then at Test level. In the spring he had been named as one of Wisden's Five Cricketers of the Year. His career was at its peak and his powers of leadership would prove to be second to none.

The Gang of Four had their sleeves rolled up and ready for business as soon as 2003 dawned and it was not long before they paved the way for the new season by releasing Clark from his post as director of coaching and setting on Kevin Sharp as batting coach with Arnie Sidebottom in charge of the bowling and Oldham responsible for the Academy.

Having also accepted that Lehmann would not be available they installed 27-year-old McGrath as captain, the club's youngest since Sellers had taken on the role 70 years earlier.

Elliott had been contracted to stay at Headingley throughout 2003 and Yorkshire were quite happy to rely solely on him for overseas aid but things did not quite work out that way. The Australian left-hander missed the start of the season with a nagging knee injury and was then forced to return home because of the serious illness of his brother-in-law.

As a result of these unforeseen events, Yorkshire signed India batsman Yuvraj Singh and he was later joined by New Zealand's captain Stephen Fleming. Hardly anything went right for Yuvraj, who was glad when the time came for him to return home, but Fleming was a useful acquisition and brought experience to the dressing room.

Before the season began, Yorkshire announced at the March annual meeting a loss on the previous year of a staggering £1,292,000 but finance director Bouttell insisted this had been expected and he predicted a positive cash flow of around £78,000 in 2003.

The Board also recognised the work of Keith Moss and other leading members of the now defunct committee by nominating Moss, Tony Cawdry, Sidney Fielden, Jack Sokell, Peter Townend and David Welch as vice-presidents and Bob Platt, Phil Sharpe and Michael Crawford as honorary life members.

The meeting voted Simon Parsons, Cawdry, Fielden and Vann on to the new Members' Committee, to which the Board also appointed four business people in Carole Rymer (Hull), Nigel Adams (York), Ian Townsend (Sheffield) and Michael Ziff (Leeds), chairman of the Bradford-based shoe group, Stylo. At their first meeting the committee elected Ziff as chairman.

March was also the month in which Yorkshire's office and cricket staff moved into their new accommodation in the East Stand, so vacating offices in the old dressing room building which was erected in the club's centenary year in 1963 and was soon to be demolished to make way for future development.

After much hesitating over his future, Gough agreed to remain with Yorkshire and in the build-up to the season he did rehab work on the injured knee which would continue to restrict his first team appearances.

Also receiving a year's contract was South African-born all-rounder Pieter Swanepoel, who had recently received British Citizenship and was now eligible to play for the first team as an English-qualified player. Swanepoel had distinguished himself the previous season as leading wicket-taker for the Second XI with 43 dismissals and he also performed the hat-trick for the Yorkshire Cricket Board in their C&G Trophy match against Somerset at Scarborough.

McGrath pitched into the pre-season preparations with great enthusiasm but with just over a week to go his plans were hit by the news that White had undergone an operation to remove a piece of rib bone and would be out for at least ten weeks.

It was just the sort of setback that a new captain did not need and White remained sidelined until June, the best of his bowling days having drawn to an early close.

CHAPTER FORTY-SIX

ENGLAND CALLS

A further surprise was sprung on the eve of the 2003 season when Wood was appointed vice-captain, despite a slump in form the previous year that had seen him axed after making only 201 runs in 17 Championship innings.

McGrath had pressed hard for Wood to be his deputy and his confidence was well-placed because the Huddersfield batsman was the only one to make it to 1,000 Championship runs, not only reaching the milestone but going well beyond it to 1,339 at an average of 53.76, with five centuries and two half-centuries.

Wood went on to lead Yorkshire out in more matches than he could have envisaged, the reason being McGrath's totally unexpected elevation to Test status. Just as Wood did not let McGrath down for Yorkshire, so McGrath justified the faith shown in him by Duncan Fletcher by contributing 69 and 81 to the two innings victories over Zimbabwe.

McGrath owed his selection just as much to his bowling as to his batting because he had graduated from occasional off-breaks to nagging slow-medium pace, which had been sufficiently effective to move him to the top of the Yorkshire bowling averages in 2002 with 18 dismissals at a better rate (27.66) than anyone else in the side. He amply demonstrated his usefulness in this department by claiming 3-16 on his England debut against Zimbabwe.

Everyone was delighted that McGrath's ability had been recognised at the highest level but he understandably discovered that concentrating on his England place meant he could not give his full attention to captaining Yorkshire and he unselfishly stood down at the end of the season.

With hindsight he may have decided differently because having been given his chance with England he was then rather poorly treated, particularly in one-day internationals where he often came in too late to be able to express himself fully. After some indifferent displays in the NatWest Series in 2004 and a dispiriting winter abroad with his country, he returned to full-time county cricket but he had to wait a few years to get another crack at the leadership.

At least McGrath enjoyed a great start to his captaincy in 2003 as Yorkshire overpowered Northamptonshire by an innings and 343 runs in the opening match at Headingley, their third highest innings victory.

Wood rediscovered his best form with 157 but even that fine effort was overshadowed by Blakey who ploughed on to an unbeaten 223, bridging a gap of 16 years between his two Championship double centuries. It was the highest score by a Yorkshire-born batsman since Moxon's 274 not out against Worcestershire in 1994 and the biggest on a home ground by a native since Vic Wilson's 230 v the same opponents half a century earlier.

Blakey, now 36, had entered the season with his place under threat from Guy but he was unable to repeat anything like this sort of form again and he contributed only 224 in his next 16 innings before having to give way.

The whipping of Northants resulted in Yorkshire being tipped for an immediate return to Division One but they could not maintain their momentum and they finished one place below the three promotion teams. It was a difficult season with injuries, particularly to the bowlers, Gough, Hoggard and Sidebottom all missing out on many matches, and the situation would have been even worse if Kirby had not stayed standing and claimed 67 wickets, well supported by Silverwood with 48.

The sudden loss of McGrath for six games and the availability of Vaughan for only three, in which he contributed 263 runs, also left Yorkshire rarely able to field their best side.

Vaughan's appointment as England's one-day captain was confirmed on May 6 but the following day he came back down to earth with a bump, caught and bowled for only ten by fridge-freezer salesman Ajaz Akhtar in the C&G Trophy encounter with Minor Counties' team, Cambridgeshire, at March. It was cold comfort on a hot day for Vaughan and it was Wood who did the celebrating with an unbeaten 118 before grabbing 3-45 with his very occasional spin.

After playing in 27 limited overs matches over two years, Bresnan was given his Championship debut against Northamptonshire at Wantage Road and Vaughan used the occasion to warm up for his first Test in charge by hitting a splendid century with 11 fours and three sixes.

Yuvraj Singh, having told the world on an Indian website that he was joining Yorkshire before the club had breathed a word about the deal, played in his first match when Glamorgan visited Headingley on May 21, but it was Wharf who stole the show. After scratching the surface with Yorkshire and Nottinghamshire, he finally settled down to enjoy a profitable career with the Welsh side and in this rain-marred game he put on 64 for the last wicket with Mark Wallace. It was a record tenth wicket stand for Glamorgan against Yorkshire and it came immediately after a record ninth wicket stand of 94 between Wallace and Michael Kasprowicz, the first time ever that Yorkshire opponents had set up two such records in the same innings.

Apart from the early demolition of Northants, things were not going well for Yorkshire in either four-day or one-day games and after opening their National League programme with a win over Warwickshire, they lost their next six matches and could not recover sufficiently to avoid relegation.

There was a further setback during this bleak period when Hoggard broke down with a torn cartilage after dismissing Graeme Hick with his first ball and then limping off after his third in the C&G clash at New Road, which Worcestershire won easily, thanks to telling contributions from their three Bradford-born players: David Leatherdale scoring 80, Steve Rhodes 29, and Gareth Batty 14, plus the wickets of Vaughan and Craven and also assisting in the running-out of Andy Gray. Hoggard's serious injury resulted in an operation and it was September before he returned.

Either side of the new Twenty20 competition, Yorkshire were twice humbled by Durham, who gained their first Championship success over them in the Headingley match and went on to complete the double at Riverside, their first against any county.

At Headingley, Yorkshire were partly undone by one of their own, 18-year-old Liam Plunkett, from Middlesbrough, who marked his Championship debut with figures of 5-53, all of his wickets coming in a second-spell burst of eight overs which included four wickets in nine balls for four runs. Also on debut was 20-year-old wicketkeeper-batsman Phil Mustard, 'The Colonel' giving an early exhibition of his attacking style by including four boundaries in his fiercely-struck 23. Yorkshire were hammered by 167 runs but their own debutant, Swanepoel, created a good impression with enthusiastic bowling that brought him three wickets.

The two teams met soon afterwards at Riverside in a much closer contest which Yorkshire lost by three wickets, despite a superb unbeaten 135 from White in the first innings. Durham batted with great care in chasing a 251 target in 87 overs and they got there with 7.3 overs to spare. Gough endured a nightmare time, struggling to take a couple of wickets at a cost of 145 runs and scoring four and nought.

Yorkshire's first match in the much heralded Twenty20 Cup was on June 14 at Headingley and although it was played on a Saturday with a 10.30 morning start, it still attracted an excited crowd of 5,342 fans to silence the Jeremiahs (Moss and myself included) who felt that this crash, bang, wallop form of the game would be no more than a seven day wonder.

Fleming dashed halfway round the world to make it in time to play in the match and probably set a record for the longest journey ever recorded for a first ball duck but there was joy in the home camp as Yorkshire gained a comfortable 45 runs win.

Joy turned to sorrow at Old Trafford where Lancashire won easily in front of a 14,862 crowd – the biggest so far anywhere – and although Yorkshire overcame Nottinghamshire in their final group game to preserve their 100 per cent home record they still failed to qualify for the later stages. This was to become a familiar pattern over the years as Yorkshire repeatedly fell short of making it to Finals Day.

Although the competition was still in its infancy, Lumb did enough to show that he would become a major Twenty20 performer. His blistering half-century in the win over Durham, for instance, came off 30 balls and contained five sixes off Nicky Phillips, four of them consecutive deliveries.

Yorkshire resumed normal service after their Twenty20 adventure by winning their next two Championship matches at Taunton and Derby to move briefly into second place but their only further success in the second half of the season was to complete the double over Somerset.

At Taunton, Fleming failed by just two runs to become only the fourth Yorkshire batsman to score a century on his Championship debut – he holed out on the boundary edge attempting to reach three figures in the grand manner. But the honours went to Kirby, who captured 8-80 in the second innings to emerge with match figures of 13-154, the best for Yorkshire since Illingworth's 14-64 against Gloucestershire at Harrogate in 1967. Kirby was full of his eccentricities during the match but interviewed afterwards he amazed the national Press with his good humour and honest answers. Some for the first time were seeing the other side to his character and they were much impressed.

Yuvraj was so consistently out of touch that he was axed for the trip to Cheltenham and both he and Fleming had to take their leave in late August to attend training camps as their two countries prepared to face up to each other.

To plug the gap left by their departure, Yorkshire signed Damien Martyn in the belief that he could help get them back in the promotion race. This did not quite happen but his impact could hardly have been greater. Having raced to 87 on his debut against Somerset at Headingley he top-edged Richard Johnson into the gap in his protective helmet and broke his nose. He was taken straight to hospital, where stitches were inserted into a deep gash.

The injury was serious enough to have sent him straight back home but he insisted on staying and travelled to Worcester to support his team in the next match which they lost by 71 runs. He declared himself fit for the last game with Gloucestershire at Headingley and played one of the greatest Championship innings of all time.

Unfurling stunning strokes full of awesome power, Martyn smashed his way to an unbeaten 238 in 222 minutes off 159 balls, with 38 fours and seven sixes, to record the fifth highest Championship knock on the ground. He and Wood (116) put on 330 together in 55 overs, the biggest Championship partnership for any wicket at Headingley.

The rain-hit contest still ended in a draw and it was cock-a-hoop Gloucestershire who were promoted while Yorkshire were resigned to at least a further season of Division Two cricket. Another Australian, Ian Harvey, scored 70 for the visitors and collected three wickets in each innings but Yorkshire were already in the process of signing him for 2004, realising that he was just the sort of shoot-from-the-hip all-rounder they needed, particularly at one-day level.

On the last day of the season, Yorkshire gave a National League debut to 20-year-old left-hander Joe Sayers, captain of Oxford UCCE, and he enhanced his growing reputation by weighing in with a determined 62, which was not quite enough for his side to beat Gloucestershire and end up on a winning note.

As usual, there was no shortage of activity over the coming weeks, starting with Sidebottom walking out and joining Nottinghamshire and Hamilton being among those not retained and later recruited at Durham by Moxon.

Sidebottom's leaving was regrettable but he had increasingly not seen eye-to-eye with Yorkshire, who had shown a reluctance to bring him back into the side after a long period out with an ankle injury and a short illness. He had bowled with his usual vigour up till then and it is untrue that the move to Nottinghamshire developed him into a Test player. He was already knocking on the door while at Yorkshire.

Plans for the complete rebuilding of Headingley continued to grow apace and in addition to the £10m already spent on the east and west sides of the ground Graves announced that the club intended to pump a further £25m into, among other things, a new north east enclosure with 2,100 seats, a scoreboard and video screen, and a new pavilion and media centre on the old winter shed site. It was also planned to redevelop the increasingly decrepit grandstand on the rugby side of the ground but, unfortunately, costs forced this to be placed on the back-burner.

In late October and early February, two untimely deaths occurred which were later marked at the first match of 2004 by players and officials lining up on the field for a minute's silence in their memory.

I was shocked to hear on October 29 that my great friend and Press Box colleague Rob Mills, cricket correspondent of the Yorkshire Post, had died of a heart attack at the age of 51, and on February 7, former Yorkshire president Viscount Mountgarret died just as suddenly, aged 67. Both men could not have been more committed in the roles that they played.

Meanwhile, Yorkshire hit the headlines for entirely cricketing reasons in December when it was revealed that David Byas was set to return to the fold in charge of cricket.

CHAPTER FORTY-SEVEN

"GOOD TO BE BACK"

Cope, now director of operations, had steadfastly taken on the overall responsibility for cricket in 2003 but come the end of the season, the Board looked closely at the restructuring of cricket management and agreed that Byas was the ideal man to put in charge. The invitation to him to return to Headingley also hinted at some regret at the way he was dealt with after he had led Yorkshire to the Championship title in 2001, the decision to relieve him of the captaincy prompting his move across the Pennines for a single season.

Byas was officially due to commence his role as cricket supremo from January 1, 2004, but he started to put his plans into operation as soon as his return was announced and one of his first changes was to release Arnie Sidebottom as bowling coach and pass the role on to Oldham, former York CC captain Ian Dews being brought in to fill the new role of director of coaching.

A piece of Yorkshire's history went with Arnie because it meant that for the first time since 1971 no Sidebottom was on the staff. It was only a temporary complete cut-off, however, because Ryan would return in 2011 and resume picking up the wickets again.

Blakey was appointed second team captain and 19-year-old fast bowling prospect David Stiff was allowed to take his 6ft 5in frame off to Kent because he felt he had been afforded too few opportunities at Yorkshire.

But the biggest news of an immediate departure had to wait until January when Gough said he was leaving Yorkshire for family reasons, although he would like to stay in county cricket. A fortnight later, he clinched a three-year deal with Essex where he would join up with his close friends and former team-mates, Grayson and Middlebrook.

Graves admitted that he and Byas had both tried to persuade Gough to stay but had not been successful and did not want to stand in his way. He also acknowledged that Gough at one stage was among several players he had spoken to about the possibility of the captaincy.

Gough and Byas did not always see eye-to-eye on everything but Byas said he would have preferred the Test bowler to have seen out his career with Yorkshire, adding: "We have to respect his decision. We don't enjoy anybody leaving us but we want people here who want to play for Yorkshire. We won't stand in the way of anybody who says Yorkshire is not for them."

What a different state of affairs it would be three years on when Gough returned as captain and Byas was replaced by Moxon. Like flotsam and jetsam, Yorkshire cricket personnel can be brought in with the tide and just as easily taken out again.

McGrath's decision to step back from the captaincy caused plenty of speculation as to who his successor would be and there was some surprise when it went to White but only because he had never put himself forward before. Just as McGrath was looking to England, White sensed his Test days were over and he was happy to take on the responsibility. In any case, he was the obvious choice. His pedigree was beyond question and he was well-liked and respected in the dressing room.

Byas signed John Blain from Northamptonshire to strengthen the bowling and the Scot was to prove an enthusiastic employee in his two spells at the club until his coaching role ceased at the end of 2011. His first season was also a generally disappointing one for all of the pacemen but he still took 30 Championship wickets – only one behind the leading fast bowler, Kirby – and his strike rate was the second best in the country.

Costcutter's six-figure sponsorship deal in March eased financial worries and at the annual meeting members received further good news in that the club were near to securing a 15-year staging agreement for Test matches at Headingley.

Introducing himself, Byas said: "Good to be back with Yorkshire after a brief but interesting spell away from here!" He was warmly applauded, as was new president David Jones, chairman of Next, who succeeded Smith, the Board member continuing as club chairman.

Much was expected of Yorkshire in 2004 but little was delivered, the chief reasons being the inability of the bowling attack to fire effectively, the loss for the whole of the Championship campaign – and most other times as well – of Vaughan and the absence for the second half of the season of the captain with a crippling knee injury. White managed only seven matches but that was two more than Hoggard, who had become an England regular with a six months' summer contract, his reputation having soared with his April hat-trick against the West Indies in Barbados.

Australia's increasing demands on Lehmann and Ian Harvey's fitness problems and international one-day calls also put great strain on Yorkshire but the man they got to cover for the pair was a brilliant success.

Phil Jaques was signed in May to become the third Aussie on Yorkshire's books and in terms of runs and appearances the Kolpak player was their the biggest asset, churning out 1,118 runs in only 11 Championship matches and guaranteeing his return in 2005. He answered the call again in 2012 after deciding to retire from first-class cricket back home.

Jaques had amassed 222 for Northants against Yorkshire the previous year and now he repaid that debt by making 243 against Hampshire at the Rose Bowl – the highest score to date on the ground – to become the only batsman ever to record a double century both for and against Yorkshire.

Early indications were that Yorkshire could gain promotion in both the Championship and the totesport League but they became ever weaker as time went on, finishing seventh in the Championship after failing to win any of their last ten matches and fourth in Division Two of the Sunday competition where they could not capitalise on a sequence of six wins in seven outings which took them to the top of the table by midsummer.

Again they made their way to a semi-final and again they were denied by Gloucestershire, despite Harvey having changed sides. They could not find their way past the wide bat of New Zealander Craig Spearman, who fashioned an unbeaten 143 in a near-perfect innings and made light work of reaching a 244 target with almost four overs to spare.

Gloucestershire proved they were still the one-day kings by hammering Worcestershire in the final and Yorkshire were distraught at not making it to Lord's after a rousing quarter-final win over Lancashire at Old Trafford when Vaughan, in one of his rare appearances, played one of his greatest limited overs innings in reaching 116 not out.

Yorkshire fell below their previous year's standard in the Twenty20 Cup, coming fifth out of six in the North Division, but the season did not go by without some significant moments, including the first team debuts of both Ajmal Shahzad and Ismail Dawood.

For the past 15-20 years, Yorkshire had been eager to promote a Yorkshire-born youngster from an Asian background into the senior side, realising that pressure was mounting on them to do so and also believing that such a move could boost attendances, although this never happened to any great degree.

Several youngsters at the Academy had already seemed as if they could make it without actually doing so. But on May 23, almost without warning, Ajmal Shahzad made the breakthrough at the age of 18 by being brought into the injury-hit side for the totesport League match against Worcestershire at Headingley.

Born in Huddersfield and brought up in Bradford, where he learned his cricket with Windhill CC, Shahzad attended Woodhouse Grove School and was highly thought-of by the cricket master Graham Roope, the former Surrey and England all-rounder, who believed he had sufficient all-round ability to go right to the top.

Roope was correct in his judgment and Shahzad immediately showed himself to be an articulate and diplomatic young man who was proud to carry the banner for the ethnic community.

Interviewing him before the match began, Shahzad told me: "It is an awesome feeling to be the first ethnic cricketer born in Yorkshire to be chosen for the county.

"I hope I will be seen as a perfect role model from the Asian community and I look upon this as the first stage in realising my ambition of playing regularly for Yorkshire."

Shahzad bowled economically without picking up a wicket and he could well have made further progress that season if a back injury had not put him out of action. He did go on to play for England but early in the 2012 season he was at odds with the Yorkshire cricket management over how he should bowl and he moved over the Pennines to Lancashire for the remainder of the summer.

Wicketkeeper-batsman Ismail Dawood was a much more experienced cricketer than Shahzad and ten years his senior. Born in Dewsbury, he had attended the Yorkshire Academy before going on to have spells in first-class cricket with Northamptonshire, Worcestershire and Glamorgan. He then became a mature student at Leeds Metropolitan University and was a member of the Bradford-Leeds Universities' Centre of Cricketing Excellence, where he came to Yorkshire's notice again by scoring a sparkling 125 off them in 2003.

This led to him being given a trial in 2004 and he made his first team debut in the Twenty20 Cup match against Derbyshire at Derby. Further one-day games followed and on July 21 he became the first Yorkshire-born cricketer from an Asian background to play for them in the Championship when he was included against Somerset at Scarborough.

Dawood, too, was both competitive and articulate, and having secured his place at Scarborough ahead of the out-of-touch Guy, he held on to it for the remainder of the season. He was 'in situ' for most of the following season, scoring valuable runs as well as standing behind the stumps, but he was not retained after 2005 due to the arrival of Gerard Brophy. He had, however, filled a gap more than adequately and I am sure he would have continued to serve well had he stayed.

Yorkshire were soundly beaten by Somerset at North Marine Road, new signing Ricky Ponting hitting a classic century and West Indian Nixon McLean bagging 11 wickets, but Dawood was not the only home player to make his Championship debut.

Fresh-faced Andrew Gale, who would rise to be captain in six years, started out with a second ball duck and England Under 19s leg-spinner Mark Lawson was preferred to Gray. Lawson took a couple of wickets and he became an increasingly exciting prospect, particularly after his 5-62 haul against Durham in the next match at North Marine Road.

Soon, Bradford-born Adil Rashid would also be baffling opponents with his leg-spin and Yorkshire for a while were richer in this department than ever before. The pair had to battle it out to become first-choice spinner and in the end Rashid won but Lawson gave him a good run for his money.

Lehmann, top of both the batting and bowling averages, had to take his leave in mid-August, along with Harvey, and their absence made room for Sayers to make his Championship debut at Grace Road where he settled in nicely. The Oxford Blue continued to impress sufficiently to form a successful opening alliance with Jaques in the last two matches, the pair contributing 162 and 69 together at Taunton and then 171 and 13 off Glamorgan's attack at Headingley.

In the encounter with Glamorgan at Colwyn Bay in late August, Richard Pyrah showed plenty of guts on his Championship debut. Appalling weather severely restricted play to the afternoon and evening of the third day but even then there was time enough for Pyrah to withstand a highly-charged burst from Simon Jones and pay him back with three aggressive boundaries.

No bowler actually set the world alight in 2004 but Dawson was by far the pick of the bunch, topping the Championship list with 36 wickets and also heading the totesport League table with 22 wickets.

Gray had often been a rival for a place but he lost out eventually and was not retained. Neither was left-hander, Vic Craven, who turned in some good all-round performances in his time and was, perhaps, under-rated.

Yorkshire could be fairly relaxed about releasing Gray and Craven but it came as a bombshell when Kirby then requested his release from a contract which ran until the end of 2007. Byas was not the man to stand in the way of someone who wished to leave and Kirby's request was granted but the loss of a bowler who had captured 182 first-class wickets since arriving during 2001 was a hard blow to take.

A misunderstanding had occurred which led Kirby to believe that he was not properly valued at Yorkshire and after giving it much thought he decided to seek pastures new. He became a splendid acquisition for Gloucestershire and later on bowled his heart out for Somerset.

There was an obvious need to strengthen the bowling for 2005 and after signing left-arm swing bowler David Lucas from Nottinghamshire, Byas brought in South African Deon Kruis as a Kolpak player. Lucas never commanded a regular place but Kruis hit the straps straight away and immediately fit like a glove into the side.

While the cricket was in full swing and occupying everyone's attention, the Management Board had been in regular talks with Caddick and Leeds CFAC over buying the cricket ground. But the subject flared up in January, 2005, when Caddick's side called a Press Conference to say that talks had irretrievably broken down, a claim immediately denied by Yorkshire.

Smith hit back by saying that although the talks, which had been going on for more than a year, were frustrating he hoped that a deal would be clinched before the start of the new season in a month's time, otherwise they would pull out of the negotiations and continue as lease-holders.

CHAPTER FORTY-EIGHT

HOMEOWNERS

Bluff and counter bluff were all part of the complex game in the negotiations that dragged on as Yorkshire sought to own Headingley cricket ground.

It did not come into Yorkshire's ownership by the start of the 2005 season but neither did the club carry out their threat to pull out of talks if a deal had not been concluded by then.

The road ahead continued to be a bumpy one, with Yorkshire and Leeds CFAC friends one minute and foes the next, but a deal was finally reached between the two parties on November 30, 2005 – with two crucial provisos.

The £12m buy-out of the ground's freehold and its associated income streams would be completed if (1) Leeds City Council during December rubber-stamped plans to give Yorkshire a £9m loan and (2) if Yorkshire members then voiced their approval at an extraordinary meeting of the club, which had been called for Christmas Eve.

It was imperative that the ground passed into Yorkshire's hands before the end of the year because the 15-year staging agreement with the ECB was dependant upon Yorkshire owning it by 2006.

Still, everything was far from straightforward. On December 14, Leeds Council for a second time put off a decision to sanction the grant, saying that they wanted details of revised negotiations between Yorkshire and Leeds CFAC to be put to members on Christmas Eve.

"The deal as it has been put to us is not an acceptable use of public funds and it would be irresponsible of us to agree it," warned Coun. Mark Harris, the Council's deputy leader. "Unless there are significant improvements over serious areas of concern then we won't be going ahead with the loan."

Time was rapidly running out and Cope, Yorkshire's director of operations, had to telephone the shock news to Smith, who was on holiday in South Africa, and also inform Graves and Bouttell.

"The priority now is to arrange talks with Leeds CFAC and the council just as soon as possible in order to arrive at a satisfactory outcome," he said.

Every interested party now had to pull their finger out and they did, the re-negotiations being put to the extraordinary general meeting, at which every one of the 206 who attended voted in favour, while the proxy vote showed 2,111 in favour and 35 against. Unprecedented harmony.

It was the best Christmas present Yorkshire could have wished for but it was New Year's Eve before Leeds CFAC were able to pocket the £9m loan with £3m to be paid at a later date.

The deal had gone through even later than the eleventh hour and both Cope and Leeds CFAC's chief executive Gary Hetherington expressed their delight.

Yorkshire, of course, still did own the hotel at Headingley or the floor level of the old winter shed but that would be bought in due course for £1m and a new pavilion and media centre built on the site.

The purchase of the ground sealed a splendid year for Yorkshire because during the summer they had gained promotion in the Championship by just managing to secure third place in the Division Two table behind Lancashire and Durham.

This had been made possible by the terrific form of McGrath and Jaques with the bat and consistently great displays with the ball by Kruis, who kept fit throughout his first season to bag 64 wickets at 30.64 apiece.

Five wins from the first nine games bounced Yorkshire into third place and they clung on to it, despite drawing their next six matches. They would have gone a whole season without being beaten for the first time since 1928 had they kept Northants at bay in the final match but they were humbled at Wantage Road by Monty Panesar and Jason Brown who had an equal share in all of the wickets in each innings, the first time two bowlers had wiped the floor with Yorkshire since Dick Pougher and George Hilliard took ten wickets each for Leicestershire at Leicester in 1894.

Had Yorkshire won the game instead of losing it they would have finished top of Division Two and taken home £30,000 in prize money. Instead, they had to be content solely with promotion.

That had been clinched in the previous game at Derby but only after they had managed to save one of the most incredible games in the history of the Championship. At 233-7 in their second innings, Derbyshire were 71 runs away from an innings defeat but Ant Botha (156 not out) and Tom Lungley (36) rallied the home side with a stand of 140 and Botha and Nick Walker (79) added a further 133 for the ninth wicket, the innings closing at 523 at which stage the lead was 219.

With 59 overs at their disposal, Yorkshire were still favourites until they slipped to 82-6, at which point they were in serious danger of not getting the draw and with it the four extra points which would guarantee promotion. Fortunately, opener Sayers had grimly denied Derbyshire and he was partnered through the last dozen overs by Guy, whose resilience made up for dropping Botha the ball before he reached his half-century.

A relieved White commented: "It did feel a bit of an anticlimax in the end but we set out at the start of the season to gain promotion and that is what we have done."

The biggest all-round contribution came from Harvey, with five first innings wickets and a century, but Lawson also collected five in the second while McGrath had earlier outshone Harvey with a scintillating 158 to become the first batsman to hit four consecutive Championship centuries off Derbyshire.

McGrath was consistently showing the sort of form that compared favourably with any other player in the first-class game and it was a surprise that a batsman of his undisputed class should have to wait so long to complete 1,000 runs for the first time.

He got there in his unbeaten innings of 173 in the previous match against Worcestershire at Headingley when rain denied Yorkshire the win that would have seen them promoted earlier than was the case.

McGrath was also instrumental in the two record-breaking wins over

Leicestershire which had laid the foundation for promotion. At Grace Road his extraordinary 165 not out saw Yorkshire reach a 400-plus target for the first time ever – their previous highest was 331-7 against Middlesex at Lord's in 1910 – and in the return match at Scarborough he hit 89 in a winning score of 400-4, Sayers making 104.

For a time it had seemed as if Yorkshire would canter into Division One of the totesport League because they opened up with three consecutive wins and enjoyed four successes in their first five outings. The last of them was against Scotland on May 30 and, unaccountably, after that they lost 12 of their next 13 matches, ending with eight successive defeats.

They were as bad as ever at Twenty20, finishing fifth out of six in North Division, but their one-day season was redeemed by reaching the semi-final of the Cheltenham and Gloucester Trophy. The last hurdle to leap over to make it to Lord's was at The Rose Bowl but a bizarre set of circumstances highlighted the folly of an impossible schedule and led to Hampshire shattering their dreams with an easy eight-wicket win.

On the eve of the match, Yorkshire had dug deep to save the Roses game at Old Trafford and give their confidence a timely boost. The downside of their resistance, led by skipper White, was that the contest did not end until almost 5.30pm and then their coach was late in arriving to transport them down to Southampton.

By the time they pulled up at their hotel it was half past midnight and they were assembled in the reception area at 8.30 the following morning ready to board their bus to take them to the ground.

The only problem was there was no sign of the driver and when an anxious Byas contacted him in his room he said he could not take them because he had not had the legal number of rest hours.

Byas made a frantic attempt to get a fleet of taxis to the hotel but this proved impossible and some of the players clambered into a truck belonging to the hotel with others travelling by various emergency means.

Still the team's nightmare was not over because the roads were so clogged with traffic that they could not reach the ground in time and some of the players decided it would be quicker to walk. White jogged the last mile or so for the toss and to explain the predicament they were in.

The start of the game was put back quarter of an hour to 10.30am but Yorkshire were all at sixes and sevens and their 197 total hardly taxed Hampshire, for whom Zimbabwean Sean Ervine made exactly 100.

Apart from saving face against Lancashire, it had not been the best of times for White and his men. Barely a week had elapsed since they had been stopped dead in their tracks at Taunton by Matt Wood – not their own Matthew Wood but Somerset's.

In the drawn Championship match he plundered 297, the only higher individual score against Yorkshire being W.G. Grace's 318 for Gloucestershire at Cheltenham in 1876, and then on the Sunday he whacked 129 off 105 balls in a Sunday League thriller of 688 runs which Somerset won by just two runs.

Not only was 2005 a memorable year for Yorkshire but it was also a stupendous one for Vaughan and England, who regained the Ashes after a 16-year gap in the most rip-roaring series of all time. When England were 2-1 up in the series with only The Oval still to go, Vaughan brought his England XI on to Headingley to play a Yorkshire XI in an Asda Challenge Twenty20 floodlit match as part of his benefit programme.

Around 15,000 ecstatic fans turned up to pay homage to Vaughan and his team but before the game could begin a mighty storm flooded the ground to a depth of several inches and the players spent the rest of the evening signing autographs.

Another noteworthy event in this momentous year was the formation in the spring of the Yorkshire CCC Players' Association with the popular Jimmy Binks, now living in the United States, being installed as the first president. Yorkshire were the last of the counties to set up such a worthy organisation and the two men who got it off the ground were chairman Stott and secretary Cope. They held office together until 2012 when Stott stepped down but by that point an annual dinner and other social events had become well-established.

At the same time as the Players' Association began to prosper, Park Avenue sadly went further into decline, the Universities' side being driven away from the ground by vandalism and rising costs to set up new headquarters at Weetwood after temporarily playing their home games at Harrogate.

Since entering the 21st century, Yorkshire had barely had a moment when something dramatic was not occurring in one form or another and the pattern was set to continue as they cast their gaze towards 2006.

They approached it without Jaques who bade a premature farewell with three of the 2005 Championship matches still to play when he was called up by Australia A to tour Pakistan. The club would love to have kept him on but Lehmann was due to return to complete his contract and the other overseas slot went to Jason Gillespie, the hope being that the wild-looking fast bowler would turn out to be just as destructive for Yorkshire as he had been for Australia.

Two other Aussies, Harvey and Cleary, also moved on and Yorkshire did not retain Dawood, preferring instead to bring in Brophy in the belief that he would give them more runs. Chris Taylor had been released early in order to join Derbyshire and Lucas was also let go after just one season. But it was not until February that the parting of the ways came with Silverwood, who had been allowed to sign a two-year contract with Middlesex.

His service with Yorkshire had been exemplary – 427 first-class wickets at 26.49 and 223 wickets at 23.07 in one-day outings – but his fitness record had been poor for some time and there were doubts over whether he could keep going day after day. Yorkshire were probably right in their assessment of the situation but it goes without saying that Silverwood would blast away his former team-mates in the not-too-distant future.

The club was still buzzing with the news of Yorkshire taking over the ownership of Headingley when it was announced on January 12, 2006, that 41-year-old Stewart Regan had been lined up to become the new and vibrant chief executive.

Born in the market town of Crook in Bishop Auckland, Regan had been managing director of the Football League Championship over the past two years and had just seen attendances for the second tier of English football soar to their highest level in more than 50 years.

Regan had been chosen from a list of over 100 applicants and one of his chief aims was to attract a younger generation of cricket fans as he felt they were crucial for the long-term survival of the game.

Although at Headingley for less than five years before moving on to become chief executive of the Scottish FA, Regan brought real energy and drive to his work and his main legacy will be that he oversaw the building and completion of the state-of-the-art Headingley Carnegie pavilion and media centre.

The day before Regan had been unveiled as chief executive, it was disclosed that Yorkshire and Leeds CFAC had signed a new partnership agreement with Leeds Metropolitan University and that the complex would now be called Headingley Carnegie Stadium. A ten-year deal had been concluded with the option of a further five years and this had been a major factor in cementing the purchase of the freehold of the cricket ground by Yorkshire.

Former athletics star Brendan Foster, chancellor of Leeds Met University, said the deal was a fantastic example of a sporting partnership taking place off the field. The ambition had been to relocate part of the Carnegie faculty to Headingley and the plan had flourished.

It was the planned relocation of part of the faculty to Headingley that was to result in the construction of the new pavilion and media centre – the building being designed for joint use but different purposes – but spiralling costs meant there was to be no refurbishment of the grandstand at the same time.

Regan was officially behind his desk on March 20, a month after Yorkshire had signed a £500,000 sponsorship deal over three years with Bradford and Bingley, who the previous summer had also stepped forward to sponsor the indoor cricket school.

At the end of his first week, Regan addressed the club's annual meeting which approved two significant nominations. Appleyard was elected president in place of the retiring David Jones and Boycott was voted on to the Management Board along with Leeds City Council's deputy chief executive Dave Page, while Graves took over from Smith as chairman.

Smith, who had been a leading light from the start in the moves to save Yorkshire from financial disaster, retained his place on the Management Board and continued to serve with a passion both for the club and its members. It was entirely appropriate that he should launch the Yorkshire Pride Appeal, which aimed to raise at least £6m and that he should be its chairman.

Not for the first time, a big build-up to a new season was not matched by results and the main thing Yorkshire took out of 2006 was the avoidance of relegation by a hair's breadth in the Championship – but only after a monumental and memorable struggle with Durham in the final match.

One-day cricket once again proved not to be Yorkshire's forte, finishing seventh out of ten in the North Conference of the C&G Trophy and bottom of the pile in Division Two of the NatWest Pro40 League. There was a ray of light in the Twenty20 Cup where they made it through to the quarter-finals for the first time but were then beaten by Essex at Chelmsford by five wickets with four balls remaining.

One frustration followed another for Vaughan, who struggled manfully to rid himself of his knee injury, but in the end succumbed to a further operation and was not fit to lead England either against Sri Lanka or Pakistan.

The most fascinating and enjoyable aspect of the season involved watching the development of two outstanding young leg-spinners in Adil Rashid and Mark Lawson. For Yorkshire to have one leg-spinner to call upon was a rarity but to have two was unique and to watch them operating in tandem for a short while was a joy to behold.

Lawson had the edge in experience, making his first-class debut in 2004 and a year later collecting five wickets in the win over Derbyshire which clinched promotion. He was also the first student of the ECB's wrist spin development programme to play first-class cricket but Bradford-born Rashid was catching him up fast and in March, 2006, ECB spin bowling coach David Parsons, singled him out as the best leg-spin prospect in the country.

Yet it was mainly because of his batting prowess that the 18-year-old Rashid was given his Yorkshire debut in the Championship tussle with Warwickshire at North Marine Road in July, Byas selecting him on the strength of four centuries in the space of a few days for the Second XI and Academy sides.

Once Rashid was thrown the ball, however, he was reluctant to part with it and the young leggy became an overnight sensation. With Gillespie and the newly-capped Bresnan doing the early damage, White did not call upon Rashid until a last-wicket partnership between Heath Streak and Paul Harris was proving troublesome and his eighth delivery trapped Harris lbw.

Gale turned his maiden century into a powerfully struck 149 to give Yorkshire a substantial first innings lead and Warwickshire were then unceremoniously swept aside by Rashid, who claimed 6-67 in the innings and 96 runs victory. In a marathon spell from the pavilion end he began bowling at 12.45pm, when Warwickshire were cruising along at 85-1, and he was still wheeling away in the intense heat at 5.15 when Bresnan ended the match with two wickets in two balls.

Rashid was unavailable for the next match at the Rose Bowl because of England Under 19s involvement so Lawson stepped up to claim 6-150 in the ten-wicket win and at the same time earn praise from Warne who, on the same track, could only manage 3-100.

There was much debate on the respective merits of the two young leg-spinners when they were eventually picked to play together and opinions remained divided after they had wiped out the Middlesex second innings together at Scarborough, Lawson emerging with 6-88 and Rashid 4-96 – the first time Yorkshire bowlers of this ilk had run through a side. In the penultimate game against Nottinghamshire at Headingley, which Yorkshire won by 68 runs to keep alive their hopes of avoiding relegation, Lawson shaded it with eight wickets to Rashid's six, but in the final encounter with Durham, Rashid was the stronger with five wickets to Lawson's solitary success.

Lawson ended up with 26 wickets to Rashid's 25 but never again were the pair so finely balanced and, sadly, Lawson's career with Yorkshire spluttered to a close in 2007. He had spells with Derbyshire, Middlesex and Kent over the next three seasons before fading out of the first-class picture.

Gillespie missed the first Championship match of the season because of

Australia's Test series in Bangladesh and when he arrived on our shores all the talk was of his batting rather than his bowling. He had signed off for his country with an unbeaten 201, a score which prompted Lehmann to say he dare not ask Gillespie about it because he would never stop telling him – and for Byas to observe that they would now have to send in a nightwatchman to protect a nightwatchman!

Lehmann was near invincible in his last summer for Yorkshire in which he scored 1,706 runs for an average of 77.54, saving his very best for the very last, like every great showman does.

It seemed certain that only the winners of the final match between Yorkshire and Durham at Headingley would avoid relegation but in the event both teams pulled off Houdini acts because title-holders Nottinghamshire could only muster a single point off new champions, Sussex.

Batting first, Yorkshire's immediate aim was to secure 400-plus inside 130 overs to take maximum batting bonus points. The fact that they did this and soared on to 677-7 declared was due to Lehmann's truly epic 339, Yorkshire's first triple century in 74 years and just three runs short of overtaking the county's highest-ever individual score of 341 by Hirst against Leicestershire in 1905.

In his own inimitable style, Lehmann batted for eight hours and three minutes, faced 403 balls and peppered the field with 52 fours and three sixes. He was within spitting distance of Hirst when he played wearily across the line at New Zealand off-spinner Paul Wiseman and was bowled. But it was typical of the man and of his respect for Yorkshire's heritage that he came in to a thunderous standing ovation without displaying any sign of anguish at so narrowly missing out. Quite the contrary, he even seemed happy that the record would stay with Hirst.

Durham were made no less determined by Lehmann's brutal assault and Nottinghamshire's capitulation meant that they, too, would survive if they could acquire five batting bonus points and hold out for a draw. An eighth-wicket stand of 315, their highest for any wicket, between captain Dale Benkenstein (151) and Ottis Gibson (155) achieved the first part of the exercise and rain removing a chunk of the third day helped bring about the second objective.

Despite the run-drenched finale, it had still been a summer of much under-achievement. McGrath had stood shoulder to shoulder with Lehmann and could not be faulted but the pace bowling was a big let-down, Kruis coming back well after injury to end with a modest 38 wickets, two ahead of Gillespie whose best days as a front line bowler were behind him.

The first win of the season in any competition closed a sequence of ten consecutive one-day defeats and did not come about until May 14 when Yorkshire beat Northants in the C&G Trophy by two runs in a barnstorming contest which saw 680 runs scored. White's sparkling century was quickly put into the shade by the audacious brilliance of his brother-in-law, Lehmann, who thrashed 118 off 86 deliveries with nine fours and six sixes. A score of 341-3 only briefly seemed out of reach as Northants skipper David Sales went crazy in knocking up 161 and it was only a great catch by McGrath at long-on that stopped his charge in the nick of time.

White said of the match: "It was a fantastic game of cricket, one of the best I have ever played in with two of the best one-day innings from Lehmann and Sales you could ever witness. It has left me speechless."

Chris Taylor's C&G century for Derbyshire in April and Silverwood's 6-51 for Middlesex in the Championship in June were the latest instances of former Yorkshire players raising their game to bring about the defeat of their native county, the trouncing at Southgate resulting in an internal enquiry into the continuing poor form.

But such matters suddenly seemed less important with the death from cancer on July 1 of Fred Trueman. Fittingly, many of Trueman's closest colleagues and friends were gathered at Headingley on the day of his death for the one-day international between England and Sri Lanka and the likes of Appleyard, Close, Illingworth and Boycott were all clearly affected by the news and gave heartfelt testimonies to his greatness.

The weather, as previously mentioned, was warm and sultry for his funeral in the Priory Church of St Mary and St Cuthbert at Bolton Abbey – just the conditions he would have revelled bowling in – and he was laid to rest at the Priory. His coffin was adorned with white roses but he would have been just as proud of the spray of flowers brought into the Priory before the service, a simple message reading: "From Lancashire friends."

He would have been relieved, had he lived, to see Yorkshire escape relegation, but the team were still celebrating their survival in the dressing room after the Durham match when White told me that he had decided the time was right for him to stand down as captain. He had taken Yorkshire up and had kept them up and he was ready to hand over to someone else.

The news took everyone by surprise but it was not on the scale of other dramatic events which would be played out before the new season began.

CHAPTER FORTY-NINE

BARNSLEY UNITED

Mystery and intrigue on a scale never witnessed before or since surrounded Yorkshire virtually from the moment that White made it known he was jacking in the captaincy. The suspense continued throughout the winter and the 2007 season was almost upon us before things settled down, by which time some big names had gone, others had arrived – and one stayed exactly where he was!

No fewer than six players left the club for a variety of reasons in the latter stages of 2006 but it was the departure of Blakey, the senior member of the cricket staff, that possibly lit the blue touch paper on all the fireworks that were to follow.

The 39-year-old wicketkeeper-batsman had last played for the first team in 2003 and after two years as captain and manager of the Second XI he spent the season just gone working alongside Byas in coaching and supervising the first team.

Byas was under severe pressure to reduce the cricket budget and with Blakey now out of contract, it was not renewed, a Board decision which Regan later admitted had not gone down well with the other players.

Towards the end of October news filtered out that Yorkshire were to hold emergency talks with McGrath, who had two years still to run on his contract but wanted to leave because he was unhappy with the way the club was being managed.

Byas insisted he had no problems with McGrath and was eager for him to stay but initial clear-the-air talks came to nothing and the subject went off the radar for a while as other issues forced their way on to it.

Lehmann, of course, had seen out his days with Yorkshire, leaving them with an unrivalled batting average and with the status of a super hero, and plans were quickly finalised to replace him with Pakistan vice-captain Younus Khan, Boycott playing a significant role in setting up the deal.

Of much greater interest, however, was the admission by Yorkshire that they were aiming to bring in 36-year-old Chris Adams from Sussex, county cricket's most successful captain, and that they wanted him to be responsible for as yet undefined extra duties as well as leading the side.

Only a matter of a few days later, Yorkshire confirmed Adams was to arrive in December on a four-year contract as captain and head of professional cricket, leaving Byas to ponder over whether to agree to be cast in the new role of head of cricket development.

At the same time, it was revealed that Lumb had decided to pack his bags and move to Hampshire, thereby rejecting the offer of improved personal terms and a contract extension if he stayed. The first signs that Lumb was discontented surfaced in 2005 when he briefly lost his first team place but he was an ever-present the following year, excelling in all competitions and looking a fine England prospect.

While all this is being digested, the really big one goes off. On November 13, Adams travels to Headingley to meet the players at an informal gathering in the indoor school and is reported to be in buoyant mood upon leaving to return to his

Sussex home. Next morning he calls in on officials at the county ground at Hove and following a discussion, he rings Regan to say that he has bitten off more than he can chew and that he is standing down from the appointment at Yorkshire. He intends staying on as captain of Sussex.

Rocked by this turn of events, the Management Board talked to each other by telephone to decide on their next course of action and the stunned playing staff was brought up to speed with one of the biggest U-turns in cricket history.

Now the McGrath saga resurfaced. In a fresh bid to keep him he was offered the captaincy, a benefit and a new three-year contract with enhanced terms and additional responsibilities. But he could not be budged.

Agreement was reached that Gillespie would return to Headingley but on the second day of the 2007 New Year, further talks between Regan and Byas broke down and Byas was on his way, the job on offer not to his liking.

Then South African Jacques Rudolph was signed as a second Kolpak player – a move frowned upon by the ECB who took a time to approve his registration – but Yorkshire were further away than ever from having a new regime in place and they decided to advertise the posts of director of professional cricket and director of cricket development.

Allan Donald and Chris Old were early applicants for the first job but even while the list was being processed the McGrath affair reared its head again, his agent stating that the player was leaving the club with immediate effect because differences could not be resolved.

Yorkshire hit back by threatening legal action and the Professional Cricketers' Association was called in to try to end the dispute. These talks stalled and an ECB hearing was due to take place, with solicitor Francis Neale named as the independent mediator.

Another chapter in the winter's tale unfolded towards the end of February when Yorkshire learned that Gough had not yet signed his contract to stay on at Essex. Contact was made with him upon his return from Australia and the captaincy, which had once been offered in an attempt to dissuade him from going to Chelmsford in the first place, was put on the table again.

It did not take long for the Dazzler to make up his mind to say 'yes' to a two-year contract as captain with an exit clause in a year's time if things did not work out. And he was full of bounce and the joys of spring when he was paraded at Headingley on February 28.

"It feels like I have never been away and I have been hugging all the people I know from when I was last here," he said. "I was offered the captaincy before I left but unfortunately circumstances took me away. I was certainly not going to turn it down twice."

He added that he had spoken several times to Boycott, who wanted him to take the job, and he had also received a text message from Vaughan, asking him to come back.

Although Moxon's name was not mentioned on this occasion, reports could not be denied that he was about to return as director of professional cricket in a dream ticket partnership with Gough, who wasted no time in trying to convince McGrath to stick with Yorkshire. His persuasive approach paid off and McGrath agreed to stay on the very day that the mediation process with the ECB was due to begin.

The final pieces in the puzzle were quickly slotted into place as former captain and coach Moxon handed in his notice at Durham and was introduced to his new charges along with Ian Dews, who stepped up from cricket development officer to director of cricket operations, while McGrath was promoted to vice-captain.

Suddenly, there was a frenzy of activity as the new season loomed and Gough could not have faced a greater challenge than the Championship match which opened the programme at The Oval.

He was more than equal to the occasion but even he could not have envisaged such a crushing victory in the first meeting between the two deadly rivals in five years, particularly as Yorkshire had not won at the venue for the past 29 years.

Surrey were humbled by 346 runs to give Yorkshire their fourth highest runs win in Championship history and records were scattered like seed in the wind. Rudolph showed the sort of class he would exhibit throughout his stay with Yorkshire by opening his account with 122 and there were maiden Championship centuries also for Bresnan (116) and Gillespie (123 not out, Yorkshire's highest score by a No 10 batsman).

They piled up an incredible 246 together, the county's highest for the ninth wicket and the fifth biggest in first-class cricket. Gillespie's century was his first since his double Test ton against Bangladesh and it came upon his 32nd birthday. There was a classy second innings century from White and six wickets apiece in the match for Gough and Hoggard but perhaps the biggest debt was owed to Rashid who hit a career-best 86 in the first innings and initiated a recovery from 127-5 by adding 190 with Rudolph, a record against Surrey for the sixth wicket. Not content with that he grabbed four wickets in the first innings, including three in 15 balls, and three in the second.

Gough was cock-a-hoop and rightly so, the former Come Dancing champion's delight being intensified through pinning the current champ, Mark Ramprakash, lbw for a second innings duck.

"There was a lot of talk about the dancing rivalry but it was with mixed emotions that I got him out because he is in my fantasy team," said Gough, before pausing and adding: "But so am I, so terrific." The irrepressible charmer was well and truly back.

The Gough-Moxon partnership could not have made a better start and nothing at the moment could stand in its way, Younus contributing a match-winning century on his one-day debut against Nottinghamshire in the FP Trophy before Moxon put one over his old club by overseeing the nine-wicket caning of Durham in the Championship.

Sayers in this game showed extraordinary powers of concentration to carry his bat for 149, from 417 balls with 17 fours over 553 minutes, to become the only Yorkshire left-hander to achieve the feat twice. He was on the field the whole of the match and two further big centuries followed in the next three games to make him look unconquerable. It did not last and a string of miserable scores soon after receiving his cap led to him being dropped along with White, who bagged a pair at New Road.

In the Durham game at Headingley, the visitors were spun out in their first innings by Rashid, who had now collected 37 wickets at 23.94 in seven matches since his debut the previous year and was rapidly adding to his glowing reputation.

Yorkshire just ran out of time at the Rose Bowl, where Younus became the only White Rose batsman to score a century and a double century in the same match, but Worcestershire were swept aside at Headingley to make it three wins from four outings and keep Gough's marauders at the top of the Championship table until into August.

The only big problem for Yorkshire at this time was trying to accommodate Vaughan as he tried to improve his batting form ahead of the Test series with the West Indies. The England captain was preferred to White at the Rose Bowl and he contributed an elegant 72 in the first innings but had to retire hurt in the second when his finger was broken by Australian pace bowler Stuart Clark.

Even Gough's greatest critics could not query his commitment to the cause or his bowling, which had been given a new lease of life, and he was dynamic at Tunbridge Wells where he made Kent follow on with 6-47, his best figures for Yorkshire since 1996.

But during a lethal spell with the second new ball, when he claimed three wickets in six deliveries, he flung out an arm in a vain attempt to catch Ryan McLaren and broke a bone in his right hand. Kent were forced to follow-on and so desperate was Gough to end rugged resistance that he came on to bowl despite his injury and in his first over had Geraint Jones falling to a stunning catch by Younus at second slip. Six overs were the most he could manage, however, and James Tredwell's maiden century ensured the draw, Gough insisting on a return to the fray after resting his injury for less than a fortnight.

Yorkshire's enthusiasm under Gough never wavered even though results tailed off to some extent, apart from in the Twenty20 Cup where four consecutive wins set up a quarter-final match at Hove which they lost. Left-arm spinner and left-handed batsman David Wainwright, who went on to become Yorkshire's saviour more than once, made his first impact in this competition and he finished joint leading wicket-taker with eight dismissals.

Players and fans alike were saddened in mid-season when Yorkshire released Matthew Wood, who had been unable to regain his first team place after losing it in 2006. Everyone felt the loss caused by his departure but the runs just would not return and after a spell at Glamorgan he called it a day at first-class level.

Gough led from the front in all ways and in the rain-wrecked match against Surrey at Headingley he emerged with 6-50, surprisingly his best Championship figures on the ground.

In spite of a run of six consecutive draws, Yorkshire stayed ahead in the Championship race until their confidence, if not their enthusiasm, was badly affected by consecutive heavy defeats, first by Lancashire at Headingley, and then, even more alarmingly, by bottom-of-the-table Worcestershire at Kidderminster, where the home side were playing while their New Road headquarters recovered from disastrous flooding.

In the Roses encounter, Yorkshire had no sooner won the toss than they were three wickets down for one run in their struggle towards a wholly inadequate 144, which was no more than a grain of sand in the desert as Lancashire rampaged their way to 517. Much of the punishment came from Stuart Law, whose 206 off 250 balls with 27 fours and two sixes, was his side's highest individual score in Roses cricket, beating Reg Spooner's 200 not out at Old Trafford in 1948.

Paul Horton also amassed a career-best 149, he and the Aussie putting on 258 in 61 overs, a Lancashire record in these matches for any wicket. Shortly after 3pm on the third day, Yorkshire had capsized to defeat by an innings and 126 runs and it was no mere blip because they were decidedly second best against Worcestershire, who were still seeking their first win.

Rashid bolstered the middle-order with his maiden first-class century but it was not enough to upset Worcestershire who were set 336 off 65 overs and got there with seven overs and six wickets to spare.

This was Younus's last match before joining up with Pakistan's squad for the World Twenty20 in South Africa and there was a hint of panic in Yorkshire's search for a late replacement to kick-start their Championship ambitions again. They brought in former Pakistan captain Inzamam-ul-Haq for the last three matches but he never seemed to get over the bitter weather at Scarborough and remained distinctly cool throughout his short stay.

In any case, it did not matter that he failed at North Marine Road because Rudolph battered 220, only three runs short of the best on the ground in Yorkshire matches, and Bresnan hit an unbeaten 101. Hoggard had seen off Warwickshire in the first innings and Gough whipped out five in the second to bring victory by an innings and 210.

If the signing of Inzamam was unexpected, Yorkshire's sixth import of the season (four overseas and two Kolpak) had hardly been heard off, Pakistan A leg-spinner Imran Tahir arriving after a work permit hitch in time for the penultimate game with Sussex at Hove.

Tahir later proved himself to be a worthy exponent of his trade but it was asking too much of him to run through a side without any acclimatisation and he was flogged for 141 without picking up a wicket. Mushtaq Ahmed then showed how it should be done by snatching five wickets to make Yorkshire follow on and they were overpowered by an innings and 261 runs in what was Tahir's only appearance for the county.

The result inspired Sussex to go on and retain the title while Yorkshire had to be satisfied with sixth place and they were left to ponder what would have happened had they ended the season in similar style to how they started it.

Bob Appleyard's two-year term as president came to a close at the 2008 annual meeting in March and one of his last duties was to present a new award, the President's Medal, to Geoff Holmes and Vivien Stone, who have raised thousands of pounds running the second hand bookstall at Headingley on behalf of the John Featherstone Memorial Foundation.

The Medal is awarded for outstanding voluntary services to Yorkshire CCC and in its inaugural year the award was shared with Mollie Staines, a lifelong supporter who became the only woman to serve on the Yorkshire general committee. She later received her medal from the incoming president, Brian Close.

The following year, the award was again shared, this time the Medals going to Veronica Denby, a founder member of the Yorkshire CCC Supporters' Association and a familiar figure in their Kabin at Headingley, and Clifford Gregg, who spent countless hours helping out in the Yorkshire members' office in the indoor school. No further award has been made since then.

Gough was quick to agree to stay on as captain in 2008 at the end of which he was able to retire, happy in the knowledge that he left Yorkshire in the top divisions of the Championship and the NatWest Pro40 League – but only after a couple of near-miracles had occurred. Otherwise they would have gone down in the Championship and stayed down in the NatWest.

Yorkshire flattered to deceive in the Championship after beginning with an emphatic innings victory over Hampshire at Headingley, when Gale hit a glorious 138 to cement a permanent place in the side and be awarded his county cap at Scarborough in September.

But their only other win was achieved at Taunton, where Rudolph stroked 155, Gale managed a half-century in each innings and the bowlers all worked well together. Then followed a run of four defeats in five matches before a sequence of five draws saw them travel to Hove for the final game fearing the drop. And their depression became more acute as Sussex reduced them to 80-6.

From such depths of despair came one of their greatest fight backs of all time to secure a priceless five batting bonus points after none had seemed likely.

It began with an 80 stand between Bresnan and Rashid but the departures of Bresnan and Pyrah left the side in crisis again on 178-8, at which stage the tenacious Wainwright joined Rashid and the ninth-wicket pair put on 140 before Rashid bowed out with 111.

The score now was 318-9 and three batting bonus points had been salvaged but the chase was not yet over, Wainwright and Hoggard dashing up 82 for the last wicket. As soon as 400 was reached they were called in with five points in the bag and Wainwright unbeaten on 104, his maiden century coming off 166 balls. Never before had Yorkshire totalled 400 after losing their first six wickets so cheaply.

Wainwright was then on the money with the ball, claiming 3-9 as Sussex were bowled out for 207 and forced to follow on and only a determined century from Murray Goodwin prevented what would have been a sensational Yorkshire win Rashid took seven wickets and Wainwright two but having struggled into the lead the home side were able to declare with nine down to end the match, 12 points for Yorkshire being sufficient for them to stay up.

A grim battle also went right to the wire in Division Two of the NatWest Pro40 League. In the last round of matches, table-toppers Essex needed to beat Kent and Yorkshire were required to beat bottom side Northants in order for Gough to lead his men up. Essex duly obliged but Northants appeared to have taken Yorkshire to the cleaners at 157-4 in their canter towards a 183 target.

Injuries and indifferent form had turned it into a generally disappointing season for Kruis but here he summoned up the energy for a blistering spell of four wickets in 15 balls, including opener Sales whom he yorked for 88 to end the match with Northants five runs short.

A new batting star had arrived on the scene in 2008 in the form of Adam Lyth, Yorkshire's first player to hail from Whitby, and he drew great inspiration from Rudolph, the only one to exceed 1,000 runs in the Championship. Rashid's star was once more in the ascendancy and his 62 wickets earned him a place on England's tour of the West Indies where he came down to earth with a bump and some of the shine was taken off his reputation. His wish to become the next Shane Warne suffered a setback from which it is still recovering.

Not everything worked out right for Yorkshire and their best-laid plans sometimes went awry. Rana Naved-ul-Hasan was signed from Sussex but never fully recovered from a serious shoulder injury sustained late in the 2007 season and was well below par in each of his two years at Headingley. South African fast bowler Morne Morkel, drafted in as back-up, could have been an inspired choice had he not gone down with a hamstring injury in what proved to be his one and only match.

And there is no doubt whatsoever that Yorkshire's confidence was seriously affected by the Azeem Rafiq affair which brought an abrupt halt to their Twenty20 progress minutes before they were due to walk out to face Durham in the quarter-finals at Riverside.

In the last of the North Division matches, Rafiq, the hugely promising 17-year-old off-spinner/batsman, was given his first team debut against Notts at Trent Bridge, a game dominated by Yorkshire's batsmen and one in which Rafiq's two overs for 18 runs seemed of little consequence in comparison to Rashid's 4-24.

Yet his appearance in the match would result in back page headlines because the former England Under 15s captain, born in Pakistan but brought up in Barnsley, had not been properly registered. And it came to light on the day of Yorkshire's quarter-final at Riverside that neither did he hold a British passport, so making him an unauthorised overseas player.

The upshot was that the game had to be called off with thousands already in the ground and after an ECB disciplinary panel later cleared Yorkshire of deliberately flouting regulations the result of the Notts match was eventually allowed to stand, Yorkshire being deducted two points and ordered to pay £2,000 costs. The decision paved the way for Glamorgan to play Durham instead but they failed to make the most of their good fortune.

Yorkshire withdrew Rafiq from all cricket but during August the ECB ruled he could play for the county while his application for British citizenship was being processed.

The start to his career for Rafiq was traumatic but for Gough the end of his career was glorious and a fitting way to celebrate his 38th birthday. In the penultimate Championship match at Scarborough – the third game of the season at North Marine Road due to the drainage work going on at Headingley – he defied sore shins at the start of the final day to bowl with all the verve of his pomp.

One sensed that this was to be his last hurrah as he plucked out Craig Kieswetter's off-stump with an absolute snorter and then beat Justin Langer off the pitch to have him nicking a catch to Brophy. The Aussie was a top-class scalp and the last of the Dazzler's 453 wickets for Yorkshire. Gough came back for a further spell but he had flung everything into that opening burst and was a spent force, too far down the line to include himself in the last-match thriller at Hove but content that he had done everything he possibly could in his two years back as captain.

CHAPTER FIFTY
BUILDING THE FUTURE

Certain aspects of the 2009 season were a mirror-image of the one just gone, the baton upon Gough's retirement having passed into the hands of McGrath who had previously taken on the captaincy six years earlier.

Remember the heroics of Wainwright & Co at Hove in saving Yorkshire from relegation in the Championship? Well, 12 months on and a repeat performance on the same ground for the same high stakes.

This time the outcome was even sweeter because the game ended in a Yorkshire victory rather than a draw but the consequence was exactly the same, with the team finishing directly above the two relegation slots.

Only two matches remained when Yorkshire travelled to Hove after having won only one fixture all season – and that success did not arrive until they visited Basingstoke in August and beat Hampshire by an innings and 22 runs to end an inglorious run of 21 outings without a victory.

Once again, the redoubtable Wainwright helped to keep Sussex at bay, he and Shahzad rescuing Yorkshire from 209-7 with a stand of 157, the highest for Yorkshire's eighth wicket at Hove. Shahzad contributed 88 and Wainwright an unbeaten 85 to a first innings score of 403, and the same pair then shared nine wickets as Sussex reached 448 through 171 not out from Rory Hamilton-Brown.

Yorkshire's second innings 284 brought a lead of 239 and with time running out, a draw seemed the likely conclusion until Sussex decided to go for the runs. They were well-placed on 44-2 at tea but everything went haywire after the interval as Hoggard and Wainwright ran riot to shatter them for 83, Hoggard turning the game with a hat-trick and Wainwright ending it with a couple of wickets that gave him 9-146 in the match and 99 runs without being dismissed.

So Yorkshire had slipped out of the hangman's noose yet again but it was all too close for comfort, even though some positives had come out of the summer, notably the emergence of Jonny Bairstow who soon proved to have the same spirit of adventure as his father, the late David.

The 19-year-old wicketkeeper-batsman, born in Bradford like his dad, had shown immense talent while at St Peter's School at York and he began 2009 for the Second XI in a style which suggested his elevation to the senior ranks could not be far away. In their first Championship game at Kidderminster he dashed up 110 against Worcestershire Seconds and then 63 off Warwickshire's attack at King's Heath, Birmingham, before moving on to Oakham, where he had Leicestershire in a whirl with 63 and 202 not out. Still Bairstow's thirst for runs was not sated because MCC Young Cricketers were next up at Stamford Bridge, where he galloped to 147, giving him 585 runs in five innings at an average of 146.25.

By the time of this last knock in the sequence, he had already made his first team debut against Somerset at Headingley and his relaxed style and abundant talent were there for all to see in the second innings which left him unbeaten on

82. He was now a permanent fixture, to be seen either behind the stumps or in the field, and at the end of the season he stood on 592 Championship runs in 12 matches with six half-centuries.

During Bairstow's Second XI rampage, other young batsmen were also starting to blossom alongside him. In the Leicestershire match, Sheffield's Joe Root, a young man with the composure and attention to detail of Boycott, scored 163 and assisted Bairstow in adding a match-winning unbroken 358, a competition record. And against MCC Young Cricketers, Gary Ballance, nephew of former Zimbabwe captain David Houghton, scored 212, putting on 238 with Bluey's lad. Two years on and all three players were fully established, Bairstow towards the end of 2011 making his one-day debut for England.

The rising sap in the Second XI in 2009 helped make it a fruitful season in which the team finished second in their group of the Championship in addition to winning the one-day Trophy competition, beating Lancashire in the final at Scarborough.

White had captained the side astutely – from the ringside when not including himself in the starting line-up – but it was appropriate that Guy, shortly to retire, should be the leader when the silverware came into their possession at North Marine Road and that he should receive it from Close.

One policy which paid dividends for McGrath and Moxon was the promotion of Rudolph to open the innings with Sayers. A serious shortage of runs from the various first-wicket partnerships in 2008 could not be allowed to go on – the tenth-wicket pair had even been more productive – and the new combination made sure that it didn't.

Both batsmen exceeded 1,000 runs, Sayers for the first time, and they added 1,288 together, a figure surpassed by only two of the other top-flight counties. The move was an obvious success but it still had its critics because there were those who felt that Rudolph would have stacked up even more than 1,334 runs had he been coming in when the shine was off the new ball.

Not only Rudolph and the younger players made an impact in 2009, Sayers and McGrath embedding themselves at Edgbaston to set a Yorkshire record for the third wicket of 342, this displacing the distinguished names of Sutcliffe and Leyland, whose unbroken 323 had been established against Glamorgan at Huddersfield in 1928. Sayers completed his first century in almost two years and stood defiant for nine hours and 38 minutes while moving on to 173 and McGrath, foot on throttle after a hesitant start, was able to celebrate his maiden double-century.

The season also saw Vaughan's career draw to a sad and unsatisfactory conclusion on June 28. He was due to have played in Yorkshire's final Twenty20 North Division match against Derbyshire at Headingley on that particular day but stepped down after he had said in a newspaper article that his playing days were drawing to a close.

In the latter part of the 2008 season, having already given way as England captain, he had tried without success to rediscover his best Test form at county level, and now he made one last despairing effort to salvage his international career.

But in five Championship matches he was a pale shadow of his former self, scoring only 147 runs in seven innings at No 3, the position which the England management had requested that he bat. This in itself presented Yorkshire with a difficulty because it meant they could not accommodate Adam Lyth, who needed regular first team cricket. When Lyth did eventually get his chance he had lost his rhythm and form.

The ideal send-off in front of an appreciative crowd which Vaughan deserved never materialised but he at least had the satisfaction of being Yorkshire's leading run-maker in the Friends Provident Trophy that season.

While Vaughan declined, so Gale ascended, making attractive runs in both Championship and one-day cricket and standing supreme in the Twenty20 Cup, his 383 runs almost 200 above anyone else in the side.

At the end of the season, Yorkshire lost another of their great players with the departure of Hoggard to captain Leicestershire and he left with little goodwill on either side. He claimed he had been sacked but Yorkshire insisted that he had been released because he had refused to sign, in the April, a two-year contract with the option of a third based on performance.

Yorkshire's priority was to hold on to Ajmal Shahzad, whose services were in demand elsewhere, and once he had agreed to a new and improved contract there was no willingness to upgrade the offer to Hoggard. Moving on probably served the best interests of player and club.

Nevertheless, Hoggard had been Yorkshire's top wicket-taker in the Championship in 2009 but neither he nor the other pacemen were consistently sharp enough to rattle opposing batsmen.

As well as all the cricket that was on offer at Headingley during the summer, spectators also absorbed themselves in watching the building of the new Headingley Carnegie pavilion and media centre, Meccano-like in its construction.

In order that the work could start, Yorkshire had raised the £4.85m required to buy out the option payments to Leeds CFAC which had been agreed in 2005 when they had bought the ground. The total cost of the project was £21m and Yorkshire's contribution of £7m included £4m from Yorkshire Forward, the regional development agency. The remaining £14m was provided by Leeds Metropolitan University, who would occupy most of the building and also the media centre as a lecture theatre when it was not required for Test matches or one-day internationals. For Yorkshire matches, the media would be shunted into a much smaller room with limited visibility for those not fortunate enough to be on the front row.

The Headingley Carnegie pavilion was on schedule to be opened the following year but already in use was the ground's new drainage system, installed with a £600,000 ECB grant. It was in service for the first one-day international between England and the West Indies on May 21, but it still needed time to bed in and it was unable to cope with the torrents of rain which flooded the ground shortly before the game was due to begin. Perversely, the sun was shining brightly when the umpires were forced to abandon proceedings, leaving 11,000 spectators grumbling into their watery beer, but on this occasion at least Yorkshire did not deserve any of the flak that was flying around.

Neither was it Yorkshire's fault that in the fourth Ashes Test at Headingley, England should be slaughtered by an innings in less than two and a half days, the game only lasting that long because of a cavalier go-down-fighting stand between Stuart Broad and Graeme Swann. The thumping levelled the series but England redeemed themselves by winning at The Oval.

CHAPTER FIFTY-ONE

GALE SWEEPS IN

At 1.53pm on September 16, 2010, Yorkshire received an emotional standing ovation as they walked off the field at Headingley to bring their season to a close.

It was a spontaneous wave of applause of a kind never heard before because Yorkshire were not glorious winners but shock losers, having just suffered a shattering defeat at the hands of Kent which was to cost them the Championship.

Yorkshire followers are not in the habit of applauding defeats and they weren't doing so on this occasion, either. They were showing their gratitude for a season which had promised little, yet achieved much – and might well have achieved far more if nerves had held for just one more week.

Had Yorkshire beaten Kent on that fateful day, and they were well-placed to do so right up to their capitulation, they would have taken the title because of the way results unfolded elsewhere. But they didn't and they had to settle for third place behind new champions Nottinghamshire and Somerset.

The sudden turndown had begun at Scarborough the previous Saturday when Yorkshire had denied themselves a place at Lord's by losing by four wickets to Warwickshire in the semi-final of the Clydesdale Bank 40, the game being played at North Marine Road because Headingley the following day was staging a one-day international between England and Pakistan.

Until that point, Yorkshire had thrilled and delighted with a brand of cricket that had warmed the cockles of the heart and restored faith and pride in the team. And a young and exciting team at that, led by a rookie captain in Gale to whom they responded by giving their all. If they had a fault it was that they came to believe they were invincible and their pain was intense when they suddenly collided with a brick wall.

For the second time in his career, McGrath nobly surrendered the captaincy at the end of 2009, believing that it had badly affected his form, a state of affairs which he felt was not good either for himself or the men under him. He was unhappy with his 825 runs, a figure inflated by the double century at Edgbaston, and his reasoning was sound because, unburdened, he eased his way to 1,219 runs.

Under Gale in 2010, Yorkshire appeared relaxed and uninhibited and there were massive contributions almost right across the board. Rudolph, in his last full season, enjoyed marginally the most successful of his Championship campaigns with 1,375 runs but even he was not the equal of the dynamic Lyth.

With his place in the side assured – at least for the time being – he became the first batsman in the country to 1,000 runs and romped on to 1,509, with three centuries and nine half-centuries, to perch himself on top of the county batting averages with 52.03.

If it were not Lyth of the younger brigade who was setting the game alight with the bat, then it was either Bairstow or Rashid who between them totted up 14 half-centuries, Bairstow possessing an ability to reserve his best efforts for run chases when it really mattered.

The bowling also benefited from youthful and willing exertions, Rashid spinning his way to 57 wickets, Patterson's accuracy being rewarded with 45, Shahzad's menacing pace fetching him 34 victims on the occasions when, like Bresnan, he was not required by England, and Oliver Hannon-Dalby coming on in leaps and bounds to secure 34 victims.

The tall and willowy Hannon-Dalby was to a large extent responsible for Yorkshire making the splendid start to the Championship season which led to their self-belief. He took five wickets in each of the opening four-wicket wins against Warwickshire and Somerset and never missed a match in the competition, his strength preserved through being shielded from all one-day activity.

Almost at the end of the programme, Yorkshire paraded another of their emerging fast bowlers by bringing in Moin Ashraf and in the last two games he collected 9-106 to give him an average of a wicket every 11.77 runs. In the first innings of what turned out to be the rout by Kent, his figures of 5-32 were the best return of the season.

So what went wrong in that final week? Everyone fancied Yorkshire's chances in the Clydesdale Bank 40 semi-final but, in a contest reduced to 37 overs a side, the batsmen did not show enough urgency in making 257-5, despite Rudolph's fourth century in 13 games, and the bowlers, for once, looked tired and powerless to stop Darren Maddy's late and brutal assault.

The amount taken out of Yorkshire by this reversal did not surface against Kent until the final day when the domino effect took hold and they hit the deck. The morning began well as Lyth and McGrath hurried the score on to 93-1 to build a useful lead of 52 and the question on everyone's lips was at what stage in the afternoon would there be a declaration?

Suddenly, McGrath fell to an almost unplayable ball from Andre Nel and, unaccountably, panic set in, the last nine wickets toppling for 37 in 55 balls with Tredwell performing a hat-trick in his 7-22.

Shahzad desperately tried to make amends by dismissing both openers with only six scored but an 89 target was simply too small to defend and Kent hit it with four wickets remaining, although they could still not avoid relegation. Another 50 runs for Yorkshire could have made all the difference to the result.

West Indian pace merchant Tino Best, South African run-machine Herschelle Gibbs, and Australian quickie Clint McKay were all recruited for particular roles, Best in the hope of creating shock and awe with his unquestionable speed, and Gibbs and McKay to add fizz in the Friends Provident t20.

Best, sometimes over-enthusiastic, was unpredictable, occasionally producing a real rocket but more often than not being too erratic. He soon had the home crowds on his side but was unable to deliver what was really required. Gibbs could not be faulted and was as professional as one would expect but although he topped the t20 batting with 443 runs and McKay, in between Australia A duty, chipped in with ten wickets they could not lift Yorkshire above sixth place out of nine in the North Group.

Raymond Illingworth had become president in 2010 and he was on hand on July 21, the first day of the Pakistan v Australia Test match, when the Duke of

Gloucester officially opened the Headingley Carnegie Pavilion by unveiling a plaque during the lunch break.

Regan had seen his vision of a state-of-the-art pavilion on Yorkshire's own ground become a reality but he was not around much longer to appreciate it. In a little over a week's time he announced he would be vacating his post at the end of the season to become chief executive of the Scottish FA.

Poor ticket sales for the Pakistan v Australia Test cost Yorkshire around £750,000 and significantly worsened their parlous financial situation. In view of this, Graves decided that Regan would not be replaced for at least a year and that, in the meantime, he himself would once again take over the role of chief executive as well as remaining chairman of the Board. One continued to wonder just where Yorkshire would be if Graves were not around to bail them out.

There was, however, some better news in November when it was revealed that Bradford car company JCT600 had agreed to become Yorkshire's main sponsors from the following April in a three-year six-figure deal.

And on March 18, 2011, the Headingley Carnegie cricket ground was further enhanced by the opening of the £300,000 museum below the East Stand in what were the club's offices before they were moved lock, stock and barrel into the Carnegie Pavilion.

The superbly designed museum was opened by Dr. Keith Howard, chairman of the trustees of the Emerald Foundation which had so generously funded the project along with the Yorkshire Cricket Foundation.

The seeds that eventually grew into the museum were planted a decade earlier when Robin Smith, then club president, suggested that Harold North should head up an Archives Committee which would be responsible for bringing together and cataloguing items which were an important part of Yorkshire's history.

North became the first Archives chairman upon its formation in 2002 and he held office until 2005 when David Hall took over for the next five years. Construction of the museum began in March, 2009, and upon its completion, Hall involved himself with the meticulous arrangement and display of many of its items. He was particularly well-suited to this type of work, having as a young man learned to dress shop windows in London's West End during his management training which led to him becoming chairman and managing director of Collier Holdings plc.

Hall also headed up the Museum Development Group and in July, 2010, he stood down from the Archives Committee to become Museum Director, updating with a natural eye for detail both the displays in the museum and in the cabinets in the Long Room. He was succeeded as Archives chairman by the industrious David Allan, a founder member, who was responsible for overseeing the transfer to Headingley of Wilfred Rhodes's magnificent collection of cricket memorabilia which had been gifted to Yorkshire by the great man's granddaughter, Mrs. Margaret Garton.

With the ground and its amenities now transformed and the club in possession of a team which had just performed so gallantly, Yorkshire should have been the kings of county cricket in 2011 – but they turned out to be among the paupers, despite having secured the considerable services of Ryan Sidebottom who returned from Nottinghamshire to see out the remainder of his career on home soil.

A year earlier, Yorkshire had confounded the bookies with the strength of their challenges, now they surprised them with an undignified fall from grace which saw them relegated in the Championship and outmanoeuvred in one-day cricket.

Not a case of being too full of themselves, in my opinion, but of still feeling vulnerable, the shock of crumbling in the final week of the previous season having eroded much of their confidence.

Desperate times called for desperate measures and so deep was the fear of relegation that Yorkshire brought back Rudolph in the third week in July to try to dig them out of a hole. He was available for four matches, scored 318 runs with all of his old panache but could not stop the downward spiral.

The season had begun promisingly with a nine-wicket win over Worcestershire at New Road. It was made possible by a scintillating career-best 177 not out from Brophy and career-best match figures of 11-114 by Rashid, but neither player got anywhere near matching these splendid efforts again.

Yorkshire did not win their second match until their tenth game when they completed the double over Worcestershire, whose late spurt was to save them from relegation, and the only other victory for the White Rose came in the final fixture against Somerset at Headingley when it was too late to matter.

To add to their general discomfort, Yorkshire conceded the double to Lancashire, who went on to become worthy Championship winners, but both of these games were among the most dramatic ever played between the old foes. Indeed, at Headingley Richard Pyrah earned himself a place in Yorkshire's history by playing a fighting innings of the very highest calibre in what was his side's 3,000th Championship match.

Yorkshire were sinking fast at 45-8 in reply to Lancashire's 328 after being inserted but Pyrah then mixed stunning strokeplay with rugged defence to record his maiden Championship century on his way to 117 off 126 balls with 12 fours and three sixes.

His heroics would not have been possible without bold assistance from Sidebottom, who contributed a splendid 52 in a ninth wicket stand of 154, Yorkshire's highest at Headingley in all first-class matches.

With Sidebottom's departure, in came Bresnan who had driven from the England camp at Lord's during the partnership to replace his stand-in, debutant fast bowler Iain Wardlaw, a product of Cleckheaton in the Bradford League.

Pyrah and Bresnan were able to add a priceless 40 together before Pyrah finally succumbed but the first innings deficit had been reduced to 89 and as Lancashire stumbled to 87-8 they appeared to be losing their grip. It was tightened again with gritty half-centuries for Sajid Mahmood and Kyle Hogg, who put on 127 for the ninth wicket, and Yorkshire were left to make 284 to win. All but Ballance, who bagged a pair, made telling contributions and the tension in the air could have been cut with a knife the nearer Yorkshire got to the finishing line.

The great irony was that Bresnan's appearance relegated Pyrah to No 11 in the order, Sidebottom having already been used as an effective nightwatchman, and it was Pyrah, of all people, who had to be last out, lbw to Keedy when only 23 runs separated the sides.

At least Yorkshire fought back in this pot-boiler, unlike in some other games where they collapsed inexplicably, most notably in the Headingley encounters with Nottinghamshire and Warwickshire.

Although the team disappointed in 2011, some of the players acquitted themselves with great distinction and advanced their careers. Bairstow's reputation was already high at the start of the season and it continued to soar until England recognition came in September.

The only irritation in his development had been a failure to turn any of his first 16 Championship 50s into centuries but all that ended at Trent Bridge in early May when he converted his maiden first-class 100 into a double century, the first time a Yorkshire player had done this since Major Booth almost exactly 100 years ago – on May 22, 1911.

Bairstow was the only player to reach 1,000 Championship runs but equally as pleasing for the club and the fans was the fine form shown by Root, who gathered up 937 runs in his debut season and exceeded 1,000 in all first-class matches, courtesy of his 66 and 10 for England Lions against Sri Lanka at Scarborough.

Ballance, too, refused to waste his opportunity once it came and he was the model of reliability, making at least a half-century in almost every match – his Roses 'pair' being a glaring exception.

Pyrah showed extra maturity with both bat and ball and Sidebottom valiantly carried the flag for the fast bowlers as well as making significant runs when they were most urgently needed. His bowling became sharper as the season wore on and his 62 wickets were a fine example of what determination and sheer hard work can bring.

 Yorkshire had been happy to start the season without an overseas signing and they were proud to point out that Brophy was the only non-Yorkshireman in the side for the win over Worcestershire in the first match. They believed they would be strong enough soon to field a full Yorkshire-born XI again but they began to realise that they still required the skill and experience of a top-class outsider to help them along.

There was no doubt that Rudolph's presence was badly missed, his brief re-appearance boosting the confidence of Lyth to mention but one, and as they planned for 2012 they signed Jaques to introduce some of the steel he had injected into the side in 2004-05.

The Board also changed the structure of the coaching set-up, the five current coaches working under Moxon being invited to apply for the four new coaching posts which were being advertised.

White decided not to apply and was soon taken on as Second XI coach by Hampshire and the headline news from the changes was that Jason Gillespie had agreed to return to Headingley as first team coach. Up to his appointment he had been coach of Mid West Rhinos in Zimbabwe.

Paul Farbrace was recruited as senior second team coach, having resigned as Kent's director of cricket in September, and he had also spent a couple of years as assistant coach to Sri Lanka.

Ian Dews stayed on in the new role of director of cricket development and the 'team' was completed by development manager Richard Damms who had previously worked with the Yorkshire Cricket Board and the county's age-group and Academy teams.

As mentioned earlier, neither Steve Oldham nor Kevin Sharp found themselves a part of the new structure and their long and valuable service to Yorkshire drew to a close, their departures not being welcomed by all of the county's followers.

In other changes, Boycott was elected as President at the annual meeting in March, taking over from Illingworth, and Vaughan was co-opted on to the Management Board in place of Boycott.

The 2012 pre-season tour to Barbados was a big success with Yorkshire competing against other counties to scoop the Barbados Twenty20 Cup and Sayers impressed sufficiently for Moxon and Gillespie to get their heads together and make him official vice-captain.

Now all that remained was for the team to gain the promotion in 2012 that Boycott had made an impassioned plea for at the annual meeting and which would see them in the top bracket during their 150th anniversary year of 2013.

CHAPTER FIFTY-TWO

DOING AS INSTRUCTED

Boycott's message to the players upon being elected as President was a blunt one. The only thing that really mattered to the membership, he said, was Championship cricket. The team could play well in 40 overs and 20 overs cricket but if they played badly in Championship cricket they would let the members down.

Immediate promotion was very important because in their 150th anniversary year they should be striving to win the Championship and they couldn't do that if they were in the Second Division.

"We have to get out of it," he implored. "The young players have to perform and some didn't do that in 2011 when they let themselves and the club down. That has to stop."

Graves had already taken a hard swipe at the players' performances in 2011 and with Boycott now spelling out in the frankest of terms the need for an immediate improvement the team clearly knew what was expected of them.

And they delivered. Not just in the Championship, where the weather-sodden summer meant they had to wait until the last match, against Essex at Chelmsford, to achieve their objective, but also in the Friends Life t20, reaching Finals Day in Cardiff for the very first time and going on to contest the final with Hampshire after an emphatic win over Sussex.

In the end, they lost by ten runs to Hampshire but their reward was to earn a place in the qualifying stages of the Twenty20 Champions League competition in South Africa in October. The boost to their confidence was immeasurable because they had shown they were at last good enough to make an appearance on the international scene.

From a consistency point of view, Yorkshire were at their best in the t20, their sequence of eight victories en route to Finals Day being split only by two 'no results' from washouts.

When the players had listened so intently to Boycott's words in the spring, neither he nor they were to know that county cricket was about to endure its wettest summer in 100 years.

The persistent rains made the Championship programme little more than a lottery and although every county was literally treading water for much of the time Yorkshire could not get sufficiently into their stride to show what they were really made of until the weather finally relented and they won their last three matches in great style.

So wet was the spring that, come the half-way stage of their programme following the Glamorgan match at Colwyn Bay, Yorkshire had lost 1,151 overs, which represented 37.47 per cent of the total play possible.

Just when you thought it could not possibly get any wetter, it did, and umbrellas were to remain pointing skywards as the big soak continued. When the second and third days of the 14th match – against Gloucestershire at Scarborough – were washed out, scorer John Potter calculated that 8,561 minutes of Championship cricket had gushed down the drain, almost 24 days' play out of a possible 55!

Yet a surge towards the end, allied with a degree of good fortune, kept them among the promotion contenders from start to finish.

Brimming with enthusiasm in his new job from the off, Gillespie exuded confidence at every turn, always seeing the best in his first team squad and never admitting to any negative thoughts or doubting for a moment that Yorkshire would not be up there with the leaders in all competitions.

But his optimism could not hide the fact that Yorkshire were second best in two of their first three Championship matches or that one or two early tactical decisions would come under scrutiny.

The elevation to the vice-captaincy of Sayers, although well-received, left some people wondering whether his encouraging pre-season form abroad would continue and allow him to stay in the side. He made a positive start before slipping away and was dropped after five matches.

His inclusion from the off meant there was no immediate place for Lyth, a rising star only two years earlier, but his time would come and in some style, his place in the record books being assured when he became the only player in Yorkshire's history to score a double century while carrying his bat.

The decision to include rookie paceman Iain Wardlaw in the first match against Kent in preference to Steve Patterson was a bit of a mystery. This move clearly did not work and Patterson was quickly restored to the side and was their leading wicket-taker from then on, earning 48 wickets at a miserly 20.81 runs apiece.

The signing of Australian left-arm paceman Mitchell Starc and South African left-hander David Miller, chiefly to bolster their t20 ambitions, could not be faulted and it led to Yorkshire finishing top of North Group and earning a home quarter-final draw against Worcestershire, which they won with some ease.

But, in the Championship, with Ryan Sidebottom out injured in mid-July, Moxon and Gillespie were much less successful when they brought in Steve Harmison on a month's loan from Durham where the former England dynamo had been unable to command a place in the side.

The hope was that Harmison would blast his way through opposing batsmen and he did, indeed, pick up a few wickets with real snorters, including twice yorking a bemused Ramnaresh Sarwan, the former West Indies skipper, in the match against Leicestershire at Grace Road, which Yorkshire would in all probability have won but for the adverse weather.

As some had suspected, however, Harmison also sent down a plethora of no-balls and wides and he was even jeered by some Yorkshire fans at Grace Road, behaviour which was roundly condemned by Gillespie who retorted: "As far as I am concerned, Harmy's been fantastic. There have been times when he's sprayed the ball around a bit but we know that the more overs he gets, the better he gets."

In three weather-hit draws, Harmison collected a total of eight wickets in 42 overs for 195 runs, but he suffered a calf injury late on in the Leicestershire match and returned to Durham for treatment rather than being able to play for Yorkshire at Northampton – the turn of Gale's men this time to be rescued by the rain.

At the start of the season, Yorkshire had opened their Championship programme on April 5 under blue skies at Headingley (they were not to know then what a great rarity this would be) despite the ground being hidden under several inches of snow the previous day.

The team were quickly made to realise that promotion would be no pushover as Kent amassed 537-9 declared, their highest score on a Yorkshire ground. There was a maiden century for 21-year-old Matt Coles and his 153 stand with Mark Davies was a Kent record for the ninth wicket against Yorkshire and the second best to be recorded at Headingley.

Bairstow went a long way towards repairing the damage by celebrating his inclusion in the England Performance Squad by hitting his first home Championship century. The fates were with him, but not Pyrah, who broke a bone in his left hand in freak circumstances in the Kent innings when he rolled over to complete a piece of fielding and his thumb was pushed into the ground. When he returned much later in the season he did exactly the same again and was left to ponder that things could only get better in 2013.

Bairstow's innings kept him in the eye of the England selectors and continuing good form and an injury to Ravi Bopara brought him his Test debut against the West Indies at Lord's on May 17. He had already played in six one-day internationals for England and six Twenty20 matches but now he had climbed to the summit. Everything had so far run smoothly for him but staying at the top proved harder than getting there. He struggled for runs in the three-match series, which England won 2-0, and slipped off the radar for a while.

But Bairstow was to return to the England fold in the most dramatic of circumstances – and to establish himself as a batsman of rare ability and temperament with a memorable performance.

Less than two weeks before the third and final Test against South Africa at Lord's, neither Bairstow nor anyone else could have imagined that he would be selected for a crucial game which England had to win to end the series on level terms.

Then Kevin Pietersen destroyed himself at his now infamous Press Conference immediately after the second Test at Headingley Carnegie, where he scored a fabulous 149, and the temporary withdrawal from Test cricket for domestic reasons of Bopara opened a door for Bairstow which seemed to have been shut in his face.

His response was to score a breathtaking 95 in front of a packed house and against the best bowling attack in the world and he was only spitting distance from recording one of Test cricket's greatest centuries when he was bowled by Morne Morkel. In the second innings he scored a handsome 54 and although he could not save the match for England he had more than proved his pedigree.

Meanwhile, in their second Championship match Yorkshire had a taste of what was in store for them in 2012 when the first day of their game against Essex at Headingley was washed out. It also signalled the re-appearance of Jaques, whose registration as a non-overseas player had been cleared at Lord's the previous day, and he soon showed he had lost none of the prowess which he exhibited for the club in 2004-05 by striking a powerful century, contributing 126 out of a score of 246.

Bopara then managed an even bigger percentage of the runs for Essex, an unbeaten 117 out of 199. He was the only one not to be troubled by Sidebottom, who bagged 5-30, and Gale's later decision to set the visitors 262 in 74 overs was proof of his promise to be positive at all times. Essex were struggling on 26-2 off 11.1 overs when rain intervened.

So strong was the spin coming out of Yorkshire about everyone working in great harmony that it came as a big surprise to the public that Shahzad's appearance in the third match against Kent at Canterbury should also prove to be his last.

During the game with Leicestershire which followed at Scarborough, Graves called a press conference to explain that there had been "irreconcilable differences" between Shahzad and the club and that a parting of the ways had been mutually agreed.

It seemed that some of those differences concerned how Shahzad thought he should bowl, which were at odds with how the club wanted him to bowl. Whatever the reasons, it was sad that the first Yorkshire-born player from an ethnic background to represent the club should leave under a cloud. But he was quickly taken on for the remainder of the season by Lancashire where he immediately settled into the dressing room. Yet he could not stop the Red Rose from hurtling into the Second Division while Yorkshire had their finger firmly pressed on the lift button for the top floor.

Graves was certainly the right man to spell out the Shahzad situation to the media. While the game at North Marine Road was still in progress it was announced that he had now taken on the role of executive chairman of the club, an amalgamation of his existing role as chairman of the Management Board and the vacant post of chief executive.

Ten years earlier, he had fronted the Gang of Four which had taken over the running of the club and now he had become the most powerful individual in Yorkshire's history and the cornerstone of its future. He was working full-time at Headingley in a salaried position and had retained his place on the ECB Management Board.

Graves had sold the last of his Costcutter shares the previous November and had been offered the role of non-executive chairman of the company, but instead he decided to throw his full weight into running Yorkshire.

The Leicestershire encounter at Scarborough was a bitterly cold affair with temperatures never rising above 8C, so cold in fact that one couple were seen to be watching from their sleeping bags! Aided by another century from Bairstow, Yorkshire beat Matthew Hoggard's strugglers by an innings and 22 runs, and when they moved on to Bristol to overcome Gloucestershire with a massive gamble which paid off they jointly topped the Championship table.

Instead of allowing the game to splutter to another rain-hit draw, Gale risked sacrificing points when he agreed that Yorkshire should chase 400 from a minimum 110 overs. And chase them down they did, winning by four wickets with 20 balls to spare to hit the second highest target in the club's history, Jaques blasting 160 from 256 deliveries with 17 fours and Ballance 121 not out from 221 balls with ten fours and three sixes, the last two big hits from consecutive blows to end the match.

This was the last positive result Yorkshire would be involved in for a long while because one cloudburst after another resulted in the next eight Championship matches all ending in draws, the stalemate finally ending when Gloucestershire were found to be in an even more generous mood at Scarborough than they had been at Bristol.

Frustration, also, for Starc, who arrived in England in early May after first flying from the West Indies to Australia, but was promptly deported because of visa problems. When he returned with everything in order on May 15 he had been through 14 airports in 12 days, earning the nickname Terminal from his new team-mates, and Yorkshire decided he was too travel-weary to make his Championship debut against Hampshire at Headingley Carnegie the following day. That came shortly afterwards in the match against Northamptonshire on the same ground when he eased himself in with a couple of wickets and showed genuine pace.

The continuing wet weather made it impossible to gauge just how sharp Yorkshire were as a team but Root and Lyth each managed a marathon innings during July. At the Rose Bowl, Root hammered out an unbeaten 222 from 270 balls with 26 fours and three sixes. Jaques, acting as captain for the injured Gale, declared the innings on 350-9, but had he instructed last-man, Ashraf, to get out instead, then Root would have become the first Yorkshire batsman to carry his bat with a double century.

Would such a rare chance ever occur again? The answer was 'Yes' and only two matches down the line. This time Root was out for a duck against Leicestershire at Grace Road but his opening partner, Lyth, batted throughout the entire innings for his unbeaten 248 off 395 deliveries, punching 28 fours and three sixes.

When Lyth returned to the dressing room he was showered with congratulations upon carrying his bat, but he had not heard of the term before and answered with a puzzled frown: "But I have been carrying it for the past one-and-a-half days!"

Rashid began the season in disappointing form and the ever-improving Rafiq replaced him at Headingley Carnegie for the Northants match. Happily for Rashid, he gradually found his touch in the second team and the two spinners both played in the return fixture at Northampton where Rashid cashed in with five wickets.

Yorkshire had the better of the exchanges with table-toppers Derbyshire at Headingley Carnegie in August, but could not make up for time lost to the weather in a crucial match. Although taking 11 points from the draw, they slipped out of joint second place.

There was surprise news on another front before this game began with the sudden announcement that Gerard Brophy's contract would not be renewed at the end of the season and that he would not be playing again. He was thanked for his services but no reason for the 'disappearance' of such a popular player was given.

Sussex wicketkeeper Andrew Hodd, languishing in the second team back home, was recruited at a couple of days notice to stand in when Bairstow was unavailable for Championship matches. Hodd did a magnificent job on his Yorkshire debut, scoring a valuable 58 and holding on to five catches in the Derbyshire first innings. He continued to look the part and after three matches had brought him 16 catches he was given a two-year contract for 2013-2014.

The second of those matches was against Gloucestershire at Scarborough where there was good news and bad before the start, Root and Ballance being handed their first team caps, but Sidebottom having to stand down with back muscle spasms and Pyrah out of the reckoning after breaking his hand again the previous day in the Clydesdale Bank 40 League encounter with Warwickshire.

It was beginning to look as if the dreadful weather would never allow Yorkshire the opportunity to get back into the top two in the table and that view was reinforced when the second and third days were wiped out after Yorkshire had ended the first day on 61 for two in reply to Gloucestershire's 215.

Somehow, Gale managed to smooth talk his opposite number, Will Gidman, into a deal which resulted in Yorkshire promptly declaring on the third morning before feeding Gloucestershire 159 runs in ten overs, five apiece from Gale and Lyth.

This left Yorkshire a very reasonable target of 314 in 84 overs and the experience of Jaques and McGrath got them over the line with ten balls remaining although it also needed a cameo 24 from Rafiq to see them home after slipping to 267-7 at one stage.

The first rain-free match was in the penultimate game against Glamorgan at Headingley Carnegie which Yorkshire won with some ease to leave them to travel to Chelmsford just one point behind leaders Derbyshire and five points ahead of Kent, who were coming up on the rails.

The true test of a good side is to be able to win by taking 20 wickets and after doing so against Glamorgan they repeated the feat against much tougher opponents in Essex who were thrashed by 239 runs, so sparking off Yorkshire's promotion celebrations on the final afternoon of the season.

Glamorgan's unexpected beating of Kent inside three days left Yorkshire knowing they were certain to go up but they refused to relax until Patterson bowled Tymal Mills to end the match, leaving them level on points with table-toppers Derbyshire, but winning one fewer game.

There were several outstanding individual performances, the most noteworthy of them coming from Rafiq who scored 53 and 75 not out as well as capturing a match haul of 8-115, including career-best figures of 5-50 as Essex crumbled.

In the Clydesdale Bank 40 League, Yorkshire lost four of the first six matches in which a positive result was possible and they never looked like qualifying for the semi-finals even though there were some good batting performances, notably from Gale and Lyth.

As we have seen, it was a different story in the Friends Life t20 as the team bubbled with a confidence which they had not shown previously in this shortest form of the game, Miller and Starc both earning their corn.

Yorkshire were the sixth team – including his country – that Miller had played for in Twenty20 cricket and the South African led the way up to Finals Day with 274 runs. Starc was just as dominant with the ball, his blistering pace bringing him 21 dismissals, seven more than nearest rival, Ashraf, and they cost him only 10.38 runs apiece.

Yet it was young Rafiq who perhaps did more than anyone else to hold the team together. Yorkshire lost their opening match to Durham at Headingley Carnegie but then won their next two before Gale had to drop out because of injury. Some eyebrows were raised initially when the t20 captaincy was handed to Rafiq but soon everyone was singing his praises as he took to the role like a duck to water.

Remaining cool and decisive no matter how great the pressure, Rafiq proved himself to be a true captain in the making. Yorkshire won four of the six games he was in charge of up to Gale's return – and the other two were wash-outs. Neither was his bowling adversely affected for he operated with considerable skill to claim nine wickets without ever being mauled.

In several of the matches, crowds were down because of the appalling weather, but in the home Roses match 10,350 turned up to watch the demolition of Lancashire while 8,000 were attracted to the quarter-final caning of Worcestershire.

And so Yorkshire march proudly into their 150th anniversary year back where they belong in the First Division of the Championship. On January 8, 2013, exactly 150 years to the day since the club was founded, the occasion was due to be celebrated at a Sesquicentennial Soiree meticulously planned by Rachael Boycott, the President's wife being determined that it would be an event to last long in the memory. And, poignantly, it was being held in Sheffield at the Crucible Studio Theatre, the building standing on exactly the spot of the old Adelphi Hotel where Yorkshire County Cricket Club had been born in 1863.

What have we discovered over this span of time and through these pages that has made Yorkshire CCC the envy of the cricketing world?

For a start, it was managed supremely well by people in high places, T.R. Barker, the first listed president, and M.J. Ellison, his almost immediate successor and founder treasurer, being distinguished gentlemen in Sheffield with a great passion for cricket, despite being born outside the boundaries.

Likewise, Yorkshire's secretaries were men of integrity who helped to build and then protect the club's burgeoning image at home and abroad. They did so quietly and with dignity and the fact that there were only five of them from 1864 to 2002 is testament to their service and loyalty.

Then, 20 years after the club's formation, came Lord Hawke to mould his motley collection of players from all walks of life into a fighting force. Hawke was to Yorkshire cricket what Sir Titus Salt was to the woollen industry and to the village named after him, Saltaire. Both looked after their men and made provision for their futures – and they, in turn, responded by working all the harder for them.

But, most importantly, cricket is imbued in the soul of all Yorkshiremen who play the game and this deep affection has rubbed off on to most of those who come from outside the boundaries to play for the county club.

What makes up the collective character of a subject is a complex thing. But take the effortless ease of F.S. Jackson, the earthiness of Peel, the toiling genius of Rhodes, the sheer energy of Hirst, the belief of Sellers, the haughty elegance of Sutcliffe, the resolution of Verity, the admiration shown to Hutton, the rough pride of Trueman, the courage of Close, the canniness of Illingworth, the strength of purpose of Boycott, the majesty of Moxon, the breathtaking audacity of Lehmann, the showman skills of Gough... take all of these, and countless variations, and there you have The Sweetest Rose.

Fans of
Yorkshire County Cricket Club

John Andrew Ackroyd

Glenn Acornley

John Adams

Malcolm Douglas Addy

Derek Agar

J.C. David Allan

Richard Allison

Michael Allison

Mr K S Anderson

Christopher J Andrews

Anne and Neal

James Appleby

B R Armeson

S R Armeson

Shaun M Armitage

Peter R Arrand

Gary Ashton

John Bailey

Brian Bailey

Martin Bambridge

Kevin J Banks

Joy and Ron Bannister

Alan Barber

Peter.B. Baren

Dr. Michael Barke

John Barnes

Dennis L. Barnett

Mr D Barratt

Jean and David Bartholomew

Mr Ian Barton

John Baxter

Ken Beanland

Andrew B Beardsell

Glen Beaumont

Guy Beaumont

Garrath Beckwith

Wilfred "Wilf" Bedford

Betty Bedford

Ian Bedford

William "Bill" Bedford

John Allen Beever

Phillip Bell

The "Bellamy Family, Cudworth"

K M Bellwood

R Benfell

G Benfell

Ben Bennett JR

Roger H Benson

Gary David Benson

Colin Frank Bentley

Kevin Beresford

Andrew Berriman

Ben Berriman

With much love to Bill

Geoff Binks

Edward Birdsall

David Birks

Stuart Black

Mr Roy Black

Ken Blackburn

Richard John Blackburn

Arthur Blackham

Paul Bly

John C Blythe

Mark Clement Bollon

Bomber

Thomas P. Booth

Wilfred Keith Boswell

Terry Botham

Richard Botting

Christopher John Bowes

Tony Bowser

Anthony Bradbury

Graham Bradbury

John Bramman

Roger Brice

P J Bridges

John Briggs

Matthew Briggs

Miss K L Briggs

Benjamin John Briggs

Ronald Briggs

Peter Ingle Britton

Ken Britton

John Broadhead

Andrew David
Broadhead

David Broadley

Robert Trevor Brook

Michael James Brooks

Colin W Brook

Lawrence Brooke

Tony Brooke

Peter Brookes

Rupert D.E Brown

Phil Brown

Alan William
Browning

Peter Clive Brumwell

Nigel Buckland

John Bull

Phil Burgess

Derick and Dorothy
Burns

Adrian J Burton

Malcolm Butler

Stuart Butlin

Malcolm Butterworth

Michael Buttery

Peter Bramley Byram

Clive Cagill

Neil Calcott

Stephen Calverley

Ken Cant

Simon R Carding

Nicholas Carlile

Nicholas Carling

In Memory of Ralph
Carr

Jason Carr

Timothy N Carrington

Andrew Cartlidge

Harry Cartwright

Phil Catchpole

Ian Chappell

Rob Champion

Chris Chew

Christopher

John C Clapham

Andrew Claughton

Ian Patrick Charles
Clay

Geoff Clayton

Howard Clayton

Brian Coates

Miranda Coates

Alan Coe

David Coe

Michael Coffey

C J Coggill

David Ian Coldwell

Shirley Coleman

Jack Collinson

James Andrew Coney

Trevor Constantine

John Conyers

James D B Cook

Gordon Simms Cooper

Paul F Cooper

David Cooper

Stewart John Cope

Colin Cope

John H Corney

Jack Cotterill

Malcolm Coupe

Lawrence Craggs

Hubert Cranston

John Crapper

Bernard Crossland

Arthur Crow

Graham Crowe

J Crowther

David Crowther

Ray Currie

Alistair Dales

Mr. Philip Darley

John F Dawson

Ron Deaton

Peter Deighton

Simon Dennis, Little
Ribston CC

James Dickinson

Christopher John
Dixon

Rob Dixon

Roger W Dixon

M M Dossor

Brian Douglass

The Viscount Downe

Martin Dransfield

John Duckworth

Maurice Duffield

Dr Phillip E Dunn

Tom Dyal

Paul Dyson

Philip Earnshaw

Frank Edgeworth

John Edwards

Roy Eggleton

Janet E Ella

Roger M Elliott

Ron Ellis

Barry Endeacott

Charlotte Evers

Andrew J Fallis

Ben Falvey - A Cricket fan

PS Fell

David Fell

Mick Fickling

Dr Michael R Firth

Paul Firth

Rob Firth

Ken Firth

John Fisher

Ian Fleming

Paul Fletcher (Fletch)

Simon Foster

Keith Foster

Stephen Fox

Carl Foxton

Stewart Franks

Donald Fullarton

Mr Nick Gale

Logan William Galloway

Ted Gambles

Richard Gant

Frank Gant

Brian Garbett

Anthony J Gardner

David Gaunt

John A Gedge

Jim Gibbins

M C Gibson

Paul Gibson

Bob Gibson

Christopher Gilbert

Richard Gilbert

Roger Gilbert

Tim Gilfoy

Gill

Cedric Gillott

Roy Gittins

Andrew Paul Gledstone

H Glover

Paul R.W. Goddard

Ian M. Goddard

Paul R W. Goddard

Richard Goddard

Tony Goldman

Nic Gomersal

Robert (The Growler) Gosling

Robert Gosling

Dudley Eric Graham

John Graham

Grant

Stephen Greaves

C R Green

Ian Greenhalgh

Craig Greensmith (Greeno)

Peter Senior Greenwood

David Gronow

Ian Gunby

D J Hagger

T Hague

John Haigh

John M Haigh

Chris Hall

John and Paula Halliley

Andrew Hambleton

Edward Hambleton

Ken Hammill

Rob Hampstead

Robert "The Rebel" Hand

Lochlainn Hankin-Appleby

Odran Hankin-Appleby

Neil Hanson

Kevin Hardisty

David Hardisty

Paul Hardwick

Chris Hardy

John Robert Hardy

Janet Harker

John Harley

Tim Harris

Paul Harris

Robert Hart

Steve Hartley

Mr Alan Hawke

Brian Heald

Robert Heap (60th)

John B. Heath

Sam Heaviside

A Denis Heeley

M D Hellawell

Henry

Mark Hepworth

Richard Hewitt

Leonard Hey

Colin Hickford

William Hickson

David Hills

Chris Hirst

David Hirst

John Hoather

Michael Hobbs

Keith Hodgson

Martin Hodgson

Norman Holroyd

James Holt

Les Hopkin

R A Horner

Daniel Mark Horry

Keith Howarth

Martin Howe

Alan Howe

David William Hoyle

Stephen Hunt

Richard Hunt

Michael Hunt

Matthew Hunt

Keith Hunwin

Barry Hutchinson

John V. Hutchinson

Andrew Yates Hutchinson

Richard Iball

Richard Ingleby

Robert Issac

J P Jackson

Richard Jackson

Alan Jackson

Paul Edward Jenkins

Tony Jenkinson

Tom Jennings

Matthew Jepson

Albert Edward Jervis

Charles Jesper

To Jim best wishes from Anne

Alan Jinkinson

Andrew A Johnson

David Johnson

Les Johnson

Mike Jones

Jeremy Jones

Pat Jones

Philip Alban Jones

Gordon W Kay

Arthur Kaye

Norman Kellett

Luke W B Kendall

Robert Kenworthy-Platt

John Kerby

Jeremy Kettlestring

P.A. Kiddle

Christine King

Darrel Kingan

The Kirkland Family

Philip Kitchingman

M B Knight

Ian Lamond

Alyson and David Land

Dick Lane

Arthur R Langhorn

Paul A Latham

Sachin Lavender

Mark Law

Mark David Lawlor

Ian Lawrence

John Melvyn Lawson

David Lawson

Peter Laycock

John Laycock

James Laycock

Raymond Leach

Stuart Leather

John Winston Leathley

Michael Evitt Lee

Vanessa Lee

Janet Leighton

Julie Leonard

Michael Lightfoot

John Lightfoot

Peter Lingard

John Lister

Dr Greg Lodge

John S Lodge

Lewis Lomax

Christopher Lonsdale

Jeremy Lonsdale

Robert Franklin Lowe

Geoffrey Lunn

Anthony Hugh Lupton

Richard Mallender

George Mallender

Tim Mallinson

Mr John Edward Mann

Michael Mann

Denis A Marshall

Peter Mason

David Massey,
Little Ribston CC

Matt

Peter Matthews

Lee Mattocks

Robert Mawson

Lawrie Mawson

Don McBurney BEM

Linda McDermott

M. Mead

Michael Meadowcroft

K D Medlock

David Mellor

Steve Melody

Ken Merchant

John Metcalfe

Tony Metcalfe

Micheal

Simon Middleton

Trevor Middleton

Carlton Midgley

Stella & Howard
Milner

D.P. Milroy

P N Mirfield

Alan Mitchell

Gillian Moody

Jim Moore

John Moorhouse

James W J Moorhouse

John Moralee

Richard Moran

Terry Moran

Terence Keith Morgan

June and Bill Morris

J.E. Mortimer

Andrew Mortimer

Michael Morton

John Morton

David Mowforth

David Neighbour

Colin Neill

Roddy Neill

Mark Newbound,
Dewsbury

Gerry Newing

Geoff Newton

S G D Newton

Ann Nicholl

John Nilen

Stephen Norman

Pat Norman

David Normanton

Keith Nuttall

David O'Kelly

Charlie O'Kelly

Edwin J O'Sullivan

Tony Ogley

Dr. Bob Oxtoby

Carole Parkhouse

Nicholas Patchett

Grandad Albert
Patterson

Andrew Paul

Paul

David Payne

Harry Pearson

Mark Robert Pearson

T. Gordon Penman

R W Perkin

Steph Phillips

Cedric Phillips

AJ & PA Phillips

John Pickering

Mr Roger W Pigott

Malcolm Pipes

Don Player

Malcolm Poad

Anne Pollard

Don Poulton

To my parents Chris &
Brian Powley

Noah Jack Prince

Russell Procter

Sam Wilkinson Pycock

Keith John Ramsden

John Rawnsley

Dr Andrew C.
Rawnsley

Michael Rawnsley

Richard Rawson

FR. Charles Razzall

Terry Rees

Graham T Reid

Geoff Relton

Sam Renshaw

John Reynard

Keith Rhodes

T J Rhodes

John Rhodes

Brian Richards

David Richardson

Roy Bennett Richens

Michael Ridsdale

Adrian Roberts

William Roberts

Paul Robinson

Arnold W. Robinson

Rick Rogers

David Rose

Simon Ross

William George
Rounding

Tony Rowe

Michael Rowlands

Peter W Ruder

Ruth

Chris Ryan

Stephen Ryder

Ian Ryder

Michael Ryecroft

Ali Saad

Sam

Gerald Sanderson

Mark Sanderson

Daniel J Sanderson

Michael W Sanderson

Stan & Ann Sanderson

Ralph Scott

Martin Scott

Joan Scott

Kevin Scotter

Tony Scotter

B Seymour

Bob Shackleton

Craig Sharpley

J Shaw

Neil F Shaw

Peter Shires

Malcolm Short

Michael Simpson

Ralph Skelton

Dave Skilbeck

Robert Smales

Dr A M S Smith

Adrian Smith

Albert A Smith

Barrie Smith

Clifford Smith

David O Smith

Dennis Smith

Harold Smith

Jeff Smith, Greetland

John B. Smith

Ken Smith

Dr. Martin A Smith

Mike Smith

P.A. Smith

Dr P G Smith

Peter Smith

W C Smith

Roger Smith

R Peter Smith

Tim Soutar

Alan South

Laurence James
Sowden

James Laurence Frank
Sowden

Mr G Spenceley

John Spencely

Patrick Spencer

John M Spencer

Joshua Spink

Graham Stalgis

Geoff Stalker

T.M. Stanley

Colin Stansfield

James Stansfield

Paul Stanton

The Stathams

George Walter Stead

David Stead

Joan and Eric Stephens

Steven

John Stevens

Gavin Stevens

Robin Johnston Stewart

Paul Stokes

Les Stones

Andrew Stott

Robert Stott

Bryan Stott

Terry Styring

John B.W. Summerskill

David Sunderland

Charles Sunley

Superbat

Phil Sutcliffe

N.R.A. Sutcliffe

Charles Swales

Timothy Sykes

Stuart Sykes

"T.C." (Tom)

Christine Tadman

John Tattersall

J K Taylor

Darren Taylor

David Taylor

Peter Taylor, Leeds

Brian J Tempest

Michael Terry

P Thewlis

Ian L Thomas

Edward Thompson

Donald Thompson

Peter and Margaret Thompson

Keith Thompson

Malcolm Thompson

Chris Thompson

Les Thornton

A J Thorp

CP Thorp

Reverend Donald Thorpe

Arthur Tidswell

Geoffrey A Tiffney

Chris Timewell

M C J Tolan

Ian Ernest Torr

Robert M Town

Bethany A Town

Jerry Town

Dave Townend

Bill Tunnicliffe

Ken Tunstall

Adam Geofrey Tyler

Alan Vickers

Alan Vincent

Rosemary Vollans

John Hedley Wainwright

Neil Waitt

John E Walker

Chris Walker

Gary Waller

Michael Walsh

Michael Walters

Stephen Ward

David Ward

John Ward

Peter Warner

David Washington

Sheila & Ken Waterworth

John Watmough

Bob Watson

Nathan Weatherstone

John R Weatherstone

Gordon Webster

Mr J H Welbourn

James Kirby Welch

James Wellock

John Wells

Richard Wells

Mark Westmoreland

Keith Whawell

G D Whitaker

Roy White

Philip James Whitehead

Ronald Whitelock

Gordon H Wigglesworth

Robin A F Wight

Eric W. Wild

Peter Wildsmith

Paul Wilkinson

Roy D Wilkinson

Ian R Williams

Councillor Martin Williams

John Williams

Andrew Michael Wilson

Richard Wilson

Stan and Stella Wilson

Daniel Winfrow

Phillip D Winter

Mary Wood

Peter Wood

Andrew K Wood

David M Wood

Sir John Wood

George Wood

Barry Wood

Anthony Wood

Howard Woodbridge

John Woodcock

Brian Workman

Andy Wormald

Richard Worthy

Gerry Wright

Terry Wright

Nick Wright

R G Young

Zig Zwierzewicz

Also available from Great Northern Books:

The Yorkshire County Cricket Club Yearbook

Magnificent Seven

Yorkshire's Championship Years

The Players' Own Story

with Andrew Collomosse

Fire and Ashes

How Yorkshire's finest took on the Australians

Sweet Summers

The Classic Cricket Writing of JM Kilburn

Winner of Wisden Book of the Year

Frith On Cricket

Half a Century of Writing by David Frith

Play Cricket The Right Way

by Geoff Boycott

www.greatnorthernbooks.co.uk